Angels Speak

The Art and Work of Crafting Consciousness

By

Anthony B. James

Angels Speak
The Art and Work of Crafting Consciousness

Contact: (706) 358-8646
Email: SomaVedaONAC@gmail.com
Website: http://www.ThaiYogaCenter.Com

Publisher: Meta Journal Press
Address: 5401 Saving Grace Ln. Brooksville, FL 34602

Trade Paperback Edition

Inquires should be addressed to:
Anthony B. James
5401 Saving Grace Ln.
Brooksville, Fl 34602

ISBN: 978-1-886338-17-3

Angels Speak
The Art and Work of Crafting Consciousness

Preamble

This book is based entirely on the original workbook Angels Speak, first published in 1994 by Anthony B. James as a personal workbook for himself and his students. The original short workbook, composed of a list of useful aphorisms, maxims and statements allegedly attributed to conscious beings, is herein discussed and elaborated on in detail. The following is based entirely on a series of 28 lectures given by Dr. J between September and November 2011.

For clarification questions and answers from various participants have been included. These ideas have been discussed in the context of practical ideas for working on oneself, and although following generally a Fourth Way theme, are also eclectic and not meant to represent any other school or tradition other than that of the author himself. These ideas and concepts have helped me to have an amazing life and a more intentional and conscious life, and by sharing what has been of great merit for me personally, I hope it will do the same for the chance reader who considers my words.

Acknowledging the contributions of ideas derived from the teachings of the following individuals As well as that sacred spirit which runs throughout and yet remains unnamed :

Georges Imianovich Gurdjieff
Peter Dimionovich Ouspensky
E.J. Gold
Mr. Miles Barth
Johann Wolfgang Goethe
William Shakespeare
Rodney Collin
Joel Freidlander
Manley P. Hall
Swami Vivekananda
The Great Oom!
Charles W. Ledbetter
Swami Vivekananda
Venerable Aachan Chaa
Colonel Milan E. Elliot
George Bernard Shaw
Fletcher Wolfe
Martin Luther and Corretta Scott King
Catherine Dwyer
Wilhelm Reich

Dedication

I would first and foremost like to dedicate this material to my wife Julie James without whose support and continued feedback it simply would not have been possible. She actually sat through all the lectures and discussions and brought her insight and sometimes confusion to what I was communicating. Julie helped me understand better what I was trying to communicate. I think she did so in a way to make this material accessible for individuals with less exposure both to my personal teachings and to Fourth Way concepts in general. Next I would like to thank the transcribers and editors who went through every word over a period of over a year to make it readable and legible. Thanks to my editor Jordan Coe for his efforts and sometimes chagrin.

As always I would give credit and acknowledgement to all of my teachers and mentors in helping me sometimes have a clue! As I have been working on these ideas since I was a child, I would like to acknowledge some of my childhood mentors whose influence before the age of thirteen remain powerful to the present day. My grandmother Faye Wallace who first taught me that we should strive to have integrity in everything we do and to play nice! Ms. Corretta Scott King in whose living room I was in for a short while every Saturday on my assistant delivery route with Westmont cleaners. I would sit in her and Martin Luther King's living room and stare at the large oil portrait of Mohendas Ghandi Gi. One day I asked her who that strange looking man was and she replied that he was a role model for her husband Mr. King. He was a man of color from India who proved that we could do much with peace. Colonel Milan E. Elliott, my archery coach who not only showed me how to be an Archer but how to find a still place within where there was no separation between my inner self and my outer world. George Bernard Shaw, during practice with the Atlanta Boys Choir which I was a part of for a time, who once told me if I wanted to be heard I needed to open my mouth!

4

Notes from the Editor

Hello and welcome to *Angels Speak*. This book began as a series of informal lectures conducted and recorded by the author, then transcribed and edited into what you now hold in your hands. Though I was not present at these discussions, and the subject matter was largely foreign to me, I was given the fortunate, and oftentimes arduous, opportunity of fine-tuning the transcription in an effort to preserve the sensation of informal discourse while making it more appropriate for the written word without sacrificing the author's intent. This was an interesting exercise for me, and even though I was able to take liberties with grammar (the book being entirely dialogue), the challenge lay in interpreting and reconstructing the wandering trains of speech and thought of the lecture participants into something more cohesive and understandable.

Angels Speak has purely to do with working on oneself, bettering yourself, not from a financial or material standpoint, as you'll find in a plethora of self-help books, but from a deeper, more intrinsic and psychological one. I was once a representative of a marketing company and attended a conference in Dallas. One of speakers mentioned it was okay to take time out of your business to "work on yourself." I thought, *Hmm, I've heard about this whole* working on yourself thing. *I like the sound of that. Yeah, that's what I'm going to do. I'm going to work on myself. That's what I need to do.* I left the conference with reassurance and determination. Twenty-four hours later I asked myself, "How in god's name does one 'work on oneself'?" I was at a complete loss, yet in the span of a few months the rough, transcribed version of *Angel's Speak* graced the inbox of my email account with its presence, and I started to understand a little more. This book has helped me in many facets of life and will certainly continue to do so the more I apply what I have learned. Think of *Angel's Speak* as a bottomless toolbox, wherein Dr. James has placed not only a vast array of tools and contraptions, but also detailed instructions on how best to utilize these items to the operator's advantage. And, because the toolbox is bottomless, there is plenty of room for you to add tools of your own design and making as you learn and grow, as you play this game we call living on Earth.

The point is we'll never get it all. The most we can ever do within each and every passing moment is to understand *just a little more*. In American society we are expected to comprehend information at a specific rate. We are essentially programmed to believe that if we do not grasp an idea the first time around there must be something wrong with us. Well, take that ideology out of your skull and throw it out, because it won't do you any good here. You're not going to grasp everything in the pages follow. A lot of concepts will be unfamiliar to you, and there's nothing wrong with that. Overtime, as you read and continue to experience life, the relevance of the subject matter will become clearer, and what once seemed insignificant will emerge as something of great substance.

May *Angels Speak* serve you well.

Sincerely,

Jordan T. Coe
09.09.2012

What is Angels Speak?

This book is a manual of practical exercises that enhance the ability to observe one's Self and reduce the expression of negative emotions. The statements come from experiences of encountering random individuals who appeared for a few moments at critical times when I was in a state of confusion. These individuals would give a few words, not of encouragement, but of advice on what I had to do.

Overtime, I realized these words of wisdom from strangers had turned out to be significant. The statements did not seem too profound at first, but in practice overtime their effect was empowering.

If angels exist, and you had an interaction with them, they would have to speak in a way you would understand, in your own language, using familiar concepts. Their words would have to be recognizable.

Because of the profound effect these statements had, I came to the conclusion that if angels exist, they would be the people who said these words, as if God was speaking to me through a flesh and blood person. That is why Angels Speak is a quirky book of statements about things to do to cultivate certain kinds of energy and practice self-observation and non-expression of negative emotions.

To lift our spirits above and beyond the limitations and constraints ordinary life places upon us is our objective.

I once heard an angel say, "Be your self, be true to your self." When I heard these words, I was in a difficult circumstance and it appeared the words were meant to be helpful. I thought I knew what they meant, but after consideration I realized I could not be "myself" or be true to "myself," as I did not know what the Self was, or even if I had one. How could I be true to something I could not verify? If the angel's words were a solution to my dilemma, then I had to ask and answer some questions. Who am I, really? What is a "Self" and under what conditions does it arise? If there is a true "Self," what is an "un-true Self?" If I do not have a true "Self," is it possible to cultivate one and under what conditions? If I could follow the words the angel spoke, what might be the result?

The "lifting" we seek must occur in the context of life that generates the limitations and constraints in the first place.

Life experience leads to a particular way of being that is derived slowly over the entire course of life. Ultimately you may find your way of being dissatisfactory and then choose to move in a positive direction towards helpful influences, or a negative direction towards despair. Negative influences causing states of suffering and dissatisfaction are infinite, while positive, helpful influences are not infinite. This is similar to healing, where a few simple techniques (like bio-tapping and energetic healing) can be applicable to a diversity of suffering. There are three primary lines of work that can change the state of dissatisfaction. Internal personal work, or work for your self, and transitional personal work, including both work for the group or community in which you are involved as an extension of the personal internal work you have been doing, and external personal work for the world/society at large. These are areas of emphasis and direction and all three may be on going simultaneously.

As you begin to move in the direction of positive influences, the question will arise, "Who or What is dissatisfied with life?" "Who or What is now subject to beneficial influences to correct this dissatisfaction?" When we talk about life in normal conversation, we assume it is known what we mean when we say "I." The problem is, there is no genuine "I," "We" or "You." This is a necessary realization because it shows that what is moving in the continuum of satisfaction/ dissatisfaction is not a concrete, singular Self. If that is not you, then what is? What is something that is not what people have been educated to believe defines who they are in life?

Previously we may not have been aware there is a separate part of us, within us. This separateness has a different orientation to everything surrounding us in life. It has a unique perspective on every action or interaction in which we are involved. At first we think there is something within us we wish to cultivate or to "get in touch with." Instead we should ask, "Who wishes to cultivate whom?" It is not a matter of trying to get in touch with our self, but a matter of our self, our eternal self, trying desperately to get in touch with us.

When you begin to have this realization of Self, you will realize whatever you think of or mean when using the term "you" is not what you previously thought, or what you have been taught to think. Up to a certain point, "you" as a possessive identifying person is separate from your true Self. Your understanding of who you are not correct and you are not who you thought you were. In fact, you are something separate from your perception of 'you'. You are separate from how and where you were raised, separate from your family's perception of who you are. You begin to see that you are not what you do. You are not a plumber, a doctor, or a teacher. You are not where you live, or what you look like. You are not your personality or the outward characteristics that define your personality.

A worship of outward personality has developed in Western culture. Even though there have been great advances in the soft sciences of psychology and psychiatry, culturally there is not a high priority placed on knowing oneself. What is "important" is what you do and have done, who your family is and what they have accomplished.

Our successes in life are judged by critical but superficial standards, such as what we wear, how big of a house we have, our job or what kind of car we drive.

When we describe someone who is successful in life we are usually describing how well this person has adapted to the mechanical process of developing a personality defined by cultural programming. It is quite possible that the most outwardly successful people may in fact be the most mechanical/least conscious. This how we end up with examples of leaders all over the world who function at a very low levels and are apparently only concerned with destruction, consumption and entertainment. As the most successful/ powerful person in the country, the outcome is ugly.

Cultural programming is mechanical and comes from the sum of dominant culture, family culture, religious/dogmatic, political, and societal culture; virtually everything that surrounds a person in life. External qualifiers like what you do and have done are what
define our "self," our "personality." All outward manifestations of acculturation and socialization are mechanical and these processes may have occurred by accident. It is not uncommon to hear a "successful" person make the statement, "I never knew this would be the result," or "I never imagined…" yet still they are considered to be successful.

In our culture there are people considered to have been "successful" who died of suicide and drug addiction or as a result of stress to their bodies. They had no apparent control over the course of their lives and were very unhappy, yet we glorify their successes and even strive to be like them.

Rather than buying into this version of success, it is important to always be inclined to look for a deeper meaning. Like in The Wizard of Oz, we must learn to look behind the curtain, to not accept anything at face value, and to look for the underlying meaning. In The Invisible Landscape, Terence McKenna writes that in order to know what the universe is about you must learn to look at the parts you cannot see or understand by conventional means…this applies to everything!

By looking deeper we are beginning to examine the Self. By defining what the Self is not we come closer to what it actually is.

> The Self is not what we do.
> The Self is not where we are.
> The Self is not what we have.
> The Self in not inherited from one's family.
> The Self has no nationality.
> The Self has no politics.
> The Self is not limited to any religion or creed.

We each come to these realizations in different ways while we are busy living our "normal" lives. We may begin to ask questions as we find that we are missing something; "Is this all there is to my life?" Our questions may come with an understanding of the brevity of one's existence in the world. We may wonder if the time, energy and effort we put forth daily will have any real consequences whether we live for one hundred years or die tomorrow. In addition, we may wonder or consider whether any part of us has the capacity to transcend the limitations of our life or exist after death.

These questions do not concern everyone. Many are content to go through life without waking up to see that there is more to life than physical existence. In the Bible it says, "To him who hath will be given; from him who hath not will be taken away." In order to obtain valuable and practical insight in pursuit of deeper satisfaction of life one must have already achieved a certain degree of awareness. If there is not enough, the tendency is to devolve and to find oneself in increasingly negative circumstances tantamount to suffering. Devolving is what is meant by, "As a dog returns to his vomit, so a fool repeats his folly." (Book of Proverbs, 26:11) If consciousness is not sustained you will get trapped in the loop of negativity and repeat your mistakes. If you have specific information pertaining to consciousness then more is available. If you have not, the little that you have may not be sufficient to bring you to Self-liberation. In other words, you have to have some, to get some.

The Law of Lift: The Law of Overcoming Obstacles

To overcome obstacles that hide the knowledge of true being, we literally have to do something impossible! The trick is to find or create a new set of rules or laws other than those that hold us down. Here is an example of the possibility of something once thought to be impossible:

For thousands of years human flight was considered impossible. To contemplate the possibility was considered a sign of mental illness! Humans were earth-bound according to the law of nature called gravity, and there were no exceptions. That is, until the law of lift was discovered. When properly applied, the law of lift enables flight. The limitations of gravity still exist, but flight is now a possibility when we work according to the requirements of both gravity and the law of lift.

With this new information comes the desire to create an airplane. We now understand to overcome gravity the airplane must have wings attached to its body. We realize air needs to move over the top of the wings for them to rise against gravity and fly. The air velocity moving across the top of the wings must be proportional to the surface of the wings; if it is not sufficiently proportional the plane will crash. It is the same with consciousness as with the airplane. It is not enough to have some realizations. We have to have a critical mass of momentum in order for the changes to become permanent (i.e. take off!).

Overcoming the obstacles that kept humans out of the sky began with some key realizations, and now what was once thought of as impossible is an everyday experience. Momentum drove the desire to fly just as it drives the desire to be conscious. Swami Paramhamsa Yogananda would say this momentum is necessary in order to become a "fully realized Self-conscious being." In our system, this momentum is of utmost importance.

Momentum happens when we apply tools overtime. It begins with small changes and with momentum you will begin to notice things. You begin to understand there is more to life than what you formerly understood or have been led to believe.

Even a word of truth can drive momentum by changing something within us, as if simply by hearing it we are a little more awake. Something in us responds to this word of truth and quickens. Tibetan Buddhists believe there is possibility of progress towards liberation and enlightenment as a consequence of hearing a single word of objective truth. Simply being exposed to a truth from external influences more conscious than your own may lead to a process, which they call "the great liberation." Many cultures have a tradition of reading their sacred texts aloud annually, over a period of days. After one is exposed to these sacred words there is a Self-generating/Self-perpetuating process to gain momentum.

Understanding the laws that both limit and liberate us in our construction of a vehicle or a methodology to work with is also not enough. We also need some help! We describe this help as "external conscious influence. Many traditions hold to this principle in their own way. They speak of deities, gods, saints, sages, and bodhisattvas as providing external conscious influence.

Consider this help originating from external conscious influence as truth. It can be as simple as a single word or image, but once heard or seen has the ability to change our perception of reality in relation to who we are.

Because of this exposure to objective truth, we begin to have an orientation toward favoring certain kinds of energy, information, and ideas that awaken us and elevate our consciousness. Something has now changed and we are not the same as we were a minute before as a result of that externally derived influence. The exposure to objective truth acts as food for our Self. As we feed this part of ourselves, we accumulate energy and start to develop a magnetic center for higher influences.

We have spoken of many things the Self is not; perhaps it will help to mention some qualities of the Self.

The Self is beyond the restraint of time and sees the world as an organic entity with a life all its own.

The Self is a vehicle whereby stellar influences are directly transmitted to the earth.

The Self is where the breath of God manifests on the earth.

Through the eternal Self, God sees and acts in the world.

Through the eternal Self, Man sees and acts with God.

The Self is beyond time and space—
This means the existence of the Self is found in the pure flow of energy that all things are a part of without limitation or duration.

The Self knows God. The Self is a direct conduit for influences originating from the world of the creative and conscious Absolute to the world of organic life on earth.

The Self knows only one emotion, love. Love is the expression of life from God or the breath of God in the universe. As the Self is a conduit for the influence of God, it can only express love. Any other expression does not come from the Self.

Only the Self is real.

Everything not of the Self is temporary and limited. Almost every facet of our personality is based on unreality. There is no conscious development based on true knowledge of our being. Our pre-occupations, vocations, habits and hobbies are not commonly based on what is best for our spiritual advancement or our conscious development of that which transcends mortal life and knows eternity. We are generally concerned with the fullness of our stomachs and the comfort of our beds. We mistakenly think the house in which dwells the master is more important than he. Not only do we mistakenly think the house is more important, we think the house is the master!

This misunderstanding makes perfect sense if you consider everything we commonly associate as being our self (our personality, interests, occupations, capabilities, strengths, weaknesses, negative emotions, and most conscious and unconscious actions) belongs to the house. The master is the true Self and is separate from these things.

The house was carefully designed as a tool to preserve and care for the master. It was always intended to be a vehicle through which the master might influence the world and MUST be taken care of.

The Self knows beauty. Beauty is a reflection of God in the world and only that which is of God may know or see this reflection. The very act of perceiving beauty brings one closer to God because the Self is the conduit between God and the world. As we perceive and appreciate beauty we fulfill our nature and function in harmony with all other living beings. As we react to more accurate perceptions we become the very hands of God manifesting love in the world. We can bring down and transform higher energies to a level where they may actually transform the nature of our world.

The principle of Alchemy is often thought of as a "bringing of that which is low to a higher place," with the traditional example of the transmutation of lead into gold. There is another form of Alchemy—that of the transformation of Higher influences, or influences which originate from a source closer to that of the conscious Absolute, into lower forms, which may affect certain changes at the level of energy from which we operate.

This gives us two parts of a formula for "raising" our own level of consciousness. First is the work of bringing up the level of energy of areas in us which are below the level we desire. Second is bringing down the energies above us to an accessible level. According to this formula, "consciousness raising" is not accurate because there is consciousness higher than ours that must be brought down to us, as well as lower consciousness that must be elevated. Alchemy then represents the organic processes the eternal Self goes through in manifesting its life energy in the natural world.

When we actively pursue alignment with sources of light and subtle energies in our life, we place ourselves in proximity to higher influences and increase the likelihood of attracting them to us. This is one reason why the work of cultivating and sustaining higher influences around us is so important.

As we attract higher influences into our proximity we can create the necessary forms of energy to bring up the lower parts of us by bringing conscious attention to the higher influences. This is important to understand because it indicates there is a price for everything, and the price is effort. The energy used to bring up the lower parts of us must be acquired from somewhere else. Information and knowledge are forms of energy, and the process of acquiring these types of energy does not begin internally.

What can we say about the Self at this point?

The Self exists.

The Self exists eternally, and as we are we do not own it.

The Self is other than our personality and the outward manifestation of our personality in life.

The Self seeks to supersede personality and to manifest actively in the natural world—we may be conscious participants in this process, either to aid or impede the process.

We are not, until the Self is.

The Self is manifested in the natural world through a process of Alchemy. As we come into proximity with higher influences and absorb the impressions they generate by consciously directing our attention, we create the energy necessary to bring up the lower parts of us.

With the union of the higher and the lower we become one. Until the union actually manifests there is no Self, there is only personality. The union describes a kind of birth process or a kind of evolution. This is not referring to the Darwinian model, based on natural selection, where various species become dominant overtime depending on their ability to adapt in their environment. There is another kind of evolution not based on the environment, an event, or location, but an evolution of necessity only occurring as a result of applied intention.

Conscious evolution has its own rules and appropriate conditions just like Darwinian evolution, but instead of environment being the primary force for selection and evolution, the primary force is desire and the application of discipline. Desire is a positive inclination to acquire something potentially helpful. This is not to be confused with craving, which is the result of compulsion and negative emotion and leads to seeking harmful things. We must have an inclination to acquire what is useful in our life to make progress. If this inclination to want to acquire comes from ego or false personality, then it is on the continuum of craving, attachment, and greed. If the inclination comes from the objective Self, it will have none of these qualities. Attraction and inclination derived from the true Self will always have positive motivations.

The reason the Self should manifest in this world is to take part in raising the micro and macrocosm consciousness of the planet. The microcosm is the Stress Adaptive Human Biological Transformational Machine, or the body and the consciousness of the body. The macrocosm is the consciousness of the planet of which the body is reflective. We want to raise the level of consciousness of our planet because our planet is alive and seeks a higher union as we do. Everything there is eventually seeks a higher union.

Once we understand what the Self is and what the Self is not we can begin to work with two primary methodologies.

First we must understand Self-observation, what it is and how to undertake the powerful act of observing the Self. The act of Self-observation is a way to accumulate useful energy to begin the necessary practice of reducing negative emotions. The mechanical expression of negative emotions is an impediment to Self-observation, but to reduce negative emotions you must be able to observe them.

Second we must learn and practice doing.

We will discuss practical ideas to help one to wake up. Take one!

Table of Contents

CHAPTER ONE: On Evolving

1. For there to be light, there must be friction.

Dr. J: This can be taken in several ways. For example, in Ayurveda, the movement of the air creates heat, and heat creates light, so heat and light together represent the element fire.

In work terms, friction is inevitable because we are starting from such a low place. We have so much inertia to overcome in the mechanical state. You cannot stop the machine on a dime and change directions. There is resistance, both internally and externally, as you begin to put on the brakes. The light is the observations, realizations, knowing and change of state that occur as a result of the effort of changing the state of the machine.

STUDENT: An example in more practical terms: You can be living a life that is relatively comfortable. For instance, I was living in my mom's house, had my job, my yoga, everything. I knew what was going to happen pretty much every day. Not necessarily, but it was really comfortable. And I always had this problem with getting too comfortable in a situation because there's very little growth. That's why in relationships you see people growing really comfortable with each other, and then I'll watch my friends break up and I'll see in myself or in one of my friends—they go through the two weeks after they break up having all these self-realizations like "Why didn't I see this before?" And it's all about being in a situation that is relatively uncomfortable to you. That's how you grow, through being uncomfortable.

Dr. J: We say in class, we are "stress adaptive," right?

STUDENT: And if there is no stress to adapt to, you're going nowhere.

Dr. J: We are adapting to stress whether we like it or not, whether we know it or not. We're constantly adapting to stress. From the point of view of the work, the friction refers to the specific resistance toward evolving. There's friction in just about any change you care to make, good or bad.

2. Shocks jar a person out of sleep; sometimes a terrible sacrifice is necessary.

Dr. J: It is as it is. There are actually three different things here. Shocks have a particular meaning in the work and they are not random. All shocks do not equally jar a person out of sleep. Many kinds of shocks may momentarily jar a person awake or bring them to a relative waking state, such as being in an accident. Seeing something extraordinarily beautiful (shocks are not always negative) can create a moment of awareness.

Shocks in the work refer to specific kinds of influences brought in with intention to instigate certain reactions that then feed the process, making it potentially more sustainable.

"Somehow a terrible sacrifice is necessary," refers to a whole range of things. For example, if you learn that everything is unreal, in order to get to reality you might have to give up everything. You literally sacrifice everything you believe, everything you think you know about your self, everything you've been told about your self and the understanding of "how the world works." The more identified you are with your belief system, the greater a sacrifice it is to let go. Many people, when confronted with that kind of possibility, might run the other way.

"Sometimes a terrible sacrifice is necessary." We don't get to say ahead of time what sacrifice is necessary for enlightenment. Nobody gets to say it for us, either. In order for it to be genuine it has to be authentic to the person. What might be a great sacrifice to me might not be such a big deal to you. "Oh, I can give that up." "Oh I can think a different way." One thing hard to give up, for example, that people will fight to the death to hold onto, is the justification for negative emotions.

"It is as it is." There is no way around it. The Work says there's no genuine possibility of self-evolution that does not involve personal sacrifice on some level, so it is how it is. Part of "being a person in the Work" is about accepting that that is how it is.

STUDENT: I think about Rumi and the Sufis and how they talk about dying. In order to get close to "the light," you have to die a thousand times. "There is always another death to die beyond the death you know."

Dr. J: My opinion is that it is exactly what they are talking about. You might understand this early, you might understand this on the way, or you might understand this late, but every time we give up something that up to a certain point we've considered to be fundamentally a part of who we are, that part of us dies. In order to be new, you undergo the process of "birthing your self." Something has to go away in order to make room for the new.

Depending on where you're at in the process, it might be up to your literal death, because there are lots of ideas and a lot of words about creating something that might actually be able to endure the physical death. If we aren't strong enough, clear enough, willful enough, deliberate enough, knowledgeable enough and/ or dedicated enough to let go of the little things keeping us from being completely authentic to our true nature, we're going to have a hard time adjusting to the change of state after we die. There is a lot of teaching about this in many different cultures. Making transitions such as dieing with intention a work idea shared with Sufi culture and Sufi ideas.

3. Contacting higher sources and levels of energy is your main work.

Dr. J: This means to contact higher sources and levels of energy within you, and more independently higher sources and levels of energy within the different centers that make us up. Once we start to understand this, we have a compartmentalization of centers. We have different native centers of influence, and each one of them has lower and higher parts. We are talking about moving from the lower parts of our centers to the higher parts of our centers and our inner self as a whole. There are also higher sources and levels of energy external to us, so how do we go about moving into proximity to them and how do we go about attracting them?

There is a hermetic philosophy (also an engineering theory), which is a "law of similar" and has to do with resonance. I want to attract higher influences and I want to do this on purpose. I don't want it to just be a random occurrence that might happen one day in my life, such as: I'm walking down a road and an angel or some spiritual influence or intelligence communicates to me and has some transforming nature or information. Rather, there's another idea that these types of occurrences aren't necessarily random. How do we attract or resonate with energies higher than our own and how do we do it on purpose? Why does it say your main work is to contact higher sources and levels of energy? There is also this fundamental idea that it is not possible for any one person without assistance and support to do this work. We need help, we need other people, and maybe these higher sources and levels of energy in the closer realms represent other people, other groups or a conscious school.

4. Commence many efforts simultaneously to achieve results.

Dr. J: There are schools that focus on one center versus another. There may be conscious schools focusing primarily on the instinctive center, or the emotional, moving, or intellectual center. The idea is if they can bring a perfected consciousness in that one area, it will be a key to "unlock" all of the rest. This theory has been tried. Been there, done that. Perhaps a better way to work is to work on many levels with many centers simultaneously, because that's how they work in us. One center does not work to the exclusion of all the others. They are all somewhat active all the time. Effort refers to intentional activities or intentional work that targets specific influences, centers, and features all at the same time.

Working on many things simultaneously also keeps you from being too comfortable, and getting too much in a groove. There is really nowhere to relax because somewhere in the interplay between the simultaneous efforts, there is going to be friction. As long as the source of friction is the intentional work, then you can do something positive with it. You can gain a lot of energy, in other words. Then it is just a style of work. The purpose of a style of work is to have many objectives, have many different aims and have sort of your primary and secondary aims. Then you work on all of them at the same time. A simple example would be: we are living here in the house.

I have big aims that have to do with working on my self. I have aims that have to do with operating a school and assisting other people. I also have aims of how I want to live on a day-to-day basis in my house, aims about the attitudes, conversations and kinds of work I want to have. All of these things are happening at the same time so there is no real compartmentalization. Because we would like to get somewhere near enlightenment in this life, we assume we don't have a lot of spare time. From the point of view of the work, we don't know how long this life is for us. Maybe it is shorter than we think. Maybe it is really long. Maybe we do have a really longtime and hopefully we do. However, what if we don't?

STUDENT: So just for kicks, our typical day goes in a relatively routine pattern. Take today for instance, and the idea of working on the different centers. What did we do today, that is working on all those things?

Dr. J: Well, the instinctive/ moving center, for example, is actually maintaining our environment. Specific kinds of things are good for the machine, like the food you prepared for dinner. Eating good food with a high vibration, food intentionally crafted and aesthetic, brings tangible energy into the machine useful and necessary for all the other functions. It supports the equilibrium and the health of the machine so the instinctive parts of us aren't necessarily too big of a distraction. If we ate food without nutritional value all day and then sat here trying to do what we are doing, it might be quite different. It might be a lot harder to focus, you might have diarrhea or some stomach thing going on or a headache or whatever, just because the quality of the food was poor. So from an instinctive point of view, that's one thing.

Moving center can virtually be any intentional movement. For example, housekeeping has intentional movement as long as you are somewhat intentional about it. There's this bridge between the instinctive center and the moving center. Today, the primary thing for the instinctive center was our comfort, the maintenance of our machine, and our food, even the movie we watched, for example. Moving center includes whatever intentional movement you did today, even though it might have been going to the post office, but if while you went to the post office and ran your errands you had a quality of intention about it, then that is feeding the moving center. You are bringing awareness to how you go about from A to B to C to D.

J: Just bringing attention to my driving, so that I make it back!

Dr. J: Right, the attention you have to have while you're driving, that's moving center.

J: I was forewarned today to watch out because the snow-birds were out, and they don't use their blinkers.

Dr. J: It's not about the specifics of what you were doing so much as to the fact you were moving and you were paying attention while you were moving. Bringing some intention to your self while you were running or walking the dog becomes an exercise for the moving center. When we practice yoga, we focus very strongly on the moving center. That's one of the benefit's of yoga as well as one of the limitations of yoga because people try to get so much more out of it and it is not necessarily designed to do that. The ancient yogis knew this very well, and that's why they created many kinds of yoga because one kind of yoga wasn't supposed to do everything. Yoga is an excellent exercise as well as dancing and martial arts.

From the emotional center, the independent work we have done deals with self-remembering, self-observation and dealing with negative emotions. Did anybody here today deal with any negative emotions? That's working on the emotional center. What we are doing this minute is working on the intellectual center. By definition, and in yogic terms, what we're doing right now is practicing Jnana yoga, or the yoga of understanding.

5. Divide your self so that one part of your mind watches the other part to heal your self.

Dr. J: This is just a simple presentation of the idea of self-observation. The simplest way I can describe self-observation is you have one part of your self that watches another part of your self. Self-remembering and self-observation happen when you start to know what those parts are. For example, if we are talking about chakras, first, second, third, fourth, fifth, six and seventh, we will start to have clear distinctions about what they are and what they represent. If we're talking about centers of gravity, instinctive, moving, emotional and intellectual, we start to know what those are. We start to see them, and we catch ourselves watching. That watching is self-remembering. Observation is when we get specific to the centers.

I like the first part, "to heal your self," because we are fractured, broken apart and compartmentalized in so many ways. We can't even begin to count all the different ways we are separate from our self. That's the nature of illness or disharmony. By watching our self, just literally by having one part watch another part, it seems like the simplest thing when I say it like that, to me, but it's incredibly powerful because something happens when you do which does not happen when you do not. You are more awake when you are watching your self. You're more in a waking state as opposed to sleep, and you can only do anything for or about your self when you are awake.

So, if you're going to heal your self, then real healing is the work you are doing when you are paying more attention. Most systems of healing never talk about this, and in my opinion that is a fundamental flaw with those systems, because you've got sleeping people working on sleeping people so everybody is sleepwalking, and they're doing a sleepwalk dream called healing, so there's a lot of play for imagination. There's a lot of play for things appearing to work that don't really work. There's a lot of room for error. If I want someone to work on me I would prefer the person who is trying to heal me is awake and paying attention.

6. Erase what is recorded on the negative side of your record by stopping the justifying.

Dr. J: First of all, what's the negative side of your record? What is your record? This is what I'm referring to when I talk about "tapes." That's my term. I'm not harking back to album metaphors here, I've moved on to cassettes.

STUDENT: We could call it CD's? MP3 files?

Dr. J: Yes, it would be tracks and files.

J: I like vinyl…

Dr. J: So the other side of your record is referring to those recordings, those completely mechanical tapes we play. We are no more conscious in this regard than a jukebox. Instead of actually selecting the tracks on the jukebox, which are mostly negative, our jukebox was made basic, so it just has one big red button on the front of it. Every time the button gets bumped, something plays, but it's random. The negative tapes may in fact have absolutely nothing to do with what triggered them. You hit the big red button and something plays.

One of the techniques for removing energy from negative tapes is to stop justifying. Justifying always happens after the fact, it's not conscious. One of the ways we know it is not conscious is because consciousness occurs before the expression. Justifying is what occurs after the identification. For example, "Generic Student, or GS", I'm trying to think of something you do that really irritates me. Let's just pretend. Let's say GS is wearing a headband while we're trying to have a little class here and work on something. As soon as I see that it brings up all kinds of stuff, because I had a student who, in the past, wore head bands in class who never paid attention, who was the worst student and ended up causing me some big problem, by hurting themselves or whatever. Or today while I was out, I was trying to get something at the store and I needed help and the person who came up to help me in the store today was wearing a headband and was a complete idiot, and not only didn't help me do what I needed to do at the store, but we ended up in a fight and I got thrown out of the store. So the second I see you with the headband, all the stories and all that stuff, whatever triggered it, whether it was a memory, an association, but the fact that I'm using something that actually has nothing at all to do with you or your headband, all of that together is a result of identification which I then justify.

J: But why do you wear a headband all the time?

STUDENT: I love my headband.

Dr. J: All right, so do I. So to erase—we don't know what erase means, is there like some eraser in our head that's rubbing things out? Or is it like in the Bio-Tapping (B.E.T.), where we say when we balance the energy, you actually take away the basis for the negative emotion, and since the basis is no longer there, it simply goes away, just like when you put a fire out and the smoke vanishes. There is now no basis for there to be smoke. We use the word erase.

7. Let go of self-deceit in order to support unity in your nature.

Dr. J: You cannot move so long as you take your self as one person. Your work begins when you feel two persons inside your self. The fundamental theory is that there is not one I, there are many "I's." There are so many I's. We can't rope them, it's like herding cats, trying to get all of these different I's to do anything or to go in any particular direction at any particular time. So that's why we start with self-remembering because it's enough to start just to get to a point where you can have one part of your mind watching another part. Inside, one part observes another part. Later, we can talk about aggregates and centers of influence, i.e. deputy steward, steward, objective self—those are all stages of organization, if you will, of I's into cohesive consciousness.

To start with, forget it. There's no such thing. All those are just myths and fantasies. If we could even just get to the point of being able to clearly see there are at least two of us, one who can watch and one who is sometimes watched without knowing, that's enough to prove the many I's right there. If there's more than one, and we've been taught our whole life there is just one of us, and that in psychiatry, if you believe there is more than one person inside your head, you could be clinically diagnosed as a schizophrenic.

Part of the reason I don't put a lot of stock in modern western psychology is because if that is true, then I believe everyone is schizophrenic. Everyone is schizophrenic because they have multiple personalities. "I" is just another word for personality. Your work begins when you feel two persons inside your self. Feel is an emotional word, and you are going to find, as we go further in this, emotions are very important. That's why, right from the beginning, we start working on them. We start working on the negative side because it is the dominant side. The dominant side of our emotional life is negative, and until you really understand that, you don't really know much about your emotions. As far as the possibility of having a positive emotional context for the work you do on your self, and for your life and the things you do in your life, well, there is not a chance of it until we begin to handle the negative side of that. We want to feel those two; it is not enough just to mentally acknowledge it. That's a starting point, when you really begin to feel it.

J: Well how does one feel it? What does it feel like?

Dr. J: However it feels. There is no "how does it feel," not at this point.

8. Push your self beyond your limits all of the time.

Dr. J: All of the time., you mentioned the comfort thing and getting out of your comfort zone and how things shock you and happen to you and how that is a stimulus for growth, right? That's essentially what you were saying? Well, even if that is not happening, you have to make it happen. You make it happen small, you make it happen big, but you have to at least have. Remember we are stress-adaptive, so pushing beyond our limits is intentionally creating stress consistently greater than the stress coming mechanically from your environment. We're going to adapt to the stress one way or another, so to what stress are we going to adapt? Up to this point in life, most of us have been adapting to stress we didn't pick. Time is coming or going. It just happened, and ta-da, we adapted to it.

Here we are. Pushing beyond your limits all the time is complex since we don't really even know what our limits are. We might think we know what our limits are, but we don't.

Pushing beyond our limits is intentionally creating pressure to wake us up. It is so easy to get comfortable. It's too easy in a relationship or situation to get into your comfort zone, and, as soon as you're all comfy and snuggly, usually that means the relationship starts going downhill. There are rare exceptions, but I think you can pause for a while at any place.

From a work point of view you never want to be too comfortable, because if you are, as soon as you notice you are too comfortable, you have to change something. One of the good parts about being in a school is that we have pressure to push ourselves a little bit beyond our comfort zone coming from different directions. Often right when I would just really like to collapse and not do this too much, here comes a bunch of students and it's time to work on your self! Oh, man, I didn't want to work on myself at 9:00 am. I would have way rather been working on myself at 6:00 pm! Don't you know that my favorite TV show is on? "Class over, click!"

STUDENT: Can I just say about that previous point: "adapting to stress" we create rather than always adapting to stress outside of our control? I think that's such an important point, because when I first started going to my yoga school I remember being introduced to the concept of just saying "no" to things and situations. Do this instead of just adapting to everything that happens to you. You can't control everything. This isn't about control or power. It's about crafting and having intention come in so that you're not a victim of circumstance at all times. I think adding intention is even more than starting to observe your self, although it is part of observing your self. That's a huge thing! As you practice this you can see the lack of this in ordinary conversation. You start to see it in the way people talk about their lives and the things that "happen to them." Because there is little or no intention there is little or no responsibility. Whatever happens is random, an accident or an event. Nothing is intentional at all. If you're observing your self you will see this is exactly what you also do. So that's a really big one.

Dr. J: There is an idea that Karma, the theory of independent origination, is entirely out of our control. This is true in circumstances we relate to in ordinary states of mind and being. However, Karma is a Law of Nature and it's not personal. By bringing awareness and intention into the present moment we can generate the precursor to future Karma in our favor right now.

J: Once you start taking responsibility for your internal life, does that help with justifying? Does it help because you have no one to blame?

Dr. J: I don't know about that because I think we are really sharp, and we can always find someone to blame. In the absence of someone externally to blame, we can even go to the point of blaming "the man."

J: Today I blamed the overhead speakers playing "Christmas music."

Dr. J: That's the man.

J: Done by the corporate. I was clear with the cashier—somebody should tell them that we're not all of one particular religion.

Dr. J: That's programming. They don't care. It's propaganda. That's "the man." There's always something external you can blame. If you were responsible enough, you would then responsibly blame your self.

J: Why, because I chose to shop at Wal-Mart?

Dr. J: No, that's just what people do. People blame themselves. Can't find someone else to blame, they blame themselves. One way or another, someone will get blamed. "I'm not taking the heat for this," wait a minute, who just said that? And, "if I'm not taking the blame," "why do I have to take the blame?" Wait a minute; both conversations are in my head at the same time. If I could ever catch myself doing that, I'm self-remembering right there. So pushing your self "on evolving," for example, goes back to friction, back to shocks. Pushing your self creates friction, because we have this inertia, we want to come to stillness. We want to find a comfortable place. We want to find a comfortable place in everything: the best seat in the theatre, the most comfortable relationship. I want to drive a comfortable car, I want to eat comfy food, I would like for K. to not be so critical of my writing when she's editing, I would like to find a comfortable place. That's my inertia, to come to this comfortable place. But as someone who is working on myself, one of the things I have to remember while I'm self-remembering is to challenge that.

J: Is that why sometimes we sit on the uncomfortable spot and go to the IMAX?

Dr. J: Well, no, that was an accident. You can't give credit to an accident for being some reflection of your consciousness, even though on another level we might say everything is a reflection of our perfect luminosity. We're far from being in a place to bask in the glory of our luminosity. We're still slugging away here.

STUDENT: Well we can just look at it all as an exercise.

Dr. J: It's all work.

9. Be or not be.

Dr. J: The real battleground is not another person or an event. It is one's own "I's." There are no issues (plural), there is only one issue. This is what Shakespeare was writing about. In one school I was in, there was quite a lot of debate about whether or not Shakespeare had been in a Fourth Way school. Shakespeare is a treasure trove of ideas that can be related to the kind of things we are talking about.

One of my favorite things I did when I lived in the northeast for a while was going to the Shakespeare wing at the Library of Congress. All Shakespeare. All the time. You can see these most ancient copies of original Shakespeare manuscripts. It was fascinating. In some work schools, the groups will get together and will actually perform Shakespeare plays. I think other schools of self-development have done Shakespeare in their repertoire of exercises "To be, or not to be." The real battleground is not another person or event. In the Tibetan Book of the Dead the aspirant is directed to affirm "that which is before me is a reflection of my own perfect luminosity," or, that which is before me is an aggregate of my own I's. What I'm struggling against is "I".

Always the struggle is within. It appears we struggle between ourselves, it appears we have interpersonal relations and struggles, it appears we have societal struggle, it appears that we have environmental struggle. But on some level, that's an illusion, and all true struggle is on the inside. There are no issues. Issues are based on identification and grounds for justification. When we make a list of our issues, everything we list is a basis for justifying not being who we are supposed to be. This applies to everything we list or could list. From the point of view of the work, none of those issues are real, because eventually, all of those issues have to go. They all have to be let go because whatever the goal is of what we are trying to create is not about the issues. I read in a magazine that the "be here now" is a new-age concept, or a new thing. But Shakespeare wrote, "To be or not to be." That's it, be or not be. So there you go, it's the real battleground. If you want to be a warrior, a true samurai, then you work on the inside. It doesn't mean we abandon the outside, because we are still in the machine, the vehicle.

10. To help you awaken, before you retire in the evening, set an aim or willful objective.

Dr. J: The definition of an aim is a willful objective. It's a work term. Awaken in the morning so you can continue your work for another day, but actually there is another idea here. Remember, we are in two states of consciousness right now. We are in sleep; we are still asleep just like we were before we crawled out of the bed this morning. Then we have another over-laying state of consciousness, which we call "waking state" or "waking sleep," which is over that. The sleep state is still here. While I'm relatively more awake, I can influence my sleeping state. So what I would like to do is, before I give over my consciousness to my sleeping state, give it some instructions. Overtime, you may have a training effect, if you will, on the sleeping state.

STUDENT: Oh, that's why it doesn't just happen right away? That's why every night before I go to sleep I try to set some sort of intention and then I wake up in the morning and I'm like, "Damn it, it didn't work!"

11. Abandon any activity whose initial impetus is or was negative emotion.

Dr. J: Seems pretty clear. It's an exercise. You get upset, you run away. Running away is an activity, in this example, whose initial impetus was negative emotion. You got angry, or whatever. So don't do that. Better to work through the anger and resolve the negative emotions than to run from them. You've heard this "tit for tat" concept? Someone hurts you so you hurt him or her; they were mean to you so you are mean to them, eye for an eye?

J: Or get them before they get you.

Dr. J: And that's proactive negativity, which is very interesting. "I'm going to be negative in anticipation of I'm going to need to be so lets just go ahead and do it now..." An eye for an eye is a Judeo-Christian biblical kind of reference. From the point of view of this work, it is absolutely self-destructive to even think that way. This is where the bible is schizophrenic, because in the Old Testament it says "eye for an eye," and in the New Testament Jesus says "turn the other cheek." No one can turn the other cheek because they are actually practicing eye for an eye. It gets in the way, because once you are identified with a negative emotional state, there is no place for anything else. It consumes all available space. It's like blowing up a balloon. So, abandon any activity where the initial impetus is or was negative emotion. Abandon actions or activities spawned from fear, and/or any negative emotions you can think of. Examples of common negative emotions might be anger, anxiety, fear, depression, compulsion, obsession, etc.

Student: That's what the stop exercise is for, right?

Dr. J: The stop exercise is to help identify the activity of particular centers. In other words, it is a photograph. For one second you see your self thumping your head, and you might be looking at your self, going, "Why am I doing that? Who is doing that? Who likes to thump on their head when they're thinking?" That's a photograph. That action or activity is in the moving center. So ordinarily we would think that right now the moving center is asleep, but it couldn't be further from the truth. Even if I'm not doing yoga or working in the garden, the moving center is still awake and active; it wants to have something to do. "Hey, what can I do? You guys are having a talk but I want to do something! I can't talk, but I can move!"

Student: But stopping that, especially for me, that part of it is crazy because I get this.

Dr. J: Well the only reason you stop it is because in that moment it creates a little friction. Right at the moment you do the stop, you have a little separation. Something is watching something. It's just for that purpose.

This is really important. If you go back over your life and you do a little survey, how many things have you done where the original impetus to do those things, say those words, was a negative emotion? Surprisingly, it might be quite a lot.

12. Release everything unnecessary to sweep your life clean.

Dr. J: Well that's pretty clear. Of course, it takes discernment. First of all, you have to have a life to clean one. You have to have a little will and discipline to do anything, and you have to have education and discernment to decide what is unnecessary. This is somewhat Impossible for people in ordinary situations of life because people don't know what it means. What about their life needs to be changed? They lack the discipline to make a change, and they don't have clear discernment as to what would be necessary. Necessary things are interesting, because if I can let go of something unnecessary, that is relatively easy. It's harder to get rid of things I feel are necessary, since I justify why I keep them. Of course, we are talking about internal parts of us.

Student: A few months ago, before I came to this place, I was writing about how I knew that looking at this life I have right now, and imagining the end of it, I pictured myself laying there and at that point there would be a lot of things that would no longer matter. Most of what I was concerned with in my day-to-day life wouldn't matter. So I was writing that considering the point I am at now, I want to get rid all of the things that won't matter, since they are not that important now, instead of being at the end and realizing with regret how much my life was consumed by minutia and inconsequential issues.

Dr. J: And then, how do you do it every day and how can you do this 5 times a day, instead of praying to Mecca 5 times a day. Nothing wrong with that, because I have no issue with prayer I think there's a lot of value in praying. I'm just saying that if 5 times a day you let go of and get rid of something unnecessary, you haven't gotten rid of it if the next time you turn around you still have it. Many times that is what we do with unnecessary behaviors and so on. We think, oh, I've gotten rid of it. But then, I turn around, and it's still there. What if it's not a behavior, but an attitude? Have you ever tried to get rid of an attitude? I can have one attitude that is not necessary right now. I can work through it, yet an hour, day or month later, I can be completely back in that attitude, as if it was never gone.

J: That was why a week or so ago, when I asked you how come some mornings I set this aim and I wake up and I do really good and then sometimes I wake up and I'm like, "Argh! It didn't happen!" I wake up like a big crabby pants. You told me it was a habit. So ever since then, I've started noticing it less, but on the days I have it, I notice it quicker. "Oh wait, here's that crabby pants again. Where the hell did she come from?" Then I look in the mirror and see the crabby pants face, because there's actually a face I wake up with.

Dr. J: So how do you get rid of that? Sweep your life clean by getting rid of everything unnecessary. Initially there is no getting rid of it. Initially, it's just a huge thing to observe. That might be enough for a while, because we don't talk about another step past these two steps, because they work together. Handling negative emotions and self-remembering work together, and it's not enough just to get rid of the negative things. You have to also have a level of observation and remembering at the same time. We work on them where we find them, when we can, because eventually the gaps get smaller where they are not, and eventually, you might start to find your self in situations where you are remembering, observing, and there is no negative emotion, no tapes playing. When that happens, right there is a possibility for something else to happen which ordinarily would never have an opportunity to occur. Reject and let go of what is useless to make way for the possibility of something new.

13. To begin again in a different way, acquire all that you can from words, then abandon them.

Dr. J: Ask your self a question, how can I apply in practical terms what I know now? Words are great. Words are what we have to work with. We talk about books, ancient texts, and we use these as a starting place. Maybe we have some oral tradition passed on from one person to another. I believe I am fortunate to have some of that. Still in all, the instructions are, after you get everything you can from words, discussion, language, we are supposed to abandon all that and begin again in a different way. We've already discussed some of the different ways we can work without using words. For example, we can feed ourselves without a lot of words or discourse about it. We can create art without using a lot of words. We can create music, dance and practice martial arts without using a lot of words. We can just do it; we don't have to talk about it. We can clean house with intention. Quite often, I find I can work out in the world, even though I might be typing on the computer. It's very interesting to me because from another point of view there is very little going on in my head. There's not a lot of inner conversation. It really is projecting.

The idea is finding practical ways to do what we know. If we know anything, how can we do it? When we do a Tantra practice, we have not a lot of words. There is not a lot of talk. There is much communication, but not a lot of words. It has to do with the difference between knowledge and being, because that is always the challenge. How do we translate what we know into who we are? Initially we come from a place of what we know is not right, so we have to correct the knowing to have an effect on the being. They are related. We do have to bridge the gap and be very creative in finding practical ways to be what we know. We have to be creative; we have to be ingenious at it.

14. Avoid that which makes you fall asleep.

Dr. J: Relatively quickly, you should be able to start having a list of things that make you nappy. By "nappy" I mean things that cause you to lose energy and forget to observe yourself.

STUDENT: The television!

Dr. J: What makes you fall a sleep? Could be mindless TV, it could be running, it could be all kinds of things. In fact what is interesting is that almost anything that could be good for you could also make you fall asleep. It depends on where you are at while you are doing it. That is the criteria. If the activity tends to make you not observe your self, then it is in that category. If you find you can observe your self or appear to observe your self, then it is not on the list.

15. Become normal by making efforts to not have a center of gravity in negative emotions

Dr. J: We do not know what normal is! The work postulates a different normal from what we've been led to believe is normal, if we've been led to believe there is such a thing as a normal state. Work ideas say we are far from normal. In fact, we are abnormal, subnormal. Negativity cannot be the basis to approach the concept of a normal life or a normal existence or a normal consciousness, whatever that is.

J: Now falling asleep is not necessarily… When you use the word "asleep," it is not sleep; it's just not observing your self.

Dr. J: It is more than that. Not observing your self, not working on your self, not working on negative emotions, not handling or addressing your issues, not balancing your centers, not feeding your machine, not crafting, creating, Implementing, or putting your self in front of the kinds of impressions that give you the energy you need to cultivate your consciousness, etc. All of that is "asleep."

16. To get anything, you must pay.

Dr. J: You pay by sacrificing imaginary values and replacing them with real values. This is right-valuation. Step one: consider your values. What do you actually think is important, what do you believe is important. How have you lived your life up to this point, where have you put your valuation, where have you put your monies, so to speak? Where does your effort go? What generates the bulk of your activity in life? What do you value? What do you act as if you value? Many times we will say, "Well, I value this, I value that," but do not live as if that is very important. How much then do I actually value it? Maybe it is just something I have learned to say because I think people will think more highly of me because I say I have these values.

J: The first thing I think of is the concept I was raised with, which is: family is family, blood is thicker then water, family comes first, and then I realized at some point my family didn't actually practice that.

Dr. J: Those are examples of false values. False because they are affectations you absorbed from your life environment. You did not come by them through any effort or validation process originating in your own consciousness.

J: Valuing myself was not what I was taught.

Dr. J: You have to learn what real values are, and begin to substitute real values for false ones. We call that process right-valuation, or the process of valuation.

Native Americans and other indigenous peoples have the right idea when they perform ritual personal sacrifices such as "Sun Dance" and "Vision Quest". An old Lakota Medicine Chief named Chris Leaf once explained to me like this, he said "It's not a sacrifice unless it's something under other circumstances you could never let go of". Under ordinary circumstances we never give up our imaginary values. That's why we need help.

17. Accept and understand, see and appreciate everything to collect higher energy

Dr. J: This refers again to negative emotion. For example, in some workbooks it says if we are able to accumulate energy, we are also able to waste it. The single most effective way to waste the good kind of energy is to express negative emotions. If you want to start collecting energy, and you want to stop expressing negative emotions, then you must get a handle on some things triggering negative emotions or the expression of negative emotions. Cultivate an attitude of coming to understanding and acceptance. Look for the value and appreciate what's before you.

Finding fault and seeing something wrong is actually a basis for expressing a lot of negativity. I know I am subject to it, for example, when I am watching something political. I get emotional in the sense of "that's just not right, that is wrong! It is awful!" I might start to express something quite negative. If I get caught up in the expression of that negative emotion because of finding fault and seeing something wrong, I'm wasting a lot of energy and I'm also probably not observing myself.

18. To receive higher influences, make a prolonged, consistent effort.

Dr. J: There are no shortcuts to create a basis for realistic expectation of receiving higher influence. Time and effort is required. Time and effort looks like a prolonged, consistent effort. A prolonged effort means an effort continued overtime. Consistent means a steady, regular effort overtime.

J: Would that be the same as accepting that you are a beginner and moving towards being an intermediate person?

Dr. J: No. It just means once you have some work to do, you actually do it. It is not about beginner, intermediate, advanced or mastery. It's about the thing you know you're supposed to be doing, then doing it regularly and consistently over a period of time.

STUDENT: The reason it's effort is because it is not easy. That's the reason why you would need to make a prolonged consistent effort, because it's something that is very easy to back away from and say, "Well, I don't want to do this anymore because this is too freaking hard."

Dr. J: At a hundred different points you can slack off and go in a different direction that doesn't look like you are making the effort.

19. To cease creating annoyances for your self, cease expressing annoyance.

Dr. J: Goes back to the saying: what you resist persists. If you find your self annoyed, it's probably because you're expressing annoyance. We do mirror each other. There is this principle of mirroring, mimicing and resonating with each other. It's phenomenal how quick you can have one person who is annoyed, and then, all of a sudden, everybody else in the room is annoyed. It happens so quickly. Sometimes it happens so fast you can't even tell who got annoyed first. Then we might even get into annoyance competitions. "No, I'm more annoyed than you are! No, you are annoying me way more than I'm annoying you!"

STUDENT: Like people in a movie theatre: "SHHHHHHHH! SHHH! Hey, You!"

Dr. J: And then some other people in the movie theatre: "I got your "shhh" right here!" (In a Chicago style accent) Where does it end?

20. Practice external consideration to learn control.

Dr. J: Control of what? What is external consideration? Anybody want to take a guess? Or based on what you might have read, what is external consideration?

Student: I don't think I can think about it in any terms of what I've read in a book. External consideration goes back to creating experiences or friction for your self in terms of the world around you and how you react to it rather than…

Dr. J: Let me give you the idea from the work perspective. For example, we are living together, working together, doing varieties of practice, some of which are more challenging than others for us as individuals. Both challenging to do and sometimes to lead, more than you might think. It creates friction. We want the friction. The friction helps us grow. However, we don't want too much friction, so part of the way we are able to sustain and maintain a working environment is we practice what's called external consideration, which is doing everything we can to make life good and tolerable and easier, while at the same time creating friction to help us grow. We try to create the friction intentionally to discount accident. Often it is too easy to get caught up in the friction, since that is our habit, to get caught up in the friction and then all of a sudden, the friction and what is causing it becomes all we are about.

External consideration is like when I'm doing a therapeutic session or treatment and I know that this pressure on this point is going to be painful because most people have restriction and inhibition and blockage and deficiency in this point. I don't jump on it. I go in gently and it's still going to be painful, but it's not as painful as if I jabbed it. When I'm done, I make nice. That "make nice" is external consideration.

For example, it is a wonderful blessing to have someone prepare a meal. The energy to prepare the meal is not the same as the energy to clean the mess afterward. In fact, they are very different. So, when we kind of change gears a little bit and we jump in together and practice cleaning up the meal as more of a group thing, that's making nice. Usually what happens is you put so much effort and intention into preparing the meal, you don't have a whole lot left over. All of a sudden, the meal is over, and there's a big mess. There is an opportunity right there to have mechanical friction because you are tired and you did expend a lot of effort on everybody else's behalf. Since you spent that effort, you haven't recuperated it yet and there's a possibility for that not to be the most positive experience. By bringing in external consideration, which is to help, what it does is it makes the whole meal experience more positive. That is external consideration. Every little thing we do to help each other work, and still come out of it in good shape, is external consideration.
J: Is it also showing compassion?

Dr. J: Only if there is a practical expression of it. Compassion is just another idea unless you are doing something. If I say I'm compassionate, "oh my, look at this mess that has to be cleaned up in the kitchen," and then kick back with my book and throw my feet up on the table, it might be empathy, but it's not compassion. It doesn't become compassion until I actually get up and help.

21. Do not expect to obtain roses without thorns.

Dr. J: It should be obvious, but as I've been surfing through social media posts and referral links online, everyone is so blissed out and a lot of these discussions are just about "finding your blissful space." There's actually very little discussion about people having meltdowns and genuine crises and issues that stop them dead in their tracks. The reality of it is, if the work you're doing is practical, effective, and addresses distortions in your energy and your different centers, then stuff is going to come up. You will have resistance and emotions like fear and anxiety. That's going to happen. It has to happen. If we said, "Okay, we're going to do a really thorough housecleaning," there's a high probability we are going to find some stuff that's not where it's supposed to be and has to be moved around. There's a high probability we are going to find something dirtier than we ever could have imagined.

This is going to require some cleaning, scrubbing, effort and work! We might even find some critters like spiders or fire ants or something we didn't anticipate would be there. It's going to take effort to resolve or restore that particular area or item. Just like when we clean the pantry and we find rotten food. We didn't know this before we started cleaning. And that's just the house! We are way more complex than this house. Chances are we will come up with things in ordinary life and circumstances to which we would never want to pay very much attention. In most cases in ordinary life, when these kinds of issues come up it is considered perfectly okay to put them right back where you found them, cover them up and go in a different direction, pretending they are not there. When you're working on your self, that's not okay.

J: You have to move the bookcases to get the spider webs.

Dr. J: As we do so, we are creating this balanced template, which is a state of being more conducive toward the true self manifesting. It's a painful process, picking roses. As much as I'd like to say lets just work on the blissful parts and the things that make us happy, the garden can become completely overgrown if we don't pick the weeds.

22. Endure passing small test to prepare your self for large ones.

We definitely have to work on handling the things we can handle and practice as an hourly, daily, weekly, monthly, yearly strategy to take care of the things that we can take care of. Going back to the house metaphor—by keeping the house in a semi-orderly state, and not letting it get too far out of whack, it becomes a lot easier when you have to really organize things to have the best space you we can (for class, for instance). If we've been doing lots of little stuff before that, it will be way easier.

If we haven't been focusing on what is really important in terms of keeping the house orderly, then we have to do something big, and it takes a huge effort. Maybe we are not even able to do it. Maybe it is too much to get done. In some schools and systems, there is a lot of crisis management, which is what to do when you have an extreme situation. There's nothing wrong with having that, but it's more practical to work on the little, manageable stuff to prevent an unruly situation. This goes back to validation. When you have a small challenge and you handle it well, you validate your methods.

When you have a big test or challenge, though you might have some resistance to applying the tools you have, you will go ahead and do it because you have already validated that the process works. It also helps with your endurance. When you haven't been working on your self and you have a huge crisis or challenge, you might handle it well to start with, but then you will crash and burn, unable to sustain the effort long enough to get through it. You haven't built up the muscles, so to speak, or gathered what it takes to be successful over a period of time. If you've been practicing and achieving some success with smaller things, you've built up some endurance you're able to hold a way of thinking or being long enough to get through it.

23. Assimilation through insistence and repetition make essence grow.

Dr. J: Digest experience through understanding. Essence is a good word. It is a work word, and it is referring to the true self. It is another term for the true self used quite a lot in workbooks. Essence is everything that does not relate to personality and ego. Your essence is the parts of you that do not have their origin in negative emotion or expressions of the ego and personality. Insistence is to insist that you work a certain way or that you try to self-remember and work with non-expression of negative emotions.

Repetition is doing this over and over again. To digest your experience through understanding is another half to the coin. Just to use yesterday as an example, without being specific, it is actually a really good thing, because you are in a different state of mind right now, to go back and reflect on that. Reflect on it, and then try to bring understanding to what you were thinking, feeling and saying or not. Come to some clarity of understanding about that. Going back is a way of eating your experience. When you have a difficult time, you go back, while it is fresh, because you really do want to remember the details and look at them with rational eyes. That is a process of digestion. It's not just about looking at the negative parts. Even when you were having a meltdown, did you happen to notice there was part of you watching you have this emotional intensity? This is important because that is actually the self-remembering process.

J: Truthfully, the part of my thought also was not only did I notice it, but I felt still like that part of myself didn't have enough to go, "Ahh! What are you doing?"

Dr. J: Well that's a different issue, whether you have enough will to change it in the moment. I'm talking about getting to a point where you could have the will to change it. For example, I am talking about the digestion, the idea of going back, not only looking at the negative, but also looking to see what the triggers were. Then look at the expression, both internal and external, but look at it from the light of where your head is not at, in a more rational place. Then look at the positive part. What were the positive things? How did you eventually come to a positive place? How did you eventually get to a place where you didn't have that anxiety or panic? What transpired that got you to this other place? Everything I am describing is the process of digesting experience through understanding.

24. Divide attention to make essence grow.

Dr. J: Divided attention is just another word for self-observation and self-remembering. Self-remembering is the sense or state of "I am." I am here, I am doing this, I am feeling this, I am thinking this, and I am saying this. In other words, it is the idea of having a feeling or observation of "I am" in relation to thought, action or deed. You could also say it is the observation that "one is doing," if you wanted to avoid using "I's" as an exercise. We don't really have one I, we actually have many I's. So really it isn't that I am self-remembering, because I don't even know who I am! Which "I" is actually doing the observation? I don't know. I do notice something, however, and that is divided attention. There is a work idea, which is to sometimes, instead of thinking "I," use the word "one." Make it less personal, in other words. Personal equals personality, and it is egocentric. Saying "I am" without discrimination or discernment of knowing which "I" is at the present moment is very indistinctive and unclear. It could be one of many I's in the present moment.

There is a work exercise often practiced in schools. I had a teacher give an exercise for everybody to do for a period of a month, whether we were in class, out of class, driving a car, going shopping, at the bank, whatever, unless it was some ordinary circumstance of outer life where people would think you were being ridiculous. For the whole month we couldn't use the word "I." So, when we are talking and I say, "What do you think we should do today?" you couldn't say, "Well, I think," because the exercise is not to use that word, and you must find something else to use. "One" is an example of this. Either don't refer to any I because you don't know which particular I is having that thought, or use the word "one," which is the same thing. Do you understand?

Self-observation is focusing on seeing the work of a particular center. In other words, you are trying to be more distinctive about what the difference is between self-remembering and self-observation. Self-remembering is the "I am" phenomenon where we practice divided attention. Self-observation is when you are doing that "I am" experience but you are focusing on a particular center. Is it coming from the instinctive, moving, emotional, intellectual, sexual, or physical center?

25. Separate your aim from the desires and habits of the body and personality.

Dr. J: Try as much as possible to make them serve your ultimate aim. By "body" I mean the tangible, physical body. By personality, I mean ego. We can't actually make the body go away. We can't discount that the body is influential, and that all the things stored in the body are going to continue to be here and are going to influence all of the centers. That means the matrix body and the tangible physical body. If the tangible physical body is where the subconscious mind and matrix body are, and where the disruptions in the energy patterns are manifesting as negative emotions, we can't just make that go away. It is still going to drive us.

If ego is the expression of our personality, which has been developed through our stress-adaptation to life, patterning our family, friends, schools, patterning our society, propaganda, and all of this kind of thing, we cant make that go away. We can't just snap a finger and make it not be so. It is stored in us. What we can do is make aims. An aim is like an objective, a willful objective. For example, one of my aims today is to reduce any expression of negative emotion. I have a corollary to that, which is to express love and compassion, joy and equanimity. So there are two aims, one on the negative side is working to not express negativity.

Really be concrete, which means I am going to try and think before I speak. I am going to try and think before I assume some negative posture. The corollary to it is also an aim, a willful aim, deliberate, intentional, that I will also today try to express genuine love, genuine compassion, genuine joy, and be mentally the most balanced person I can be. You want to ask your self always, what is your ultimate aim? Ultimate aims are big picture aims. One example of an ultimate aim is to become enlightened. Maybe that's too big of an ultimate aim, because you can't even imagine what enlightenment is.

If I understand there is a man number one, two, three, four, five, six, and seven, I might think there are different levels of consciousness, and if I were to say my research on my self has shown me to still be in the man number three category, then I have an ultimate aim at this point, just to become man number four, which is a person who is able to express their true self and their true nature, and who has higher functions working in all of their centers and who has the capacity to not be controlled by the expression of negative emotion. Whoa, that seems very godlike to me right now, a person who is like that would seem very godlike, balanced mind, balanced higher functioning of all of the different centers, who is not ruled by the expression of negative emotions. I set that as one of my ultimate aims.

In the past, I had an ultimate aim, which was that I would never again be violent or express violence in my life. There was actually a point when I first set that as an aim and didn't think it was possible. I was not just going to work on controlling my anger, I was going to make an aim that I would no longer have violence as part of my expression of who I am in life, period. When I set that aim, it seemed quite ultimate, as if I had made an aim to be able to levitate. I didn't think either was realistic for me at the time, but I spent ten years working on it, and now I've had fifteen years where I haven't had an outburst or an inclination to be violent whatsoever at any time. What do I do with that? Well, I just move on to the next aim.

As I discover something else needing work, then I make that into an aim. Introspection is a good thing when you're doing your writing, meditation or little survey. It is useful and okay to have a wish list of aims. You don't have to share them with anybody. It's not about what anybody else thinks might be good for you or not good for you, but just your own personal aims. It is really important to do that, and you should have ultimate aims and short-term aims. I did three different kinds of aims. I did a daily aim, an ultimate aim, and an ultimate aim now to learn what is man number four and to be that man number four. Of course, that is a work concept. Unless you know what man number four is, it doesn't really mean anything. For me it means a lot.

26. You must immediately give to others what you have received to advance.

Dr. J: Make your soul grow by learning to give your sincere attention to others. By real contact with others, something can begin to flow through you. To advance you must accept responsibility and show charity. Notice the word "immediately." It's part of the validation process. As you acquire information of what seems real to you and understanding of your self through your own practice, it is quite important that you share that with other people. Initially, that sharing is in your work group. You want to be open to the possibility of expanding that circle and testing and trying and experimenting, because it is quite valuable. Nothing says they have to accept it, or that you immediately give to other people what you have received and they will accept or understand it. It's not about that.

This works on so many levels, I think we could spend at least an hour on this point alone. For example, one of the concepts of Angels Speak was that, starting from a very young age, I would have chance encounters with people who seemed to be strangers or seemed to be not a friend per se, but someone I knew. At very particular moments of time, they would say something to me that would just jar me, because I knew what they were saying to me was absolutely true. I didn't really have anywhere to put it or any way to understand it. These words accumulated overtime. This prepared me to begin to study, research, and practice trying to be this person I suspected was possible for me to be. I had this validation, experience and understanding and now I'm a few years in the future talking to you and I have a chance to share with you something valuable I have been given, so I just do it. You don't understand it and you don't accept it; externally there is no validation you are getting it or agreeing with me.

Even the most ignorant, unconscious lead alchemy person still has a true self. They still have an essence; there is still part of them connected in this great web of life and this non-local mind. It is still there, it just may not have a way to manifest yet. So, those words go to that part of them. It may not be your play in their life to see the response. Some of these people I interacted with when I was quite young, even before I was a teenager, while I was a teenager, and later on, I never saw them again. They have no validation that what they told me had any effect whatsoever.

For example, I'll tell you a true story. This will be a new one for you! I title this story, "I was Martin Luther King's Laundry Boy." I was! When I was ten and eleven years old, I had a summer job with Westmont Cleaners in Atlanta, Georgia. It was a part-time gig, and every Saturday my mom or dad would drive me to Westmont cleaners, which was the local laundry with which we did business. They would drop me off at eight o'clock in the morning. There was the old man and his wife who ran the cleaners. He had a white van and they would go out through various neighborhoods.

We would go to the houses, knock on the doors, the ladies of the house would open the door and there would be several of these great big laundry bags, and it was my job to help schlep them to the van. We would do this from eight o'clock until three-thirty in the afternoon. I got paid by the hour, some ridiculous slave labor wage that would be totally illegal now, and they would buy me lunch.

One of our stops was 210 Sunset, which was Martin Luther King's house. I didn't know who Martin Luther King was, and probably lots of people didn't know who he was at that time. What I would do is go in, and Ms. Coretta, quite often, wouldn't be ready.

We'd get there around eleven or twelve on Saturday, and she had babies who are now senators and congressmen. I would go in, and if she wasn't ready, my boss would leave me there and go to the next house then come back in a little bit and pick me up when I had dragged the bags outside. I sat in the living room, and in the living room they had nice furniture and a glass topped coffee table on top of a white, bear-skin rug which was a real polar bear. I thought it was the most amazing thing I'd seen in my whole life at that time. Behind the couch was a five-foot wide life-size oil painting of Mahandas Gandhi.

I'd get on the floor and get right up in the face of the polar bear and I thought, "Look at this polar bear's head!" I thought it was so fantastic. It had very soft fur. Then I would sit on the couch and look at the painting of Mohandas Gandhi. He was a dark skinned, small frame man in his robes with a baldhead, sitting with his little glasses. It was a beautiful painting! I think it's in their foundation museum now. I would look at that painting every Saturday for almost two years, until the assassination.

So, one day I asked Ms. Coretta who it was, and she says, "Oh, that's Mohandas Gandhi and he was a man who believed in human rights and the rights of people. He was a spiritual teacher who practiced and taught non-violence, which my husband believes in. He is one of my husband's mentors, so to speak. Even though we are Baptist and my husband, he's a Baptist Preacher, we want to follow people who practice non-violence. He is a role-model for my husband, that's why he is in our house, because my husband is trying to teach people how to be non-violent."

At the time, I was like, "Wow, that is really cool." It was also the first time I saw anybody that looked like a yogi or anything like that. So fast forward, here I am, fifty-five years old, how important a concept is non-violence in my life? What was my personal struggle with the concept of violence in my life? How it affected other people as well as myself. Just those few words and being in that house at the time meant very little to me. I really did not know what she was talking about. So you may be that person for somebody else. The first person who I remember really talking to me about why it was important not to be a violent person was Coretta Scott King, who I knew as "Ms. Coretta." I always wanted to go back as an adult and see her and talk to her, and I never had the chance to do that before she passed away, and I sort of regretted that, but this is what I'm talking about: you must immediately give to others what you have received.

Make your soul grow by learning to give your sincere attention to others. That means not just attention, but sincere attention is real and genuine attention, the best attention you have. From real contact with others, something can begin to flow through you. In other words, I gain something, something actually happens to me when I share sincerely. It's not just something you do; you actually gain something from it. Something comes back to you. If you want to call it karma, maybe that energy could be Karma, but there is something.

By real contact with others, something can begin to flow through you. To advance, you must accept responsibility and show charity. In other words, to not share your sincere self, to not share the things you are validating that are critically valuable and useful for your self, you are being irresponsible. It is irresponsible to not share. Why? Because guess what, why am I charitable to people even sometimes when they are not the kind of people I would normally want to even have a conversation with? It's because I was one of those people at some time in my life, but somebody, or a series of some bodies over my life, in spite of my bad behavior, in spite of my wicked, stupid thoughts and ways of being, genuinely shared truth with me from their essence, from what they truly believed.

Here I am 45 years later, and every word that came out of her mouth to me sitting on her couch in her living room, I verified as being absolutely God's truth. So that word of truth had an impact. Responsibility means we have to share. Why do you have to teach yoga? You have to teach yoga because you have proven that yoga has helped you and is valuable to you and is good for you. Because of that, you have to share. What if I don't want to be a teacher? Well I'm sorry, tough, and too bad. Call it some other name, call it a "sharer." Call it something else if you have hang-ups with the word "teacher." Maybe you should tap that. Maybe it's too formal. We don't have to have words for it. However it comes about, you're going to have to give what you've got to somebody else. Why am I teaching you? Why do I even make the effort? Because I have to. It's part of this process. It's a law of the universe.

Q & A

STUDENT: No, I can just see very clearly those instances in my own life where people have been like that for me and I can also clearly see the other instances where I've been like that for somebody else. It is kind of a challenge to not be attached to their understanding in the moment, because I can look back at my life very easily. I remember clearly all those people in my life who have been that for me. And I know that something happens. It's not right in the moment. You don't just change instantaneously. Something in you does, but it might take a long time to realize it.

J: I've had that too. That is why I am sitting here.

STUDENT: That's why we are all sitting here, right?

Dr. J: Exactly

STUDENT: That's why we're having this conversation, that's why we are recording this conversation, to share it with other people.

27. Free your self from fear to progress.

STUDENT: You know, it's crazy. I think sometimes you don't even realize how afraid you are, and so once you start working on that, and really looking at the spots where you are blocked because you are so afraid, of whatever it is that you are afraid of. It's like yesterday, before I went to sleep last night I just wrote a couple of things down and I sat there thinking about how I felt. I was imagining myself standing on my own two feet, more powerful than I ever could have possibly been. Not even realizing in the past how afraid even just a situation like what happened last night. Everyone who listens to this is going to wonder what happened last night! So I would just get back into this place, and I wouldn't be able to qualify it as fear because I didn't know what it was. I can qualify it as being fear in seeing myself now and seeing the actual powerful experience it is not to have fear. It's like this moving forward thing, and I can see myself in these certain situations that would make me uncomfortable, especially dealing with guys from past relationships. I know I'm going to see some of them when I go home, and I can for the first time imagine myself standing in front of them, not feeling questioned or judged because I know where I'm standing right now. I'm not afraid. This could change, it may not be completely permanent, but I know I feel like that right now, and it's different from any other way I have ever felt. I didn't think of it as fear, I thought of it as, "Oh, this is a situation I don't want to touch, oh this is going to suck, oh I don't want to do this, oh this really just makes me feel terrible." I don't have to feel that way. And that is progress.

Dr. J: Fear is a negative emotion. If we say as some do, that "the cause of all negative emotions is a disruption in the body's energy system." In the moment, that is why we tap, to correct the disruption in the energy system. Also, fear is more than just a negative emotion. It is our habit. Just correcting the imbalance in your energy system does not change the habitual pattern of being a certain way or thinking a certain way in certain situations. The only thing is to not feed the habit, and/or to substitute superseding habits. Substitute habits more highly functional than the old habit's, which are not so functional. Fear is the number one negative emotion we generally express, whether we say it out loud or anyone else ever sees it or not. Inside of us, it's got to be right up there as one of the top three negative emotions we deal with.

28. Work is a struggle with conflicting things.

Dr. J: The moment this occurs in you, try to self-remember and try to not identify or go into the emotional parts of your self. Let me say this in two parts. First is a statement: work is a struggle with conflicting things. What does it mean to work on your self? One of the definitions of what it means to work on your self is to work on conflicting things within your self. There are things which conflict inside of us. There are things that just are not in agreement with each other, and they are conflicting with each other. There are things we know are not right we cannot do anything about. We are in conflict with those parts. There are parts of us that want to run rampant and have completely different ideas about how we are supposed to be, which are in conflict with other parts, which think we know how we are supposed to be. The idea of getting into that pile of conflict is one of the actual definitions of what is work. The moment this occurs in you, in other words, from the moment you start trying to struggle with the conflicting things, which is what I was saying is the definition of work, there are some things you have to start trying to do.

Try to self-remember; create that "I am" state. Try not to identify or go into the emotional parts of you. Right there is a partial definition of what is identification. This is a work term, and we use it a lot. Don't identify.

What does identify mean? It means when you have conflict, you relate to it or part of it with a negative emotion. When something comes up for me, and whatever it is, I then attach something negative to it. I have just identified with it. Fill in the blanks. It can be anything. How you know you are identified is that you have flipped and you attached a negative emotion to a conflict inside of you. The reason why we don't want to do this is because it is a lower emotional state, not a higher emotional state.

The second we attach to and identify with the negative emotion, thus adding negative emotion to what is causing us conflict, we lose control of it. Just like that. A long-term aim of the work is to have higher emotional states. One of the ways I would define a higher emotional state is an emotion lacking identification. It is an emotional state not based on attaching negative emotion to something you are in conflict with. The problem is, most of our strong emotion is actually negative. We might have positive emotion, fleetingly, but the thing about it is that it doesn't matter, positive or negative, it's the attaching of emotion to something with which you are in conflict internally. Two things we try to do, called struggling with conflicting things within us. The first thing you try to do when you are struggling with conflict within you is to self-remember. Try to create the "I am" state. Have something monitoring the playground. You are lost in the playground. But bring a monitor in, bring something in that can at least pay attention to what is happening in the playground. The second thing is to try not to go in the conflict as much as possible. Reduce attaching emotion to it. As soon as you attach emotion to it, you just got on the horse and gave it a big whipping. That horse is taking off! It's going to go until it runs out of gas. It's the only way you can be unattached to the emotion.

How do you detach emotion from something you have attached it to that is conflicting inside of you? Well, right now you can't. Once that emotion holds onto whatever is causing you the conflict, you can't detach it. It will literally run until it loses the energy of attachment. That is your next opportunity to make things right. This is also part of the idea of why it is when I have conflict and emotional attachment or identification, that later I feel so exhausted. Why am I always tired or feeling like I've been run over, or feeling exhausted after I've had an event where I got identified with something and expressed a lot of negative emotion. Why am I tired like that? I'm tired because that wastes energy. This energy waste occurs until the emotion leaves or separates from what is causing the conflict. Then it takes longer to gain it back than it did to waste it, and that is another reason why we work on not expressing too much in the way of negative emotion. Twenty minutes of expression of negative emotion can literally deplete you for hours or even days.

If you think about times when you have lost it emotionally and then really try (this is the digesting the experience part) to

37

come back and think about how you felt later, even after the fuss was over, how did you feel? Did you feel tired, sedated, depleted? For how long? In the past I might have had some conflict and then became emotional about it, blew up, or worse, repressed it, taking it all inside without expressing it at all. I wouldn't be right for days! So much of my energy had been depleted.

J: That's how I feel today.
Dr. J: What's how you feel today?

J: First of all, last night I literally felt like it wasn't just the expression of the negative emotion that I had last night, and the accumulation of all the fear. In addition to that, physically, I literally felt like I had been beat up. I had a headache and my whole body hurt. This morning I woke up…

Dr. J: Try to talk about this without being emotional.

J: That's where I am getting to, and this is where my struggle is. Even though today, I know that I need to not express negative emotions, but at the same time, my body and my headache, and my throat is bothering me.

Dr. J: Try to say it without emotion. Keep working on it. This is an exercise, that's what we are doing.

J: I feel more susceptible to the negative emotions because there are all these other physical things. I'm irritated by my headache, and it hurts to walk. At the same time I also understand that it is a habit, because for so long I went without any physical therapy to walk without pain, that when I would wake up and have pain, I would automatically just go right to the negative, cranky, bitchy, oh I have pain sort of thing. I'm catching myself more, when I wake up and have pain, noticing that I go to that habit. I'm like, well wait a minute, I don't really want to be negative, and I'm working on not being negative. At the same time, the habit keeps coming up.

Dr. J: Yeah, let it! In other words, the trick is, don't attach any particular emotion to it. First of all, understand that it is a process. You should feel depleted; you should have some physical symptoms of depletion of your energy. That is perfectly normal. That is the way it works! Now you have an idea that makes sense. If you got beat up, you should feel sore later. Being sore later doesn't mean anything at all about what is going on now. It means nothing at all. But the habit is to associate a current feeling with what is going on now. The physical feeling is actually a symptom. The headachy, tired, low energy, etc, is the normal consequence of having an expression of negative emotion and identification for a period of time. Even just half an hour or an hour can actually deplete your energy for many hours and sometimes for several days depending on how extreme it is. Knowing this doesn't make you feel better.

J: That was one of my questions, shouldn't knowing this make me feel better?

Dr. J: Nope. It's just like, if you just went out and ran ten miles, and you know, I can tell you right now if you go out and run ten miles you are going to get really sore. You're going to have lactic acid and some muscle cramps and spasms and your shoes probably aren't ready for it so you might get blisters on your feet. You might have some aches and pains from other beats and bangs and your knees might hurt. I'll tell it to you now before you run and you'll say, "Yeah, ok whatever, it's just an idea." You go ahead and do the run, and sure enough, not only did you get all that but you got overheated, you got dehydrated, you vomited, you got lots of aches and pains from the lactic acid. You have muscle spasms and cramps and blisters and a bad headache from the lactic acid accumulation. And guess what? You're going to have it for three days! After the fact when you're saying, "God! Why do I feel so bad?" And I say, "Well, it's because you haven't been running at all and you ran ten miles yesterday!" Just knowing that will not make the lactic acid not be there. The inflammation and stress to your knees from the repetitive motion of running when you are not used to it will still be there. What do you do? You take care of your self, you acknowledge that you expended a lot of energy and you did a lot of effort. You are not critical or judgmental about your self because it's over, it's in the past now. Today, part of your job, care and maintenance of your self and the machine in which the self happens to be walking around is to take care and be kind to your self. Don't go back and recreate scenarios. Drink some water, do some yoga and stretching, eat some really good food. Laugh your face off. See something beautiful. You have to reward the machine, doing something that is good for your self and acknowledging that you had some effort.

Work is a struggle with conflicting things, the moment this occurs in you, try to self-remember and not identify or to go into the emotional parts of you, and I explained how that emotional attachment is key to identification.

STUDENT: The last thing I was thinking about right before we stopped last time, was an illustration. An illustration you've seen so many times, especially in cartoons. I picture Garfield, the devil on your shoulder picture. I remember a cartoon where I'm seeing the cartoon character that is faced with some choice and there's a devil on one shoulder and then the angel pops up on the other shoulder and they start fighting each other. Then another devil pops up and another angel pops up and there's this big quarrel, and you're just sitting there like, "Hmmmmm, that's interesting." That's kind of what we are talking about, being that person who is just watching this happen, watching all the devils and all the angels on your shoulders fighting each other.

Dr. J: Especially if you can catch those moments where you are actually the witness and you see these different I's warring it out, so to speak. That's a good example. It's an example of a lot of things: self-remembering, because you have this sort of meta-observational point of view, where you're watching the different points of view wrestle it out. As far as struggle with conflicting things, a lot of times, those are the conflicting things. Do what's right, and do what feels good. "I like this, I don't like that". But, sometimes I like that, and I never like that, but sometimes I do, on and on, no end to it. Lets go to the next one.

29. Evolve by transforming denying force and negative emotions.

J: What is denying force?

Dr. J: Good question. First, just take the words at face value. Denying force, the force of denial, the force that denies. The influences that seek to impede, disrupt, dislodge, unseat and move you in a direction other than the one you want. Denying force is that, whatever that is. We have a lot of internal denying force, which is our own internal resistance to working on the things that need to be worked on, our own internal resistance to what we think of as a good, practical, productive thing for us to do. The resistance to being honest, the resistance to your self or with anyone else, the resistance to practice, the resistance to have discipline, the resistance to engage in education which might be necessary.

Denying force can also be external. It can come in the form of third party influence, completely outside your self. Accident can be denying force. For example: you are going somewhere to do something you have an aim to do and you are in an accident. That accident is now denying force. You were going to train with a teacher and suddenly something happened and you no longer have any money. That sudden deficit of income appears to be an impediment and it is going to try to deny you to train with your teacher.

There is denying force in every center. Instinctive center wants to be comfortable. When you challenge instinctive center to work, and initially there is no momentum in that work, the instinctive center wants to maintain its equilibrium and does everything possible to stop you. You'll get sore, you'll get sick, you'll feel tired, and in the emotional center you will get caught up in rounds of negative emotions. In the moving center you will have difficulty with coordination or strength. In the intellectual center you will get caught in loops of understanding or the lack of understanding.

We all get caught up and we think that because we don't completely understand a thing, it is a good reason not to do what is necessary. That is a terrific impediment to actually doing something. What if the understanding is something that only occurs after you do something? We will send our self an intellectual challenge. It will be spontaneous. It won't necessarily be well thought out, because there is no complete understanding of anything. We will put that as a condition toward doing something we need to do, and the end result is simply not doing what we need to do. As a result of that process, we never actually get to the place of understanding, which would be a consequence of actually doing something we needed to do.

For example, building will and being is really based on success. It is based on setting aims, working toward them, skirting and handling all of the denying things that come in to keep you from achieving your aim, and then having success in little things, then maybe in bigger things. It only comes at the end of the process and doesn't occur at the beginning. We want to think we need to have some complete understanding or even a feeling of understanding of what the end result of the process is as a precondition to even engaging in the process. It is a complete impediment to actually making progress.
Denying force can be other people. You might think you want to do something, or you have an idea you want to do, need or work on something, and then another person comes in and says, "You shouldn't do that." However much consideration we give to what they say is however much their input becomes denying force. It can be our friends, our family, a random stranger. It can come from anywhere. It can come from books! One book says that it would be good to do XYZ, and another

book says you should never do XYZ. That sets up a conflict, and that conflict becomes denying force. Who is to say what's right? I'm not being specific in any particular examples. I'm just giving examples of denying force.

Justification can be an example of denying force. We justify not doing what we need to do, saying what we need to say, or being what we need to be, or being disciplined or practicing or studying or other things like. There is always a good reason. Whatever the good reason is, it is a perfect example of denying force.

You can only evolve by transforming negative emotions. Negative emotions, both those that we capture and hold and store and express within our self and the negative emotions of people we come in contact with, are considered one of the top Impediments to transformation of any kind.

30. Think about your self less to remember your self more,

Dr. J: It's pretty self-explanatory. We don't even know who our self is, so we are consumed with our notions of our self, as if that is something of substance. The more we think about these ideas, the one thing we discover is that whatever is initially our concept of our self in reality does not have much in the way of substance. It's ephemeral in the sense that as soon as you start to get a hold of it, and try to weigh and measure it, it disappears. It doesn't have substance or hold up to scrutiny. We don't want to have our efforts and attention on the less than substantial parts of us (in some workbooks, they use the term "unreal") in the hopes of catching a glimpse of something real. Being a student and working is learning how to differentiate and have discernment between true self, your self, real vs. unreal parts of us, in hopes of bringing energy, attention, consciousness, etc to the more real parts of us.

31. Doing begins by completing small aims, not expressing negative emotions, and stopping useless talk.

Dr. J: The first part we have talked about. In order to get energy to complete big aims, practice small ones. We have talked a lot about not expressing negative emotions, but there is a third thing here that comes in as a work idea, which is stopping useless talk. Useless talk is any kind of talking or conversation that is in and of itself an impediment to self-remembering. Any kind of talking that generates or supports the expression of negative emotion. I'm not saying that when we talk about negative emotion it is useless. That is not an example of useless talk. Useless talk might be talking about somebody else's negative emotions behind his or her back without the subject's input. You may not even know if what you are saying is true. Useless talk is also repeating anything you don't know to be true.

STUDENT: Can't it happen inside your own head too?

Dr. J: Yes, always internal and external. Denying force—internal and external. Negative emotion—internal and external. Useless talk—internal and external. For example, you catch your self in what I call a "thought-loop." It's like when you get a song in your head and you can't get it out. It just keeps going and going. That's an example of useless talk. We find ourselves repeating chains of talking in our head. It could be a single work or it could be a whole conversation playing over and over in our heads. All that is useless talk.

J: Well thank you for explaining the first part of that, about wanting to talk about negative emotions in order to work on them. For myself I never really understood what useless talk was. I know there is some kind of chatter going on in my head. I've sorted that part out. But I always wondered if the wanting to talk about the negative emotion or issue in order to work on that issue was considered useless talk. I've had a lot of these conversations in my head because it seems to be the only place I can have them. I didn't understand useless talk. It's like if I have an emotion or negative thought, do I positively express it in order to understand it better?

Dr. J: It also refers to things not having a lot of substance, like how long do you want to talk about last week's football game? It was a great football game, but I mean really, how much do you want to talk about it? How much gossip or repeating stories do you want to engage in? Somebody "done something wrong." Ok, great! How much do you want to talk about that? Especially considering it may not be about you or have any effect on you. It may or may not be true. Any kind of negative talk or conversation, how much do you want to talk about it?

STUDENT: What if it's not negative, but still useless?

40

Dr. J: Literally just inanities and gibber-jabber and just chatting to be chatting. Just talking to hear the sound of the voice with nothing in particular to say, that is useless talk. Useless talk is like if you sit here and first you have one idea, "Well, I once had a dog who was blue! And I don't really like this table because it has a mark on it. I wish I could move that lamp. What are we going to wear? What are we not going to wear? What's on TV tonight?" Engaging in the inanities of just talking for the sake of talking. Doing this takes up a lot of space and takes up a lot of energy. Sometimes if you were just quiet, there would be something to work on and sometimes there might be an opportunity to talk about something having value and substance. We fill a lot of time talking about things without substance.

In some schools, they are very strict about this, and they may set objectives there be no conversation from sunup to sundown not work related. If whatever is about to come out of your mouth isn't something directly related to the work, you can't say it. Boy is that hard! We want to talk about stuff that doesn't have a lot of importance or substance, and then we justify it, because it makes us happy, it makes us laugh. You say, "Well, that is my interest. You are not validating my interest!" We are not necessarily required to validate every crazy Impulse passing through the pea-brain. It's nothing personal. It comes from this understanding of three-quarters of the thoughts in your head at any given time have nothing to do with you. They are just passing through. We call it associative I's, or associative thinking. It's like the ticker tape of gibber-jabber, which is running through the head in the background at any given point in the day. To feed into that ticker tape and start endlessly expressing it is pretty useless and distracting. It is distracting for you, who is doing it, and it's distracting for anyone else who might be trying to hold on to a long thought.

Useless talk is usually pretty short and sweet, one way or the other, negative or positive. It is short and sweet because it does not require a long thought. When you really think something through to express it with depth and consideration, you will notice there is quite often a pause. There is a gap where there is no talking. That is because you are thinking! Thinking takes space. If there is constant talking, there is very little thinking. From the work point of view, that is considered useless talk. This is actually quite hard to work with. Ouspensky listed it as one of the three very most important things to work on. Completing aims, not expressing emotions, and stopping useless talk.

32. Ignore the many I's and feed your essence to become one.

Dr. J: Well, there you go. The many I's, the masses, the untrained, unwashed, unkempt masses of your egocentric personality. All of your egocentric personality constructs. All the different likes, dislikes, all the critical and non-critical ones, just the masses of all of the different things inside of us. Feed your essence, true self, core self, the original, authentic self, of which there is just one. Right now, it is one Immersed somewhere in a sea of I's. Overtime what we want to practice is learning how to simply ignore voices, which we have already determined through our process of validation and verification and practice are not expressing something coming from the authentic self. Overtime we want to ignore them and pay attention to the clusters of I's resembling more the I we want to be.

33. Be the same person, rather than a different person, when circumstances change.

Dr. J: It's really about becoming authentic. If we say the self is not what happens to use, the self is not the events to which we are subject, the self is not where we are or who we are with, or what we drive, wear or where we live, then there is something about the self that should be the same no matter what the circumstance. The practice is, let's say you are not one now but you want to become one. Try to be means to practice. When circumstances change, practice being the same person you were before the event, rather than a different person as a result of the event. No matter what the circumstance is, all you have to do is wait a minute, and it will change.

Try to see how quickly we become a different person when the circumstances change. To what degree do we change? There's something here just as a flier I want to put out, there's this "way of the fox" thing. The idea is, just because I am working on my authentic self, and I am working on honesty, disclosure and integrity, especially with my family and my core group, it does not mean I have to be the same with people who are trying to hurt me, or who are going in a completely different direction. If I was my self in that situation, it would instantly make me a food item or cause me to have harm. There is a lot of confusion about this. Even though we want to be the same all the time, it doesn't mean externally. The important thing is that I am the same all the time in my head. That is the critical part.

Let's consider circumstances of life, for example: I am in an alley and somebody runs up and bangs me in the head with a 2x4 and puts a pistol in my face and tells me to do something I don't want to do, or would never do. Way of the fox says that maybe I'll go along with it long enough to survive. Just because I went along with them, I didn't change according to the environment. I craftily created whatever I needed in order to survive.

That is also why it is important to have a dedicated group of people with which to work, because if you are not in a dedicated group, then you are in a situation where everybody around you is always on a need to know basis. If everyone around you is on a need to know basis about who you truly are or what you truly think, then you don't have much time or place to practice your authenticity of your self, because you are constantly in survival mode, constantly hedging your bets, protecting your self, keeping escape options available, etc. In this way you are never truly able to express your self even externally. When we have a safe group to work in, we can practice being more authentic than usual and more truthful than usual. Maybe we say something like, no matter what you say, even if I disagree with you with every fiber of my being, we have an agreement we are not going to hurt each other. So at least we have that going for us!

Whereas out in the world, in public, even in your family, you may not have that agreement. It may not be an agreement if you say something completely authentic yet it is completely antagonistic to what everybody else is thinking or believing, that they might not try to hurt you. Being a smart person, you are simply not going to practice being authentic in a dangerous environment. Unless it is something you are practicing. I'll give you an example of that:

One of my martial arts instructors (I won't say who) said we needed to authenticate our level of practice. He told us to meet him at his house, we got in his car, and he took us to the deepest, darkest, most dangerous criminally inclined neighborhood in a major metropolitan city (I won't tell you when or where), and he took us into a bar, which was a place where drug deals, prostitution, gambling, and other kinds of illegal behavior and nefarious activities were commonplace. He told us we had to stay in that bar for two hours and not get killed, and we did it. It was a place where the second we walked in the door it was obvious we didn't belong. We had to do it on purpose, and we had to survive. And yes, there was a fight, yes we did get away, and yes we did all survive. The point of it was that he did this on purpose as an exercise. I wouldn't ever do that to my students, but maybe I would!

It's only an example, but there might be a time and place to practice being authentic even in front of someone with a gun.

34. Separate from identification, imagination and negative emotion to develop your higher intellectual functions.

STUDENT: The first time I heard anything mentioned about separating from imagination or imagination not being good, I brought it up from one of the workbooks and I was talking about dreams. I think I understand it to a better degree now, but it is not as if this is some unimaginative system, though that is what it came across as. I was like, "What! No, I like my imagination." But there are parts that distinctly do not serve me. There are parts that don't distinctly serve anything.

Dr. J: A work idea is that everything is according to alchemy. There are four different kinds of imagination. Lead imagination, copper imagination, silver imagination and gold imagination. Lead imagination is coarse, negative and dark and can actually generate harmful kinds of thoughts, feelings and consequences. Lead alchemy art celebrates the worst parts of us and is abusive. The truest forms of pornography come from lead alchemy imagination.

Child pornography, horrible things which we don't really want to think about. There is a lot of creativity and a lot of imagination there, and there is an entire fantasy world there and a blurring of lines between realities, which is very negative. Copper imagination might go from there to just not having much in the way of substance. That imagination doesn't lead you up and down in any particular fashion. Silver imagination always lifts; it has an ascending energetic quality. Copper is kind of neutral, and silver is the kind of imagination that leads us into being creative, where the creativity expresses the more genuine parts of us. Gold alchemy is the imagination of possibilities that can transcend ordinary life completely, even to lift a person into transcendent states. We talk about music, art or any kind of creative expression this way. Even in dreams. Dreams are poo-pooed in this system because until you can sort out what parts of your dreams come from your organs and tissues, from dinner and the things that happen, dreams are just the replaying of tapes, voices of I's which have been sublimated through the day until we start to separate sleep state from waking state. That's another thing about imagination, a lot of what is commonly thought to be imagination is actually you observing your sleeping mind which never woke up. Remember the waking state is an overcoat; it is a secondary state that comes and superimposes the sleeping state. The sleep state is still happening, so we are partially in a dream state right now while we are having this conversation. There is a part that is in a continuous dreamlike state of unreality.

A lot of what we think of as creativity actually comes from that place, and there is no consciousness in it and it doesn't represent higher parts of functions. All the parts have a creative part, so it's one of those level of practice things, where initially, creativity, in the sense of imagination and dreams and that kind of thing, are not considered very important, and that is because there is no discernment of what they are. As you go further along, it requires a great deal of imagination to overcome things such as denying force. Denying force comes at us from so many directions, that in order to take one step and put one foot in front of the other, we have to be creative. There is a good function of imagination and creativity but we separate the idea according to levels of consciousness.

J: What does "higher intellectual function" mean?

Dr. J: Every center has four parts. Each Center has an instinctive, emotional, moving, and intellectual part. Higher intellectual function is the intellectual part of the center.

J: Why do you say that?

Dr. J: Because that is how it is. It is an exercise. Here's another way to say it: if you want to know what higher intellectual functions are, then separate from identification, imagination and negative emotions, and you will start to see higher intellectual functions. That is how you learn what they are. Here is another example of getting the cart in front of the horse: I want to have higher intellectual understandings of things, but I haven't separated from identification, imagination, or negative emotions. I want to have an intellectual understanding, I need to understand this before I practice trying to separate. Well guess what? You can't get there from here. The way you see those functions is as a result of doing this other work. That comes later.

35. Deliberately undertake an emotionally difficult task to obtain understanding.

STUDENT: I think we all know that is true! I mean, isn't that what we are doing?

Dr. J: Quite often. It's an algorithm. An understanding is something that happens after deliberately undertaking emotionally difficult tasks. The phone is ringing, I know who is on the other end of it, and I'm not going to answer it because I know there is going to be a negative or emotional conversation, so I don't pick up the phone. A practice idea is to go ahead and answer the phone, and I am going to have that conversation because I don't want to.

J: And you're not going to express negative emotions.

Dr. J: Well no, you're always going to be practicing whatever you are practicing, but that is not what I am saying. I am saying the reason why you answer the phone is because you are practicing undertaking emotionally difficult tasks, not because you're not going to express or do anything in particular. Your practice is to self-remember, so the phone rang and you saw your self run away to the other room. That's interesting! My little fear-self skipping "like a bunny" off into the corner somewhere just because the phone rang. I'm afraid to answer the phone. I'm going to answer the phone because I am afraid. Why? Because by doing that kind of thing, I will get to a place and gain some insight and understanding about myself to which I would normally not have the ability to get. I am going to learn something about myself I didn't know five minutes ago. If we are working on our self, we are almost in a continuous state of addressing emotionally difficult things and that is one of the differences in between the work in the world. In the world, not only is it not ok to undertake emotionally difficult tasks, but also you might even score brownie points by how slippery you are.

36. Participation in the evolution of a higher cosmos is the way to evolve.

Dr. J: This requires three lines of work. The three lines of work are work on your self, work with and for your group, and work for society, to participate in the evolution of a higher cosmos. A cosmos, by definition, is an entity with three forces. A male, female, and reconciling force, or first force, second force, third force, or positive, negative, and neutral. Evolution of a higher cosmos means we are in a cosmos right now. From the microcosm viewpoint, there are three of us, and at different times we are all functioning as a cosmos. We have male, female, reconciling or active, passive, and receptive roles we take turns fulfilling.

A cosmos is like a little universe. Our solar system for example: Sol with the eight planets is a cosmos. It is complete. From the point of view of the work, the purpose of one cosmos is to generate another, to be the genesis of another group, which becomes the genesis of another group. That next group could still be us. As we work on ourselves and change our states of consciousness, we are evolving. If that is true and we are growing and evolving, then the nature of our cosmos will change. It is not random; we don't participate in this evolution unwillingly or randomly. It is not about just having a peaceful moment. Now, it is about wanting to change. I am different now, because I set an aim ten years ago to be different now. I am different now because I set an aim to be different then I was two years ago. I am different than I was two years ago, because I set an aim to be different now. The way I am now is a reflection of that evolution (hopefully) in a positive way.

We want to create a higher way of being with each other. That includes our self, our group and our society. When I think about my personal evolution, that is why I still maintain a sense of activism from a societal or medical point, or a global or ecological point. I am activist minded and I do some work on that level because I realize it is a very important line of work I am supposed to do. People like me are supposed to do that. By doing so, and if you do so, if you are working on your self and to have a better relationship in our group, and you are doing concrete things to make society a better place, then we have an engine for evolution.

Three forces create motion; something new can occur that didn't exist a minute ago. In a family the three forces are the mother, father and children or progeny representing the extension of that cosmos. The child then becomes the first active part in the next cosmos, ad infinitum, then we go a million generations and we have a planet full of people. That is the evolution of the cosmos. We are doing the same kind of thing in our evolution, except the baby being born is our self.

37. Work is not letting anything unnecessary occur in you.

Dr. J: Use only the amount of energy necessary in what you are doing; otherwise wrong work of centers occurs. This also has to do with self-remembering. You'll notice we put out extraordinary, disproportionate amounts of energy. There is no reason why all of my thinking and energy and everything about me should be all about something that is happening. Things will change in a few minutes, anyway. So there I am, I've spent all my energy, money and resources, and now things are different, so what do I do? I have to start over. One of the difficulties in supporting the work of consciousness overtime is we overspend and waste so much energy.

J: I understand that. An example is many years ago when I would picket for LGBT rights and March. It takes a lot of effort for me to physically go out and March today, but that doesn't mean I have stopped my conversation about rights for the LGBT community.

Dr. J: But actually this is more specific than that, because it talks about wrong work of centers. Remember we have four centers. They are the instinctive, emotional, moving, and intellectual. I'll give you an example in the moving center. We want to train and balance and bring healthy energy to the moving center. I may injure myself if I do too much exercise, yoga, martial arts or dancing. Then I may not be able to practice for a year or two. Or maybe I injure myself so badly I can never practice again. That is wrong work of centers. It is important to work with the moving center, but if you do too much of it and put too much emphasis on the moving center, you create the possibility of having that intention cripple you and keep you from success in being your balanced self. I am just using that as an example, but it could be anything.

STUDENT: For me it seems like the best example is breathing, because a lot of people go around every single day with this shallow breath. This has to relate to every center, that is the way you subsist, you breathe oxygen. You can't do anything, or have any centers without breath. So if you are going around and you are taking little tiny inhales, not inhaling all the way into your lungs, your energy is not right. At the same time, if you are sitting there all the time taking huge inhales and exhales, you will hyperventilate and fall on the floor!

J: Not to mention people are going to think something is wrong with you.

Dr. J: And that will shut you down. It is a wrong work of the centers. You don't breathe enough, and you asphyxiate. You breathe just enough to survive, and you are in a constant state of asphyxia and acidosis, and that causes wrong work in the centers.

44

38. Accept every thing as it is to self-remember.

Dr. J: To self-remember more, you must be successfully working against and transforming negative emotions. We've talked about the second part quite a bit. The first part is like in the book "The Hitchhiker's Guide to the Galaxy". No matter what happens, "don't panic." Be here now, which was the title of Ram Dass' first book. Accept everything as it is, because one way or another, however it is, is however it is. We use that as a starting place. It doesn't mean as individuals we may not want to change or improve our circumstances. Change or improvement from what? If you don't know what the actual circumstances you find your self in, then any judgment or decision you make is not going to be valid. That is what we do, we leap from the frying pan into the fire and maybe where we need to be is in the frying pan just a little longer! We should go for that extra-crispy rather than jump out at the first sign of something uncomfortable. Maybe the heat is going to transform us into something that can survive the fire. If we jump out of the heat too soon, the fire burns us up.

STUDENT: Can I just ask a question? Negative emotions are something we talk about so much, so it is not a mystery to me. Everyone has different ways of working with it. The bio tapping is one of the main things we do here, so especially in some of these workbooks, by Gurdjieff and Ouspensky, what did they do?

Dr. J: Well, they did everything we would like. In other words, the tapping is a way to look at the idea of influencing the energy field of the body. That's one additional technique. The primary technique is learning how not to express them, and the reason why is and this is different from repression. Repression is more than non-expression. Repression is based on suppression, which is hiding, storing, and putting away out of sight. That's not what we are saying to do. When we say don't express negative emotions, we're not saying pretend they are not there. We're not saying hide them so not even you can find them in the dark with both hands. What we're saying is, observe them with absolute clarity because that comes out of self-remembering. You start to observe the negative emotions. Why? Because now you're paying attention, so you're going to see them.

The first step is not expressing them. Now, expression is thought, action, and deed. So not expressing them in thought means not dwelling on them. Observe them, but don't add to them or take away from them. There's this idea that what you resist persists. When I have a negative emotion and wrestle with it, and I manipulate and dwell in it, I get attached to it and identified with it. That is feeding the negative emotion. It is giving it energy it doesn't deserve to have, which could be used for something else. Conversely, if I have a negative emotion I'm dealing with and I very clearly observe it and don't attach it, justify it, rationalize it, it actually does the opposite. By not feeding it, since it's not actually real, it doesn't come as a true or genuine expression or essence of my true self and doesn't have its own independent energy source or center. There's no food, other than the attention it can survive on, and eventually it simply dissipates for lack of attention. It dissipates if for nothing else, for lack of attention. So that's one of the primary techniques, to not expressing negative thought, action or deed.

I pay attention to anything I do in which the genesis is negative emotion, then simply stop doing those things. There are things I catch myself doing in which the only reason in the world why I'm doing it is because of attachment or identification with some negative emotion. Even if I can't make the negative emotion disappear, guess what? I may have enough will power to not express it with an action.
That starts to rob it of it's power.

The thing about it though, is expressing negative emotions just feels so good sometimes. It is so easily justified. Well, I did this because you did that. Well, I was rude to you because somebody was rude to me. I'm going steal from you because somebody stole from me. I'm going abuse you because somebody abused me. It's a perfect rationale. It's a perfect defense. Even if I do that, say I was really abused in the past, and then I abuse someone else, and I've got my compatriots here and they're like, "Why are you treating them so badly?" "Because somebody else treated me really badly and that's why." Well guess what, we could probably find a whole crowd that would go, "Oh that makes sense. It makes perfect sense." Does it make sense at all? Only in an egocentric, personality based world based on the lack of authenticity and lack of integrity does it make perfect sense. As soon as we start practicing being authentic, there is no longer justification for being bad to each other because we're expressing some negative emotion. All of a sudden, it's not good enough. It's not reasonable to do that. But guess what, we're going do it anyway. The trick is, as we work on ourselves, to try and start to catch it. In other words, I realize the reason I'm talking to you this way is because I'm actually thinking about something else. I realize the reason I'm being a little distant or mean or lying to you is because of something else. So, I don't necessarily need to explain all that to you. What I need to do is simply stop being bad to you. Just stop it. If I'm lying to you, I just stop lying.

Now, I may not be strong enough to work through it all and it may not even be appropriate to disclose to you why I was lying to you. What's important is when I see it happening in myself, I just stop it. If I can stop it, that should tell me something. It takes a little bit away from the negative side and gives me a little energy on the positive side, and eventually I may even be able to stop the thoughts or have some control over my thoughts. Let's say right now we don't have control of our thoughts or our emotions. If we don't have control over our thoughts and emotions and as Napoleon Hill said in his little book Think and Grow Rich, "as a man thinketh, so he is."

So, we have no control over our emotions. We have no control over our thoughts. We can't say we have any control at all over who we are. Part of this consciousness game, part of this transformation game, is the hypothetical idea of being able to control your self, regardless of circumstance, regardless of environment. Hypothetically, that's possible. So, all of these little things we are doing here are practicing that, and the more you are able to do it, the more apparent it is when you see others who can't do it, who aren't doing it.

When we first start talking about man #3, #4, #5, when you first read those distinctions and go through it, you might think, "I really can't tell what the difference is. I don't really get it. Why is there such a big difference between man #3 and man #4? Woman #3, woman #4?"

But what is the difference? When you first start thinking about it, it's very hard to tell what the difference is. But, then you start practicing and you start to say, "Well, part of the difference is that man #4, woman #4, is able to control some of the manifestations of negative emotion. They are able to tell the truth if they want to. They are able to not lie if they don't want to lie. They're able to not cause harm if they don't want to cause harm." And you say, "What would a person look like who starts to have those magical abilities: not being Impelled compulsively to lie, both to themselves and to other people, not being compelled to express negative emotion and constantly engage in useless chatter. What would a person like…well, what a minute, I now I start to think…well guess what if I could imagine a person like that, that's a very different kind of person." You start to see the difference between a 3 and 4 is actually humungous. That's why we don't worry about being like Jesus. It is enough if we could just think of getting from 3 to 4 much less from 3 to 7.
Anything else?

39. On every difficult occasion, say to your self, it was for this that I exercised; it was for this that I trained myself.

Dr. J: Part of this, is that you want to affirm your process. This is a really good thing, that when you're in difficult circumstances or you're caught chasing your tail and you're trying to sort it out, that you remind your self the whole reason I engaged in this process was to get a handle on stuff like this. That's the whole reason I'm here, okay. Because affirmation helps to validate the process you're in. Otherwise, you tend to forget, we tend to forget, and we might justify and run away because we forgot the reason why we were wrestling with it was on purpose in the first place. It was to handle this. I just forgot.

So how do you keep from forgetting? You have to practice affirming almost constantly. It's a constant thing. In the Bible, there's a passage that says one of jobs of a righteous person is to pray without ceasing. Pray without ceasing. Remember when I talked about Puja, that one of the definitions of Puja was affirmation. I could now say it differently. One of the aims of a righteous person is not so much to pray without ceasing but is to affirm without ceasing why they are engaged in the struggle.

I want to craft the aim to affirm, to create this constant state of affirmation. This is why I work on myself. I know it's troubling dealing with you. Generically. I know it's very troubling dealing with you. some more than others. But I have to say that this is why I work on myself and you provide me an opportunity to work on myself. And because of that you are worth more than your weight in gold. Because who else can do that, safely? Who else can do that? Who else can help me work on myself?

J: It almost seems to me that in some regard to metaphysics and spiritualism and new ageism, they've almost got that definition of affirmations wrong.

Dr. J: In what way, how do you mean?

J: Like, some of the…sometimes…I've read some affirmation books, and it's like over and over and over again just saying words, a bunch of words, but with no practical or physical reinforcement. Like even when you're in a challenging situation I've attempted to do affirmations, and the only thing the affirmations have ever done was eventually I might have calmed

46

down. It's like counting to 10.

Dr. J: Yeah, but you might have calmed down anyway.

J: Exactly. But now I have this great mantra I'm going remember for the next 30 years, which is helpful. You know, because I've memorized it now.

Dr. J: This is a different process. To literally say to your self, "On every difficult occasion is literally to just have the thought." Just have the thought. The thought that this is what I've been practicing for.

J: Things like that would be the best affirmation to ever have or to repeat to your self.

Dr. J: And even maybe a better word than affirmation is acknowledgement. And that's also another definition of the word Puja. It's an acknowledgement. When I'm in a difficult circumstance and I think it was for this I practiced, well who said that? In other words, there's part of me engaged in what's happening. Maybe even identifying. But what part of me has the capacity to be a part of it and acknowledge this circumstance was something I've practiced for? So, it's actually a reflection of self-remembering. You have to self-remember to do that.

40. Increasing your understanding and affection make your task easier.

Dr. J: I really like this one. First of all, increasing your understanding is balancing for your Kapha Dosha and affection. Affection is like a magnetic principle. It's like being drawn toward something. When you say you have affection for something, you might say you like it, you're drawn toward it. It pleases you. You get a good feeling about it. Increasing your understanding and affection refers to the work. Increase your affection for working on your self. In other words, you want to want to work on your self. You want to be drawn toward it progressively more. If you find your self ambivalent to working on your self, then you are less likely to be diligent on working on your self. If you actually get bored with it, for example. Oh I'm bored, all this work on myself. I don't want to do that anymore. Well then, you will simply stop working on your self. And so it's hard to work on your self when you don't have affection for the process.

When you don't have affection for the possibility it might place before you, working on your self is hard, difficult or bad becomes your primary way of thinking about it. I find, for example, as a result of working on myself, I have had moments of joy and happiness greater than I ever experienced in my life before, because it's one thing to have a fun experience when you are not paying attention, yet it's another to have a fun experience when all of your faculties are alive and awake. We talked about this; we used this example with sex. Drugs, sex with a stranger, met at a bar scenario vs. conscious sex engaged with a loving partner not under the influence, eyeball to eyeball, chakra to chakra, with whole manifestation of mind, body and spirit. Guess what, different possibility. Not the same. But then, you can apply that to anything, right?

J: Cooking food is another good example of that. Eating food.
Dr. J: All right, make your food preparation task easier by increasing your understanding and affection. As you learn the value of eating good food, you learn the joy of food and start to learn about the nature of different foods and how they all have their own little personality and their own little way of being in the kitchen, and in the pot and on your plate with each other. They all bring something different to it and you start to creatively compose and develop a relationship dynamic, a conscious interaction between you and the food. Then what that food does as it comes into your body is different than if you just stopped at Taco Bell and shoved a deluxe burrito down your gut in 20 seconds.
J: Or even not so much. Just making some rice but, doing it just like, "Well I'm just going eat it."

Dr. J: Well the difference in food quality is vastly different. But the other thing is, you eat one way, it hurts you. You eat the other way, it never hurts you. In fact, it will protect you. In other words, the food puts the chi out and actually surrounds you with a protective field. It's like in that one documentary we saw with the green light. It surrounds you with the green chi because you're being more conscious with your food.

J: You're having a relationship with it.

Dr. J: So what does this not apply to? I don't know? Specifically here we were talking about the work and working on your self. If we bring that kind of idea to virtually all other things we do, then that's also supporting the idea of working on your self. Eating more consciously is absolutely supporting working on and transforming us. All the great teachers I've studied were really into food. Many of them were very good cooks. That's why. But, what do you do when you can't rely on someone to make that really good food for you? Well, you must cook it your self. And what if you are with people who don't know anything about food? You have to teach them.

41. Face the difficulties that you tend to avoid to advance.

Dr. J: To advance you must face the difficulties you tend to avoid. That is a correlation with the "approach an emotional difficult task" idea, but you must also face the difficulties you tend to avoid. A little cataloging starts to happen when you begin practicing self-remembering, in that overtime you'll notice patterns of what you avoid. Some things will be obvious, and we use different terms for them. Sometimes we call them our issues, you know. So if I have an issue, a specific issue, in a specific area, I will tend to avoid addressing that. And actually there's going to be many, but some will be more obvious than others. That's one of the things you start to notice when you work on your self and practice this idea of self-remembering. You start seeing a catalog of difficulties, difficult areas, issues, that your inclination is to avoid. You want to avoid talking about them. You want to avoid working on them. You want to avoid other people talking about them. You want to avoid other people bringing attention to them.

Our idea of working on our issues is compartmentalizing and trying to hide them and not have them come up, and in the work it's exactly the opposite, and anything you can identify as an issue, put that on your list of things you need to work. As we start to bring energy to issues, consciousness to them, and as we start to bring progress in resolving them, then we can see other issues a little more clearly. What happens overtime is, there comes a point where not only is it no longer an issue, but it's as if it never was, because all the energy it had to change my thinking, emotions and actions is no longer there. But to advance you must face the difficulties you tend to avoid.

42. Find ways not to be preoccupied with your self to receive more.

Dr. J: To receive more, find ways not to be preoccupied with your self. As much as we like to believe it's all about us—life is all about me, you're a witness—from the point of view of working on your self, it's not productive to be in that space, because it leads toward encapsulation. It leads toward isolation. It leads toward separation. It does not genuinely acknowledge the value, strength, insight and the possibility of new ways of being that originate from other people. Also, there's the inner part, which is when we're preoccupied with one part of ourselves. We're not really preoccupied with our whole self. We're not preoccupied with our essence. We're preoccupied with our life as reflective of manifestation of our personality and ego. That's what we're preoccupied with. We're not really preoccupied with our true self.

Thoughts, comments, questions?

J: I'm going need some work on that one hehehehehe.

STUDENT: I just like what you said about how this is my life…right. My life and you're just an onlooker, okay? Get that? You got it? It's just so funny. Everybody's all thinking that at the same time.
Dr. J: It is funny when you think about it.

STUDENT: Whether or not it's true and this makes sense, it isn't productive. It could be true. It can be true in a productive way, but thinking of being in that spot, and thinking about it in that way, it just can't possibly be productive.

Dr. J: We're trying to say, you know, part of creating right relation is trying to come up with ideas and ways of thinking about ourselves that are more productive than others. This is on the list of things we do which is not very helpful, not very productive.

STUDENT: Unless you're trying to take over a country or start a cult or something.

43. Serving one purpose, not many to unify your self.

J: What's the definition of purpose in this statement?

Dr. J: You could say purpose. You could say aim. You could say line of work. I have many functions in life. All of them need my attention. I have more than one purpose in life, all of which need my attention. In the process of bringing attention to all the roles I play, all the aims I've set, the end result is that I become more integral to myself. I become more holistic.

44. To work you must expose your self to higher influences and not lower.

Dr. J: Destroy your peace and make your self uncomfortable. The peace you destroy is the unreal peace. It's the lethargy of being asleep as you go through your life. It's the false sense of security that if nothing's happening, everything must be okay. When we see that, as thoughtful and deliberate and intentional people, we challenge it and bring light to it. Constantly making ourselves a little uncomfortable helps us find what's more genuine.

J: Earlier today when we were talking…it almost seems, the way you said it just now almost seems exactly opposite of what you said earlier today, which was, "everything's good so why are you being a drama queen," to sum it up or paraphrase it. I'm now confused because I don't understand that at all.

Dr. J: The peace I'm talking about destroying is the false sense of calmness and security. If things are okay, then you want to acknowledge that also. In other words, you don't want to tear the world apart because it's being peaceful. I'm not saying because we're sitting here in a peaceful house I need to start being mean to you, or start expressing negative emotion.

J: I guess my question is, how do you know what the difference is between the peace?

Dr. J: Well, I think you don't know. It's something you are going to have to learn, because we don't know what peace is, because we don't know when we're right and when we're not. We think when we're not right that that's acceptable and we justify it. This is something we learn overtime. It's not something you're going to get on the first pass.

The other thing, by the way, is this is practical. It is very practical. For example, you might be perfectly comfortable in your body right this minute. All the more reason why tomorrow we should do an intense yoga practice. That's going to make you uncomfortable. It should be enough to challenge you. If it's not enough to challenge you, then it's not enough to work. If we are going to bring energy to the moving center, then we need to bring enough energy to the moving center to make it uncomfortable, to take it to the point of not being able to cope. That's the place where growth occurs.

J: I don't mean to be difficult, but is this your statement?

Dr. J: Yes.

J: Why did you choose to word it, "destroy your peace?"

Dr. J: Because it's fake! It's false.

J: But if you don't know if your peace is fake or not, why would you attempt to destroy something if you're not certain?

Dr. J: Well, maybe you wouldn't. See, you can only do what you can do according to your level of understanding. If you don't understand it, you can't do it. Destroy your peace literally means challenge your ignorance. It means push your self in ways you wouldn't ordinarily be inclined to do. When you're negative, you cannot do this. So what you were describing earlier was a situation when you were just negative. Well, you can't do this in a situation like that. You can only do this when you're exactly the opposite, when you're calm, clear, at rest. You can't stay in that place. If you find your self in that place, you have to find something new to work on. You will never know the difference if you are all identified and locked up in negative emotion. There is nothing else. There's nothing peaceful.

If I made someone uncomfortable. That's my job, when I'm doing this. If while I'm doing this, if you can sit there and the whole time we're having these discussions, you can be all self-centered and comfortable and feeling like you got to handle on everything and that you understand everything, then I'm not doing my job, and the work's not working. If it's working there should be a hundred times, as we go through this, where we are nailed to the wall, just like a bug in a science experiment. Because if it's not happening, and it should be a little different for each of us, then this is frivolous. It doesn't mean anything. It should bring up stuff. Otherwise, the exercises are not practical.

45. Separate from, not identify with, the habits and feelings of the body and personality to regenerate.

Dr. J: So, here's the thing. As much as we want to work on the issues and approach them, intellectually, we need to keep reminding ourselves these habits and failings are not really part of us. We get attached to our weaknesses. We get attached to our failings. We define ourselves by them. So, when they're challenged, we must defend. We must identify. We must judge. However, to regenerate you must separate, as in not identify with the habits and feelings of the body and personality.

To use J's example: I feel I can't understand a word of this. If I'm practicing my self-remembering, I should be thinking, "I have no idea who said that. Who doesn't understand? What doesn't understand? Who doesn't understand? Who has the issue?" If I was being rational, then I'd have to say, "There's actually quite a lot about life I understand clearly." The thought, "I just don't understand anything," well, who doesn't understand anything? There may be an "I" that actually believes that. Guess what? That's not you. From the point of view of work, that's not you. In feelings of the body, for example, sometimes I say things like, "I have a bad back." I've got all kinds of justification with that. I've been in accidents. I have injuries. I once collapsed and was paralyzed. I've got all kinds of reasons that would make perfectly rational sense for someone like me to be able to say that I have a bad back. But then, from another point of view, I'm not a bad back. I'm not something that could be limited by a bad back one way or the other. My true self, the authentic expression of my essence is not dependent on whether my body functions or not.

My body could completely fail and my essence would survive. My essence would prevail. This is just a different way of looking at it, but it's very helpful to do this. The Tibetans say to meditate on your own death. Meditate on the worst thing that could ever happen to you, which is your own death to the dismemberment of all of your parts. See it as clearly as you possibly can. See every part of every part literally turning into goo and being eaten by the worms and turning back into compost, and understand the whole time there's a part of you not touched by it.

As a practice of regeneration, we want to separate from this identification with our habits and feelings.

46. To be out of patterns, consciously choose an active role, without deviating, that you intended to before hand.

Dr. J: There are a lot of ways that's taken. In some schools, they actually organize plays, people are assigned parts, and you have to learn the part. You have to literally act a role like an actor on a stage. At one school in California, they rent a theater once or twice a year and put on a performance of the students. They're not actors, they're students. They act and if they have other talents like music or playing piano or singing, they'll do the musical or singing parts. They take it literally. In the past, conscious schools were theater schools. There is some understanding the Greek mystery schools, were consciousness schools, and they were using the plays to model the different ways people are and the ways personality and false personality, contrasted with essence, actually manifested in life.

Then there's another idea, which is, be out of patterns. Consciously choose an active role, without deviating, that you intended to beforehand. The role is something you ordinarily would not be inclined to do or think you could do or be successful at. It could be like, well, I never cook and I don't like to cook. I might decide to act like I'm a cook, take on the role of a chef and learn how to mimic and act and be a chef. It might teach me something about myself I wouldn't learn another way. Being a teacher could be a role. Being a student could be a role. We all have roles. We have our societal roles, business roles, housewife, boyfriend and girlfriend, husband, wife. Those are roles. They're play acting. They're conscious affectations of ways of being. But the idea is to do it consciously, without deviating.

J: Are you saying that you intended to beforehand?

Dr. J: "Intended to beforehand." Before you take on the role, you decide to do so on purpose. You intended to do it.

47. To advance, you must bequeath knowledge, skill, understanding, loyalty and affection to others.

Dr. J: Our individual progress is not contained or limited to ourselves. It's why you can't go and transform by your self in a cave somewhere. There's a certain amount of information you can get by solo meditation or solo practice. You can get some insight and understanding. After a point, it becomes a self limiting situation. This is a very old and traditional rule in work groups, by the way. That is, according to your understanding, you actually have to give away your understanding to others. You have to do it in such a way that they get it. This is a model of your own progress. It's another way of determining your level of practice, so to speak.

J: Does it have anything to do with the friction part?

Dr. J: No. I'll give you an illustration that's personal for you. There was a time when you didn't know anything about fertility cycles, and then you went through a process of education and increasing awareness, knowledge, and understanding about fertility cycles, for your self. Then, there was a point where you started to regurgitate that information. Now, you are at a point to where, not only can you sort of regurgitate the facts and the general information about it, but you actually can do so passionately and with great affection, in such a way that other people want to learn about it and want to take it even further than what you've given them. That's you doing that process, exactly how it is described here. You are bequeathing knowledge, skill and understanding based on your own practice. You practiced it, you got some validation, so you trust it and you're passionate and have affection for it. You have loyalty and affection because you see it as something valuable everybody should know. You are able to convey that, so a lot of people you share this information with get passionate about it for themselves. Then the process starts over again. This is exactly the same.

48. Your first desire should be to master your self, for without that, nothing else is possible.

Dr. J: But only those results will have value, which are accompanied by self-remembering. Otherwise, you just replace one mechanical thing with another. All self-help systems not including self-remembering as a component are, according to the work, doomed to failure. There is some value in these systems, because they may help people to be less violent, to have better relationships, to have better communication skills. They may in fact help people to be much more congenial as human beings than they may have been before going into them. From the point of view of transformation, the lack of self-remembering becomes a stop point, where the system runs out of gas. There's a point where only doing mindless repetitions and affirmations runs out of gas. Where's the self-remembering? Where's the non-expression of negative emotions? There might be a benefit to mindlessly repeating positive statements. It's better than mindlessly repeating negative ones. But, it's only so much better before it runs out of gas, and when it runs out of gas, people go the other way. They become disillusioned and say, "There's nothing to this. I might as well not even try." Then you see people in a yoga school or what they think is a consciousness school, and they follow some guru all over the world, and yet there's a point to where, all of a sudden, it just runs out of gas. When I look at schools and listen to lectures from various teachers, self-remembering is hardly referenced.

Devotion is great. There's a lot to be gained from devotion. Prayer is great. There is a lot to be gained from prayer. Yoga is great. There's a lot to be gained from yoga. Asceticism is great. There's a lot to be gained by focusing inward. Yet, they all come up short at some point because focusing inward, in and of itself, is not an answer, because what are you focusing on in the inward? You can't distinguish real from not real if you can't distinguish positive from negative. If you can't distinguish the functions of the machine from each other, then you're focusing inward on something that is a mystery to you. There is no reason why it should sort itself out. So you end up replacing one mechanical thing for another. You go from one positive mechanical thing to the next positive mechanical thing, endlessly "jack of all trades, master of none."

I've met people who have done every positive transformational class there is. They've read every book. They've done all the classes. They've done workshops here and workshops there. They could give you a list of all their conscious accomplishments, like how many yoga classes they've done, how many gurus they've studied with, and then guess what? They are still a complete mess. So what's missing? How could that be true? How is that even possible? If all of these things really worked the way they're advertised, surely someone who's done 20 or 30 workshops and read hundreds of books and worked with gurus here and there, must be very enlightened as a person and have self control. Why is it so common to find this? Three things are missing.

First, you have to be in the right kind of school. Second, there has to be self-remembering. Third, you have to work on your negative emotions, no matter what you're doing. How you could have done all this transformational work and yet have no transformation makes perfect sense. There were key things missing. Normally, you'd never be able to sort this out on your own. We're also in this enlightened age where we're taught you can be enlightened and elevate your self all by your self. You don't need anybody else. It's not true.

STUDENT: That's the myth of the self-made man.

Dr. J: The myth of the self-made man.

STUDENT: I had a first grade teacher, you know, the self-made man, somebody drove him to school on the school bus. The self-made man, you know, the guy stocking the shelves at the grocery store. Everybody along the way somehow helped this "self-made" man, but he refuses to acknowledge, and thinks he did it all on his own.

Dr. J: Right. I call that spiritual elitism, and I see it in the transformational world, where there are a lot of variations on it. Too many to list.

49. Save your energy by avoiding that which wastes it.

Dr. J: Examples of what to avoid might be negative emotion, worry, restlessness, haste, useless automatic actions, unnecessary tension, vehemence, unnecessary talk, wrong work of centers, and identification.

Saving energy is the same thing as making energy, because it's very hard to make energy. While we're coming up with skills to make energy, the very best thing we can do is not waste the good energy we have, the energy for attention, for working on your self, and the energy for self-remembering. Now, worry, restlessness, anxieties and things like that are where the tapping is useful and beautiful. Tapping is a great way to dissipate that anxious energy in a fairly short period of time. We want to get to the fundamental causes of them.

Restlessness. Just being restless for the sake of restlessness, or getting in a hurry to do anything, is a waste of energy. Maybe you could go at a more comfortable pace.

Useless automatic actions are ticks and twitches, thumping your foot. For example, sometimes I'll be teaching class, look around the room and see a student tapping his foot the whole time I'm talking. I'll look over and see somebody else rubbing her forehead repeatedly, or somebody else doing finger games or constantly shifting, shifting, shifting. Doing these things while trying to share information is like heating the house with all the windows open. There's energy dissipating into the ether, with that restlessness and unconscious expression of energy. This is why all forms of meditation stress learning how to be still. Fidgeting is not allowed. If you can fidget in a Zen meditation class, they'll smack you on the head. Literally, they'll smack you. You can't fidget in a Tibetan Shamatha meditation class because someone will come over and put their hand on you and they'll say, "Stop that." So meditation classes try to bring attention to those eccentricities and unconscious movements of the machine. If I'm leading a class and taking everyone through a Savasana, and I see someone chewing gum or fidgeting or thumping their foot back and forth the whole time or constantly adjusting or constantly moving, I'm going to stop them. I'm going put my hand right on that body part. I may not say, "Stop this," but I might say something like, "I want you to focus on your breath. Take a big breath and see the breath move into your foot," if their foot was moving. My actual intention, though, is to make you stop, because while you're fidgeting, that's where your consciousness is.

In Thai Yoga Therapy, we have this thing called "Kwan". One of the reasons why we fidget and why one part of our bodies will seem to have a mind of its own, is because there's displacement in the consciousness of our bodies. The Kwan (innate or intelligence) is not balanced. We want to bring it back into the core.

J: What is vehemence?

Dr. J: Literally the word means to show an intense, violent or passionate feeling. I take vehemence to mean adamant, but negative. For example, if we are talking about something intellectual, but somebody is being very emotional and they're trying to make an intellectual argument using strong emotion instead of being rational, that's being vehement. That's what it means.

50. Avoid guessing and speak of only that which you are sure.

Dr. J: How sure are you about what you're saying or what you've been talking about? In class, it's important we to avoid a lot of guesswork and have the conversation be more practical. We learn a lot of stuff from books, and we read a lot of books and get a lot of ideas from movies and videos. Certainly quite a bit of that is valid, but when you speak about information as if you know it and have verified it, that's called guessing. In reality, you don't know this information. You are relaying someone else's experience they may or not have relayed to you objectively. One of the reasons we watch a lot of documentaries from different points of view is because overtime you realize hardly anyone is objective in the way they present their issue. There's always a bias, a skewing of the point of view based on their experience.

When we're in class talking about particular applications or situations, or even techniques, I keep coming back to the idea that I have to speak more from actual experience. The more you engage in hands-on practice and other aspects of the practice, it is not guessing or hypothetical when you speak about what you are doing. It's a genuine expression of your experience at the time. It's less about what you've heard and learned and more about what you know.

51. Practice good housekeeping by restoring and reclaiming lost time and territory as quickly as possible after a bout of expressed negativity.

Dr. J: What is good housekeeping? When you're negative, when you have a bout of expressed negativity, make every reasonable effort you can to correct anything you've put out of place as quickly as possible. 99% of the time this has nothing to do with anybody else, because 99% of the time we express negativity internally and we don't involve other people. It's a conversation going on in our heads.

When you notice you've been in that place, don't just let it go. Make an effort to restore the energy the expression of negativity has cost you. It takes a certain amount of energy to transform your self into working on your self. One of the primary ways we waste energy is through the expression of negative emotions. If we really understand that, then if you find your self having gone through a bout of expressing negative emotions, engage your self and restore your self back to equilibrium, back to a more intentional way of being that is not wasting energy. If it's an outward expression and involves other people, the first thing to realize is that it has nothing to do with them. When you say, "Well, you made me express the negativity and lose control," that is absolutely not true. It's never true. There is no reason why any behavior, by any other person in the world, should cause you to lose it. All the rationales for why you "made me lose it" are based on a lack of information and knowledge, because if you had a little bit more knowledge, you'd understand that negative emotion is self-generated. It comes from within. Another person cannot make you negative. It's a blame game and a control game. Allowing one's emotions to be susceptible to the actions of others is a sign of lack of control. It's a sign of weakness. Now it's no judgment or criticism about being weak, because everybody's weak.

When we observe, as soon as we find a clear point to where we start to remember ourselves and exert a little control, we make every reasonable effort to correct any damage to the environment. Now that may involve other people, so for example, if I was rude in my expression of negative emotion, well then one of the things I'm going to do is to apologize. I'm going to try and establish some reconnection. If we were really close and were working on some emotional intimacy, but then I had some issue come up, and I push you away and I cut you off and I'm distant, as soon as I see I've done that, I make an effort to come back to some equilibrium in the relationship. Whatever that looks like, and I think it would look very different from person to person and from moment to moment. For instance, if in my expression of negative emotion, I do something to someone to cause more work. Well, as soon as I come to my right mind, and I see I've done that, I correct that and help them out.

We have this tendency to be embarrassed about coming out of a negative state because we are admitting we were wrong or that we were in that negative place. We do it in our head. There's a lot of resistance to correcting, because the negative expression might have been really subtle. For example, I took on a negative attitude and was expressing negative emotion in myself, and I have several different ways I show this. I subtly sabotage or overtly disconnect or push away. I'm not quite so helpful or I'm not quite so communicative. I don't participate at a high level and I have resistance when I come back to my right mind. By right mind I mean the mental state where I begin to go about trying to step it up and trying to restore what might have been lost. I'll say, "Well, it'll be okay." I might have all kinds of rationale for my previously bad behavior. We'll justify it in our heads instead of stepping up and making the extra effort out of acknowledgement that while we were in that negative space we were actually wasting energy, whether anyone else noticed or not. In that negative space we are actually losing energy and losing connection, right? It's not enough simply to move on. It's not enough to say, "Oh, I'm better now...let's just move on from this moment forward."

Okay, simply moving on is better than nothing, much better than being more negative. However, moving on is still not really working in a correct way because the issue of both the recurring patterns of negativity, and the lost energy because of this, has not been addressed. We have to make a conscious, extra effort to bring the energy back up to at least as high, or at an even higher level, than it was before, and if everybody's doing that, then it will look a certain way. This is a housekeeping idea.

If everyone is not doing that, it's going to look a certain way. What it looks like overtime is losing ground, because if I express negativity but don't seek to correct the loss of energy, if I just come back to my normal self and continue, I actually lost energy there. It's not enough just to come back to your center and get back to your good faith and good way of working and good relationships and all that. When you get back to that space, you have to make an extra effort to restore and bump the energy up, and begin to build resources overtime.

52. Recover quickly from negative emotions to deviate less from your aim.

Dr. J: This relates to what I just said. The first one was about restoring and reclaiming. This one is that by recovering quickly, if I'm in a negative state and realize I'm in a negative state, I have to immediately start taking aims to correct it. As soon as I see it, I start to make it better. What does make it better mean? First, by just observing I'm in the state. Second, by stopping any negative expression I can stop, certainly from doing anything that negativity generated. The end result is less deviation from the aim on which I was working. If there's less deviation, if I can respond more quickly and come back into how I am or how I want to be, there's less restoring and reclaiming to do. There's less energy expended dealing with the negative emotion.

STUDENT: Well, it's just an interesting way to go about it. Without this sort of idea in your head, without any of this knowledge, when something bad happens, you just fall and get stuck. Say you start crying and have this big thing, and then you just feel terrible afterwards, like you have a headache and your face is all puffed up and you just feel like you're done and that you have to wait for it to be over. There's no thought about well, how do I recover from this? How do I not let this get me? It just seems like this normal thing that happens every once and a while, more to some people than others. That's what I grew up with, that's normal. I mean in daily life, that's normal.

Dr. J: Yes, in ordinary life things are not going to be right until they're right.
Dr. J: We're not always on a receiving end and succumbing to what other people do to us. We're part of that chain of suffering and causation with other people as well. The person who's being bad or negative toward us was treated negatively by somebody else who was being treated negatively by somebody else, this ultimate chain of negativity with no breaks. The practice of restoring and reclaiming breaks the chain. It has the possibility of breaking the chain. First of all, it breaks the chain of what's happening right now. You might have a moment of clarity right in the middle of the most negative expression you could ever imagine. You could be at the point of utter and complete emotional collapse, and if you've been planting these seeds and practicing, right then, you could have a moment of clarity of self-remembering where you exert a little control and start to reduce the deviation, and start making attempts to restore and reclaim the territory. What happens is, overtime, you'll look more resilient and you'll look more temperate. In other words, less highs and less lows and more temperate. For example, I think this is what Johann Wolfgang Goethe is described as talking about in "Conversations with Eckermann", a book by Johann Peter Eckermann.

Goethe tells
Eckermann you want to "seek moderation in all things." You want to avoid extremes. Why? Because when we're identifying in a negative emotional state or we're expressing negativity, we are not in a moderate place. We're all in. Whatever it is, we are all in it. And if we don't like it, no part of us likes it.

There is a positive side too. The Chinese have a disease condition, which is the opposite of depression, called over joy. It's a liver Imbalance, and in Chinese medicine it is just as much a sign you need treatment as if you were in a deep, dark depression. Why? At some point, it is going to swing the other way. It is extreme. You are going to fall off of it, and it's unpredictable. Who knows what that's going to look like. It might look like you fall into hysteria or psychosis or neurosis or into depression. Then we have that manic-depressive cycle. You go into depression, then over joy, depression, over joy. Since you are always in rapid motion, which is ruled by your emotions, there's no middle ground, it's in the middle ground where we get to work on ourselves.

A lot of this is about deviate less from your aim. Well, one of my aims is to make progress. Progress means I'm making little Improvements, hour by hour, day by day, week by week, month by month, year by year, and in order to guarantee we are making progress we have to find that middle ground where we can work consistently more hours of the day and try to sustain ourselves in a place we can observe ourselves, and not be completely controlled by our emotions. Right now, all the emotions we have are based on identification. So, even though we might think we have positive emotions, we don't. If they were positive emotions, they wouldn't come and go.

How you know your emotions are not based on your true self is because they come and go. As long as whatever emotions you are feeling come and go randomly, as long as somebody or something else—phone call, email, random overheard word, checkout lady at the grocery store, incidental random occurrence, traffic—as long as any of those things are controlling your emotions, then none of your emotions are genuine. They are actually all based on some kind of identification. It is possible to have real emotions; we just don't what they are yet, because so much negativity qualifies what we think of as our feelings.

One of our objectives is to redefine what an emotion is, what our feelings are. Lets see how much our emotions rule our thinking, especially associative thinking. For example, consider thought constructs and patterns similar to the following: "I like you today - I don't like you today." "I want to be close to you, but not really." "Right now I feel really close to you. However, a minute ago you asked me a question and it just 'made me mad' and now I don't want to be close to you."

I don't see the reactive thinking quality of these patterns of thought or how mechanical they are. Unconsciously, I travel from one loop to the next seamlessly, without much in the way of transition to grab my attention. The next minute, not only am I not happy with you, I don't even like you. I'm like that for half an hour. It continues…and then a minute later or a couple of hours later I forgot that I really didn't like you at all and once again I'm all into you. Suddenly, I'm in a different state.

We can go from one random associative thought, one in juxtaposition to another, all day long, all week long, all year long!

All of it is mechanical. We have a possibility of having some genuine connection, genuine emotion. However, it's going to be something other than all of that stuff, that random associative thinking and feeling, whatever that thought or emotion is.

We're looking at these ideas as exercises as ways to help us create states of mind, states of being, states of observation, where we get glimpses of something that is not all of these things. These are the genuine things.

One of the first rules of chi development, of chi systems like Tai Chi, Chi Gung, Chong Fa, Fa Lun Gung, Wing Chun, Mai Pa Fun, Tsing-I, Bag Gua, so on and so forth, is to cultivate chi, to do the things that bring energy to you. The second rule is stop wasting chi unnecessarily. In other words, be conservative with how you spend or how you distribute or how you project your chi, which leads you to the third rule or stage, which is collect the chi specifically. Collect the energy.

I do things to store it. I do things to collect the chi called "chi gathering." So, in "Chi Gung" we actually have exercises called "gather the chi". There are different things you can do. Hug the trees. Do your Tai Chi. Do your yoga. Go out and do the Orgone vision exercise to see chi in the air, because that also helps collect chi through your eyes. Next is to store whatever you have acquired. There are all kinds of ideas about how you store chi, because you are building up your reserve like a battery stores current. You build it up and you build it up until you get to a point to where you can begin to direct the chi within your self.

In classical chi gong, for example, you direct the chi from organ to organ. Then you direct the energy from organ to meridian. And so on and so forth, macrocosmic orbit to microcosmic orbit. And once you are able to store and then to direct the chi, you should be able to distribute chi within your self. Practice that for a while, then the last step is projection, where you begin to send chi out of your self into your environment. It could be to another person, or it could be generally to the environment in some way.

First we discover the presence of chi, that there's energy everywhere and everything has energy, and "may the force be with you". The second thing is that you can actually collect more of it than you currently have. Third thing is that not only can you collect the energy, but you can store it. Fourth thing is not only can store, you can begin to direct the energy intentionally with your consciousness around your body.

In yoga science, for example, there are the five Pranas (Vital Life Forces specific to areas of the body) and how we direct the five Pranas through seven chakras through the Prana Nadis, through the ten Sen lines, through the Marmas, muladras and the various techniques of doing that which is asana, pranayama, bandhas, locks, Udjaya breathing, through focused visualization, etc, etc. But that's not it, that's not enough. First direct the energy within us, then actually project the energy outward.

The energy necessary for consciousness works very similarly. First, we have to find the obvious ways we are leaking energy. Second, we have to start to learn the ways we can acquire the energy necessary for raising our consciousness and our ability to sustain attention long enough to see ourselves for who we are. How can you store energy in a part you don't know you have? That's why we have to include an anatomy and physiology of the consciousness. That's why we talk about centers, instinctive, moving, emotional, intellectual, or we talk about chakras and meridians and we talk about all these different parts. We do this because the more familiar we are with them, the more we begin to have a chance of seeing that they are actually functioning and real. I'm not just imagining I'm gathering energy. I'm not just imagining I am focusing energy and bringing energy and storing energy within myself, and or wasting it, because I'll see the waste of it too. I start to see the evidence of the energies ebb and flow within me. I see I have a little bit now and then I messed up and I got all caught up in some negative expression and I see it's gone, how I wasted it. I now see how I feel when I'm empty.

I need to start to learn how to have more control of this energy for being and consciousness within me. Where are the release valves? What do those look like? How do I begin to acquire that energy? Then, how do I move it within myself? And this is coordination between centers, okay. And then lastly, expression is a form of projection. Expression is a form of projection. If I'm working on myself and I'm making some progress and I'm gathering and I'm storing and I'm circulating and I'm starting to have sustained moments of self-observation, then the practice of it is with you. The practice is what we do together. In other words, I'm beginning to project that consciousness to the people around me, and that has a stabilizing effect on them.

So, the trick is that we, as we're working on this process, and we're all doing our own work, that as we work together, we have a more stable template, a house that we're working in. We're able to make this little, incremental progress, but then we start to have lots of up and downs every day. At this point, we're spinning our wheels because it takes longer to gather the energy than it does to spend it. That's one of those principles. It's not equal. I can spend a year gathering a certain kind of energy and I could literally lose it in a day, depending on how extreme I became. In one day I could lose much. I could open all the valves of negative energy and let it all go. It's like a balloon, ppppfffftttttttttt, and I'm now empty. It takes lots of little breaths to blow that balloon back up.

53. Work is a line of efforts leading to a definite aim.

Dr. J: It is determination to stick to a thing until it comes naturally. The definite aim can be anything from I just want to remember myself. I want to learn what it really means to have integrity. A definite aim could be, I want to experience love. I want to know what that really is, genuinely. Not what I've been told. I've heard that love is a power. Well, I want to know what that power is. I want to have a direct personal experience with what that power is. Is it just a story people tell? Is it a fairy tale? Is it real? People describe love, for example, as being eternal, as being consistent, as being strong, as being able to overcome obstacles, being able to heal, even heal disease. Well, what does that mean? I mean in my own experience of life. What does that mean? I want to know that. Okay, that's a definite aim, okay. You want to think about aims are goals. Aims are goals. It's good to have aims. It's good to have goals, as far as working on your self. You can go with the flow, okay. But , I've done kayaking and white water canoeing before.

The way it works going on a class 4 rapids is that sometimes you go with the flow and sometimes you don't. Because the flow goes over a cliff and not in a good way or the flow is heading for a boulder in the middle of the river, which is throwing up a 20 foot buzz saw of water which they call a rooster tale, which if they run into it, will turn you, ass end over elbow and separate you from your canoe, paddle, and vest, helmet and maybe your life. Sometimes the flow carries you into an eddy current, which is like a whirlpool and you can't get out. You get stuck in this swirly thing. You can't get out, so you have to be able to look ahead and that's what aim is. Aim is this intentional practice of trying to look ahead about where you want to be in the next minute.

We have different aims. Like most people's aims are to have a good job or have a better car or to find a boyfriend or girlfriend. Those are shortsighted kinds of aims because they're really concrete and easily achievable. Generally speaking, anybody can get a job. People can get a place to live. If they can't, they can at least make one out of cardboard and tin cans if

56

they have to. It's actually easier to do that than to know what is the true nature of love. That's considered to be a pretty lofty aspiration, right?

We want to have definite aims. We want to have big ones and small ones. This requires enough will power and determination to stick to something until it comes naturally. For example, virtually nothing we're doing, on the internal work…working on negativity, working on our issues, etc., comes natural to us. In fact, quite often, it seems completely counter intuitive. It's so hard at times that it might seem like it's against our nature. Well there's also this idea that if we practice working on our issues, that we actually get much better at it. That it seems to come more naturally overtime, if you're consistent in your practice. So, same thing with achieving aims. It gets easier to achieve your aims when you actually practice doing them. It gets easier. I know that I have issues, but what I want to do is to have an aim to work on my issues when they're in front of me, at least just a little bit. Work on them. Make some effort. Because then what happens overtime is I have lots of little successes and it just becomes natural because of the habit. It becomes more of my habit to correct myself than it is my habit to let myself go.

54. To develop conscience, verify.

Dr. J: Conscience is an emotional realization of truth. We talked about this a little bit previously.

STUDENT talked about the little angels and demons on the shoulders, right? Conscience is an emotional realization of truth, and we want higher emotional states because we want to develop conscience. We want our conscience to be more present with us. In order for that to happen, we have to verify things. In other words, we have to prove them.

Verification means to prove. Validation, verification, support higher emotional states as you witness them. For example, if I think what I feel is love, then I want to prove it. I want to keep pushing it a little bit and not just accept it blindly. If someone says they love you, it's not a bad thing to go prove it. Why? Because, if you just accept it without verifying it, without allowing it to prove itself, you'll never have a conscious understanding of it. You'll never understand it as being true. Otherwise, love is hypothetical and will come and go. It's important you throw down a gauntlet. I love you. Okay. What does that mean? Prove it. Verify it. Validate it. You say you love me, but can you make it real? Can you prove you love me? The truth of it is, if you can't, no matter what you say I'm not going to believe you.

J: Well, wait a minute. Aren't you working with someone else's expectations of what love is.
Dr. J: No, I'm working with me. I'm not working with you.

J: If you're saying you love somebody, from where you are you're proving it, and they're still looking for verification.

Dr. J: Well, how do you know that? How do you know you don't just Imagine that you love them? Maybe you've been led to feel that when you're attracted to someone, love them. Maybe you've been led to feel that when someone's congenial, love him or her. You know, who knows what you mean when you say you love?

J: Okay, well then, how do you prove love?

Dr. J: However you do. I'm just using it as an example. According to P.D. Ouspensky "Conscience is an emotional realization of truth". In order to develop conscience, you actually have to verify what you feel. You have to verify genuine emotional states, whatever they are. So, you do it however you're going to do it. How do you prove love? Well, you test it. Is it consistent? Does it have an element of integrity? Does it have an have an element of honesty? Does it have an element of clarity? Does it have an element of healing? Does it have an element of acceptance? Does it have an element of critical assessment? Does it have an element of consciousness? If it doesn't have any and all of these things, it's not love. It could just be hormones. It could just be chemistry. Love is supposed to have enduring qualities. One component of love is that on some level it has an enduring quality. So, if it comes and goes, poof, just like that, it's not love. It's something else.

I don't prove love by measuring what I think love is. I prove love by observing the absence of what love is not. It has to work that way, because I am identified with everything. I have agendas, even though I like to say I don't. I always have agendas because I'm a person. I have agendas. I lie to myself. I have negative emotion. I have obsessions and compulsions and greed and parts of myself I would never admit to myself, much less to you. All of this acts as a filter between you and me. You're doing the same thing. I'm doing the same thing.

Generally speaking, when we say we're having or experiencing love, most of the time we don't know what we're talking about. We can learn, however, what we're talking about overtime. There's a way to prove it. Like I said before, the way we prove our love is not by looking for what we think love is or what we've been led to believe or what our opinion is. We need to find things we can agree on that love is definitely not. If we observe the qualities of what love is are definitely not present, then perhaps what we're seeing or experiencing is love.

I think that's part of the problem, when you start talking about qualities like love. You actually can't define it. There's no clear, succinct definition of what love is.

J: Right, because I've heard that love is not fleeting, but then we see all the time how we love sometimes and then sometimes we are pissed off at you.

Dr. J: We don't know the difference between affection and love. We don't know the difference between lust and love. We don't know the differences and distinctions that occur between all of these states. Some of these states are physical/ chemical, some emotional, some intellectual. We need to look for the distinctions before making declarations of what love is.

We really can't have conscience and emotional realization of truth if we're not engaging ourselves in the process of verification and validation. We can't do it.

55. To quiet doubts, meditate on what is beautiful and do not disdain what you have received.

Dr. J: What are doubts? They are those voices of the little I's, which reflect old patterns and judgments. Why do we doubt? We doubt because we constantly compare every little thing about where we are and what we are being asked to do with previous work and life and efforts, expecting this will tell us what the result will be. Only we cannot know this ahead of time, as we have not actually done the work yet. This places the ultimate validation of success and experience a bit out of reach. It is unknown and unknowable and therefore suspect. We doubt because we do not have the end result of the experience and the validation, and not knowing causes us to have concern or even fear. What will be lost? What will be gained? Only direct experience and visceral validation can solve this, and that is unrealistic to expect in front of the actual experience. It's an empty basket.

Better to concern our selves with what is happening now. Better to focus on something, to think about something with intention capable of giving energy. Because you have not and cannot have this advance verification and validation, watch carefully the thoughts wanting to disqualify what you have felt, seen and experienced, as if your past work can be nullified because you cannot see the future.

56. We are all connected in some way.

Dr. J: This connection should be explored with consideration, compassion and loving kindness. It's pretty self-explanatory. One is just this acknowledgement that everyone working together is connected to everyone else, whose working in some way. Actually, "some way" is not enough. "So many ways" would be more accurate. This connection or these connections should be explored with consideration, compassion and loving kindness. We can't work together consistently from morning to night, from one day to the next, from week to week, month to month, year to year, if the way we're working together doesn't have the qualities of consideration, compassion and loving kindness, for without these qualities in mind, as we're working with each other, it's too easy to create a fence. It's too easy to hurt feelings. It's too easy to sustain progressively defensive communications that don't allow us to honestly and sincerely address the actual issues we have coming up for ourselves and between us. We can't take it for granted.

We have to remind ourselves that if we get off a little, when we're in a work environment, to try and come back to an even keel, a level place having these qualities as opposed to any other place.

STUDENT: The only thing I can think of is that sometimes it's hard to distinguish in between when you're around other people, whether or not you have a legitimate conflict coming from within you? It's difficult to try to figure that out sometimes I ask myself, is this mine? Or wait…am I just making this up or am I reacting to this because of this or is this conflict theirs? That's one of the things I find to be the most challenging. I don't know what do with it sometimes.

Dr. J: The critical words I heard in that are "around other people". I don't see any reason why it might be a bad thing to have these qualities in our communication with everybody. I don't see a downside to that. It's difficult to sustain, in my opinion, these kinds of qualities with other people because it presupposes they're working on themselves. It presupposes they have any idea or capacity in themselves to try and come from these places. The simple fact of it is many people don't. If they do, it's really kind of random. It can come and go easily. It can go away suddenly and dramatically. There's nothing you can do about it. From a work point of view, it's productive as an exercise to try and work with other people, but it is not productive to expect anything from people who are not actually doing their due diligence.

In other words, when we say we're working on ourselves, it's more than just trying to maintain an attitude. It actually means we're reading the workbooks, we're going through the materials, we're practicing different kinds of exercises, and we're specifically and pointedly addressing specific issues to come to some resolution of them. This is not a given outside of a work environment. It's not a given at all. In fact, even to try and do so with a person who's not engaged, in the work, so to speak, might come across so many different ways as completely random. It might come across as being judgmental, as if you're trying to control them, as sort of a holier than thou kind of attitude. There are many impediments.

Part of the value of being in a school is at least we're in some agreement that we are each doing something related to the others in the group. Outside of these environments, all bets are off as far as how things go, at least at this point. Why? Because we cannot assume people we don't know are working on themselves, are going to respond to anything that we're doing in a positive way. There's no guarantee of that. In the past, I've seen students become very excited about the work and about working on themselves and the different ideas and what not. They would try to communicate to their friends or to their family. Well, nobody had any idea what he or she were talking about. In fact, on some level, without some kind of preparation, most of what we talk about has to come across as being kind of crazy, because there's certainly no support for it in the mainstream culture. However, we do sometimes see evidence of it there.

We can't have or be attached to any expectation these conversations, in this way of being, will be very well received. In fact, the history of the world is full of examples of people who are very accomplished, who had achieved a lot of personal growth, who, in their attempt to communicate their ideas to the populous and popular culture, were killed by popular culture in some way. Not only did they not accept what they had to say, but got sharp sticks and fiery things and went after them. That's a reality we have to be aware of.

One of my aims is not to be crucified or burned at the stake or thrown on top of sharp objects because of my philosophy and psychology and the way I want to work. Out in the world, I practice discretion. I really try to look at people before I say very much about what I think or what I understand about these things. I tend to speak in more general terms. Even in a class, when we have our CTP programs, I'm somewhat judicious about how far I go into what I say, as far as approaching people about these ideas, because my understanding is that until I know they're open to them, I pretty much assume they're not. That positioning, if you will, is not arbitrary. In the past, I was that happy person who was so excited and wanted to share everything I was doing with everybody, and the response was not pretty overtime.

Again, this work presupposes an understanding of vocabulary. Look how much we talk about the meaning of words and what we mean by the words we use. Well, part of the reason we think overtime that we can understand ourselves is because of those conversations. If we don't have them, we can't expect to have the same kind of results and the same kind of clarity, or the same kind of depth of communication as if we did have them.

57. As you reveal and facilitate (photograph) the release of obstruction in those you love, you reveal and release obstruction and restriction in your self.

Dr. J: Helping others to have clarity and to understand their psychology is the same as working on your self. Additionally, reveal and facilitate release "in those you love"; in those I love. Because I love them, I want to engage them and I want to try to educate them. I want to try to help them. I can't always do it. I do make the efforts. I really do make a distinction between the amounts of effort I put into it as being quite different from one person to another. When I look at someone I really care about and I see obstructions, I still maintain that part of the reason why I am able to see those obstructions is because either I have had the very same issues in myself at some point and/or I still do. It's either I did have them or I still have them. If we didn't on some level share the obstructions, as common parts of our development, we wouldn't see them in other people.

They'd be invisible to us. That's also a source of compassion. I have to be compassionate on some level with the most idiotic people with which I would care to have a conversation, because I have to be honest and say I've had some pretty idiotic conversations myself. I've said some pretty idiotic things. I've held some pretty idiotic beliefs and I've certainly at different times in my life, been the poster child for idiocy, literally, with the tall pointy hat and the whole nine yards. I have to have done that. I know I have. So I have to have some compassion. As I'm working through those issues with the people I care about, I'm still working on what the remnants are of those same kinds of obstructions I generate within myself. That's humbling. Part of the system, I think, is that overtime, with practice, humility definitely comes into the equation. Also, if I were to think in real terms of people I've worked with and known, who I felt were more advanced than me, in this system, every single one of them was a very humble person. This doesn't mean they weren't powerful. Some of these people were very, very powerful. Even still in life, they still have powerful positions and jobs and authority and responsibilities. Also, at the same time, they are humble people and progressively more so overtime. I think that's just inevitably something you see as a result of this.

J: Here when you're using the word obstruction, how are you using that?

Dr. J: I'm referring to any impediment to waking up; any impediment to not being asleep. That's what I mean by the word obstruction. It doesn't necessarily mean "issue", because an issue, actually, if you're up for it, can be a great step toward waking up, because sometimes issues trip us and in that tripping we are stimulated. We're more awake and aware of it than we might be at some other time. Actually, release of obstruction, for example, photograph. As you reveal and facilitate, or photograph. Photograph means to isolate the mechanical behavior, to take a snapshot of it. We want to bring attention to and use that as an Impetus for self-remembering; to use that as leverage against identification, justification, and all of those kinds of things.

58. Working compassionately on others is the same as working on you.

Dr. J: As you work on your self, your work on others will change.
I literally mean this as actually having a conversation with someone that genuinely is coming from the point of view of helping them understand something mechanical in themselves and assisting them to be able to separate and self-remember.

I also mean it in the sense of concretely and practically working on someone to help him or her. When I talk about compassion, it's the practical expression of love. Working on someone, from this point of view, working compassionately on someone else, is a moment of a genuine expression of love. There's no downside to it. Whether they receive it or not is irrelevant. Whether they acknowledge it or not is irrelevant, because we don't do this for kudos. We don't do this for acknowledgement. That's not why you work on your self, so you can get reward or acknowledgement from others. That's not why we do it. The act of helping, in and of itself, is still the same as working on your self, and of course, overtime, if you change, if you make progress, if you're consciousness is being elevated, what you do with other people will change, the way you do with other people will change. It's inevitable. I think about trying to work with people twenty years ago, and oh my god! It just shocks me to think what I must have been asking people to do, at the level of consciousness of whatever kind of exchange or work we were doing, compared to the possibility now, because I am so different than I was twenty years ago. I can't even conceptualize it even though at the time I thought I was all over it. I thought I was the bee's knees. I thought I had major accomplishments in some of these regards, but in comparison, in contrast, not so much. I am very different than what I was doing and what I was thinking when I was doing what I was doing, even just general attitudes.

Now whether or not that might have been noticeable to someone else, I don't know. Someone else might look and say, "Well actually you apparently look the same, you apparently work the same, you sound the same, you teach the same kind of things." You might say, "Oh he's apparently the same, right?" Well, that's their perspective. Mine is very different. My perspective is that what I do and the way I do what I do is very different.

59. To be of any real value, theories on balance, harmony and management of energy must be verified and proven as facts.

Dr. J: Giving the work validation significantly increases your capacity to do more. This is an important one for me. So we talk about these things. We talk about balance. We talk about harmony. We talk about energy. We talk about balancing things, managing things, changing things, correcting things. Well, that's all talk. That conversation has some value, but it has so much more value if you can prove these things exist for you. It is so much more valuable. We really try to be creative in coming up with ways to prove it. Oh, so you think there's energy? Prove it. Oh, you think you can balance energy? Prove it. Oh, you think negative emotion is derived from disruptions in the body's energy system? Okay, prove it. Prove it to your self. I'm not saying prove it so that proof will be acceptable to anybody else in the world. That's not what I mean. See, that's the whole thing about validation. People get caught up in a loop and they think to prove or validate or establish something as a fact, that what I'm talking about, is science. I'm not talking about science. What I'm talking about is you have to be creative and diligent. You have to work hard to prove the things you believe are true as facts to you. You must acceptably verify them to you, not to anyone else's standard. You can't take it for granted that somebody else says energy exists or harmony is beneficial or that you can affect these things. Whether anyone else understands it, believes it or can prove it, is really not your issue.

The benefit here is all about your own personal process of verification and validation. It's your own personal thing. That's why I always say I've done the work for myself, and I've great confidence in this process. I've great confidence there is energy and that you can balance it, and that there are negative emotions and they are related to energy disturbances, and that we can change their nature and we can dissipate their capacity to cause distortions in our personality or separate us from being in the moment. I've personally verified that. Like today, when we were doing sessions, for example the tapping. Even just watching the shift occurring, okay? Watching that connection happen is validation for me; watching the shift take place, as we're working. That's good for me. I don't have to go get some scientist to come over here with laboratory equipment and hook somebody up with wires and do blood tests. There's nothing wrong with scientific verification and validation, but it is not the only criteria for validating something. Why? Sometimes we deal with concepts and words science has yet to catch up to. In other words, they're behind us. They're not ahead of us. That's a mistake people often make; that science is actually ahead of our consciousness, that it's somehow discovering and validating the possibilities of the universe ahead of our consciousness. Actually, it's the other way around. Science is always a little bit behind trying to figure out why something we've already observed works or how it works.

My personal process of validation, which is a work idea, is that it has to be personal. Given the work, validation significantly increases your capacity to do more. Why? Well, if I know something is true, then I can operate from that point of view without constantly having to revisit it and put in time, effort, and energy into recreating the whole validation process over and over and over again, the gerbil wheel of "I don't know if this is really true or not. I don't really know if this works or not. I don't really know if it's really something valid for me to focus my energy or life on, this idea of elevating my consciousness or spirit." If I've already in my life seen changes, and I've verified them and proven them and I've developed confidence in my ability to discern these kinds of things, then I can spend more time and effort and energy on doing the work, and less time on proving it. Proving it is important. In the initial stages, you kind of have to prove it in everything. You can't take anybody's word for anything relating to this. Ultimately you can't, because if it ever has any value at all, that value only occurs when whatever is happening here, whatever we're talking about when we say "the work", when it becomes personal, becomes your work. That's where the value is. Everything up to that point is conjecture and practice and hypothetical. We want to get out of hypothetical and out of conjecture and get more into concrete terms of verifiable and reproducible results. We want to get to that place however we can. We want to get there as soon as we can.

60. Begin with small aims and small successes to build a foundation of trust and accomplishment, from which to do serious work.

Dr. J: I like this, and again, all these comments, keep holding them in your mind as they relate to evolving. One thing here is actually postulating the possibility to do serious work. Serious work is the work we do that is not all wrapped up in superficial things; in other words, making fundamental changes to really core parts of us. How do we get to a point where we can break out the big guns and work on the really major Impediments? Well, we do it by making small aims. Remember what an aim is. An aim is the same as an objective, as a work objective, but start small. For example, today I will be considerate and compassionate in my communication. That's a work aim, complementary to my goal of evolving. I am either successful at it or I'm not. Okay. If I'm successful, my success shows I just validated I can make a small aim and complete it. So, I've got a little bit of discipline and will. That's confirmation.

Now, at the same time I'm working on small aims, if I deviate from it and fall short and I'm not able to fulfill the aim, then the friction in the discovery my inability to do what I say I'm going to do, that perhaps I don't have the discipline I think I do, or the strength, the energy—this then is a good opportunity for self-remembering. The reason being is I'll see myself when I trip on these small aims. When I'm missing them, I should notice I'm missing them. At some point then, I make some effort to correct them and I'll reformulate the aims and perhaps try again. So we start with the small ones first and, as we have success overtime, build this foundation of trust and accomplishment. Who am I learning to trust?

STUDENT: Your self?

Dr. J: My self. My "self" knows whether I'm trustworthy or not, no matter what I say, my self knows. There are a lot of ideas here based on the idea that if you're practicing self-remembering, one thing you are no longer going to be able to do is successfully lie to your self. It's just not going to work, because you are going to know you are lying to your self, especially when it comes to aims. That is why we don't want to set our aims too high or make them too big because, when we set big aims, we know whether we have the capacity to accomplish them or not, to a point. How we know is by trying to do the small ones. The small ones define our level of practice, so to speak. When we have more and more success in accomplishing our small aims, then we can stretch our muscles occasionally and go for bigger ones.

We'll know whether or not ourselves believe we have the truthful possibility of being able to accomplish that, based on experience, not on imagination. Well, I imagine I should be able to be more loving, but if I haven't been practicing and I say, "From today forward I'm going to be more loving," and even as I'm saying these words, my "self" is in the background going, Liar! You won't be able to do that. You'll be lucky if you last a day. You think you're going to always be this way from now on? I don't think so, not going to happen. Why? There's no reason you should believe it could happen. If you can't do it in small things, you're going to have a hard time convincing your self you can do it in big things. Guess what? We need ourselves to be convinced because we need ourselves in whole embodied commitment to break through on the big issues.

"Accomplish" means just like the word says. I said small aims. The day came and went and I accomplished my aims. My aim was successful. That is concrete right? That is a penny in the bank of your evolution, and it counts. That's one way we build our energy reserves to make bigger efforts. The thing about bigger efforts is we don't usually get to predict when we're going to have to make those efforts. They tend to come to us; we don't tend to go to them. That's why it's important to make small aims to keep putting that penny in the bank over and over, as much as possible, because unfortunately we don't come with a meter. We don't really know what our reserve is until the challenge comes to us. We either have enough to step up or we don't. We want to keep that in mind.

STUDENT: It would be really interesting if we did come with a meter. It'd be kind of helpful.
Dr. J: It'd probably be more depressing than interesting.

61. The more you accomplish in each day's work, the greater the results you can look forward to.

Dr. J: Each restatement creates different impressions. Each way of stating the principle ties it to something else and creates a slightly different impression. Certainly, when I wrote this, I wasn't writing just to one person. I was thinking mostly about myself, but every step away from that has been the thought of how do I communicate this for different types of people, different body types, different chakra types, different personality types, different alchemies. What way is that person going to be able to relate to it? It's simply more of a restatement: the more we accomplish in each day's work, there's that validation, there's that accomplishment, and the greater the results you can look forward to. Why? Well, because you have more to work with. So, it's reasonable you'll expect to do more, accomplish more, if you have more to work from. When we think of great leaders, great spiritual beings and so on, and their capacity for accomplishment in real time, it's only reasonable for them because they have a lot to work with. They bring a lot to the party, so we expect a lot from them. We don't expect so much from us because we don't know how much we have. We don't really have a history of accomplishment.

For example, in talking about healing, one of the theories is to develop your self as a healer. It's important to get your hands physically on as many people as possible. Just do it. Get your hands on as many people as possible. Try to craft that healing mind every time you do so. Why? Overtime, through that process, and if you're paying attention, you will get validation. You'll get verification there's something occurring when you do that. As you start to prove that's true, all of a sudden you see your capacity to do the healing work increases. It's a slow process, for how many people do we get to lay hands on daily? Sometimes more, sometimes less. It's a necessary thing we do it. I question healers who never work on people. People call themselves healers, but they don't do very much hands-on healing work. I question that. I go back to the idea that you have to verify, validate, and prove everything. How do you prove you're a healer? Well, by healing people of course. There's no other substitute in the way to do it. At some point, that nasty proof should come into the equation, because if you really try to be a healer, and did healing work without ever being able to prove any beneficial effect to what you were doing, at some point, you have to admit you're not very effective as a healer. You have no proof.

Proof is not so hard to come by. Most of the reason we don't have the validation we need to do more serious work is because we're not actually making the small aims and making the effort to carry them through. That's all there is. It's very practical in that way.

62. You do not know anyone's limitations much less your own.

Dr. J: It's impossible to verify another person's level of consciousness, externally. I can't definitively prove, one way or the other, whether your consciousness is higher or lower than mine, past a point I want to say. The reason why is how do I know you're not an angel sitting here on my couch, or in the chair in my living room. How do I know you're not an angel who has affected a disguise and come to live with me in order to teach me, the whole time I'm thinking I'm the teacher?

Dr. J: How do I know? How do I know? How could I prove it one way or the other, if part of your teaching strategy is to portray your self as an ordinary person, as a traveler, as a student, as a wife? How do I know? I have no way to prove that one way or the other, not in any short-term consequence. So, you're apparent lower qualities or difficult qualities might just be challenges to give me an opportunity to practice what I preach. It's possible. In the work, we admit there's a possibility of angelic intervention, angelic beings, conscious beings who literally intercede in our life in practical ways, i.e. Joshua on the road and the angel telling him that if he wants to go on to town, he's got to wrestle him. Whoever wins the wrestling match, whoever pins whomever on the ground, gets to do whatever they want. He ends up getting his shoulder dislocated because he gets in this big fistfight with an angel. Okay, well what was the lesson? You would think an angel would have been able to whoop him easily anyway. I mean, these angels fought wars that supposedly took place over vast ranges of the universe, whole galaxies involved, sky full of rain of fire, so you would think an angel would be able to whoop you in a wrestling match if he could destroy worlds. That would be kind of unreasonable, wouldn't it? No, no, no, because the angel takes the form of the limitation of manifestation in order to what, be able to relate to you, because I can't relate to an angelic being who's a destroyer of worlds. I have nothing in common I can relate to within myself. I have no similar capacity. There's no resonance. Just because you can blow up a sun, well, good for you, isn't that special.

If you come to me as a person of fairly similar level of consciousness or being, well, I'll wrestle with you and I might learn something. How do I know? See, I can't judge that, so what do we do as we try not to? And see, I can't even judge my own level of consciousness. That's the really funny part. I come closer to self-remembering because I observe that sometimes I'm paying attention and sometimes I'm not.

How clearly can I see my soul? You could shoot me in the head right now and it wouldn't even matter. How well can I see that? Well, not so much, but it's there so I can't even judge my own level because it's very hard for me to grasp sometimes the immortal parts of myself. If I can't with myself, how am I going to do that with you, you being anyone and your limitations, like if I'm critical and I think I know your limitations? Okay, well that's not true. Most of the time when I judge someone else's limitations, all I'm doing is stating the projection of my own limitations. It's pretty much what I'm doing.

It's good to hold that thought. I like the angel thought. That comes up a lot in the Sufi tradition. There are a lot of stories about angels and genies. Some of the stories are so quirky because the interactions they have with these supernatural beings are pretty mundane, sharing food, going for a walk, taking a bath, hitting the waterfall, having a conversation, getting in a fight. The superseding idea, though, is that all of this is happening under the direct influence and presence of a conscious being.

63. Your constant work is in selecting the highest aim.

Dr. J: If I have a choice of aims I'm going to set for myself, small ones, if I have any choice, let's go for the higher one. In other words, don't set your aims low. Don't always go to the lowest common denominator of what you know you can achieve. Don't always play to that "I know I can pretty much get along so that's my aim for today" idea. "I'm going to get along with everybody and have a fairly positive environment to work on." If I think I can do better and set a slightly higher aim, than that's what I should do because it's about the friction. Does that mean more often I'm going to fail? Well, yes, but when I succeed it's going to mean more.

64. It is said study to find oneself approved, however it is better to transform negative emotion than to study.

Dr. J: There is a saying, study to find oneself approved. Approved means when you're tried or tested, when you're in a circumstance where there is a challenge or trial to your aim or objectives or work on your self, you're able to meet that trial. However, it's better to transform negative emotion than to study. Study can mean all kinds of things, like reading, talking, working, but one of most important things we can do is transform negative emotions. If you have a choice of reading or dealing with some negative emotion, it's better to deal with the negative emotion. You're going to get more bang for your buck, in other words.

65. Evolution is dependent on how much you are willing to give.

Dr. J: It is diverted or held back by the consumption of lower influences. I made a note with this, the word alchemy. Manley P. Hall in his work titled "Words To The Wise" defines evolution as a "Law of Nature". He defines it as the expanding of natures from within themselves, outwardly." He further states "Evolution is the process of becoming ever more sufficient to the need of that energy resident within the evolving form". So evolution is dependent on how much you have to start with and from and how much you are willing to give. At a low level of alchemy, like lead alchemy, you're not willing to give anything toward it. You can't even imagine why you would.

STUDENT: Do you mean "give" as in give up?

Dr. J: Give as in willing to make efforts, willing to actually submit to the life you're creating. I want to evolve. I want to be a better person. I want to have a finer understanding of psychology. At the same time, I am not willing to change anything. Let's just have a very clear understanding about that. I want to know everything there is about psychology, yours, your psychology. Focusing on the issues and concerns of others is easy. How easy is it as far as my own issues go? I don't want to know anything at all about mine.

STUDENT: You should just go to college then?

Dr. J: From the point of view of my false personality I want to be able to audit life class. I don't want to be doing life class. I'm auditing. I'm here to help you. Let's not get me involved. My issues are my issues. Your issues are your issues.

STUDENT: Like the 380lb Diabetic, nutritionist?
Dr. J: Exactly.
Dr. J: Evolution is diverted or held back by the consumption of lower influences. There's this idea here that according to your willingness, you will either submit your self to or create in your vicinity higher influences. You'll either put your self in front of them. You'll attract them to you or you will create them. Okay? However, evolution is diverted or held back by the consumption of lower influences. If you surround your self with lower influences…and remember what's an influence? An influence is any thought, action or deed. An influence can be environmental. An environment can be a bad place to people who are not evolving. You could spend all your time with devolving or stagnant people. Well, that's not going to help your evolution.

You have to spend time with people who are A, already evolved, or B, at least are positive to the idea of possible evolution, in order to sustain your own work. Guess what? That takes a certain amount of discipline. It takes a certain amount of effort.

There's the alchemy part. What level of effort do you want to bring to the party?

Justification is one of the determinants of alchemy or level of practice, if you will. If I justify the bad influences I subject myself to, then I'm saying, at least in that particular area, that I'm going to sustain a level of development relating to the influence I'm subjecting myself to. So, at some point, I need to have more beauty in my life. I need to have conversations with people who are working on themselves. I need to live in a better place to have partners to help me work. What does that look like? Bring them to me, create them, or move to them, or whatever it looks like.

What's it worth? No really, what's it worth? That's the level of alchemy. Lead is not worth anything, so you're not going to do it. It might just be an idea, and eventually that idea goes away. Eventually it goes away because that's your level of work: lead alchemy. Okay? There's nothing more significant than gold alchemy. There's nothing more significant, so you want the outside to be like the inside and the inside to be more like the outside.

Copper and silver are somewhere in between. I'm sure there's some fluidity in between because our progress is inconsistent and all parts of us do not leap to the next level at the same time. What we find is, as we create a center of gravity, center of influences, which are higher minded, we have better alchemy, as far as their attraction. Those parts of us gravitate toward finer and more refined types of situations helpful towards sustaining ourselves and building up that bank account. Okay, move to the next.

66. Evolution and progress may look suspiciously like consistency.

Dr. J: To be the same everyday means to function from the higher centers, remembering your ambition and aim to be conscious before all things. Consistency is important. What we want is to have our consistency be in progressively higher ranges. There are always going to be highs and lows, but overtime the lows should not be so low and the highs should be higher. We're always going to have inconsistencies in how we are based on our level of consciousness, but there should be a progressive consistency of a way of being that is sustainable overtime. It should be enough that you can tell. You have to be able to see it. Why? Well, there's the validation, that consistency overtime. Being able to sustain a way of being overtime proves to you it's possible to do that. Now we don't have to ask the question, is it possible? Now all we ask is how do we elevate it? We've already proven we can support it overtime, so how do we move it or bump it up? Go ahead.

STUDENT: This makes me think of when I first started talking or writing or anything about having balance in my own life. It was at a point where the balance was so out of whack that the highs were so high and the lows were so low, and they were so far out of proportion it seemed like there were all these different parts of me that were just like irreconcilable. Balance was impossible and as something to strive towards, it looked impossible. I couldn't get balance and so when I think about it now, because I've been thinking about this idea of consistency as more of like a daily aim, because when I look at it, I can see the variations a lot smaller in where I, you know, those ups and downs you're talking about, but it's helpful, I think, to not even look at it so much as balance, because that's kind of like this teetering on something, you know, and I guess for me anyway, using that as vocabulary didn't really work. This makes a lot more sense in terms of consistency. Once you find that consistency where you're not just high and low and high and low and high and low, you can really start to focus. I like the picture of that better in my own head. It's a good example of a sort of daily aim, I think.

Dr. J: I also think it's important, if you have any of this, to redefine the word consistent in such a way it doesn't equal boring. Sometimes that's a cause of resistance toward developing some consistency. It's like, well, my life is up and down but at least it's not boring.
STUDENT: Right.

Dr. J: Okay? Well, not boring does not equal evolution. Boring or not boring is not on the list of qualities we're looking for, as far as personal evolution. Consistency, overtime, is the evidence of your foundation. It's the proof of your foundation in daily life that something is changing or has changed. That's the proof of it. To be consistent when external circumstances would challenge that is absolutely proof.

67. Every conscious connection in our machine is strengthened and perfected in use.

Dr. J: Yes. Every conscious connection in our machine is strengthened and perfected in use. We want this to happen, so we need to use and focus on those conscious connections. We're talking about bringing motion to our work, being more intelligent and really using our brain. Think about it. To be hypothetically a model for the way of being we talk about when we have these discussions is not something you can do with half your attention. You have to pay attention. You have to use your intelligence. You have to be really smart, but in six different ways coming and going. You have to be smart in your moving parts, in how you work from your instinctive parts, in your emotions, in dealing with what your mind brings you. You have to bring intelligence to every part of you. It's like when we talk about Tantra or Thai yoga or negative emotions, or we talk about talking about these things, we want to do everything that's related in the most intellectual way we can. It's not always going to sound the same. We want to come from the intellectual parts of centers and the high emotional parts of centers. With practice, we get better at it. That's the thing—with practice we get better at it. We become more inclined to come from the high parts of our centers versus the lower parts of our centers. They rule us less. At least, if they are ruling us and taking charge or driving us in some direction we ordinarily wouldn't want to go, we notice it more. We notice it more, which again, the friction between those two leads itself toward self-remembering. That's helpful.

All the good parts are strengthened and perfected in use.

68. Before evolution comes balance.

Dr. J: A long time before we can say we are evolved, we have this consistency and reliability. We have this practical expression of who we are. We have all the evidence of all these things a long time that is way ahead. It seems that just getting to a point of being able to be a balanced person and to be balanced in our bodies, emotions and minds and who we are as people, is a lot to ask for. For many people, it's not achievable and probably comes across as being impossible. Guess what? The impossible has to actually happen as a precursor toward the next step past impossible, which is absolute transformation and evolution of your consciousness. That's why we say this work is not for everyone, because right off the bat, right out the gate, we are setting our sights on something most people might think is impossible. It is said that for anything to be balanced, everything must be balanced to some degree.

J: Right, because a lot of people think that it's impossible to overcome the human experience.

Dr. J: Well, I'm just talking about being balanced.

Dr. J: You know? A lot of people would say it's kind of unrealistic.

They say no ones balanced.
Nobody could be balanced, okay? I disagree. I think that, back to what you were saying, and this was in my mind when you were talking about the word balance. The word balance might not be such a good word, because what is really being referred to is a sustainable equilibrium which is not so low and is a little bit higher progressively overtime, a progressive dynamic equilibrium that takes into account that it's a complex equilibrium. There's input toward these highs and lows literally from many different directions. There's input from the physical self, from the moving self, from the instinctive and emotional parts, from the mental parts, from the sexual nature. All of these things are contributing to where are you right this minute. How equal are the parts? See that's another word for equilibrium. How equal are the parts? Right this second? And the next and the next overtime, that's balance or Imbalance. If they're too far apart in the mindset, so to speak, you have one part of you operating at a very low level and another part that's relatively high. That's not balance. Balance is the extremes coming closer together overtime.

Equilibrium, sustainable equilibrium, dynamic equilibrium, tells you it's changing. It's in constant motion. It holds in the place in the mind as the reconciler of opposites. There's no such thing as a balance point. Part of the question I have with certain forms of meditation like Zen, the way I've had it explained to me and I've been in classes with Zen monks, so hearing it from the horse's mouth, where there is a constant pursuit of stillness, belies that everything in life is in motion.

When there is nothing motionless in the universe the constant pursuit of stillness, or achieving the still place as the goal, doesn't work. Everything's in motion relative to everything else. In this work, there's no approaching stillness. There's only

66

"ride the tiger". It's not about "approach the stillness", it's about "ride the tiger", because we're in motion. We're moveable.

69. The beginning of balance is being able to view without judgment.

Dr. J: There's another idea about self-remembering and self-observation. It is a process of viewing your self without judgment, because as soon as you judge, you identify. The judging part means identification. When you look at your self and you attach to it, for example, you notice something about your self, and the next moment you're emotional. Okay. Well, you just judged whatever you noticed about your self. You just attached some significance to it, some emotional significance. Usually, that attachment happens very, very quickly. That's how you know it's an identification and judgment. You didn't notice something about your self and then really consider it and what it means as a pattern in your life and where it comes from. What's the origin of it? We didn't do that. We just noticed it and it was bad—good or bad. See, that's the thing about it, good or bad. Take, for example, judgment. Sometimes when I think of the word judgment I think of it in a negative context, like judging myself. When I notice something about myself and I immediately decide it's a positive thing, well that's judgment too. I judged it to be positive.

When I'm self-remembering, if I'm self-remembering, there's no judgment or identification. It's a moment without those things. Being able to have those moments is the beginning of balance. Finding your self where you have a moment of clarity, where you see your self for who you are or you see something you're doing, that your machine is doing, but there's no particular attachment, good or bad, positive or negative, one way or the other, in that moment it's just an observation. Well, we want to notice when we notice. We want to notice when we have those moments because those moments are evidence something's changing. We want to be able to eventually sustain those moments.

70. Work on your self as a sculptor who cuts off all that which is not necessary until finding the essence of the thing.

Dr. J: It's like in the Four Principles, from JKD/Kali teacher Danny Inosanto, originally from Bruce Lee, which now I'm wondering if that's original to Bruce Lee or Yip Kai Mann, his teacher. Research Your Own Experience, Absorb What's Useful, Reject What's Useless, Add Something Specifically Your Own.

Reject what's useless may be the most important of the four. There are lots of things about us, about the way we are, that we know are not helpful. We know. We don't need to prove it, but we keep them around anyways. We cluster them up and keep them safe and allow them out occasionally. If we were a sculptor and the essence was the stone, and we're like Michelangelo carving David, we realize as we are carving our David there's an extra arm sticking out of our statue. We sit back and say, "Hmm, something's not right with this statue. It's got an extra arm. Hmm, it's not really what I'm going for. I'm going for a likeness of a person and most people don't have that extra arm, so I'm going to remove it." Then the statue is more aesthetically pleasing.

If you were the sculptor looking at the statue and 10% is incomplete with a big hunk of stone hanging off of it, you don't get all attached to that hunk. You don't think, "Well, that's part of the original stone I started with so I'm going to keep it." No, what you do is you chisel and whack that sucker off, even though by doing so you are not finishing the sculpture. You still have to take what's left, after removing the stone, and work on it to integrate that final piece into the whole sculpture. It's not finished until it's finished top to bottom. Well, we have to do the same thing. We have to be open—when we discover things about ourselves, ways of being, thoughts or attitudes or actions or habits, that are not necessary and don't serve us or anyone—to the possibility of cutting those loose and letting them go. We have different kinds of tools to help us do this. One of those unnecessary things, for example, is recurring negative emotion. Okay, well, we have a way to address that. If part of what holds me back is because I don't take care of myself, causing me to be out of balance in that dynamic equilibrium overtime and giving me constant physical issues with my body, if that is a resistance to what I know I need to do to take care of myself, well I just have to cut the resistance loose and start taking care of myself, whether I want to or not. Otherwise, it's a complete Impediment to having space to be able to work on myself. So, you can take this in a practical direction. All right, any thoughts?

J: You might have already covered it, but when you use the words, "essence of a thing," what does the word "thing" mean?

Dr. J: The essence of a thing? For example, I read somewhere Michelangelo (that's why I was using him as an example earlier) told people he saw the character of the sculpture in the stone before making the first cut with his chisel. He saw that image in the stone and called it the essence of the stone. The process of sculpting was removing everything that wasn't the essence of the stone. He wasn't carving a sculpture or statue. He was removing everything that was not the statue. He removed what was not true to the essence of the stone and when he was done, there was David, tah-dah, there was the Madonna. It's the same thing for us. It's not that we're trying to make our essence. We already have an essence. That's our true self. We already have it. As a sculptor, he was talking about the essence of a thing, meaning the stone or marble. Everything, by the way, has an essence. This table has an essence. This coffee cup has an essence. Everything has an essence. We have an essence. The way we get to our essence is mostly, at this stage, about cutting away and doing everything we can to diminish the power of what's not the essence or not supportive of the essence being manifest.

STUDENT: I think it's really good to look at it in terms of a sculptor and his sculpture because he sees a big massive rock and yeah, he sees David, but he still has this big massive rock. He could have just gone straight through and gotten this perfect statue, but I kind of doubt that. First you have this massive, daunting thing and you got a little chisel and a hammer. Some parts of the rock are denser than other parts and some parts take longer, and you could misstep and cut off the wrong thing. There are flaws in the stone. It could take way longer than you expect and even when you're halfway done, it could seem more daunting, then when you had barely started, because you were looking at an idea, at the essence, you get in the mess of it and you got stone all over the floor and you got all these different parts, and blisters on your hands.

STUDENT: It's a perfect example because it's great to talk about the work, but when you're in the midst of it, it's not this fluid process at all.

Dr. J It's not a linear or fluid process at all. And back to the sculptor metaphor. We can work with that in a lot of ways. For example, as the essence emerges from the stone, on some level, it may get easier. See, there might have been a point where I didn't know whether I was carving an animal, mineral or vegetable. Then, as the Image begins to emerge from the stone, I say "Ah", it's a person, a male person vs. a female person. Or whoa, wait a minute; it's not just one person. It's a couple of people. Oh, wait a minute. They're naked. Oh, no actually they're fully clothed." As they come up, what are they clothed with? "Oh, it's a robe. Oh, I get it."

Dr. J: Yes, as the essence is revealed it's easier to work on it because the revealing image it's self can then guide you. It becomes a self-fulfilling prophecy. Initially, the essence is completely hidden from us, then as we cut away the non-essentials, through all the different techniques we talk about, using every bit of skill, intellect, strength, will, whatever we have, using all our faculties, as we start to cut away the unreal and the real starts to emerge, then the real begins to be an influence in and of itself toward its own emergence. The essence begins to dictate the nature of the work. There are a lot of ways this is talked about. We have the idea of magnetic center, which can evolve into deputy steward, which can evolve into steward, literally, the master of the house. Previous to the master, we have to find the house. Previous to finding the house, we find there are servants. That's evidence there might be a master, because why would there be servants in the house without a master? As we go through each level, we start to have a clearer idea of where we're going.

71. The way of the warrior is to fearlessly cut away what is not your true self.

Dr. J: Back to the Hagakure ("Hidden by the leaves", commonly known as The Book of the Samurai), a commentary on the bushido code and a practical guide for being a warrior, written by samurai Yamamotto Tsunetomo. The way of the warrior. That's a term from the bushido code of the samurai. Basically, in the Hagakure it states that bushido is the "Way of Dying," or living as though one were already dead. This rings true to what we also read in the Bardo Thodol, or The Tibetan Book of The Dead. The first rule of making one's pathway via the Bardo, or "Betweens," is to realize one is deceased and let go of what is no longer reality in order to move forward, even though it is commonly understood the Bardo Thodol is instructions for the afterlife or between reincarnation state of being. We see the metaphor carried over into this present reality, our present manifestation of consciousness between moment to moment. Between event to event, thought to thought, state of being to state of being.

In the book Go Rin No Sho (The Book Of Five Rings), Samurai Master Miyamoto Musashi states, "The way of the warrior is a resolute acceptance of death." The way of the warrior is found in the resolute acceptance of death. The way of the warrior is to fearlessly cut away what is not your true self, because whatever is not your true self is temporary and is going to die anyway. It's not going to survive. It's not. There's something that might, and we call that the true self. Why wait to go through this practice of divesting your self of that which is not real after you die, when we could get on to it while we're here?

Furthermore, Sensei (teacher) Miyamoto Musashi, in his book the Dokkodo (The Path of Aloneness or The Way to be Followed Alone or The Way of Walking Alone) listed 21 precepts in basically how to live a conscious life.

Musashi's Twenty One Precepts

1. Accept everything just the way it is.
2. Do not seek pleasure for its own sake.
3. Do not, under any circumstances, depend on a partial feeling.
4. Think lightly of your self and deeply of the world.
5. Be detached from desire your whole life long.
6. Do not regret what you have done.
7. Never be jealous.
8. Never let your self be saddened by a separation.
9. Resentment and complaint are appropriate neither for oneself nor others.
10. Do not let your self be guided by the feeling of lust or love.
11. In all things have no preferences.
12. Be indifferent to where you live.
13. Do not pursue the taste of good food.
14. Do not hold on to possessions you no longer need.
15. Do not act following customary beliefs.
16. Do not collect weapons or practice with weapons beyond what is useful.
17. Do not fear death.
18. Do not seek to possess either goods or fiefs for your old age.
19. Respect Buddha and the gods without counting on their help.
20. You may abandon your own body but you must preserve your honor.
21. Never stray from the Way.

We talk about this other times when we talk about this idea, that working on your self is a little bit like dying. Again, it's because we're cutting away something, which right up until the minute we started cutting it away, we thought was us. The ego, the false personality, doesn't want to die. However, in order for the essence to be revealed and ascendant, the personality has to be the servant, completely.

I don't want to say the personality has to go away entirely. I think the personality, again, serves a function in life, and we need it. It's actually a part of the machine. Our machine is perfect, and if the personality and ego expression relating to the machine is a natural part of the machine, then that means it serves a natural function. It acts as sort of a skin, if you will, which allows us to maintain a certain kind of integrity as we beat and bang around the world with other people. Personality can serve a function, in that regard. For example, if I'm not in control of my personality at all, I might find myself in a group of dangerous people and say something stupid to them, compelling them to kill me. Oh, that didn't work that well.

J: Like stupid racist jokes. Or insulting a stranger!

Dr. J: "Oh, I wonder why they tried to shoot me?" Well, if you weren't being such an idiot, they might not have tried to do that. There might also be, for example, a need to lie to survive? What if I need to lie to survive? "No, no, I'm on your side. Don't shoot me." Well, I should be able to do that on purpose if I have to. If my personality is in charge and I have some ego about disclosure... Let's say I'm all attached to being honest. Oh, there's that person in front of me with a gun. The reason they are going to shoot me is because I'm not one of them and don't agree with them. So, I tell them, "Guess you're going to have to shoot me because I'm not one of you." So they do. Maybe on some grand scale I proved a point. Oh, I was honest even when someone was going to shoot me. Great. But now I'm done...on to the next. Maybe I'd like to be here a little bit longer and don't want the hoopleheads to shoot me. Sometimes I might have to have a little control over my personality in order to make that work.

STUDENT: One of the things they haven't talked about, I don't think, at all, that always came up in political theory and things like that, is self preservation and how, from an early age, if we're going to start talking about essence, and we're going to start talking about negative emotions and chipping away at all this to get down to the essence, well, self preservation was kind of the thing that led us to acquire all this in the first place.

72. To resonate with the higher energies and intelligences of the Ray of Creation, draw near to harmony.

Dr. J: Ray of Creation: draw a line from the absolute to you. See all the laws of nature your subject to and all the levels and hierarchy from there to where you are from heaven to earth.

What is the Ray of Creation? One simple way to think about it is to draw a line from the absolute, and by absolute I mean the origin of everything (if that's the big bang or god or the original "architect of everything there is"), through all the universe and all the worlds, all the galaxies, through the solar system to this planet to you. The ray of creation represents all the laws and external natural influences that are literally the world in which we live. See all the laws we are subject to.

Being in resonance with the Ray of Creation means we are in harmony with it. We really don't know what that means. It's a difficult question and it's one people have been trying to answer for a very long time. The idea here is that we can resonate with higher energies. There are higher energies available to us. There are higher intelligences available to us to access, which emanate from this ray of creation. The key to being able to perceive them or to harmonize or resonate with them is the balance—that we are capable of within ourselves—between all of the different centers, whether we speak in terms of our primary centers like instinctive, moving, physical, emotional, intellectual, or whether we talk about centers step up or down and transformers or transducers we refer to as the Chakras. As we balance these different parts of us, think of them as antennae having the capacity to communicate with higher powers. As we balance them with each other, we create the possibility of getting a better signal, receiving more information. The information is always around us. We are surrounded by higher intelligence. We are separate from it. We are diffuse. We are an interference pattern in the ray of creation but we play a part in it. As we reduce the interference, come more into equilibrium with our inner harmony, we are able to be right with god or goddess. We are able to have real time, direct, personal communication and exchange of energy and information with consciousness, intelligence and energy greater than our own.

73. As you draw toward harmony, higher energy draws nearer to you.

Dr. J: There is such a thing as the affinity principle in that like attracts like. As we have a more harmonious way of being within ourselves, and as our consciousness is more fully and comprehensively integrated into all the different parts of us, then that draws higher energy nearer to us. It might be similar to statement #72.

Of course, the inverse is true. As we disassociate, fracture and crystallize in negative expression and negative emotions, as we identify and are consumed by imagination, it's exactly the opposite. Higher energy is not attracted to that. What we say is, when we are in those states we receive information or communication, that's how we know there is such a thing as grace. That communication is in spite of us. It's not because of us.

This has often been misunderstood. People would find an insight into some higher consciousness when they were at their most negative, in their worst possible state of consciousness. There was this mistaken understanding of that being the only time higher powers try to communicate with us. In fact, it's exactly the opposite. We are surrounded with communication. We are surrounded by conscious influence and the absolute attempting to communicate with us in such a way to help us be part of the ray of creation, to fulfill our own destiny. We do have a unique, individual destiny within the context of the ray of creation. It's very difficult for us to do that in this lifetime when we are not able to take our cues from higher powers. We are not able to follow their lead, so to speak. We are surrounded with information, so sometimes when we are in desperate circumstances, something causing us great pain most likely, we will get a very clear hit from it. The situation is not what generated that. What happens in desperate situations is there may be a moment where we are so upset and out of equilibrium that the power of the ego slips. We might be so desperate, out of sorts and helpless that we might for a minute realize everything we are, know and have cultivated, in the sense of ego and personality, is false and has left us and failed us. In that moment of humility, where we "give up the ghost," there's an opportunity for this influence and communication. It has always been there. Now it can impinge on our reality. We suddenly have a realization. Of course, it might be too late to do anything about it at that point. It's better to work on conscious equilibriums as far ahead as possible and in the calmest of circumstances so that we begin to familiarize ourselves with the nature of the communication and our ability to integrate and respond to it, so we can have it in calm and desperate times. Take this exchange of energy out of the realm of chaos, unpredictability and accident.

74. The most extraordinary nourishment available for conscious evolution is the written legacy of conscious beings.

Dr. J: This is the nature of dharma or dhamma, as the Thais say. When we study teachings which have been passed down to us through generations, whether in the form of exoteric teachings—books, materials, art, sculpture, music—or esoteric legacy information through oral tradition, lineage through schools, that database, repository of knowledge, is nourishment for our conscious evolution. It's not random or chaotic. It's virtually impossible to do by one's self. We need help.

One of the first areas where it appears help available is in the "brain trust" in the great body of knowledge of the ancient, spiritual traditions. I think there is some truth in all of them. I don't care what the name is. That's irrelevant.

I think the purpose of religion is and has always been to encapsulate and codify in such a way as to be able to pass on to future generations elements of morality, truth and the possibilities of achieving higher awarenesses and understandings of life not commonly available. The problem, of course, with formalized religions is what happens when people get a hold of that truth and begin to use it as an extension of the ego and false personality, a weapon, for developing of the ego.
Just because people, in religion for example, have misused the truth doesn't mean the written legacy passed down through the great religions of the world is bad, just because at some point or another they were misused and the meaning was lost for a period of time even to the present day.
In Buddhism, for example we have the historical Buddha, the writings and teachings, commentaries, dissertations—all that together we call the dharma. This dharma or similar teachings exists in all the great religions of the world.

In Christianity, you have Jesus as this consciously evolved human being. You have the legacy of his teachings, maxims, metaphors, sayings, content, the written records, which are referred to as the bible, Nag Hammadhi Codex, dead sea scrolls, apocryphal literature, the Qumran tablets, etc., which then lead to the modern bibles, commentaries on them and on each other to the present day. All of that together is the dharma of Christianity, including the teachings having been passed on through Christian societies, both exoteric and esoteric, through oral traditions, monastic orders, secret societies and so on. You have the same equivalent for all the religions, for the Islamic world, the pagan world, etc. All this material is not created equally but contained within the dharma. The written legacy of conscious beings is useful information nourishing to us.

With discernment and discrimination we can access any good tool in order to feed ourselves to give us the energy we know is required to consciously evolve.

75. There's no question. You must control extreme emotions in order to awaken.

Dr. J: There's no question. Extreme emotions feed false personality and negativity. You might say, "Well wait a minute. If you are extremely happy, that will feed negativity?" Of course, yes it will, because why are you so happy? What's on the other side of extremely happy? Well, there's the let down. There's the crash. There's the pendulum swing, the seesaw of emotion from positive to negative, back and forth. This is all mechanical.

Extreme emotion drives us into sleep. When we are in that state, we are being pushed toward identification and justification. We can get locked up in a cycle of that. It affects the physical machine by generating hormones. It generates enzymatic states and changes pH. High emotions, positive or negative, do the same thing. They stimulate the production of adrenaline and "sympatheticatonia", or the tensioning and tightening, shortening and contracting states. They have effects on the organs, the nervous system, and some of these are quite long lasting. For example, the excess of adrenaline in extreme emotional states deteriorates and becomes toxic very fast. Overtime, it can cause neural degradation and hypersensitivity.

If we are really committed to awaken, one of the ideas is to monitor ourselves with these extremes. We simply don't submit to them and use all the tools we have to head them off at the pass or interrupt them. It's quite okay to interrupt dramatic, extreme emotion if you are working on your self, even though you might think it is justified by some particular circumstance, what someone did or said or how someone looked at you. So what? There is no right justification to allow oneself to be overcome with emotion, the same thing as losing control. However, do we gain a higher perspective when we are cultivating a loss of control? They are simply incompatible.

76. Higher beings will not grant awakening to those who consistently place themselves first.

Dr. J: These people will receive special lessons. Technically, when I'm praying and seeking the influence and support of higher consciousness, whether you call them saints, sages, gods, spirit, absolute, C influence, etc, I want to make sure while I'm petitioning that I'm working on reducing the role of ego. My tendency is to make my personal needs the first thing to consider. The one thing I don't want to be is too special. I don't want special lessons. I like my lessons to be smaller and more frequent. I like the intervention of conscious beings, of god andgoddess, to be much more constant in much smaller increments than having these earth shattering, life changing, devastating realizations.

If ego is what we have to work with, and I'm going to equate ego with the sword, then "those who live by the sword die by the sword." There are two parts to a sword. There's the pointy, sharp part and there's the back of the blade and handle where you can control it. The thing about the ego is when we are in a place of preferring and feeding the ego, the sword is double edged with no handle. Can you see a problem in trying to use it? It won't be pretty. The ego is something to be controlled. It's just another function of ours. The righteous use of our functions is to be controlled by the higher parts of us. When they control us, what do they do? They separate us and cut us away from everything meaningful. They cut us away from the possibility of our progress and of receiving information and communication from within and without. They cut us apart from each other and the world.

77. There is a law that the higher must and will serve the lower.

Dr. J: I always thought this was interesting. Why are higher beings concerned with us at all? Why does god care about us at all? If you study the Ray of Creation, you will see that from the origin of all there is, we're kind of far away in the boonies. Between us and the original influence that created this universe, there are over 90 orders of magnitude of laws. These are the natural laws under which creation manifest.

Why, considering that, would spirit or god or goddess, conscious creative absolute, be concerned with us at all? The answer is that everything is connected. Even though we are far away in the boonies of the universe on this little backwater planet called Earth, far from the galactic core, and we're very immature as a species, broken down and undeveloped, spirit is concerned. We have a part to play. Our consciousness and spirit make contributions to the consciousness of all there is. It's like the Native Americans say, "mitakuye oyasin" (Lakota, we are all relatives). We are not just relatives with each other but with all that there is. We just don't have a sense of it in real time, much less between each other or within us. We have no conception of that.
Because of this connectedness of all things based on levels of scales everything above reflects everything below and vise versa. I take this to mean that on some levels higher orders of intelligence and being above our own are still dependent on us for that evolution as well. If this is true then higher mind and spirit must be aware of us and interested in our progress.

The essence of higher consciousness is oneness, equilibrium, universality, more perfect understanding of the natural order and laws of the universe and the integration and reconciliation of all seeming opposites. The root word of integration is integer, which means one. As we reduce the fracturing and crystallization of personality and ego and negative emotion and so on, we become more one-like and begin to have the possibility of fulfilling our role in the ray of creation. We can then ask what is our role?

78. Virtue is not of chance but painful art. (Petrarch)

Dr. J: We sometimes have the mistaken impression that to be a good person is something natural. We will even look at other people as role models and say, "Ahh. They're seemingly virtuous." There's no such thing as virtue that's not cultivated as a result of education, practice and discipline. Virtue is a quality of being which comes from integration of mind, body and spirit. If we don't have that, we are not capable of being virtuous. We might externally appear virtuous but are not internally. We might be in public and not when we are by ourselves. We might be with one set of friends but not another. We might be with friends but not with significant others.

Virtue is constantly being qualified. It is the measure and sum of our work. I think being virtuous is impossible without a lot of work.

79. Your effort must be your own. Rely on others less for your progress.

Dr. J: There is a continuum. When you are a new student and learning how to work on your self in a conscientious and diligent way, you need a lot of help. You need discipline, corrections, you need to get busted, educated, and you need help being organized. Where do you start? What are some logical steps in your practice? How are you going to work with others and in what context? You need lots of help. As you make progress, you need to take increasing responsibility for your progress and rely on others less and be dependent on others less for the cues. Why are you waiting for someone else to tell you what to do when you already know? Why are you waiting? What's the resistance? What's the hesitation to do what you need to do? Why are you waiting on someone else to be the responsible person for your personal evolution?

Eventually you have to take full and complete responsibility for your own progress. It doesn't mean you're not still in community. It doesn't mean you're not still in school. It just means a level of practice issue. Advanced students, one of the criteria we would use to determine if someone was advanced or not is simply to look at them and see how much they rely on everyone else for their progress? What's the self-responsibility? Where's the self-generation? If we don't see that, if instead we see dependency, that's a level of practice. The dependent has a lower level of practice than the self-disciplined, self-originating, self-responsible, self-initiating person in the work.

80. The lower often thinks that it is the higher.

Dr. J: Lower parts of centers think they are in charge and get away with it because we don't address them with the higher parts of centers. They are like unruly children who think they run the house when the parents are gone. They really believe they are in charge. They do anything they want because they are not under supervision.

When the intellectual is absent, the lower parts run amuck. They honestly think they are in charge at that time. The lower is not the same as the higher. Just because the lower can be in charge, can assert itself, can take dominion and be dominant for a period of time doesn't take away from the fact that it was never meant to do so. The prudent course of action is to do whatever it takes to correct that as quickly as possible when it's observed.

The parents come home and realize that while they've been gone, the kids have run amuck and destroyed the house. From the moment they walk in the door, things change. There might be a couple minutes of reestablishment of equilibrium as the parents remind the kids that they are the kids and they are the parents. That might not be pretty. The kids might throw up some barriers of resistance, using phrases like, "You're not the boss of me". Of course, the parents are Immune to those kinds of arguments and they just reassert control and start to restore the house.

That's the way we have to be with ourselves. Whenever we wake up a little bit and realize the lower parts of us have been rummaging around and creating disarray, we have to take that parental role—in other words, relate from the higher parts of our centers and make all necessary corrections to get back to the best possible way as fast as possible. Then that's not even enough because then we have to take it one step further. Restoration is not enough. The next step is education and practice in order to reduce the possibility this state will continue or happen again.

81. Connect with something higher.

Dr. J: Value that which is higher to raise your energy. We find ourselves in a state of mind where we are not considering something with more essence than where we might be right now. We have to constantly seek this connection to something higher.

There is a concept in the bible that says, "Pray without ceasing." [1st Thessalonians 5:17] It's a very powerful statement. It's one of these written legacy types of statements we allege comes to us from higher consciousness.

How does one pray without ceasing? We have to develop or cultivate an attitude of prayer. We look at what is prayer. We think Puja, acknowledgement, affirmation, Boddhicitta, and generating perfect thoughts. We think of petitioning for help, asking for blessings, consideration of beauty and listening and connecting.

Connect with something higher. Value that which is higher to raise your energy. When you notice your energy is low, the discipline is to do something about it. Part of the reason we have so many resources here like great books and materials, documentaries and art, the beauty of nature we have access to, these are all part of the reason why we have all this. All of these things are tools that can be used to connect with higher energies. To not do so when we are in a depressed or negative state is a level of practice issue. How resistant are you to pull your self out of lower states? Then make use of what you have available in order to support that. Just do it, especially when you don't want to or don't feel like it. That's when it's most valuable. That's when you're likely to get something good. If nothing else, what you will get is simply that your energy will rise as you stimulate higher parts of centers.

82. Work towards making your work self-sustaining.

Dr. J: There's an idea that as you work and practice discipline on a day to day basis and bring energy, attention, consciousness, breath and pressure to your resistant, negative issues toward areas of your personality that are armored and buffered and held sacred from any help, you start to see the opportunity to be self-sustaining. That work becomes more habitual. All habits are not bad. We need to cultivate habits practiced by human beings who are not taking a dirt nap. We need to cultivate habits similar to what we would imagine to be the habits of those who are more awake than we are. As we do so, we become more self-sustaining. These good habits give us more freedom, more flexibility to develop ourselves because we are not constantly burning out from the old habits. It's hard to sustain when you are completely weighed down by lead bricks, old habits, old attitudes, negative emotions, identification and imagination.

CHAPTER TWO: Expect To See The Miraculous

1. Expect people to respond well and to be able to continue on their own.

Dr. J: In spite of what we know about the obvious deficiencies of ordinary people, including ourselves, we cultivate an expectation that people will respond well and that it won't always be negative. It won't always be resistant. With a little correction, people will respond and be able to continue on their own. As a teacher, this is super important. As a teacher, if I did not have this expectation, every time the opportunity would come for me to teach a class, I would ask myself, "What is the point?" If the students are not going to respond well, and if at some level they can't continue on their own, then it's just a fruitless exercise. As a teacher I need to cultivate an expectation of a good response, and whatever I'm doing, if it's genuine, that it will continue after my direct influence is no longer there.

Relate that to expect to see the miraculous. When people respond well and then you notice they are continuing to work on themselves and to practice and cultivate a discipline after your direct supervision is gone, that is a miracle. Considering what I know about the inner workings of people including myself, it is miraculous to find someone who is able to respond well in training and then continue.

2. When confronted with a situation beyond your ability or control to alleviate, apply common sense and proceed practically.

Dr. J: *At the very least, don't panic and do no harm!* That's worth reading again. How are you going to know if it's beyond your control or ability? Well, you won't know if you are consumed with imagination and negative emotion and identification because you're going to take everything personally. You're going to think on some level you have some control or influence to control every single thing that happens. You will stress and worry about unnecessary things and it will consume you. You need to apply common sense by proceeding practically. Where does common sense come from? It comes from higher parts of centers. Intellectual function is able to look at a situation and make a determination whether or not it is really in your control. Having determined that, go with it.

We were talking about hurricanes. It's beyond our ability to control a hurricane off the coast of Puerto Rico. We apply common sense. We realize Puerto Rico is distant and the chances of a big storm that far away directly affecting us are quite small. Common sense says to panic at this point and start breaking down the wagons and getting ready to roll out prematurely is not helpful.

The first thing in every situation is to not panic. Panic refers back to extreme emotion. Panic will not help you survive, much less help you thrive in fluid environments. Do no harm. When you're in a state of extreme agitation over a lack of control, keep your focus so you don't break it. Why? It will pass. Things will change, just wait.

In The Hitchhiker's Guide to the Galaxy by Doug Adams, it says, "Don't panic" and "Don't lose your towel." The towel is common sense.

3. Fear of suffering is a large component of imaginary suffering and promotes sleep.

Dr. J: This is a funny one to me. I've experienced it. When I was afraid of possible future suffering, even to the point of imagining how awful that could be, I wouldn't do something or wasn't present to a moment because of that imagination. I'd think to myself, "Since I can't resolve it and I'm overcome with emotion about possible future suffering regarding some issue, how about this? I'm just going to pretend it's not an issue. I'm going to ignore it and go to sleep. I think I'll just take a nap."

You're saying, "The world is coming to an end?" That sounds pretty serious. I think I'm just going to go take a nap.

It's interesting how tired we get. This tiredness is an impetus towards sleep, when we are confronted on some level with something we don't want to address, with something we imagine is causing or will cause us suffering. Sometimes it's not actually causing us suffering. In fact, in many cases when we talk about working with issues, at the end of the process we have more energy than we started with, and instead of having suffering we have strength and clarity and communication and closeness and intimacy and integration and awareness, understanding and a better practice. Because we project suffering and imagine more suffering relating to dealing with our issues, we simply don't do it. That's a form of going to sleep.

4. Long ago a wise man said truthfully, "He whose powers are not equal to the necessary and the useful will busy himself with the unnecessary and the useless." (Johann Wolfgang von Goethe)

Dr. J: One of the things we do in school is observe useless, busy work, which is a diversion from bringing focus and attention to something that needs it. It's interesting how often we can find ourselves having been so busy that there's no time or energy to do something we knew we had to work on, because we were so busy doing lots of unnecessary stuff. Outside of a work environment, you see individuals completely consumed with their lives. There is very little time from morning to night for what's necessary. They are just going through the motions. A great deal of emotional and mental and physical energy is all unnecessary. They go off into directions that will bring no benefit and no concrete return.

5. "My main desire is to concern myself with what is everlasting, so as to win eternity for my soul." (Goethe)

Dr. J: We are practicing learning what is really temporary. What are the parts of us, our qualities that are subject to events, the whims of nature, the whims of other people and our sleep state, the whims of our bodies and our parts? We try to differentiate all of that from what is not transient within us, whether you call that your soul. In yoga, there is a concept of Atman, spirit, our true selves, and our authentic selves.

I'll close with this reading from Goethe: "When we regard ourselves in the many situations life brings, we find from first breath to last we are conditioned by external factors. Yet it is the highest freedom left to us to perfect ourselves within so that we shall come into harmony with the moral world order and attain peace with ourselves no matter what obstacles may emerge. This is easily said and written; yet it is no more than a goal before us to the achievement of which we must thoroughly dedicate ourselves. Every day challenges us to do what is to be done and to expect whatever is possible."

CHAPTER THREE: Develop True Personality and Diminish False Personality

1. Cultivate true personality by developing an impartial attitude.

Dr. J: What is impartial and what is an attitude? If we go to a quote by PD Ouspensky regarding "attitudes", he states, "Attitudes are like wires that connect us to events. To change the attitudes to which we are subject, we must first change our attitudes". Our attitudes are polluted by the tapes and emotional buffers which are the result of unresolved, negative, emotional issues and the disruptive energy patterns held in the tissue coupled with programming and the affected thoughts and feelings we have been given, indoctrinated into us as literal ways of being. To develop an impartial attitude is to work on many different aspects of oneself, both releasing the limitations these conditions represent while simultaneously leaning how to observe oneself without attachment.

2. Cultivate true personality by formulating and remembering your aim.

Dr. J: If on some level I have this idea that ultimately my progress as a conscious being is somehow intrinsically tied to the consciousness of other beings or people, then on some level I am bound to work toward the enlightenment for all beings. On the microcosmic viewpoint I work for my own "*realevation*" (my made up word combining realization and revelation) and enlightenment. On the macrocosm, any activity geared toward helping others increase their level of being is going to be helpful for me.

The aim of being a teacher serves both of those.

On another level, let's say we have the aim to be a good student or apprentice. That takes a lot of work to hold as an aim. It is very hard to be a really "good" student. How do I know this? Well, because I've been a student under masters most of my adult life. I have to tell you—as much kicks and giggles and fun I've had with some of my teachers, quite often, being with master teachers, in and of itself, was some of the most challenging experiences of my life, literally requiring every faculty I had in order to sustain my attention, dedication and commitment in order to get the teaching they had to offer. It wasn't easy. It was never easy. Sometimes it was. I know it might sound like a contradiction.

Dr. J: That's the only way I have to describe it. This relates to the idea of cultivating formulation and remembering your aim. There was a point, when I was at the Buddhai Sawan Institute in Nongkam, Thailand in the early eighties, where I had gotten into a disagreement with Phaa Kruu Samaii because I had gotten injured and he wouldn't let me out of class or give me any time off that I thought I needed to recuperate from this injury. I had injured my forearm close to the elbow joint. The injury was getting worse and increased to a point where my hand hurt just to do the simplest motion. To extend my arm created a crazy amount of pain. So I asked him if I could take off a couple days of class because of the injury. He looked me right in the eye and said, "No." I responded with, "Well, I'm injured and I'm not well. You can see I'm injured. My arm is swollen and it's really painful. I can't really do everything everyone else is doing or what is required of me and I think I need to take time off." He looked me in the eye again and said, "No. You are required to be in class. You are required to participate. Either you're in class participating or you're not. If you leave class without permission, don't come back. We will assume, because you're not in class, which you have quit. Since you will have quit, there will be no reason for you to come back." LL kinds of negative emotions surfaced. His comment made me so angry I can't even tell you. It hurt my feelings. I felt like he wasn't listening to me. I felt like he didn't care about me. I got mad at him. I wrote a couple of letters over the next couple of days to some friends of mine at the time.

I had seen him heal people by just laying his hands on them and do miraculous things, but in this moment he was not a good person being, in my mind, properly responsive to my needs. I wrote all this down in a letter. I'm going to quit because if I can't heal myself, I'm going to have to quit, if he won't give me the space.

However, after cooling a bit and finding more my right mind, I didn't quit. I kept going to class. I kept practicing in class but changed what I was doing to cover for the injured arm to use it as little as possible and use the rest of my body to make due. Everything I could creatively come up with I did to not stress this arm. What I noticed was, after several weeks, my arm didn't hurt anymore. He was still the same person as far as his responsibility and commitment before I hurt my arm, when I hurt my arm, and after my arm healed. There was no variation or deviation in him discernible whatsoever at any time. He never changed what he was up to.

I went through this roller coaster of emotion, cogitation, mental agitation, and at various different times I was calling my teacher names in my head. I would never call him a name to his face because I couldn't run that fast and I had a bum arm. That's not good. Nor would anyone else have abided any bad behavior. A couple of times I tried to engage the other teachers in conversation about it. Every single time, they asked, "Well, what did he say?" "Well, he said I had to keep coming to class and just work through it." They said, "Okay. You have to keep coming to class and just work through it." They would parrot whatever he said. Then, of course, I got mad at them because they weren't being sympathetic to me. A couple of other students, I have to say, were sympathetic.

J: You were looking for a mutiny.

Dr. J: Yes. One other student got so mad at Phaa Khruu not giving me the space to heal that he quit. He never came back so he never finished the training. He forgot why he was there. He forgot his aim. He had been there longer than I had. He was a senior student to me.

By emphasizing cultivating true personality versus the egos point of view, I learned that who I am in the school has nothing to do with how I feel. That is one of the lessons I learned during that time. Once I learned this lesson, in all future permeations, I have had that as part of my formulation for my aim as far as being a student. Being a student is not relevant to how I feel.

3. Diminish false personality by ceasing to crave the attention of other people.

Dr. J: Look what I can do! (like the character "Stewart" on the MAD TV, television sitcom). Crave is the operative word. It doesn't mean the attention of other people has no merit or value. In fact, we need nurture and support. We want people around us to be somewhat solicitous, affectionate, positive and attentive.

We have an aim but then we put a condition on it to gain the attention of other people.

4. Diminish false personality by not exaggerating real qualities you may possess in your essence.

Dr. J: That's the function of humility. Humility does not mean being a dish rag. I did a research project on the word humble and humility. Let me explain what I did so it will make sense. I was studying the bible. I kept reading things like, "the meek will inherit the earth," and other statements by Jesus and other references. I read about how powerful humble people were. In the bible it says, flat out, that the most humble person in the bible was Moses [Numbers 12:3]. I thought, "Wait a minute!" Moses was a prince of Egypt or equivalent to the firstborn son of Pharaoh as to how he was treated. That seems to be an elevated position for the model of humility. That's number one.

Number two: he was a man of power in the sense he was first counselor of the Pharaoh, which doesn't seem to be a humble position. In fact, at one point, he was the equivalent of the CFO of the Egyptian empire. He was in charge of the allocation of grains and resources, what farmers and farms got what grains and how much. He was basically in charge of who got food when. People had to come to him daily to get money, food and what they needed to run their farms under the authority of the Pharaoh. To not follow his directions was a felony punishable by death. This was a position he had until he was in his thirties moving into his forties.

Then he becomes a spiritual leader and goes through an evolutionary process. He gains great power, prestige and authority with his community of Jewish people to the point where he not only is a counselor to the Pharaoh but begins to dictate policy to the Pharaoh. He might have said something like, "I know yesterday you thought you were in charge and this is the way things are going to be. As of today, I now represent the new god and these people. I'm here to tell you that whatever you were doing up until yesterday is no longer the law. Starting today you will do things differently." This of course was rejected. He then goes through a period where he dictates to the Pharaoh with threats of violence, as in, "If you don't do exactly what I'm telling you, here are the ten bad things that are going to happen to you. In fact, the first one is going to happen tonight after midnight. If you don't change your mind by tomorrow morning, then we'll have a conversation about the next bad thing." He even gets in a fistfight with the court magicians of the Pharaoh, where they challenge him directly and he turns his staff into a giant king cobra, which then attacks the other priests and consumes their weapons in public.

Then he bails with his people, the Jews. The Egyptian army goes after them. There is the whole parting of the Red Sea thing. He commands the elements. Not only does he do that, but also after the Israelites get to safety on the other side, when the Egyptian army chases them, he uses those same elemental powers and completely destroys the army. He kills thousands of men. Wow, that seems pretty assertive.

Then he goes up on top of a mountain and talks to God, and He gives him the Ten Commandments. He then goes to his people, who don't really believe him. He tells them everything they believe and everything they are doing is wrong. They are now going to have to do things a different way. He basically says at the gathering of the Baal Festival, the celebration of the transition of Marduk, the celestial Taurus, that not only do they have to stop their ceremonies and celebration but also to destroy what they've used to practice their spiritual belief, or they will die. He threatens them and comes through with his threats. They argue with him, and he has whole families destroyed [Exodus 32:20 and 32:28]. It's a really interesting story if you read it. The ones who survived were like, "Whoa. I'm with Moses. Yeah, Ten Commandments, whatever. Just don't kill me." I thought, "My god. How is this a humble person?" This is the example Jesus used of the most humble person before God.

I used Strong's Concordance, a book that lists every single word in the King James Bible. It indexes every single word used in that version. You can go through Strong's' and take the word humble, for example, and see there is a Greek word, an Aramaic word, a Hebrew word and an Egyptian word that are all translated in the KJV as the English word humble. I then went through the original Greek, Hebrew and Aramaic translations of the bible with Strong's Concordance and cataloged every instance of the term in any of those languages in the entire bible. Then I went through and wrote down the definitions in context every time the word was used. Then I read the whole thing together and came up with my definition of humble. Many people use the word humble as defined by the bible but they don't actually know what it means. According to my research, the word humble, in the bible means, "to know who you are according to your essence." If I were saying it in a biblical way, I might say you would be humble if you know who you are as God sees you, not as you see you. If God is essence, and that objective, undifferentiated, cosmic consciousness manifested as your soul or spirit, then what is the vision of who you are if you could imagine from the point of view of this part of you that reincarnates, that lives from life to life? If you could see your self from that perspective, from the point of view of essence, you might find you would look a lot different. That's why Moses was considered the most humble person in the bible and this is in spite of his predilection for violence!. He apparently understood, with knowledge and being, who he was. He then acted accordingly. It's not saying what he did was good or bad. There's no particular reference to Moses being kind, gentle, loving or compassionate. In fact, there are many examples of him being quite overbearing and violent in a way. Taking it from a point of view of metaphor, he was willing to sacrifice anyone or anything to be himself.

The same insight can be gained from the Bhagivadgita, for example, in the passage referring to Arjuna's confusion over his duty or sacred obligation to Krishna. It states "Therefore, Arjuna, you should always think of Me, and at the same time you should continue your prescribed duty and fight. With your mind and activities always fixed on Me, and everything engaged in Me, you will attain to Me without any doubt." (Bg. 8.7)

If I think of myself from a work point of view and that my inner Moses/Arjuna is that essence, essential nature, and true self, then what I want to do is have a realistic appraisal of who I am. I don't want to have imaginary views of who I am. If any part of me has the capacity to communicate with the absolute, then it is this part.

Back to the statement, "diminish false personality". That's everything that's not the essence…"by exaggerating real qualities that you may not possess"…to neither exaggerate nor diminish the essence. The corollary to this, I might say, is neither to undermine nor diminish the real qualities you do possess in your real essence. We need both.

5. Diminish false personality by not giving energy to what is not useful to your aim.

Dr. J: There's another idea. We've talked about doing things that support aim. When you see something happening within your self that is not supportive of the aim you've set, even if you can't stop it, at least don't give energy to it and expand and elaborate on it. There are many ways in which we give energy to that which is not useful to us. When we give ourselves either tacit or explicit permission to be less than what we know of as our committed way of being in any situation, we are doing this.

6. Develop true personality by not being afraid to make mistakes.

Dr. J: Being afraid to make mistakes is no reason to not do something. True personality accepts there is a trial and error process to crafting an essential nature. We have to learn not just how to communicate with our essence but also how to trust and utterly rely on it. That is not an easy process. Since we don't know the extent of our essence or what it is trying to communicate to us, half the time we think we are talking to our essence we are really talking to aspects of our false personality. That means we are going to make mistakes. When I do anything based on false personality versus my true essence, I'm going to mess up. Every thought, action and deed will not be perfectly correct. Some of it will come from the ego. This is a process.

We have to challenge ourselves. If something doesn't work out then we can't beat ourselves up. Take the correction. Get the insight from it. Check in to see if there is a realization, because that can happen at any time, and then come back to reapplying ourselves.

7. Minimize false personality by diminishing the expression of associative I's, first I's, opposite I's, likes, dislikes and subjective opinions.

Dr. J: Associative I's are when you have a thought (generally negative) and then you have another thought late into it but slightly different and you're off of the original thought. First I's have to do with when someone says something to you. That first thought is negative and it happens in less than second. That's called a first I. It is not measured or conscious. It's reactive. Opposite I's have the Immediate and opposite point of view. Think of backward man. If you say, "I think it's light outside." Immediately I say, "Oh, I don't think it's that light." I just said the opposite of what you said. It is not a conscious consideration and is also reactive. Consciousness in action mostly requires deliberation, which creates a time gap. Sometimes we say things like, "Think before you speak." What it means is to create a space to come into the conversation consciously before the mouth starts operating. I am mostly talking about the negative and reactive I's.

Likes and dislikes and subjective opinions—all of these things can be restated as imbalances in the Doshas [Classical Indian Ayurveda, Ayurvedic term denoting both defilements of ego and balance of elements in the manifestation of human forms or body types]. I like this, I don't like that...nah nah nah nah nah. We never say which I. We say, "I don't agree with you. I think the opposite." But, I never think to myself, which I disagrees or thinks the opposite. When I abruptly react to liking or disliking something, I haven't considered which I likes or doesn't like it. Subjective opinions are opinions based on other people's opinions. Anytime we're expressing opinions, they are not our opinions because we haven't thought about it at all or done any research on it. We express it anyway solely based on someone else's words.

When you are learning something (this is a teacher/student thing), there's a point where the student has to bow to the opinion of the teacher, even when they don't understand or agree with it. That has to occur. If it doesn't happen, the teacher can't teach. It's tying the teacher's hands. It's like, "I'm only going to let you teach me something new on the condition I already know and understand and agree with everything you are going to teach me." If I put that on the table first, I won't get very far with that teacher. I might get as far as the door.

J: Yeah, if you're going to tell the teacher what they are going to teach you, what's the point of having a teacher?

Dr. J: However, there's a point in time. Don't ask me where it's at or when it occurs, because I can't tell you. However, there's a point in time, based on experience, when you begin to have opinions not subjectively based on the opinions of the teacher. That's very valuable. Initially, however, there is a period of time where that's not how it happens. We can't have agreement in opinion be a condition of the teaching.

We still want to have discernment because that's how we chose the teacher in the first place. Having done so, if we have an aim to study, then we have to voluntarily allow for our opinions to be displaced by other opinions, at least for a time. This is very hard. It was very hard for me as a student.

8. Develop true personality by increasing your understanding.

Dr. J: We know, for example, if true personality is like that blissful body. We talk about the innermost body in Ayurveda as the blissful body [Anandamayi Kosha]. One of the ways that body communicates and is also fed is by the body being fed by the knowledge body. Knowledge does feed essence. Understanding feeds essence. Understanding is the being part. First is the acquisition of information that's true. Second is the process of manifesting or being or practically expressing that understanding. It increases the level of being. Being then feeds essence. A good work aim is to increase understanding.

I will increase my understanding, then formulate how to do that. It may be to practice more diligently or at higher levels. It may be to really study the workbooks. You may study the flows and Vinyasa of Thai yoga [Vinyasa = therapeutic postures done in a particular sequence] so that you can do them easily backwards and forwards. Why? That knowledge will increase your understanding. Your understanding will increase your level of being which will feed your essence. All of that will diminish false personality and develop true personality.

9. Develop true personality by not criticizing what you don't really understand.

Dr. J: It's a work idea that it is not valid for students to criticize what they don't understand. In and of itself, it is not acceptable. The only way to understand it is if you had already done the work. There's this thing we do where we jump ahead and place a criteria before the practice. We will not practice until we understand it. If the understanding is something that can only come as a result of the practice then that's never going to be up front. It will always come later. It can therefore never be a basis for criticism.

From the point of view of the world and the way most people go about doing things, it's very different. It is not like academia. The way higher education is formulated in the Western world, it is not designed to develop essence, being or understanding. It's designed to impart knowledge and technology mostly toward practical functions, which produce income. That's why, for example, liberal and fine arts are rejected in higher education even though they're still there. Seventy or eighty percent of the budget of large universities do not go to the fine arts departments. It goes to business and industry, depending on the school. In early institutions at places like Harvard, Yale or Stamford in the 1800s and early 1900s, a small percent of their college curriculum was geared toward industrial application or things having to do with business, jobs, commerce, corporations, drugs, military and/or things that feed those industries. The balance of the curriculum was very high emphasis on humanities, romance languages, fine art and culture, philosophy and so on and so forth. Now they don't. That's reflective of our society.

In conscious schools, the emphasis is always more on understanding than it is necessarily on ways of making money from the understanding.

10. False personality generates unnecessary suffering.

Dr. J: One of the chief attributes easily recognized in false personality is the constant generation of negative thoughts. Literally nonstop and in endless variety, these negative thoughts define and control our attitudes and are able to generate emotional states. The events and emotional states are seemingly outside of our control, and support suffering and unease with life. When you see the endless stream of negative thoughts, emotions or both, know that the false personality is in front of you. Observe its workings close and be ready for the opportunity to apply a practice or discipline to curb this influence. With practice you might even be able to stop thought long enough to reset your machine towards a more favorable way of being.

11. True personality transforms real suffering.

Dr. J: We have this idea of voluntary suffering. To do all the things I'm talking about and have been talking about is hard. It's not easy. It causes friction and struggle. False personality will generate suffering in and of itself. True personality takes the intentional voluntary suffering and transforms it into food, which feeds the essence. There's a difference between those.

12. Develop true personality by not believing the many I's.

Dr. J: To not believe the many I's, we have to be practicing self-observation to see there are many I's and that they come and go constantly and continuously. Every single one has an opinion, attraction, repulsion, and if we believe the aggregates of them, we can be pushed or pulled in any of a hundred directions at any moment of the day or night. In order to not do this, the only possible way is to practice self-observation. We need to monitor that these opinions, feelings, thoughts, and attitudes are coming and going randomly and constantly. We need to see them for what they are, as transient and insubstantial. The I that can observe is far more substantial than all the transient I's it observes. There is something different about that one. If I have a way of observing myself where I can actually catalog, without being attached, all the different opinions, attractions, repulsions, attitudes, different states of mind, body and tissue, whatever is observing and watching all that is much less transient and more reflective of the kind of consciousness that comes from essence than everything I'm watching.

13. Reduce false personality by reducing competitive and comparative I's.

Dr. J: Competitive I's are, "I have a better way. I know better. I should be doing it this way versus that." Comparative I's are constantly contrasting what we think or have seen in our past with what's in front of us in the moment. This is something Thich Nhat Hanh has written about. There's a Buddhist concept, which has to do with being in the moment. He and Ram Daas say, "Be here now." When we are here now, we are not engaging in comparison thinking.

14. Develop true personality by not expressing negative emotions.

Dr. J: We've talked a lot about negative emotions and how that feeds false personality or how it may be false personality. When we make efforts to curb and or reduce the expression of these negative emotions, it is evidence that true personality is there. Any part of us able to work and to make tangible progress is more closely related to true personality or the authentic self. Not expressing negative emotions intentionally, in spite of every impetus to do so, actually adds to and develops the substance of true personality.

15. Diminish false personality by not expressing negative emotions.

Dr. J: Those two go together. Not expressing negative emotions does two things at the least. It both contributes to developing true personality and diminishes false personality at the same time.

16. Reduce false personality by realizing that you are not.

Dr. J: That is the moment work begins. It's a difficult thing to realize, that you're not because everything you know and have been led to believe your whole life has tried to bring merit to this idea that you have some substance, that you're permanent, unified, that there's just one, singular self unique and distinctive from everyone else. Yet, not only are you not particularly special or unique in the world, in a sense, but within your self there is nothing cohesive or unified. There's no single personality construct completely in charge all the time. Whatever "you" is, if "you' is referring to some idea of the manifestation of a true self, sometimes referred to in the work as essence, then you are not. The idea of realizing you haven't become yet is important because we're under the illusion there's nowhere to go, since we already appear to be here. There's no progress to be made in ourselves or personalities because that progress is, in a sense, being taught to us as inevitable rites of passage. Getting wiser simply with age and enlightenment is just an organic process of existence.

Every sacred teaching referring to anything remotely about this subject says that's absolutely not true. The only way you become that which you profess to be is conscious, deliberate, conscientious, disciplined, enlightened, through effort over a period of time. To realize you are not is actually the beginning of work on your self.

Work begins when you realize you're not. Only the work moving you toward becoming something you're not is what qualifies.

17. To come to conscience, cease pretending to be what you are not.

Dr. J: We define conscience as an "emotional realization or understanding of truth." To come to conscience, to come to a place where having an emotional realization of truth is a constant influence and environmental force in one's being, is to cease pretending what you are not. On some other level, we absolutely know we are hypocritical. We know we are not consistent. We know our understanding of life and our capacity to understand virtually anything going on with us at any time, depending on circumstance, is so entirely and completely limiting. On some level we all know we are somewhat helpless in front of it. If we were really, as rational adults or people, if we really considered how helpless we are to our own personality, psychology, biology, our errant mental functioning, our lack of control of external circumstances, we'd have to say that any control we might have is purely incidental. If we thought about that for more than a minute, we'd probably have to shoot ourselves because we'd be in the depths of
despair.

We don't want to shoot ourselves and we can't exist in the depths of despair for too long, because eventually we get hungry or have to go to the bathroom or someone comes and interrupts our depths of despair with their issues about their depths of despair. What we do is pretend we're more in control than we actually are. As we grow older we learn this art of pretense, first from our parents and teachers, then as we start to go out into the world, we learn more pretending skills, play acting, playing in life, from our friends and peers, our jobs, churches and we eventually are so successful at pretending we are in control of ourselves and our lives we begin to believe it.

To come to an emotional realization of truth, we have to cease or stop pretending to be what we're not.

This is a vulnerable moment. It's a moment of peak vulnerability because if I realize I'm not, but with the hopeful possibility there might be something that is, and if I stop pretending to be what I'm not and don't have any alternative to carry me over in the interim, I might feel just a little bit like a trapeze artist released by the thrower and are going into freefall. There's probably that first moment of release where they are in motion, committed to the leap, but they're not 100% guaranteed there will be someone on the other end to catch them. A leap of faith must take place. That's really risky.

Conscious schools have always said that one of the reasons why they have tended to be small, especially in their inner core, and also why they don't advertise as such, is because most people are simply not willing to make the leap of faith or for very long. Most of the time, what we'll do is stop the pretense for a moment. We have a realization and stop the pretense. We step out and realize there's no floor under us, and then as quickly as possible, almost seamlessly, as if we don't even notice the transition, we step right back into the role we were playing a minute before, which was a fabricated role in the first place from our false personality.

18. To diminish false personality, stop justifying and glorifying your self.

Dr. J: False personality doesn't have a real center of being in the stress-adaptive, human biological, transformational machine. It has a manufactured seat, provided for it by the substance of the ego. The ego is reflective of all kinds of negative features among them justifying and glorifying the false self.

One of the ways we avoid bringing attention to the parts of us that hypothetically are not entirely based on the ego, is by justifying and glorifying the personality and ego. When I glorify myself, what I am doing is feeding my false personality with the praise and opinions of others, when I'm avoiding bringing light and scrutiny to the false personality through the art of diffusion and diversion. To justify it as being appropriate in the circumstances I'm in. This is the kind of thing where something happens and we lose it. The losing it is spontaneous, immediate, complete, out of control, absolutely mechanical in every way, recitation of tapes and negativity that comes from the past and so on. Later I will go back and I will justify the bad thoughts and behaviors as somehow having been appropriate for the circumstance, that there was some spontaneous appropriateness of being and behavior, when in essence it was all completely negative. Since it was immediate, mechanical, without time lag and negative, I know it has to come from the machine, from false personality.

Part of the false personality's job is to clean up its mess and tidy up loose ends. It does this retroactively. That's the process of justification. In fact, if we're under current pressure, like a deer in the headlights, we start justifying instantly and immediately. It's a spontaneous and instant reaction, even if it's imagined scrutiny that someone might actually for a moment see as we really are. There's no judgment or criticism in this work about being the way you really are. However much we are completely dominated by ego and false personality—wherever we are—that's where we start. That's where we have to start. Whatever issues are present in that moment with the false personality, those are what we work on to reduce the power of false personality. From that point of view, it's necessary, but only in the context of self-work.

19. For false personality to be passive, work I's must be active.

Dr. J: This can occur only if a third force such as emotion is present. The corollary to this is, if work I's are not active, then whatever is active are I's that represent false personality! We do the substitution game. On the one hand, we are trying to reduce the power and presence of anything in the moment we can identify as the ego and false personality. At the same time, we are trying to feed and support work I's. Work I's are those personality constructs, which represent in real time the essence and true self and are trying to construct an inner being more conducive to being a home for the true self to manifest within. This can only occur if a third force such as emotion is present. To say it in a personal way, it's not enough to know I need to work on myself. It's not enough to believe I must work on myself to diminish ego and false personality. I have to have a certain kind of emotion about it. There needs to be a necessity.

Here's a way to think about it. You're in shallow water and you fall out of the boat and you're in the water and you know you can swim to the boat or the shore. Either way there's no possibility you're going to drown unless you do something really stupid like bang your head on the boat. You'll handle that situation without a whole lot of emotion. There won't be a lot of inner benefit from having resolved this "trauma" of what falling out of the boat might mean. If you fall off the cruise liner in the middle of the ocean, as the cruise liner is sailing away, your thoughts about swimming and staying above the water will have a lot more emotional content. Whatever efforts you make to try and extricate your self from the water will be much more intense, focused and comprehensive. There won't be one atom of your body not striving and straining with every possible bit of effort producing toward doing anything else in the whole world but getting back to that boat. There won't be any other alternative or possibility. There will be no daydreaming. There will be no distraction. There will be no, "Oh I kind of forgot where I was for a minute." There will be no, "I forgot to keep swimming." That's the third force, of emotion.

In the consciousness school way, we say we don't know what positive emotion is because we are almost entirely made up of false personality (representations of false emotion). If there is such a thing as positive emotion, it's the emotion generated toward the efforts absolutely necessary to save your self and move your self forward in a conscious way, to diminish the incredible power false personality has over you. Whatever that emotion is, it needs to be there.

We have exercises to intentionally create situations for us to generate emotion, which stimulates and feeds the parts of us that may have the capacity to help us learn how to control false personality.

20. Work on chief negative feature by trying to change precisely where it is most difficult.

Dr. J: False personality is where you are identified and where you become most negative. Sometimes we use another term for chief negative feature. Sometimes we just call it "The Chronic." Work on The Chronic by trying to change precisely where it is most difficult. This is really interesting. There's no path of least resistance when you're working on your self. There's no path of least resistance. It never gets easier. The only thing that happens is, as you have more tools, more discipline, and more energy to work on your self, the tasks set out in front of you in real time are more genuinely challenging, in the sense of reaching deeper into those unresolved parts of you that have yet to see the light of day.

The last person in the world who's actually going to be able to identify their most chief negative feature is that person. That's because it is deeply embedded in the areas of our existence that are emotionally the greatest difficulty for us and where we are most identified with them. Because that's the way it is, that's the part of the forest that is so frightening, scary and challenging for us. Even if we look in the forest and sort of scan the tree line, we won't see it because there's this trick inside of us that when we come to something in front of us that represents part of our chief negative feature, we simply skip over it or around it. We don't see it. It's as if it's not there.

The beautiful part of being in a school is other people in the school working in a similar fashion almost always can see our chief negative feature. It's only invisible to us. This is one of those "ostrich sticking its head in the sand" kinds of things. I think, because I can't see how big my ass is, that I don't have one. Something scary is coming this way, so if I just put my head in the sand, then I can't see it so it can't see me. Something scary is some manifestation of our false personality or the chief negative feature. It's what's most disgusting, disheartening, depressing, and what makes us the angriest. It's the one issue or groups of issues that absolutely, left to ourselves, under no circumstances would we ever want to touch it with someone else's ten foot pole. The reason it's called chief negative feature is because it's the royal thrown room of the manifestation of false personality. False personality has to create this imaginary, psychological, mental, and emotional existence. At the very core of it is this inner sanctum of negativity or falseness. It is armor plated with many bodyguards and many thick walls. We will do anything. We will hurt anybody or escape with ingenious evasion tactics to keep from bringing scrutiny to that place. Why? Because if that part of the temple or castle is conquered, if that room is broken into, there's a possibility the false personality might not be able to survive. The thing to understand about ego and false personality in respect to its own survival is it is not passive. In respect to its own survival, it is active, because we haven't developed enough work I's, or what we would call true essence. True essence in life is passive in respect to false personality. If you think about this for one second, it instantly tells you why the world is the way it is.

We can't change the world in that regard. The only way I'd have a chance to change the world is if I had already done so in myself. Doing that, making those changes within myself, is the hardest thing in the world. Maybe I'll never be completely successful, so I how am I going to be able to do that for the rest of the world when I'm not even able to do that for myself? We have to try. False personality is where you're identified.

Identification is any moment, event, situation, person, feeling, thought, or even any expression of the five senses, where, as you experience it, you lose your self completely. You become identified with it for however long it's influential. That becomes and is who you are. The reason we know it's identification and not something genuine is because it just goes away at some point as easily as it came. It happens like a snap of the fingers. "Oooh. I like that!" Boom. That's who I am. That's what I'm up to. That's what I'm doing. Then at some point, oh, I'm on to the next. I don't even see the transition. I do not see that I was over here on to this at one moment and now I'm over here on to this in this moment. They might be completely and totally contradictory. I don't even see the transition. Why? I was identified the whole time. I just changed from one focus of identification to the next.

Identification is an attribute of your chief negative feature. What do you identify with? What are you inclined to lose your self in? Chief negative feature is always going to be the kinds of things and thoughts people bring up in you in which you are the most negative. That's where chief feature exists.

This is why, when we have discussions and it comes up that somebody else is doing something wrong, even as we discuss it, we don't want to get too emotional about it. We don't want to get too angry or too anything. Why? We don't want to get too identified with it because then all of a sudden, whatever that was, some word or dastardly deed perpetrated against ourselves or what not, we get so identified in the moment we cease to exist. We are no longer observing ourselves. We are no longer working on ourselves. That doesn't mean to not pay attention to what people are doing and react appropriately and keep your self safe and do the best thing you can do. It means, if you're going to say one of your aims in life is to work on your self, you can't afford to get too identified with anything negative. It doesn't matter a word or even a war. If it takes you away from your focus on developing your true self and core essence in harmony with the greater powers that be, whatever that was, you have now become food for the moon. You have become an expendable soul, in the sense you've lost whatever might be uniquely individual about you. You've also lost connection with the part of you having the possibility to become something quite special.

21. To diminish false personality, allow your self to be controlled by a line of work.

Dr. J: There are three lines of work. The first is to work on your self. The second is to work for others. The third is to work for the school. This is to diminish false personality. False personality is only about me, myself and I. If it appears to be working with other people, it will only do so as an expediency to get something from them. It could be something tangible like goods, services or money. It could be aggrandizement. It could be to get power, control and authority. It could be all kinds of things.

If false personality is supporting the school, the same applies. The only reason false personality is in the school is to steal something from the school it can't get on its own or can't obtain by doing the work necessary to get the benefit from the schoolwork. False personality might appear to be working for the school, and at the very same time might be engaged in a dozen different kinds of activities that might terminate or interfere with the school and make it difficult for others in the school to work on themselves.

False personality can appear to be working on itself. It is really fond of talking about all the progress it has made by working on itself. Quite often, when someone is lost in false personality, they will give you their resume of spiritual accomplishments and how elevated they are. If they're talking about healing power, well they can heal anybody although they never have and there's always a reason why they haven't. If they are a good student, well they are such a good student they mastered the whole system by the end of the first class, even though they don't know what they don't know. False personality is not trustworthy in the sense of helping others because there's always an agenda, a hidden motive, and it's something about some self-serving quality.

If we want to diminish false personality, we need to be. We need to allow. Here's a hard word for many of us to swallow. It's the word submit. Submit to a line of work. In first line of work, submit to work on your self. That means you actually do it. If the exercise is to remember your self, reduce negative emotions, practice good housekeeping, and not lie, cheat or steal, to create no harm or violence, then actually do those things. You make efforts to do those things. A line of work is controlling that. Even in points where you know or feel like not doing that line of work, you do it anyway because you submitted to doing that line of work, and for no other reason.

Submitting to the second line of work means you have to start regurgitating what you know with integrity. You have to start taking greater responsibility for those who come behind you. It never ends. There's no place where you're not reaching out and trying to lift up, help and support others. Sometimes you need to discipline and correct those who come after you. It's not for your benefit but for theirs. Your benefit is indirect and intangible. It's only a result of authentic care for others. If there's no authentic care for others, there's no benefit from the second line of work.

Submitting to the third line of work, which is work for the school, is where you act as if there's the idea of acknowledgement and affirmation of the actual benefits one has gained from schoolwork and school teachers and the other students doing the same thing. It's also about being proactive in mindfulness, about taking active measures to guarantee the perpetuation of the school as a place where you can continue your work. That's keeping the first line alive and creating opportunities for others to do the same, because they all work together in a school. New people are work for people ahead of them. School suffers all students. All students are stress for school but school doesn't exist without them. Students drive the work, and eventually advanced students become the work. It's passed from one generation to the other.

There's this idea of submission to the work. That means submission to the ideas, philosophies, teachers and to the idea that in order to be a school you have to live differently. You have to live slightly different than what the world would have you to believe is the best way for a person to live. In fact, on some levels, in some ways, work in a school and for a school (as part of the three lines of work) is the antithesis, or exact polar opposite, of what the dominant culture at any given time will say is the best way for a person to be or to live. It's difficult because we are programmed to think otherwise.

22. Diminish false personality by acting from an inner source of certainty rather than imitation.

Dr. J: You must find your way. False personality imitates certainty and confidence and ability and competence. False personality mimics the qualities of attainment of higher levels of being. False personality mimics spiritual achievement, sincerity, honesty, integrity, and disclosure. It provides things, which are similar but are not the real thing. It's artificial food. It looks like food and smells like food. It has a similar tastes like food. In fact, sometimes it tastes better than food, but it's not actually food.

Overtime, instead of being nourished, we're injured, damaged, held back, inhibited, restrained, and confined. We are coached into being something we were never meant to be by this mimicry and Imitation, which is one of the skills of false personality.

By acting from an inner source of certainty, the only way it's possible is by proving what you learn in real time and space. It's only possible to act from an inner source of certainty when you start to become what you know. That's that transition space between acquiring information and then challenging that information in real time and real space. You then acquire an increase of being. Once you acquire a little bit of that increase of being, you're no longer pretending, Imitating, or mimicking the certainty of the conviction of your understandings. You simply have conviction and certainty because you know. That's totally different than pretending to do that.

The danger with pretending is that when you pretend to have being and essence greater than that which you actually have, you fall into this trap of sleep. You lose the incentive to try and do something about your situation because you've pretended you've already got it handled so well you think you don't need to do anything. That only lasts for a little while until it all comes crashing down like a house of cards.

23. To develop essence, consider everything. (Socrates)

Dr. J: Here are the translated words from Socrates: *"The unexamined life is not worth living."*

Earlier in my life I'd heard and read this statement before. When I was in college and I did my Philosophy 101 and we studied the great philosophers of Greece like Socrates and Plato, Aristophanes, Epictetus and so on. When we studied Socrates we read this quote, "The unexamined life is not worth living." [Plato's Apology: 38a] I realized years later it was simply gibberish at the time. I'd had no earthly idea what those words meant.

I didn't understand why in particular I would want to examine my life. I'm the one having it right? It's not like I have to take an extra step to see what's going on because I'm here. I don't get it. What's the point of self-examination? When I would examine my life, all I ever saw was crap and negative stuff. At first I didn't want to do the self-examination or consideration of my life because it was just depressing. Later, I didn't want to do it because I didn't want to be negative.

To develop essence you have to consider everything. If one minute I'm one personality construct and the next minute I'm another personality construct, and there's no continuity between the two, how am I going to consider everything if I can hardly consider anything for more than a minute? The only way I can consider everything is if I craft somehow supernaturally a part of me that doesn't change. That's that self-observant, self-remembering self we sometimes call Steward or Deputy Steward. The idea being there's this meta-mind, which has the capacity to always watch and consider.

I think this is the metaphor of Santa Claus. Santa Claus as a myth is quite valuable. I don't believe the Christmas Santa Claus story for a second because I know the history of it. It was a concept evolved from many different ideas and traditions, some secular and some religious mainly coming out of the early 19th century. The common image became popular in the United States and Canada in the 19th century due to the significant influence of Clement Clarke Moore's 1823 poem "*A Visit From St. Nicholas*" and of caricaturist and political cartoonist Thomas Nast.[3][4][5] [http://en.wikipedia.org/wiki/Santa_Claus] was later adopted by the Coca-Cola ad agency and department stores like Macy's in New York. The mythical figure and story then became dominant in our culture.

The original myths by the Dutch about Sinterklaas and St. Nicholas, where there was this idea (even previous to that) that there was a supernatural agency which knew if you were naughty or nice. In fact, it knew everything about you and at some given point in time, there would be a reckoning. Oh wait a minute, that kind of sounds like heaven and god doesn't it. The funny part about it is this idea of a supernatural agency keeping tabs and holding accounts on every positive and negative thought, action and deed predates Christianity by only about 4000 years. It was very clearly described in Sumerian literature about Tia-mat and Marduk. It's also illustrated in the Tibetan book of the dead. It's pre-Christianity written about 500 years before the life of Jesus. In my personal opinion, Jesus knew the Bardo-Thodol by heart because he quite often appears to speak in transliteration of it and it's imagery and understandings.

It refers to one of the Bardo realms where you've passed away and gone through several stages of the Bardo and you've come to the place where the benevolent deities and friendly guides have not been successful in getting your attention and getting you to pay attention and be responsible for your self. At some magic point they fade away and are out of the picture. You find your self in a wilderness and you're confronted with the king of the Herukas. Vajra Heruka, the most horrific of the Herukas, unlimited number of arms, legs and faces, all of them angry (and/or happy but not in a good way). He is seen to be carrying the female Dikini with her legs wrapped around his waist. As he walks, magically the bodies of dead beings appear under his feet and he crunches their bones as he walks forward. In every hand, he's holding some kind of an Implement of torture like a knife, a sickle, a flame, a sword or some other sharp pointy object that can cause distress. You try to get away, but of course he's fast as the wind of a tornado. But also with the sound breaking class and the tinkling, tumultuous, cacophonic sound of cymbals and bells, big and small, however the case may be, this magnificent, demonic creature of course catches you and knows why you tried to get away.

He draws you out and makes you stand in front of him. In one hand he pulls out a big pile of black stones and then a big pile of white stones. As fast as bullets, he starts throwing these stones on the ground. Every time he throws a white stone, it's for the record of a positive, loving and compassionate thought, action and deed. Every time he throws a black stone, it's something that wasn't a loving expression of thought, action and deed. When he gets done, if the black pile is bigger than the white pile, he grabs you and he starts to tear you apart. Since you were already dead before this began, there is no escape of death as he flays you alive and rips the skin, muscles and tendons off your body. Then one by one he plucks your organs apart from each other, takes all the little bones apart until he's separated every piece of every piece of every part from every part.

He then desiccates you and grinds, bites and chews all the little parts to dust. With a snap of his fingers, he reconstitutes you in front of him and does it again. He does it again and again and again until…you get the point. The point is to answer the question. He asks you a question, "Who are you?" There is only one correct answer. The Bardo-Thodol, which is meant to be a guide for us, so that when we find ourselves in tricky places trapped in front of wrathful deities, that we already know the answer to the riddle. That's what the sacred books are about. We say the derivative teachings of conscious influence, those that actually know, are trying to give us a clue.

The only acceptable answer is, "That which is before me is a reflection of my own perfect luminosity." Knowing the correct answer and taking responsibility, in other words, responsibility for every harmful thing and infinite possibility of thought, action and deed my own origination cycle of the creation and continuation of suffering for myself and others.

In order to get to that point, we have to consider everything. How are we going to get a clue of what's real when we don't know what's not real?

CHAPTER FOUR: How to Work with Negative Thoughts

As a human species, we are wrought with negative emotions, behaviors and physical states as evidenced in the war-torn world of relationships, ravaged lands and misguided communities we live in today. So what do we do? Because negative thinking is a natural part of the "Human Biological Stress Adaptive Transformational Machine's" way of being, we must make dedicated and conscious efforts to not be helpless in front of it. We need a plan. Otherwise, we constantly allow negative thoughts to run wild in our heads, like leaves in the dark, windblown this way and that.

The key word above is "allow" our negative thoughts to run wild. This is both a pro and a con. The bad news is we give space to the continuous liturgy of negative thoughts.

Because of their consistency and constancy we believe them to be inevitable and true. This is a misconception. The good news is because we "allow" them to remain and become the causative factors for depression, fear, anger, and anxiety, we can also "UN-allow" them or replace and substitute other kinds of thinking for them.

So what's the plan? Here are nine basic principles to follow on a regular basis to work with negative thinking:

1) Ask your self, "Self, do you want to be happy or sad?"

As conscious beings we want to understand that thoughts come from the mind. The mind is an organ just like any other organ. It generates thoughts mechanically and constantly just like the other organs (read Candace Pert's, PhD., "The Molecules of Emotions"). Most thinking is unconscious and mechanical and can be considered white noise. Thoughts come and go without effort or direction and are usually unrelated to circumstances of life or our actual being. For example, they might be a result of communication from the lining of the stomach stating whether it's full, empty or a bit too acidic.

When we "give in" to negative thoughts and mindsets, we make a choice to do so. When we notice we are thinking negatively and do not make efforts to control, overcome or detach from them, we choose to submit to them and to the attitudes that reflect their dominance. When we don't make efforts or make feeble and inconsistent attempts to control or direct them, we set ourselves up to be victims of them. The longer we hold onto, wallow in, and allow the thoughts to continue, the less control we have over their effects until no outside agency or person can help us. Outside help might prove a short intermission, but we always come back to the patterns and habits we practice most.

If we actually want to be happy, we must make efforts everyday to choose good thoughts and to develop good thought habits. Think good thoughts on purpose even when you don't feel like it. Think good thoughts especially when you don't feel like it.

The positive, elevating, emotional experience is on the other side of the generation of a more positive thought life. We cannot wait to work on our thoughts contingent on feeling positive or motivated to do so. That may come later. Observe your thoughts as they arise, literally from the beginning. When you see the negative thoughts remember to ask your self, "Do I want to be happy or sad? Do I want to be angry or depressed? Do I want to be fearful or anxious?" If the answer is no, then right then is the time to let go or to begin the conscious effort of substitution of the positive for the negative. Once you let them take over, there is a negative, self-reinforcing momentum of thought that can take place, where every similar negative thought you have ever had in your life reinforces and justifies it. You can be in charge of your thoughts. Ask your self again, "Do you want to be happy or sad?"

2) Don't cherish negative thoughts.

We love negative thinking patterns and the individual negative thoughts themselves. We nurture them and hold them dearly as we come to realize either consciously or unconsciously that they define us and give us our character and personality. They create space around us. To a great extent, they define the manifestation of our public persona and personality. They are such constant companions that we rely on them to act as buffers between our inner selves and the outer world so we don't have to busy ourselves with the whole "paying attention" part of life. Our inner negative thoughts are reflexive and give us reaction in real time to almost everything that happens. The problem is that the reactions and reflexes are skewed, twisted and negative!

We are the source of our own self-fulfilling negative Karma. Our negative thoughts contribute to all of the other negativities within us and generate together negative emotional states and negative behaviors, which in their own way support further negative consequences to the karma we generate for ourselves and for others.

We must see the loop we are tangled up in and start to see the negative thoughts for what they are, unreal and not supportive of living a life with intention and of well-being. We need to consider the power of not acknowledging negativity and allow the thoughts to move on and let go of them. They are not valuable.

3) Let go of attachment to thoughts.

See thoughts on the screen of your mind like clouds crossing the sky. They come and go and constantly shift and change. Sometimes they appear to be more real than others. Some are closer and some are further away, but they are always transient. Your true mind is not the clouds. It is the tableau in the background; the clear blue sky we sometimes see peeking between the clouds. This is one of the teachings of meditation in Vipassana, Samatha, and Tratak. Find the still quiet place where there is no thought, yet there is fullness of being. Learn and practice meditation. There are so many types and schools both traditional and modern. If they teach you the art of controlling the mind and finding the between, transition and empty places, that's a good thing. Those inner spaces by definition are not negative.

4) Spend time with positive people.

In the Yoga text, the Charaka Samhita, there is a reference that states in order to balance Kapha Dosha, you need to spend time in the company of agreeable men and women. The primary negative characterization or fault of imbalance in Kapha (Prakruti/ Humour or Body Type in Ayurveda) is called the defilement of "ignorance." Sometimes the very best way to break a descent into ignorant, negative and disagreeable states is to physically get up and move to a more positive place, in the company of more positive people. Simply trying to work through our issues mentally does not work because we are trying to use the part of us causing the problem to fix it! You cannot use a broken or faulty tool to fix the problem the broken, faulty tool caused. You have to introduce another element. Call it distraction therapy." Since most thoughts are impermanent, sometimes even what seem to be the most negative ones will go away if you can change your focus for a few minutes. Often having fun or simply placing your self in the middle of people enjoying life and sharing joy can do this. Joy is powerful medicine.

5) Spend less time with negative people.

Negative thinking is not only self-reflective and looping, but can also be reflective of a common state of mind of the people you're with. Others help to reinforce the negative mental loops. If you're in the company of people constantly expressing negative thoughts, words and deeds, peer pressure alone will persuade you to copy and mimic the group's (or person's) negativity. Run for the hills! Get out of there if you want a happy thought life. By this I literally mean change your physical location. For example, Jimmy Buffet sings, "changes in latitudes can generate changes in attitudes." When you find your self with someone constantly expressing negativity, ask your self, "Why am I here with this person?" Ask your self, "What can I do right now to change the track of conversation or the direction on to a more positive one?" There is no elevation based on climbing on top of the faults of others. We cannot make ourselves better by making others bad. You are not a helpless victim of other people's negative thoughts. Simply move away from them.

6) Don't waste time not working on your self.

What are you doing? My mother used to say, "An idle mind is the devil's workshop." She was right! Nature abhors a vacuum. If you don't work on your self everyday by doing something to elevate and bring realization to your life, then your ego (false personality or unconscious mechanical expression of unresolved negative emotion and thought patterns) will drive you. If you can define a person as a "Human Biological Stress-Adaptive Transformational Machine", then consider that mal-adaptation to internal and external stress is how we became the poster children of negativity and expression of negative emotions.

You might also consider that you can organize positive stress to become the origination of new and future ways of being within your self, which are entirely different than those you experience today. How much of your typical day do you spend collecting ammo for inner negativity? Ask your self, "What do I watch? What do I read? Who do I listen to everyday?" If you were to determine a percentage of your average daily negative input to positive from external sources what would that percentage be? 100% to 0%? 90/10? 80/20? Rightfully use your mind for a moment. If you are a stress-adaptive organism (organized system), then what stresses are you consciously adapting to? Is it any wonder you feel helpless in front of your negative thoughts?

7) Think positive thoughts on purpose.

"If you can't be with the one you love, love the one you're with." If you can't think a single positive thought, then think someone else's. Ingenious, right? This is one of the values of having a small library of uplifting, inspiring, positive books, sacred literature, poems, mantra and songs, art, and sculpture. If you're stuck in a negative thought loop, then reset the programming with some Mantra medicine. Memorize mantras, poems, and wise sayings. Create a repertoire of positive archetypal thoughts and sentiments to draw on when in need.

Being locked into a train of negative thinking is the "valley of death" and leads to despair. The "Lord's Prayer" and the Metta Sutra are both antidotes for negative thoughts. Repeat either or both as often as necessary. "What if I have to do this all the time to stay positive?" you might ask. So be it! Some sacred traditions say one of the tools or techniques of enlightenment is to pray without ceasing. As long as the fire of negativity smolders, then keep pouring on the water. When the negative thoughts move on and release you from their repetitive burdens, continue your self-work and efforts. How about working on negative emotions?

8) Don't think anything you would not say in front of people.

Whenever you see a train of repetitive thoughts about a specific person or group, ask your self, would you share those thoughts or actually say them face to face with that person? Then ask your self, would the consequence of saying those thoughts or words be positive or negative? If the answer is negative, then check those thoughts. If you hear your self actually expressing those negative thoughts in words, then check your behavior. At the least find the control to the mouth and close the lips until you're able to make progress with the thoughts. Simply expressing negative thoughts, or as we like to say, "venting," is creating karma. People tend to respond to our negative expressions, and that can cause damage. The Tibetans are famous for saying that karma results from all three: thought, action and deed. To restore equilibrium and reduce harmful causation, or like my old Vipassana teacher, venerable Aachan Chaa used to say, "thinking right is a precursor to being right."

9) Move into the heart space.

The mind organ quantifies, calculates, weighs and measures, recognizes patterns, compares and contrasts, critiques pros and cons and imagines. The heart is a different organ and has a different center of influence. The heart is concerned with connection, transformation, movement and emotional realizations. It is the seat of our conscience, our emotional realizations of truth and the feelings of connection that stem from them. When the heart sees from essence, it realizes the true nature of things, situations and of others in a less critical way. The heart knows we all struggle, we are all finding our way, and we all want and need love. When we look at others and the situations of life from the perspective of the heart, we bond with them and experience more of a sense of oneness and common experience with less or no judgment and criticism. The mind of the heart is empathetic and compassionate. When we see our own lives and those of others through empathy, negativity barriers and boundaries dissolve.

More on Negative Emotions and False Personality

Dr. J: There is a statement in the Work. It says, "You remember that there is no real center for negative emotions. False personality acts like a center for them."

This hit me as a significant statement. What is false personality, where does it come from, and what is it's role? Why does it even exist? There is no real center for negative emotions.

Some questions came up. Do all negative emotions spring from false personality? How could it be otherwise? False personality, from this point of view, might be a special organ, in a sense, for negative emotions, for displaying them, enjoying them, producing and reproducing them. The concept in tapping is "the cause of all negative emotions is a disruption in the body's energy system." When I say something like, "the body's energy system," I am including everything I think of including the terms, "tangible, physical body", "matrix body", and "stress-adaptive human biological transformational machine". You might want to ask, "What is the energy?" or "What is the quality of energy that all of the disruptions are the manifestation of?"

Everything is energy. There is nothing that's not. For this discussion, separate from the tangible, physical body, the energy body is represented as the frequencies, which we describe as the five Koshas or sheaths or five Vedic bodies in the matrix body. How do I correlate the five Vedic bodies with the M.E.I.S. body, (the mental, emotional, instinctive, and sexual bodies)? Maybe it's better to use, instead of bodies, the words "characteristics" or "attributes of frequencies" or "vibrations". They each have their own frequency. I'm not the first person to describe the different bodies as subtle variations in frequency. When we talk about frequency, we're talking about energy.

Gary Craig states this so well in his principles of EFT™ or Emotional Freedom Teachnique™ when he says: "The cause of all negative emotions is a disruption in the body's energy system."

If all negative emotions originate in false personality, then we have to consider that disruptions in the body's energy system equal false personality. They are the same thing. False personality has different terms. Artist and teacher EJ Gold calls it "The Chronic". He doesn't say false personality. We also sometimes speak of false personality as the "unreal", that which is unreal in us. We can speak of false personality as the parts of us that are not conscious, not realized or what is not operating in harmony with the essence or true being or the foundation of being (which we call the essence, the soul, the atman, etc).

I had some other questions. Why do conscious beings need, teach, and give medicine? Why would such a fully, self-realized, conscious and self-aware being need or have an attraction to teach and give medicine? What is the definition of medicine? Is medicine just for suffering? What is suffering?

Is false personality, or The Chronic, the source of suffering? Is the dissonance between the resonance of vibration or frequency that is the manifestation of the self, soul, or pure essence…and the dissonance, disharmony or whatever is not that being manifested as the cause of suffering? In other words, is that what the cause of suffering is?

STUDENT: I had a sidebar question. Is this idea of Satan or evil, in essence, an attempt to describe or personify The Chronic? What is sin? What is sinful? What is sin within us? What is the part of us that is fully self-aware, but also fully antagonistic to the process of creating harmony between all of the inner and all of the outer parts? What is that? Where does it come from? How does it manifest?

Dr. J: In many different systems, whether it is Sufi, Ayurveda, Fourth Way, esoteric Christianity, etc. there is an idea of false personality, which is expressed in various ways. It is the unconscious parts of us. It is the mean parts, the critical parts, and the parts that do not love. One way of saying it would be, "If love equals the frequency of god, then anything that's not love is not god. Anything that's not god is not real. Anything that's not love is not real." False personality is the antithesis of oneness. It is the antithesis of love. By its very definition of existence, it's antagonistic to oneness. It thrives on discord. It thrives on disharmony. It acts as a center for attracting all of the parts of us that are out of sorts or out of place and disruptive, disharmonious, and separate from resonating with the essence, core, or true self.

What is the role of negative emotion? Negative emotions are symptoms of disruptions in the body's energy system. We're made to store disruptions in our energy system. We are also given tools to resolve these disruptions. Trauma, for example, is stored in the tissue. It creates an interruption, short circuit or Imbalance in the free flow of life force, which we sometimes call Prana or chi or Qi or Kundalini (whatever we want to call it). These are all words trying to describe different qualities of the nature of our life force manifesting in our bodies, our lives, our beings and the different parts of us (mind, body, spirit, emotions, instinct, movements, sexual functions).

If negative emotions are the symptoms and aggregates of disruptions…what I mean by "aggregates" is…let's say you have a point in time where there's no disruption to energy. You'd have to be quite young for this to happen. This is the essence of the pure child who does not yet have the development of personality. There is a push and pull on that child. Initially, the push and pull is externally motivated. It is force coming from outside the system. Then there are little traumas stored in the tissue. These little traumas, according to affinity principle and resonate harmonics, attract similar storage of similar information and we begin to have this information, the trauma, stored as disruptive energy patterns, which, in and of themselves, become a kind of energy vortex that attracts, preserves, and stores any similar influence all the rest of our lives. That's one of the functions of our tissue. One of the functions of the physical body, including organic tissue, organs, circulatory system, soft tissue, etc., is to be a freakishly complex and accurate tape recorder. Every moment and every infinitesimally small part of every moment, it is on some level, recording everything that this probe, our Stress Adaptive Transformational Human Biological Machine, is exposed to from the first moment of life to the last moment of life. As long as we are in the tissue, that tape recorder is recording all the good and all the bad.

The mechanism for storing the good and harmonizing influences is the same mechanism for storing the harmful, disruptive influences. Overtime, the way this is played out is determined by the importance of the tissue in our lives. In other words, our organic lives are very important. What's stored in the organic tissue has great influence.

Maybe overtime it has disproportionate influence, especially regarding negative emotions, which are disruptions in the body's energy fields. Eventually negative emotions have the capacity to completely take over the machine.

Overtime, false personality comes into being for everyone. It has to because it is the outward manifestation of the accumulation of energy disturbances, which generate negative emotions.

When I use the term "negative emotions", all negative emotions are not negative. That's confusing. It's really confusing because it is equally a symptom of negative emotion to have a "good feeling" or to be attracted to anything that takes you away from being in harmony and resonance with your true self. That's the confusing part because we tend to think the negative emotions are just fears, phobias, depressions, anxieties, neuroses, psychoses, schizophrenias, etc. Negative emotions are actually the expression of anything that is not concurrent with the expression of the fundamental true or original essence or nature, which we think we might have, but is apparently very hard to find, in most circumstances.

It seems like part of the strategy of why there are all these systems of religion and great philosophies of the world is that apparently it takes a lot of work and effort on a group and individual level in order for people to come to grips with this idea of what it takes, in real time, to manifest who you really are in your essence, not your personality. The point of view of the essence would have to be quite different from every other part of us. When I say "I", that changes from moment to moment, hour to hour, day to day. It changes so fluidly and freely that the shift from one "I" expression to another is almost always invisible. Sometimes it's not invisible when it's more of a radical shift. For example, in one minute, "I" am very emotional, but the next minute "I'm" not. The "I" that had the very emotional minute or day is still Anthony and the "I" who's having the less emotional day is also Anthony. In the moment, when I'm caught up in the emotion, I cannot see myself being any other way than I am at that moment. Whatever I'm feeling and expressing in that moment is who I am. That's what I am. I don't see any problem with that or any incongruity with that.

The thought that has to come up is, "I am not that today. I am completely different." I can do that from moment to moment, day to day, week to week, month to month, and year to year without seeing any incongruity with it. All of the variations of who I am are under the umbrella of what is Anthony. Anthony's still here but "I" is fluid.

The idea is that there is no such thing as a unified "I". You have to really think why that is. It's because whatever is "I" exists against the template or in the field of influence of false personality. False personality is the outward expression of the aggregates or accumulated influence and interactions of all of the disruptions in our energy system. When we think about different tools to live a certain way, think a certain way, act a certain way for example, the eight fold path. What is that? What is self-remembering? What is self-observation? What is the value of that? What is the value of not expressing negative emotions? What is the value of bringing consciousness to issues and then applying tools to those issues to resolve them? What is the end result of that process? What is the objective of all of this work in the first place?

When we're working on negative emotions, that is one direct and concrete way we identify what is false in us and what is false personality. It is a concrete way to get a handle of false personality by bringing a tool to bear. We have many tools.

Let's use the tapping, for example. We do an end-around and work on correctly the short circuit or energy disturbance to dissipate the symptom. The symptom is also part of us and that's why there's a lot of resistance to applying tools. Why don't I tap when I'm having a negative emotion like confusion, fear, anger, neurosis or anxiety? Where does the inhibition to resolve issues come from? Where's the friction and resistance to doing something that will resolve that which is impeding my intention and higher expression of self originate? What part of me would prefer I remain anxious? What part of me wants me to remain confused or angry or compulsive or neurotic? What part of me is served by and would fight to preserve being irrational and out of control? What part of me profits from that? It is the false personality. The false personality, in Ayurveda and Tantra, is called "the ego". In Christianity, it's called "Satan", "Satan's minions", "the Deceiver", "the whore of Babylon"…what is "Babylon" if Satan is the whore of Babylon? It's the great aggregate of all of these little components, which are creating these outward expressions of tension and negative emotion. It also includes what we think of as positive.

It's one thing to be distracted from working on your self because you're being persistent and resistant and contrary and lazy and anxious and fearful. Those are not so hard to identify. Sometimes it even comes as apathy. For example, why don't I work on myself in this moment? Well, because I don't feel like it. What part of me would not want to feel like it? What part of me would think that by justifying not working on myself simply because I don't feel like it is a good reason to not do the work? That's false personality.

Where we really get lost is in the positive. This comes out in Classical Indian Ayurveda in the Dosha teachings about attraction and repulsion as being manifestations of the ego equally. The things that really attract us, on some level, are just as much evidence of the ego as the things that really repel us. We feel like we can justify the repellents because we can say it's bad, disgusting, unattractive, evil, etc. It doesn't resonate with me. We have all these ways to justify the repellent side and feel a sense of satisfaction that by being adverse we're being more conscious, when in reality it's almost equally all the things we are really attracted to. In the moment, when we are attracted, we become completely separated from observing ourselves and bring consciousness to bear to manifest our true personality. It doesn't matter how good a thing is, if it takes you away from your self. It is no different in that regard than the "bad" things.

It is possible to be an entirely good person in every way and only attracted to good things, yet still not be a self-realized, conscious being. The end result does not appear to show progress in self-work.

It seems, from a point of view of working on yourselves, that certain kinds of attractions and repulsions are more acceptable than others, in that there's a happy medium somewhere, that by having some attraction or repulsion, we can find the middle ground, which is stable enough to allow us to work on ourselves.

As soon as we go too strongly into attraction or repulsion, we move out of the middle ground and we find ourselves back in a place where we aren't working on ourselves.

I've got these ideas in my mind. One is the cause of all negative emotions is a disruption in the body's energy fields. I could say that all negative emotions originate in false personality. That is stated over and over by virtually every teacher.

J asked, what is "the work"? Well, "the work", as simply as I can say it, is bringing consciousness to the questions, "Is there anything real? If everything is not real, is there anything that is real? Is there anything in me that's real? Is everything in my not real? Is there anything in me that is evidence of something more substantial than all of the insubstantial parts of myself?"

Self-realization…one of the critical components of realizing the self is learning to define and discover what a self is. There are a lot of wrong assumptions about what a self is. There has to be because the part of us that drives our minds and emotions is false personality. It's in charge of the machine. This is in the biblical metaphor where Satan is cast down to earth. Satan is given by the Lord (in conscious schools, the Lord is the manifestation of the true self) dominion over the world. Humanity exists, not in the Lord's world, but in Satan's world. Our current manifestation of self doesn't exist on some higher plane right now. It exists in the lower plane of the tangible, physical reality of the human biological transformational machine and its world. That world is ruled by false personality. That's why everything is "Maya" or illusion. That's why the great teachers and saints say there's nothing real. Everything is unreal because almost everything is an expression of false personality one way or the other. Yet, there is a suspicion there may be something real.

The work is whatever it takes to overcome the dominion, the enslavement, the oppression, and the bondage of the true self by false personality. At the same time, the work includes an investigative process to see something real and then use technologies of all different kinds like Tantra. In conscious evolutionary psychology, tapping and yoga, which are used for self-discovery, the treasure we are looking for is infinitesimally small and infinitesimally valuable all at the same time. We use the tools to feed the parts of us that are in harmony with the pursuit of self-realization. Why should we practice coming to understand what we are?

Let's use self-realization as an example. Sometimes, in talking with many students, I see that they think self-realization is something a guru gives you or something you get from a book or some teacher. You can get parts of it, hints, and evidence of it, but actually, self-realization means to know your self. It doesn't just mean to know part of you. There's a conscious school teaching that says, "To know the part is to know nothing. To know anything is to know everything." In self-realization, it's the idea of the realized conscious knowledge of all of your parts and functions. It is a mastery of the entire machine. That's why it takes time and effort using specialized tools to become self-realized.

To realize and know all of our parts, we have to have a lot of information. We live in this stress-adaptive, human, biological, transformational machine. Our consciousness lives in this machine here and now. The machine has parts. The parts have different functions. They have functions that are individual and other functions that are corporate. They have functions that are synergistic and sympathetic to each other. In one way or another, they all work together to operate this machine and keep it alive in this world while performing all of its mechanical functions.

Most people know very little about the machine. Most people don't even know, though they suspect, they have different parts, what they are and what their jobs are, even mechanically. What does the liver do? What does the gallbladder do? What does the stomach do? What does the brain do? What do the eyes do? What does the skin do? What is the job of the skin? Most people don't know. They are separate from the realization, awareness, and knowledge even of their most mechanical parts. They do not have this awareness, even the simple knowledge that the machine requires not just food, but different kinds of food in predictable and reliable manners. The machine is subject to the environment. The machine is subject to what the Chinese call external pernicious influences, which could include poisons, toxins, wastes, pollutions, radiations. The machine and its functions are subject to that. The function of the parts, some more than others, are subject to that. You have to have specific kind of food for the machine to operate at its maximum capacity. You have to have efficient waste disposal. There has to be sufficient and appropriate intake of necessary foods.

There has to be support for the elimination and byproducts from the metabolism of those foods. Most people don't know that. Take that as one thing about self-realization. The lack of that knowledge alone will separate you from your life. You can accidentally kill your self if you don't know that. You kill your self slowly, a slow suicide, by ingesting poisons or by not removing certain wastes and byproducts. Simply by not drinking enough water, you can hurt your self. Most people don't know they need to drink water every day. They are not self-realized in their physical bodies. They accidentally kill themselves sometimes with even the simplest behaviors because these behaviors are counter to the necessity of survival.

One of the things we understand as criteria for a conscious school is that it has a very sophisticated understanding of the maintenance and support of the physical body. Okay, so that's number one. It could be yoga, esoteric Christianity, Sufism, Buddhism, or Native American traditions. On some level, they all have that understanding. They have to.

We run into other things about negative emotions. Science tells us that the outward expression of emotions is a chemical phenomenon. I had this question, "Well, wait a minute. If the cause of all negative emotion is disruptions in the body's energy system, what is the role of the chemical expression of emotions?" According to scientists, like Candace Pert, pheromones, the neuro-physiological chemicals cause everything we can identify as an emotion. There is nothing that you can name in any degree or variation, positive or negative, that cannot be quantified as interplay of chemicals in the body.

If the cause of all negative emotions is a disruption in the body's energy field, there are intermediate steps. The energy is disrupted. It is stored in the physical tissues. So the disrupted energy, which is stored, is what creates the environment to generate the proportions of pheromones and chemicals, which then become outwardly expressed emotions.

If all negative emotions originate in false personality, then false personality is not just the negative emotions. It is any emotion, positive or negative, generated by the energetic disturbances, which cause distortion in the physical tissue, which generate chemical imbalances, which are then manifested as either positive or negative emotions.

We have an energy body. Our energy body can be disturbed and that disruption can be stored. We call that memory. We have many kinds of memory including physical, instinctive, emotional and intellectual. Instinctive memory starts with encoding in the DNA, which is the genetic memory from the species. It is a biologic Imperative. It is the differentiation and organization of our cellular being. It includes the matrix of instructions and commands, which are stored in the DNA of the machine. One example is the viruses stored in the DNA, in the filing system, so that when we're exposed to one of these viruses, in excess, the DNA triggers a response and sends the file on this ancient virus. We've been dealing with this virus for 100,000 years so we've already learned how to deal with it. Here's the formula, the recipe, for how to deal with it. It sends off the encoding to the Immune system and programs the T-killer cells to produce the exact protein and amino acid and pH to control that virus. That's in the instinctive memory.

Instinctive memory doesn't just come from the past. At the cellular level, we're still recording. Every generation has to have that function in order for there to be a thing like genetic or racial memory generative of a species. Not only am I playing back tapes from my DNA in the instinctive part of me from the ancient past, I'm also recording in my DNA in real time what's happening now.

We have an energy body. We talk about the matrix body. The matrix body can be disturbed with the disruption stored. We can take energy of any kind and disturb it or change it. Let's take a laser, for example. Photons don't appear to like each other very much. What they tend to do when they are generated is to run off in every direction as fast as possible. They disperse from their center of origin. The only reason we can see light is because there are so many of those photons all trying to get away from the sun all at the same time. It is a density of the photons that gives us the appearance of light. A laser uses an artificial method including a diode, a prism, and a gas-filled chamber to organize and force some of the protons to go all in the same direction at the same time. If we organize even a few of those photons to do that, we get a laser beam, which is extremely dense and powerful. A strong enough laser could hypothetically burn through anything. There's actually nothing more powerful than light. When we can organize light to do something, we've organized a force of nature.

We have a matrix body and an energy body. That free flow of energy in the matrix body has a natural inclination of how its energy wants to manifest. It can be disturbed, distorted or blocked. Just like I can close the shades and block the light or a proportion of it. I could make this room stone dark with heavy drapes. I can disturb and interfere with the free flowing process of the light photons coming from outside.

That happens inside of us all the time. Originally, it doesn't happen consciously. It's a process of storage. What happens as the energy is disrupted is there are critical points when it is disrupted enough that it begins to take on a life of its own. It becomes sentient at that level. In other words, I have an energy disruption, which originally might have been caused by trauma. Then I have 10,000 other traumas that cause similar disruptions, which are stored in similar layers and patterns in my physical body. There comes a point with enough disruption where the physical body becomes distorted. The distortion pattern can be visible from the outside. It can increase to a point where I can no longer walk, stand or where I lose function of a body part. That distortion in the physical, tangible body starts to change the way these pheromones, molecules of emotion, are transmitted and received. It begins to cause distortions in emotion. The distortions in emotions are random. Some of them will be positive for a time. Some will be negative. Overall, they tend to be more negative. Why?

Ok, let's say I have an energy distortion pattern that causes me to hold stress and tension in my shoulders. One of the symptoms of that is that my shoulders are hard. The term for this is hypotrophy. When there's excess muscular activity in a body part overtime, the body part responds with overdevelopment. That overdevelopment is called hypotrophy. An extreme example is the Dowager's hump, where you have an elderly person with this huge muscular looking mass in their shoulders and back. It grows until it starts to push them over. Eventually you will see an elderly person with so much hypotrophy they are bent over at 90 degrees. If you ever put your hand on that person you think they would be soft like a couch potato, because "granny doesn't work out that often." But actually, it's not like that.

J: I know my granny feels like a bodybuilder.

Dr. J: It feels hard as a rock. Her back feels like a tabletop. It feels as hard and tight as the biceps-femoris muscle of any bodybuilder or professional you've ever seen or given a squeeze. That muscle is every bit as hard.

Now here's the thing. When I'm young, I have this hypotrophy, a symptom of sympatheticatonia, stress, and spasm, which is uncontrollable. When I'm young, I can look at myself and think it makes me look buff. Someone can come and give me a squeeze and tell me I feel strong or muscular. In reality, if you laid hands on me and felt this, you're instant thought would have to be, that's evidence of chronic spasm, which is evidence of stress, which is evidence of disruption in the energy system in their body. It is also partnered with certain kinds of emotion that is mostly negative.

There is also a positive aspect to it. Certain kinds of tension may enhance our survivability. In other words, being a little bit paranoid, uncomfortable with strangers and other specific types of tension, anxiety or neuroses (paranoia is a kind of neurosis), might actually be self-serving to the machine. It might be productive, but only up to a point. Past that point, those very same functions that were positive overthere become entirely and completely limiting over here.

96

The cause of them, what's generating them, is the same. The judgment that this is positive and this is negative comes from personality. It's all interpreted.

Energy can be stored. It can be disturbed and this disruption can be stored. We can that memory. We have memory in the DNA. We have memory in the physical tissue. We have an emotional memory and we have an intellectual memory. The disruptions themselves (in each of these areas) create an expression of us or false personality, just like the matrix does within the context of the whole. These are all tied together. The matrix is our energy body. It is the software and circuitry that drives the physical body. It's not separate from the physical body. It is a mistake to think that. They are utterly and completely interdependent. That's why I can make changes to your energy body by pressing on points, putting an acupuncture needle in you, or giving you an electric shock.

This understanding I'm talking about is in esoteric Taoism, which is a fundamental and underlying principle of Traditional Chinese Medicine (TCM). It's in all the teachings about the organs, the six hollow organs and the six solid organs. One way or another, in TCM, all emotions come from one or more organs. The physical organs themselves and their energetic counterparts, I call them the shadow organs. You have a tangible physical organ and then you also have an energetic organ. They overlay each other. The organs generate emotions. The simplest example is the description of anger coming from the liver. You ask, well does anger make the liver Imbalanced or does the liver make you angry? Well, actually it doesn't matter from the point of view of self-realization. It's enough to know the emotion relates to the energy field, the matrix body, and some part of us in the tangible physical body. It's a chicken or the egg story. Does the organ create the emotion or does the emotion disturb the organ?

Initially, there may be little or no disruption, as in a child. There is little separation between essence and being. That's why all the teachings talk about becoming child-like. People misunderstand. It's not the idea of becoming simple or naïve. It's about trying to find ways, tools, methods, disciplines, practices, habits, thoughts, actions, deeds, etc., which support essence, the fundamental true nature of our being over the infinite expression of false personality. The young child has less false personality. They are truer to their core nature. They have so much clarity in that regard that it's not even a conversation a child would have in their head, which is to wonder if the way they are being in their head in a given moment is in harmony with their essence.

As personality grows, it mimics the adaptations of the matrix body into life. That's what growing personality means. It includes your tangible, physical, stress-adaptive, human biological, transformational machine adapting to life. If the disruptions to the body's energy are not released, distortion occurs. As soon as there are distortion patterns, they start to store in the tissue and false personality starts to manifest. In other words, the unreal part of us starts to take over the operation of the machine. This separates essence (spirit, soul, true self) from the matrix and supports the continual growth of false personality.

The energy disruption areas (locales or specific points) become self-organizing and self-aware in the sense of seeking to preserve their state of being or integrity, even to the point of defending, fighting and resisting being integrated into the whole. Once that process gets rolling, the aggregate of that acquires a sense of self-awareness. As the aggregate becomes self-aware, it then seeks to grow, to elaborate on permutations and variations of its expression. It seeks to preserve its life. Any threat to its integrity of being in control of the system is seen as a challenge and it answers the challenge with a fight, sometimes to the death. The false personality will do anything to survive, even pretending to adopt conscious practices in order to avoid scrutiny beyond a certain point as a self preservation technique.

We see this in churches. There is peer pressure to behave a certain way; what the group has defined as the way a spiritual person acts. So you have attitudes, inclinations and ways of being contrary to the group ethic of how a spiritual person (someone working on themselves) is supposed to act, but you live in that environment. As a method of self-preservation, any smart person will very quickly learn how to mimic the behavior of the peer group to avoid scrutiny about whether or not you are actually practicing the spiritual path.

The flip side of that coin is the idea of the thought police or the spiritual police or their equivalent. In this case, it might be a pastor, preacher or minister. It could be a healer. Their job is to observe and root out any aberrant behavior, no matter how subtle, that indicates that the external practice is an affectation. Because we have that push and pull, the external pressure causing us to adapt in the first place and testing us to qualify the adaptation. In that environment there is something unique and pure trying to reassert itself. That looks like a fistfight in real life. It looks like a total, running, knives out, and Spartan swords in both hands fight. The problem is that the essence in the untrained, undisciplined person has no more chance of thriving in that environment than one of those gladiators thrown into the arena with no weapons or training. The chances of the essence's survival in order to eventually take back control of the machine are very small.

When I look at shows like Spartacus, I think about stuff like this in the back of my head. I think, "Ok, what if I take this as a metaphor for Spartacus. He has the essence of truth in an environment where everything is contrary to the survival of the essence of truth. How does that kernel of self and truth take over the machine? What would that look like in real life terms?" In the end, whether conscious or not, it looks like everybody dies.

Everything/one that's unreal dies. In other words, false personality thinks it's in charge. It thinks it's in charge of everything including bad and good. The problem is, in and of itself, it is only a symptom of the disruption of the energy manifesting into life. Every minute it's in charge, it is stealing, containing and distorting the life, expression and manifestation of the self. It's very survival is entirely based on the assumption that under no circumstances will the true self be allowed to emerge.

The stored energy disruption distorting the tissue, distorting the energy, creating the impetus for the manifestation of negative emotions, is the formative process of the false personality. At some point, very early on, I think it's still in childhood, false personality is developed enough to begin to operate the machine according to the Imperatives of its survival. It becomes self-organizing. It seeks to be aware the integrity of itself. Itself, however, is entirely based on interference patterns and distortions.

That's the challenge with anything spiritual. I hate to use the word "spiritual" because it is a fundamental premise of everything religion. Yet, at the same time, there are no deities involved here. If there were, what would they be? Satan would be false personality. God is essence. All the multiplications of gods and deities, saints and sages, and so on are all actors in the play meant to give us insight into the ground of being in which we find ourselves, this world our machines are tromping around in while doing its job. The job of the machine is to be a crucible, a forge, a furnace, a stressful environment in order to strengthen, educate and provide, like a bird makes a nest for the egg, a protective environment until the spirit can break the egg.

Initially, like a chicken or lizard lays an egg, the egg is, at a point in the chicken's life cycle, a glory of the manifestation of life. It is in essence part of the womb because it continues to be the function of the womb even after the egg is expelled from the chicken's body. The egg is a protective environment that separates the outside from the inside because the outside is very dangerous. The embryo would not survive for a moment without the protective casing of the shell. The embryo develops in this restricted environment, the egg, which is in a dangerous environment called the world. At some point, the embryo develops into a chicken. The chicken has a special part of its beak, which actually goes away. It only has this for a short time. It has a special, sharp pointed part of its beak, which is specifically designed to break the egg. It actually has a tool it develops embryonically, which at a certain stage in its development will allow it to break free of the shell. It's part of the chicken's programming. Just like a baby, as the chicken develops inside the egg, initially the egg seems like a spacious environment. As it grows, the shell starts to put pressure on the bird until it can no longer take the pressure. It then starts to peck on the shell. In just a few moments, it completely destroys the environment that was absolutely necessary for its life right up to that moment.

Lizards also have a sharp horn on their beak they use to break open their eggs. Lizard eggs are pliable so they can change shape. If the lizard just pushes against it, it doesn't break. It has to have the right body part to hit the egg at the right place to tear it open.

There has to be this process of deterioration where these creatures have to entirely destroy their contained environment of the shell and separate from it to continue living. They do this in order to become what they were meant to be. There can be no more attachment.

Our shell, our egg-like environment is this tangible, physical body ruled by false personality. That's our egg. All systems of religion, all systems of consciousness are about coming to realize who we are. Almost everything we think we are as a person and have thought our whole entire lives is wrong. It's not coming from us. This idea of the immortal self, the shen, the spirit, the core—if there is such a thing then everything that's not that is a distortion and unreal from its point of view.

Every functional philosophy has to have, at some point, a complete challenge to everything we believe is valid about us as people. We have to break the shell and release it from us. The trigger for that break-through (that's why I say stress-adaptive, human, biological, transformational machine) is stress. Stress is what causes the shell to build; that's the false personality. On some level of life, we need to have certain characteristics in order to survive. That's the purpose of false personality.

I was trying to think about this. I asked, what is the purpose? Why did great nature and biology and spirit make us with this messed up part of us, which is the expression of false personality and ego and all the negative parts of us? There has to be a function. There has to be something that is absolutely necessarily for our development in it we could not develop without it. That's what it is. The stress from the outside creates that first encapsulation, but the development of these disruptive energy patterns and their distortions in physical tissue, their chemical analogs, their emotional, mental analogs and symptoms, those altogether become the egg and the shell. The fetus in development is the shen, atman, essence, or true ground of being encapsulated in this flesh body.

The function of conscious schools is to teach people we are a self-encapsulated construct almost entirely designed to manifest negative emotion, energy disruption, chemical Imbalance, postural distortion and all of the mental, emotional and instinctive counterparts to all of those things. At some point all of that was meant to help us survive long enough to get to a place where we feel enough stress to push back. The push back looks like questions. Why am I here? Who am I? Is there a god? What is my true nature? What is my purpose in life? What is love? Why is my life the way it is? Why has my life been the way it is? What is the role of other people in my life, those I care about and those I don't? What is the role of society and what is my part? What's the role of nature? How do I relate to nature? How am I like and unlike nature? Is nature my friend or enemy? Am I supposed to control nature or work with it? What nature am I working with? What does it mean to have integrity? What is truth? What does it mean to lie? Is it possible not to lie? Can I have integrity?

All these questions are manifestations of the pressure essence is putting on the shell. We don't know what the shell is. We can't see it. It has to seem pretty strange. From the point of view of a chicken, lizard or reptile, the internal environment of the egg is all there is in the whole world. There is nothing else. I'm sure it grows incrementally with a feeling of dissatisfaction being in this world. Influences come from outside the egg, right? The egg is permeable to light. The egg is permeable to sound. Certainly reptile eggs, and to some degree I suspect chicken eggs, are permeable to water. In other words, reptile eggs have to stay moist, otherwise they dry out, die and break prematurely. The snake or lizard won't survive. They are dependent to some degree on the environment outside the egg bringing something to the egg like air, light and water. The embryonic chicken or reptile has to be aware of external sounds so, in a sense, as their developing inside their eggs they are still getting information from outside the egg, giving them pressure.

There's pressure on the inside creating a sense of discomfort, stress, dissatisfaction and sympatheticatonia. At the same time, there is information coming from outside, which suggests there might be something outside of the only universe they know. There's a critical time, in a human being…the cracking of the egg part doesn't happen quickly like it does with a chicken. Chickens don't live very long, so maybe in proportion to their lives, life in the egg and breaking out does represent a substantial part of their lives. For human beings, it takes us a long time to break out of the egg.

Here's another thing. If the chicken starts to break out of the egg but for whatever reason is not strong enough to completely destroy the egg and get away from it, the chicken will die. If a lizard gets to its stage to break out of the egg but is not strong enough to complete the process, it will die. In both cases, the animal dies. With a chicken, the feathers only harden after release from the egg. They have to be exposed to air. Lizard skin has to be exposed to air. That's why all reptiles, even though they might be sea creatures like sea snakes, have to spend part of their growth cycle in the air. That's why sea turtles live their whole lives in the ocean except for two times. One is when they are laying eggs and one is when they are hatching. In those two cases, there is no other option but to be exposed to air on dry land. No other variations are acceptable.

As humans we have similar criteria, in that we have to feel the confinement, pressure, dissatisfaction, discomfort and see the symptoms of it. Examples are physical, mental, emotional disease, sexual dysfunction, instinctive dysfunction, energy Imbalance, etc. Those are symptoms of the shell creating pressure. We have to find our beak and use all the tools we have to break free of the limitations of the shell, which is our internal and external world completely ruled, dominated and defined by false personality and ego.

Consider the term "Self-realization", the realization of the true knowledge of the self. I think I first heard that term from Swami Paramhamsa Yogananda in his book, "*Autobiography of a Yogi*", so I'll give him credit at least for introducing me to the term. I'm sure it's not the first time it was used because he was in the "Great Oom's" Clarkstown Country Club and Yoga school. They were talking about this when Paramhamsa Yogananda was a teenager. I'm sure they didn't make up the term because they were given access to teaching about this by master Hamid and so on.

I first read the term "Self Realization" in Paramhamsa Yoganandas' book.

What is that? True knowledge of the self, including all of its parts—this is important. It's not enough to say you're trying to be self-realized or you're seeking self-realization, as if it's just a spiritual process, something that has to do with your spirit, separate and distinctive from all of your parts. For, the environment in which the true self is contained, the egg, is complex. Remember, we are stress-adaptive human biological transformational machines. The reason I say it that way is I want to stress that the purpose of all of this is to create an environment which is suitable for transformation. That is the point of the body and our life here. It is in and of itself part of the shell. It is meant to be a pressure environment wherein the goal is not to break us. The goal of the pressure environment is to make us, not break us. It's not a perfect process, in the sense of it's a one shot deal.

It's like we're on a merry-go-round and the way to get off the ride is to grab that brass ring. The merry-go-round has three rings. If you wake up on the merry-go-round and you're on the inside of the carousel, after a couple of revolutions you realize there's no way you can get the ring and get off this ride from where you're at. So you move to the next outer ring. You say, "Okay, it's a much better place to be able to get to the ring." You realize there are more than two rings. So you do a couple of revolutions in the middle ring. You're like, "You know what? It's better than the one I was on before. There's still no way I can get and see what's going on outside the carousel better, but I can't get to the ring from here." You do everything you can…bump, bang, whatever. The other problem with this carousel is that all the other seats are full. So to get from the inner ring to the middle ring you have to bump somebody off their horse, or somebody's got to get off the outside ring to make space for the next one to move out. Eventually, you move to the outer ring. Then at the outer ring, you're yelling, "Woohoo! Now I can actually reach the ring and get off the carousel." The problem is that it's in motion. Maybe your balance is not so good. Maybe you don't trust your reach. In other words, in order to reach that ring, it's not just that you have to reach out and grab it, you have to lean way over there. You have to time it so you can lean in as far off that horse as you can to be able to reach the ring.

So, guess what? It takes you a few turns on the wheel, even when you're in the outer ring, to be able to get that ring. Lo and behold! You grab the ring off the carousel, the carousel stops and you get off the ride and find your self in the world—a greater world, a different world. Maybe you're on a different restatement of the carousel. It's not a perfect process in the sense that it's just a one-shot deal. The self-realization must include all of the parts, the physical, emotional, instinctive, sexual parts, the matrix body, the spirit if you believe there is one. The combo code for enlightenment may very well be the conscious knowledge and awareness simultaneously of all of the parts and at the same time the awareness of what is not the parts. That's pretty complex as an issue.

Awareness of the existence need, or necessity of self-realization, comes from outside the system, as the system is literally run by false personality. False personality is the environment we exist in and it creates the stressors that are the incentive to develop, but our clues for a life not entirely ruled by false personality must come from outside of the system.
This is where, in Fourth Way concepts, we talk about conscious influence, C influence. It's an influence, a conscious influence that comes from outside the system, the light and sound in my egg metaphor. The more the fetus develops, the more pressure there is, the more uncomfortable and unsatisfying life in the egg becomes, yet at the same time, it's not just about having the urge to break free. There also has been a constant Impetus and input into the system that tells some part of that creature there's something outside the egg. If that didn't happen, no matter how constraining the egg got, there wouldn't be any reason to expect that creature to break its egg. It would have to think, if the chicken or lizard was rational, that to destroy what has contributed to its life up to this point would look like death.

There would have to be some fear.

STUDENT: Not to mention the interesting thing about the metaphor of the chicken and the egg is that it's alone inside the egg. It's different from our experience in that way. I mean, it might have some sort of idea there's other interaction going on because the sound does enter in and there's movement and shadow and things like that. It's essentially alone inside this encapsulation.

Dr. J: Right. The awareness of the existence or need or necessity of self-realization comes from outside the system. Outside the system…what is that? You want to say "outside the system" is some level of consciousness which is extra-solar. In fact, what if the planet is a conscious being? Who are we to say the planet is not? Gaia. What if the sun is a fully self-realized, conscious being aware of us? We're limited in our ability to communicate. We're contained in this shell of false personality and so all we get is the mumbly jumbly, murmured thumping sound or feeling of pressure or a sense of light. From the point of view of looking out from inside the shell, it's not real. It's very hard to define. What C influence is, that objective consciousness, is actually our self trying to talk to our self—back to the theory of recurrence and reincarnation, of having a consciousness, integrity of consciousness that supersedes life to life. If that consciousness is aware of this role play that's going on and this developmental process, which is recurrence or reincarnation, if that consciousness was trying to communicate to us, what would that communication look like or feel like?

It would have to seem supernatural. It would have to seem as if it's literally like god speaking to us. It would have to seem as if it was the deepest sense of emotional realization of truth we could have. It would have to be a communication that was a re-occurring message in life. From the point of view of an immortal self trying to communicate with a mortal self, currently in incarnation, one message would have to span the whole life. If I'm talking to one of my incarnations, it's like flipping cards (in a deck). The flip of the card is one full incarnation or the life of that card. My intention in moving through the deck would seem to last for the entire length of the card's life in motion. This thread of consciousness and communication telling us to move toward the light. The sleeper must awaken. Work on your self. It's important that you pay attention to what's happening in your life. It makes a difference what you think, feel and do. Those may be well the expression of this external influence, which could be god or not god, just you.

False personality is generated or is a consequence of the storage of disruptions in the matrix. It is a symptom of disruptions of the energy fields of the matrix. Disruptions taking place in any or all of them (M.E.I.S. body, matrix body, etc.) playing together, some of which is us, our personality.

False personality is concretized as according to the affinity principle. The aggregates of the disruptive fields grow strong enough to generate harmonics and these harmonics are powerful enough to change the state of the whole machine.

Everything about us is not real, but something real remains. Is there hope or grace? What's the point? That's it right there. It is really important to know. No matter what, even though everything is unreal, there's something that's not unreal. There's something that remains tangible and real and will remain real and tangible after your physical body dies. It's not even limited to your life and body. There is something that will persist and it is here now. It's not something released in the future after we die. This is where people have it wrong. I'm sorry, the idea that when you die you go to heaven—somehow you are released into your true nature and reality of oneness with god only after you die—it's missing the boat, because heaven and hell are here now. Hell is the separation from the knowledge of our true self. That's classic Ayurveda, by the way. That's what Ayurveda, the science of life, is all about. It's to return you to oneness with knowledge of god and with being. That's in the Charaka Samhita. The teaching is that it does not happen in the future. It's not contingent on dying. It can happen now.

The evidence of the real is the inclination and desire to be more real and know the truth. These thoughts, inclinations and desires are essence resonations. They come from the source and try to acquire control or wrench control of the machine from false personality. That's the breaking the egg idea. The inclinations to go against the grain of everything we've thought we're supposed to feel and believe is evidence the true self actually exists. The goal of the true self is to acquire control of the machine and use the machine with purpose. The purpose is liberation from all bonds and constraints, restrictions and inhibitions imposed by any part of the false personality. First purpose is liberation. Second purpose is to have control over the machine with consciousness. This is, by the way, the true meaning of Reishi, Baba, and Sadhu. It's a person who has acquired, through diligent practice, labor, knowledge, education and the discipline of applied practice overtime, the ability to control their machine.

If you get stuck there, you are still not done. That might seem saint-like, just to be able to gain control of the machine. That's Boddhisatva saint-like with people falling at your feet, even inside your own head. That's not enough. The next step is then to use the machine for the purpose it was designed for from the beginning, which was to be a vehicle for transformation under the direction of the true self. Now something's happening and can happen. Now, a person is no longer subject to the machine. They are not the machine. Now the machine becomes an expression of who they are. Instead of being an impediment, it becomes a sword, a vehicle, a springboard to transfiguration and transformation.

This is all hypothetical until we get control of the machine. We can't get control of a machine we don't know how to operate. It's no different than jumping into a car, never having been in one, and not getting it that you have to put the key in the ignition or that you have to turn the key once you do, or that is has a steering wheel lock. So far, I got the key in and turned the key in the ignition but it still won't go because I didn't realize I have to crank the steering wheel back and forth in order to turn the key. It's a Toyota and they have a break lock on the ignition. I have to turn the key, turn the steering wheel and push the brake while putting pressure on the key to make the Subaru start, not a Toyota. If you don't do all these things simultaneously, an older Subaru will not start.

J: My Chevy love was the same way.

Dr. J: If you jumped into a car and thought, "Well how hard can it be?" You put the key in, turned it on to hit go and you're not up to date on gears, and it's not automatic and only cranks in neutral? You got six gears. You have many gears to be wrong and only one to be right.

So, trying to control the machine. We have tools to do this. We have psychological tools. We have emotional tools. We have moving and instinctive tools. We have sexual tools.

In the system I teach and practice in my own personal life, I've tried to select what I felt were the very best tools, for each of these areas. That's why I choose to do the things I do and emphasize what I emphasize. If tomorrow I was given a new set of tools, I would immediately start applying them, like several years ago when I was given the insight on the importance of tapping as a concrete way to bring energy, attention, consciousness, breath and pressure to negative emotions.

It happened to me when I was in Thailand when I started that whole process of trying to do what I'm doing right now, to flesh out a simple energy tapping system so I could make use of it. I knew from the first moment I was given it, that it was important. It needed to be incorporated into what I was doing. I had always had problems with some aspects of supposedly conscious teachings. Even the schools I was educated in, which were very good schools with great lineage, authenticity, discipline and history, were missing the physical work. They didn't have physical work or really fine understanding of the machine. Nobody did. I knew more about that than anybody I was working with. I would put it aside because I thought the psychology is what's important because that's where the emphasis was. It was psychology and so called "higher emotional expression", which you cultivate by studying and meditating on fine art. The instinctive, sexual and emotional was missing. I realized overtime, when I studied other conscious schools, for example, that they had less emphasis on psychology and more emphasis on moving center. One such school incorporated themselves as a school of dance. The Harmonious Development of Man at the Chateau Le Prieure at Fontainebleau-Avon was a dance academy, Mr. Gurdjieff's school of dance. Other schools of conscious development also study dance. They have this idea of movement.

According to the Gurdjieff International Review inscribed in a special script above the walls of the Study house at the Prieure were 38 Aphorisms.

38 Gurdjieff Aphorisms:

1. Like what "it" does not like.
2. The highest that a man can attain is to be able to do.
3. The worse the conditions of life the more productive the work, always provided you remember the work.
4. Remember your self always and everywhere.
5. Remember you come here having already understood the necessity of struggling with your self—only with your self. Therefore thank everyone who gives you the opportunity.
6. Here we can only direct and create conditions, but not help.
7. Know that this house can be useful only to those who have recognized their nothingness and who believe in the possibility of changing.
8. If you already know it is bad and do it, you commit a sin difficult to redress.
9. The chief means of happiness in this life is the ability to consider externally always, internally never.
10. Do not love art with your feelings.
11. A true sign of a good man is if he loves his father and mother.
12. Judge others by your self and you will rarely be mistaken.
13. Only help him who is not an idler.
14. Respect every religion.
15. I love him who loves work.
16. We can only strive to be able to be Christians.
17. Don't judge a man by the tales of others.
18. Consider what people think of you—not what they say.
19. Take the understanding of the East and the knowledge of the West, and then seek.
20. Only he who can take care of what belongs to others may have his own.
21. Only conscious suffering has any sense.
22. It is better to be temporarily an egoist than never to be just.
23. Practice love first on animals, they are more sensitive.
24. By teaching others you will learn your self.
25. Remember that here work is not for work's sake but is only a means.
26. Only he can be just who is able to put himself in the position of others.
27. If you have not by nature a critical mind your staying here is useless.
28. He who has freed himself of the disease of "tomorrow" has a chance to attain what he came here for.
29. Blessed is he who has a soul, blessed is he who has none, but woe and grief to him who has it in embryo.
30. Rest comes not from the quantity but from the quality of sleep.
31. Sleep little without regret.
32. The energy spent on active inner work is then and there transformed into a fresh supply, but that spent on passive work is lost forever.
33. One of the best means for arousing the wish to work on your self is to realize that you may die at any moment. But first you must learn how to keep it in mind.
34. Conscious love evokes the same in response. Emotional love   evokes the opposite. Physical love depends on type and polarity.
35. Conscious faith is freedom. Emotional faith is slavery. Mechanical faith is foolishness.
36. Hope, when bold, is strength. Hope, with doubt, is cowardice. Hope, with fear, is weakness.
37. Man is given a definite number of experiences— economizing them, he prolongs his life.
38. Here there are neither Russians nor English, Jews nor Christians, but only those who pursue one aim— to be able to be.

I realized I also had in my possession great moving tools, in addition to my understandings of the Fourth Way's great psychological tools. The moving centered or focused tools I had mastery of are the Thai based "*Ryksaa Thang Nuat Phaen Boran Thai*" (Ancient Thai Classical Ayurveda) and martial arts such as Kabri Kabrong, Muay Thai, Kali, Escrima, Aiki JiuJitsu and the like in which I had achieved all Black Belt or equivalent recognition and expertise after much training and travel. I also had great emotional understanding of the role of emotions, but not necessarily as functional applications in dealing with them as we have, for example, with the tapping, because we can really address that mind-body interface whether it's the energy source of the disturbance or whether it's the energy source causing the physical distortion, which causes the pheromones to be out of balance to cause the emotions. It doesn't matter, does it? We can affect the structure, which affects the energy. We can affect the energy directly, using the emotion as the doorway to get to the energy. That's quite sophisticated.

So we have all these tools. We have our health and wellness science including nutrition, physical health, detoxification, pathology and social consciousness. Part of the reason to continue being socially active is so we can have a safe environment to live and work. If our society "goes to hell in a hand basket" then we're going to be too busy trying to keep our hair on our head and not get harmed to be having these kinds of discussions.

It's hard to have these kinds of discussions when somebody is chasing you with something sharp. That's the whole idea of the society. If our society breaks down, it's not going to make it easier for us to practice. It's going to make it harder for us to practice.

J: The only discussion we will be having is to not panic.

Dr. J: Yeah, not panic. We have exercises for all of these things: sexual, instinctive, moving, emotional, psychological, which we call yoga. We have yoga exercises both on the mat and as self. Examples are Pranayama, meditation, asana, and Tantra. We have education. Education has an Impact on all of these things, like when we talked about the 5 bodies and how important education was. We have to have that as part of the self-realization. We learn we have parts, we have names to these parts, what the parts do.

Tools like tapping and then actually applying them methodically and in a disciplined way.

The other day I noticed I started having an infection in my eye so I immediately started taking colloidal silver and spritzing myself in the eye with it. I made a Fennel Seed infusion (tea) and when cooled and strained added it to my regimen. It healed completely and went away. I had a problem. I recognized the problem. Why? I acknowledged the information. I knew what the problem was as well as the solution. Without hesitation, I applied the solution to resolve the problem because I have better things to be worried about than an infection in my eye. I don't want that to be what my life is about right now. It could have become a bad infection if I had rubbed my eye without washing my hands and not doing the health practices I know would help it. It could have escalated at that point and maybe even become infectious.

Bring awareness to negative aspects. Don't lie to your self.

Work on non-expression of negative emotions. Create opportunities to bring up negative emotions and then apply work ideas to resolve them.

This is the most difficult part. Why do we have to live and work together? The pressure for enlightenment comes from outside the system. The pressure to force me to confront my unresolved issues comes from you. Tag, you're it. You're in that place, even though you might be doing it accidentally, because maybe you're just not paying attention or thinking or being in some negative emotional state. When you are close to me, it brings up my stuff, if I'm paying attention and practicing self-observation.

Then my discipline, which I develop overtime, is to as quickly as possible apply the tools I have to resolve that to the best of my ability. My ability is changing. In the past, ten or twenty years ago, I knew a lot of this but my ability to apply the tools conscientiously was not too good. Sometimes I could do it and sometimes I couldn't. I would go through the process and see my baggage, whoop, there it is! I better get to it! The fire extinguisher is in the case. All I have to do is run over, break the glass, grab the extinguisher, run over to the fire, pull the trigger it'll put the fire out and life will be good. But I would look at the glass case with the extinguisher and I would say, "Hmm…I think I'm going to go to a movie." I wouldn't break the glass and put out the fire. I would pretty much just walk away. I knew the process but would have a hundred reasons why I would not apply the tools. I did try and then I would fail. I got better at it. Overtime, my discipline has grown so that the response time between the problem and applying the tools is shorter and shorter. There is no longer the huge gap there used to be. I practice that as a discipline. Roll with the punch, get up, and get right back in and get right back to whatever the issue is. Bring awareness to it.

That's why we have to live together. That's why you have to have a school to become enlightened and be fully self-realized. There is no possible way to do it otherwise. The reason is because you lie to your self. As long as we have the capacity to lie to ourselves, we cannot be self-generated, self-realized conscious beings. That is the perfect impediment. The problem is, I might be able to lie to myself but I can't get away with lying to you all the time and vice versa. I can pretend I'm not being negative. I can do all that in my head. I can't always get away with that living with you. I go into justification and what happens? Somebody gets called on it. Dag nabbit! I guess I have to address that, think about it, take responsibility and do something about it. What did I mean by what I said and did? What was I thinking? Where was I coming from? All of that is pressure for self-realization to bring up issues.

The whole role of intimacy, relationship, sex, sexual tension and that whole continuum of expression is it is a jackhammer for bringing up issues.

Dr. J: The psychological tools are feather dusters. The emotional tools like tapping are pretty good. They are like wooden mallets or soft hammers. As soon as we get into sexual tools and ideas, talking about intimacy, relationships, jealousy, disclosure and truthfulness we use the jackhammer. The sex part bridges the gap between the instinctive, moving, emotional and psychological centers. It is the one part that has strong access to all the other parts. You know it because they all come up instantly. All you have to do is go there and you suddenly get to the heart…bang bang bang.

In the instinctive, we deal with that. It is our fundamental repulsion and attraction. It is the sex center that stimulates us to have any interaction with another person at all, originally. That's where the original instinct from our DNA comes from, to make us want to move closer or further away from anyone. It is faster than emotion or mental awareness. We have to have tools for all of these things.

Our sexual tools have to do with our conversations on various relationship models such as monogamy vs. polyandry, relationship dynamics, intimacy, disclosure, truthfulness, and how to be with each other in a good way. It also has to do with ideas about Tantra and being able to bring energy and the same awareness of realization to that part of our self as all the other parts on the continuum of expression. We need to have as much sophistication in that area as all of the others because we have to have realization about all of our parts. We can't say any one part is separate than the rest. We can't be for example…I see descriptions of Tantra classes, but there is no discussion on psychology. Well, that's not going to work because at some point, that's going to be an absolute limitation. I see teachers who specialize on the emotional parts. It's all about the love. Love, love, love, love, love, love…I'll just give you my love…you don't even need to then you'll have it and we'll be done with it. Well, there's a limitation to that because everything I know says the expression of love occurs between and in human beings. Human beings are tangled up with sexual, energetic, physical, moving dysfunctions, which result in illness, distortions in tissues, chemical Imbalances, negative emotions, false personality and mental defects (wrong thinking). How is that a vessel for unconditional love? It's messed up. That's no more suitable of a vessel for unconditional love than my strainer is a vessel to transport water to the garden.

Work in layers. Think about the mental, emotional, instinctive, sexual and matrix. The thing is, on some level we have to work on all these at the same time. That's the point of self-realization as an exercise. We want to work on all these things individually in order to have sophistication with them. We need to have sophistication in the moving center. We want to have sophistication in healing because that helps the instinctive center and the moving center and it provides a safe place and less distracted place for people to work on their emotions and their minds and their sex. We have the tapping, the psychology, the Fourth Way, the Tantra practice, the nutritional practice, and all of these things that occasionally we bring a lot of focus and a lot of energy to because we want to really master each part individually. The purpose is not to be a "*Jack Of All Trades*". The purpose is not to have five separate masteries. The purpose is to have five masteries that when applied simultaneously create a very specific kind of working pressure to break that egg. That's the purpose. Until we're working synergistically, and by that I mean taking periods of time where we try to bring everything to bear at the same time and place, then we are not doing the work. See, false personality is involved because it is involved in everything. This strategy to crack the egg of absolute dominance is the sword. Each of these tools is part of building the sword. Some of the tools are sharpening the sword. Some tools are learning how to move the sword. Nothing happens until you apply the sword. Application means taking everything you have and bringing it to bear in one spot, one place, in one moment and doing it repeatedly. See, it's not enough to even do it one time. There is such a thing as creating pressure for break-through realization. That can happen at almost any time when you are working on your self. Take the concrete result of those intuitions, skills and tools and become an expert in their application. Then take all of them to craft ways to apply them, consciously and on purpose, in the moment.

I think that is the purpose of ritual. If nothing else, ritual is this idea of saying, "We will be this way at 5 o'clock today for one hour. We are going to try and bring everything we know, every skill and ability we have, to the best of our abilities and knowledge, to bear simultaneously in one place in time to be able to crack that egg." The downside, it's repetitive. In order to make that work and build that up, I believe we create a kind of food. We create an energy that author, teacher, researcher P.D. Ouspensky described in his book The Fourth Way as a higher hydrogen. When you make certain long term disciplined efforts applying all of the tools, that in and of itself generates a kind of energy, which is required for elevation of consciousness.

It's not something that happens really quickly. First of all, you have to have the masteries of the tools you are going to use for each and every part. You have to know what the parts are, what they do and what the appropriate tools to bring awareness to that part are, and then work with it. This all takes time. I have to learn my psychology. I have to learn my yoga. I have to learn how to master my movements. I have to learn my tapping. I have to learn my Tantra. I have to bamboozle a group of willing souls to want to work with me all at the same time. This all takes time. All of the timing has to overlap for everyone so we all do it together to make it happen.

J: No wonder we have to do so many lifetimes.

Dr. J: False personality equals tension in the system or the inclination to collapse. It's real in favor of the not real. Now back to Wilhelm Reich. I love Reich because he talks so much about the role of tension and what tension is in organic life. Every cell has this expansion and contraction phase. Everything made up of cells has an expansion and contraction phase. Everything that's alive has a balance between contraction and expansion. As soon as the contraction phase overreaches or becomes more dominant than the expansion phase, as of that moment, disease exists. As of that moment it is on a spiraling decline, which will lead to its termination or premature death. The way you can tell the healthy cell from the unhealthy cell is that the expansion is proportional in rhythm and harmony with the contraction. In the unhealthy cell, there is always more contraction until it dies and hardens. It turns in on itself and becomes solid. We call that death. When the cell stops expanding, it dies and becomes hard and dense.

The inclination toward contraction under stress is sympatheticatonia. That was his term. A sympathetic nervous system lends itself toward tension. Atonia is a dysfunctional state of being in sympathy with tension evidenced with a reduction or loss of function. The theory that Willhelm Reich worked with Orgone and his vegetal therapy (his manipulative therapy he developed) was all about releasing and expanding and supporting the opposite of contraction in all of the parts including the sexual, emotional, mental and physical parts. He said that all pathologies of the mind and emotions are reflections of biological inclinations toward contraction, which was a result of stress.

So I'm thinking, well that goes back to what's the origin of the false personality. If the inclination in storage of energy disruption in the body, the actual distortion caused in the tissue is a contraction. When I say the energy disruption causes a distortion in the tissue, the actual distortion it causes is a contraction. Cells contract. They resist motion and stop moving. That Impedes the flow of circulation around them in every way, for example in the Immune system, the nervous system, circulatory system, lymphatic system and actual tissue and structure to the point of bending the bones and causing distortions in posture and sometimes Impinging energy to vital organs causing organ damage.

The psychology is then a reflection of all of that. I believe that Reich was the first person to coin the term, "unwinding". A lot of people think that's a new term that started with cranial sacral therapy. He wrote about unwinding in 1928. That's 60 years before cranial sacral therapy was developed. It was about how to create an environment that brings more energy into the system to dissipate the short-circuitry and stimulate growth, expansion and the release of trapped energy in every part of us. What is the aftermath of that? Well, it looks like a balanced mind with balanced emotions and a physically healthy body. There is a healthy sex life (not just about intercourse), meaning one with one's own sex and sexuality. It can also play into gender…like the other day when we were talking about it. Gender inequity is a sexual dysfunction. If we are balanced sexually, there should not be any gender disparity or dysfunction because all of us are on a continuum of gender. There is no such thing as a male, male or a female, female outside of genetic identification. Everything else is in personality and socialization. If we have dysfunction there it comes out in a lot of ways. It looks like racism, violence, gender distortion (like friction between genders for no reason). This is all very negative

Genuine I and true self, essence, etc., creates or is supported by releasing of bonds, expansion of expression of awareness and release of constraints, and it represents the expansion phase of the manifestation of the self in the physical body, stress adaptive human biological transformational machine, matrix body and shen or spirit.

Q & A: More on False Personality

STUDENT: Question. When you talk about becoming what you know and no longer pretending, is there a process of pretending in order to go in that direction? You have to pretend in order to convince your self.

Dr. J: That's a very good question. No, it's not pretense. It's called genuine effort. As far as working on your self in a constructive way, we're going to fail. We're going to get an idea, have a little insight, maybe even a realization, and we're going to try to learn a tool. We'll be given an exercise and try to apply it and it won't work, not at first. In fact, sometimes it goes horribly wrong. That comes back to this idea of voluntary suffering actually creating a kind of energy in and of itself, which is useful. It jumps ahead and benefits us a little further down the road. Initially, we're trying not to ever pretend. When we're working, we want to be as genuine and authentic as our corrupt personality will allow us to be. We struggle with it. Sometimes it's messy because you have everyone struggling with it, all at the same time and place. It creates pretty wacky situations. The point is that there is a benefit. As a result of practice overtime, which is part of my definition of the word discipline, you become more disciplined and get some of those essence benefits, which are from those little successes that do happen. There are little moments of insight and progress that happen amidst the mess.

STUDENT: Another question. When you talked about, "conscious schools are small because most people are not willing to take the leap of faith." How is that "leap of faith" different from blind faith in, say, a religion?

Dr. J: In conscious schools, it can't be blind, ignorant, uninformed or uneducated. We have a fundamental working principle, which is "believe nothing and do nothing you don't understand as being something appropriate for you to do." There is no place where students are asked to trust. There's no place where I or any teacher like me would say, "just have faith, it's going to work out," in relation to what we're talking about here. In the work we are always coming back to the statement of not to do anything unless you can verify it your self. The learning curve is a little bit steep in Fourth Way psychology because there is a learning curve! That's why it's difficult. It's also why we have workbooks. That's why we have a lot of material to cover, because there's the initial step of absorbing information and struggling with ideas in your own head and seeing how you relate them to your life and the ideas being proposed, and then voluntarily submitting to particular kinds of work with a hopeful expectation of progressive outcomes. That's not blind faith.

STUDENT: Question/fear: the idea of submitting to a school and it's ideas, philosophies, teachers, etc. What is the definition of commitment if you commit with a certain understanding and then there's a possibility in the process of that commitment you come up against philosophies and ideas you disagree with or see as false personality and not true. How do know the difference?

Dr. J: Initially, I want to say that it's really hard, maybe even impossible, to know the difference. This is especially true for beginners or students because we haven't developed faculties of discernment. Faculties of discernment are imaginary until you have direct experience. Let's put it this way. If there are 1000 schools claiming to be sources of true insight and information, probably 998 of them are run by false personality. For example, hypothetically I'm the poster child for false personality. I want to guarantee my longevity and sustain this state of false personality and basically control the machine.

There is a positive connotation with working on one's self. What I might do is create a school for working on oneself that didn't work. That would be the perfect hiding place. That's what you see out in the world. That's why you see schools that profess to have certain levels of consciousness or paths of enlightenment or whatever. Really what they are is a way of inculcating systematic expression of false personality. On the higher levels, there may not be any work at all.

The only way to learn how to discern a false school for a true school, sadly, is based on experience and having a really good education so you have criteria for discernment. It's more than even criteria though, because anyone can learn the words. In fact, we could probably teach several hundred of these words to a chimpanzee if we were dedicated enough. That wouldn't make the chimpanzee a conscious teacher because it would have a working vocabulary of two hundred words of consciousness instead of words like eat, food and banana. If we taught them words like spirit, consciousness and chakra, well you'd have a monkey that could say those words but the monkey wouldn't be enlightened.

Anyone could learn the words, but one thing we like to say is that it appears false personality has fatal flaws. One of its fatal flaws is it's inconsistent. It's not able to sustain particular lines of serious work or positive expression for long periods of time. It always breaks down and it does so horribly here and there. Most schools that do not have substantial being eventually self-destruct. Even ones that last for a very long time, like multiple generations, doesn't guarantee they are real schools, because false personality is such a perfect chameleon. It's quite possible for multiple generations to mimic the constructs of previous generations ruled by false personality. We call that society. We call that culture.

In "real" schools, there is no place where you are ever free of the work. There's no, "well, you've reached the 35th level and now you're done." There is no 35th level. There's no grand wizard level. The highest are the servants of the lowest in more genuine schools. When the highest are separate and apart from servants of the lowest, that might be evidence of the school not being genuine. It has nothing to do with what they feel or what they think. If you're ruled by false personality, what you think and feel are expressions of the false personality. You could be utterly and completely genuine in your utter and complete lack of consciousness.

For example, I'm sure Hitler believed in what he did. I don't think he was a hypocrite. I think he actually had integrity in what he believed, that he would improve the world if he was in charge and if there were no Jews, or blacks, etc. The quarter of people who worked with and surrounded him, I think they were also genuinely believing people with conviction, and were authentic, authentically insane. They were poster children of mechanicality and a broken, fractured path ruled by ego and false personality.

This idea of submission—this is a hard word. In conscious schools, submission is always voluntary and self-generated. It cannot be compelled. It can be required, in the sense of there is a certain way of being that works in a school and another way that doesn't work. If you can't at least meet the external criteria for creating a homogenous, positive environment suitable for working, then you have to go. Everyone is free to come and go as they please. It has to be that way. If we're here together, if we're working right now, then we're doing this because we feel right now this is the best thing we could be doing. If we didn't really think that, we should probably be doing something else.

STUDENT: At the beginning you talked about false personality and enlightenment in that it's just a process of existence and we get wiser just because we get older.

Dr. J: I said it as if that's not true. We definitely do not JUST get wiser because we get older. We just have more opportunity.

STUDENT: In the concept of false personality, what we tell ourselves as part of it. The semantics of the word experience. In the context of false personality, experience can be regarded as accumulation of moments in time and space that equal "experience" and therefore are valid. How is that different?

Dr. J: It's not even that in the context of false personality. Experience is actually irrelevant. False personality can just imagine experience and then believe that's as valid as having had the experience.

STUDENT: What's the difference between the imagined experience and the real experience?

Dr. J: The real experience is based on doing something and not imagining you could do something.

STUDENT: So it's within the linear concept.

Dr. J: It's not linear. It's not nonlinear. It's the difference between knowledge and being. Knowledge is always in your head. Being is entirely based on doing something. False personality wants to create a world where its validation is not dependent on doing anything. It imagines, it believes that imagining doing is every bit as good as actually doing and that the benefits are the same. This kind of traditional work says, well that's just not true.

J: You had mentioned earlier the third force called emotion…has to be in play in order to reduce and control the false personality?

Dr. J: Well, I didn't say emotion was the third force. I was talking about it in relation to three lines of work and that if there was such a thing as positive emotion, it was whatever emotion supported doing three lines of work…whatever line of work was being done.

J: You gave the example of the difference between falling into shallow water and being able to swim out versus falling into water you know that you are either going to sink or swim.

Dr. J: Yes, there's no emotion in the first one—no particular emotion.

J: My question is you keep saying "particular emotion." What does that feel like? What is a "particular emotion" if you're out of control because of false personality? How can you tell?

Dr. J: It's however you would feel if you had just fallen off the boat in the middle of the ocean and you realize that if you did not apply your self with every intense faculty at your disposal, you would die. That emotion is prescient and drives you to make extraordinary effort. You would then apply that effort until you literally saved your self. That's positive emotion. That's quite different than all the other emotions we think are so positive, which are more like, "feely good, fluffy, warm fuzzies." We think positive emotion is having a "warm fuzzy". From the point of view of the work, positive emotion is what drives you to do whatever is necessary to change your self. That's a positive emotion. What does that feel like? I can't tell you. Why? Because it's situational to you. That's the thing about this work. It's personal. We do it together because it's been determined over a long period of time you can't do this by your self. It's not possible. So we do it together. At the same time, we still have to work toward being able to bring emotion to bear to making intense efforts, especially for particular periods of time, to make breakthroughs and have certain shifts in consciousness, which are only available with emotion. If there's no emotion, there is no change of state.

STUDENT: Is the practice of generating that emotion voluntary suffering?

Dr. J: That's part of it. The analogy would be that you jump off the boat on purpose.

STUDENT: With support.

Dr. J: The support would be knowing how to swim and yell really loud and how to hold your breath under water, knowing how to float. The support would be where you put your self in situations where you know you're going to be stressed but you submit to that stress ahead of time. You put your self there on purpose. The stress is genuine. The feelings, emotions and fears that come up are real. You put your self in front of them or in a place they will come up on purpose in order to access a different kind of emotion, which is not there in accidental circumstances. It's different. Like the metaphor with the boat, I was saying, "it's like that but that's still not it." It's hard to describe. It's like trying to describe a genuine realization. It's very hard because it's completely personal. How do you describe something to someone else that is only relevant to your inner or outer life? It's kind of impossible.

One thing about the work is at one level of education and experience and understanding, there appears to be contradictions. At another level, those contradictions have to be resolvable, because if the work is really a true work, then everything in the work has to be able to relate to and have harmony and cogence in relation to everything else in the work.

J: What does the word "cogence" mean?

Dr. J: ...in resonance with, similar to, in harmony with, of a similar frequency or intensity or nature.

For example, I'm driving down the road going my way. You're driving down the road going your way. There may come a point in time where our cars are right next to each other on the highway. We have completely separate and unrelated lives. There might be a moment where you could have a little conversation with the driver of the car that's next to you. In that moment, you're cogent with the other driver. You get it?

J: Well that was certainly easier for me to understand than jumping off the boat. I thought to myself, I'm not even going to be on a cruise ship so why would I need this metaphor? I appreciate the other one.

Dr. J: Yeah. Well, they're totally different.

J: When we talk about polar opposite, this work being the polar opposite of the way culture lives, that's also another form of voluntary suffering. When we decide to do the work and we know we're going up the stream with no paddles, we know there will be challenges.

Dr. J: That may not be true or a correct understanding of what I was saying. In knowing how disparate the inner life we are trying to cultivate is from that which the dominant culture is trying to perpetuate around us, the last thing in the world we want to be is in controversy with the outer culture. The further along we get, the more on the outer layer we want to be in harmony with the outer culture. We want to be in harmony with the outer culture. We want no friction with the outer culture and outer world. That's what Gurdjieff talked about in Life Is Real Only Then, When "I Am", the way of the fox. Our business is our business. Our business is building a self and developing our essence. What we're doing is in spite of the outer culture. If we push against the outer culture too hard, then of course that's much bigger than we are and can crush us like a bug at any time. It's important there not be suffering or friction between us and the outer culture. The suffering and friction happens on the inner layer in the struggle against false personality. In fact, you observe the outer culture like you observe the false personality within your self. What we need to do is observe it. It doesn't mean to withdraw from society. In fact, it's exactly the opposite. The whole definition of the Fourth Way is that it's the way in life. It's not the way of the fakir, the yogi, and the ascetic, of withdrawal from life.

It's the way in life. It's unique in the sense of "in life but not of it." That's where those kinds of teachings are stated in many spiritual disciplines. "We're in the world, but we're not of the world." That's what that means. It's often misinterpreted.

CHAPTER FIVE: Exercises for Voluntary Suffering

1. Occasionally, if you are tired, try to make an additional effort.

Dr. J: This is really valuable. How often are we tired? How predictable is our "being tired"? How often are we tired in particular circumstances, with particular conversations or people? It's a work idea that sometimes when the self-observing mind says, "I'm tired right now," the usual solution might be to withdraw or do something different or go somewhere else. That's an inclination. Occasionally, at the same time you observe you are tired, you decide to do something that requires effort. Instead of resting, lying down, withdrawing or going into a quiet place, do the opposite. Do something that requires more attention in the moment.

Let's say I'm sitting here and I've been working all day. I realize I'm feeling tired. I think, "Aww, a nap would be nice right now." A move towards sleep. Instead of doing that I go, "Actually, instead of moving towards sleep, I'm going to take these few moments I would use to nap and instead I'll pick up a workbook and read it." the whole time acknowledging I don't really feel like reading.

Another one might be, I'm feeling tired right now and instead of taking a nap or withdrawing, I'm going to go do a Hatha yoga routine or even 15 minutes of pranayama. You do these things, especially if you catch the thought, "I don't really feel like doing that right now." Find some I inside that can make a decision to do something that's constructive, practical and positive. Give that I permission to be in charge, in spite of the tiredness, and then go do it.

What happens is really interesting. Almost immediately you get energy. It's like that alone sometimes causes such a shift. Why? You are making an intentional effort contrary to the rolling inclination toward rest the machine has sometimes.

2. Try to be in a strange situation in which you have no role.

Dr. J: This is an interesting one. It has to do with intentionally putting your self in strange situations just because you don't know what they are, you don't know how it's done, you're not the expert, and you're not completely in control. Think of situations that ordinarily you would avoid. Then, occasionally (not all the time) put your self into that place on purpose. This could be anything. Usually your clues as to what situations might be valuable go back to your likes and dislikes. If you make a list of everything you don't like to do, there's a lot of value right there. Simply doing things that are appealing that we already know we like to do won't generate a lot of energy. There's no real benefit, from a point of view of consciousness or energy, in doing that. As an exercise, it's more valuable to look at things that don't appeal to you.

For example, I could frame it this way. "I really love music. I'm not such a big fan of hip-hop." So you know what? Once and a while, I'm going to go to a hip-hop concert where I don't even know who the musicians are. I suspect I might not like them. The age bracket for the group might be wrong. The demographic for the concert might be optimum for me. Guess what? I'm just going to go do it because I will put myself in a place where I had no role. I don't know how to act exactly. I don't know ahead of time how it will make me feel. There's a possibility something new might happen that is unpredictable.

That's what I'm always trying to do. I'm always trying to predict ahead of time how things are going to affect me. A lot of my choices, on a daily basis, are all played against certain criteria. I already know what I will like and dislike. I just steer myself between my likes and dislikes and my whole day could be gone like that. There's no friction one way or the other.

Moving here was a little bit like that for me. I had no idea what to expect. I had no position in the community or anything. I got a lot of information really fast by doing that. I was sometimes quite uncomfortable while I was in that process. It's a good thing, as a practice, to look for those opportunities.

You might have an area of responsibility in the house or in your job or something like that. You volunteer to do something you ordinarily would never volunteer to do. Why? Well, because you normally wouldn't. If you are working on this particular practice today, then you volunteer to do exactly what you don't want to for the sake of the exercise.

That's why I like the practices in Angels Speak. There are a lot of practices here. "I think I'm going to do this one today." Then you think about how to be creative. You know it's something you don't want to do and ordinarily would never volunteer to do. It's going to be something I don't know how to do well. It has to have some criteria. I don't know if there will be any benefit for me for doing it. I'm just going to volunteer to do it anyway. Then I will follow through and actually do it. If I fail, that's terrific because it's irrelevant to the exercise. If I do this, from the point of view that I will somehow gain something positive from it as criteria for doing it, well that's not the exercise either. I'm doing the exercise because it's an exercise. You can't predict the benefit of the exercise ahead of time.

3. Dissolve candy in your mouth without chewing it.

Dr. J: I got this as an exercise from three different teachers on three different continents in three different systems. One was Buddhist, one was Fourth Way, and one was Vedic. They told me the same thing. They gave me this idea that we have habits, even when we are eating. There is a certain way you eat candy, for example. Just like there is a way you eat a popsicle or a Tootsie Roll. Maybe you're mechanical pattern is that you suck on it or lick it until you get to the core and chew it up. Once in a while, instead of doing that, chew it up right away. With peanut brittle, instead of biting it and feeling the crunch I just let it dissolve. In other words, I do the opposite of whatever my normal pattern of eating would be. Eating candy is pretty mechanical. It is an interesting concept to bring consciousness to eating candy.

Sometimes we get concerned with the big issues of life and trying to bring consciousness to bear to resolve the really big issues. We miss all the little opportunities of mechanicality where we can bring consciousness to them. Maybe we don't get an ounce of being from it. Maybe we only get a gram or a teeny tiny little bit of being from it. We miss the opportunity to work on our everyday mechanicalities when we save up our pennies to only work on the really big issues.

If we consistently bring more consciousness to the little things we do and develop a habit of that, then being is increased. As we gather more energy from the increase in being, we have more substance to bring energy to the bigger issues.

4. Find a place where you indulge your self unnecessarily in pleasure, rest, food, etc., and set tasks to oppose these tendencies to help you remember.

Dr. J: There you go. There's a theme in some of these exercises. Find your comfort thing. I prefer to eat my food from a bowl. This meal I'm going to eat from a plate. It seems like a little thing. I prefer to eat from a bowl. With intention I'm going to go against my preference. I prefer to drink water when I eat. Instead of drinking water when you eat, don't drink. Do something different on purpose. If you always sleep on the right side of the bed with your head facing north, once in a while, sleep on the wrong side of the bed and flip your self around to sleep facing a different direction. Watch what happens. There's friction and an inclination, which the machine has toward even facing a certain direction. Sometimes when we're doing this Fourth Way thing, I like to sit on the couch or I like other people to move around a bit. If we're not careful, we'll notice that we'll always sit in the same position every time we go to have this discussion on consciousness. We're falling into a pattern. It might not be a pattern like violence or self-destruction, but it's still a pattern. When we're most comfortable is when we're liable to fall into our most mechanical patterns.

If I want to make progress on my big patterns, I want test them on the small ones. You might have some addiction or compulsion or some negative expression that's really serious. I have clients who had something like that but I couldn't get some of them to sleep on the wrong side of the bed. If I told them the secret to learning how to deal with their obsession or their compulsive eating disorder was to actually turn their bed 90 degrees or sleep facing the opposite direction, they couldn't do it.

J: Immediately when you said that I thought to myself, well I'm at the wrong side of the headboard. My feet would be at the headboard. Then I went, wait a minute, we don't even have a headboard.

Dr. J: Right. My point is, if you can't with intention go against the grain of the mechanicality of how we are when we are just hanging out when we are comfortable, how are we going to have sustained attention and energy to handle to really big things?

112

That's one reason I want to change all the furniture around in the house. It's not because I think it will make it more practical. We've had the furniture in the house in this place long enough that we are all comfortable with it. By changing it around, it will make us feel different. We will have to pay attention as we walk across the room in the dark so we don't fall over. I'm so comfortable now I don't even have to have my eyes open. Every light in the house can be off and I can still walk all the way around the house and find light switches or find this or that without even thinking about it. How can I do that? Well, I have a tape. It's ingrained. It's in there.

I had teachers who, when I would go over to their house, would occasionally put everything in a different place. It would make me uncomfortable. It was all the same stuff but they would put it all in a different place. I would go for a lecture and couldn't sit still because it would bother me that everything was in a different place. Sometimes my favorite chair wasn't in the room. I didn't like the new chair I had to sit in.

5. Occasionally, try to move continuously and intentionally for a few minutes. Then be still and observe your I's.

Dr. J: There is no particular rhyme, reason or timing. I know some people say you should have a movement exercise, meditation or pranayama you should do at the same time everyday. In our way of thinking about these things, we never say that. That's why I never do that. Anything I do in the same way at the same time everyday very quickly goes into mechanical expression and will develop a formatory aspect to it. It is better to vary the time, the length and the activity itself a little bit. Here is something that usually only happens in schools.

It's very hard to do this on your own. We all fall into predictable patterns. We want to have the predictable day. Quite often, especially if you're in business and working with the public, we have to do some things like that. On a personal level, when we're in a school, sometimes I introduce what might appear to you to be random activities for no particular reason. In fact, it might appear as if I'm not paying attention. Everybody is busy doing something else. Part of the reason I do that is because it is uncomfortable. The part of the teacher that is not paying attention, creating friction, actually has merit because of its unpredictability.

The hard thing of course for me is to do that for myself. The nice thing about being in a community and having you guys is that quite often you interject some random thing in my day that is not exactly, at that particular moment, what I would want to be doing as my first choice. When I submit to that, however well or not well, there's an opportunity for random friction to generate a little more consciousness in the moment. At least for a few minutes we are paying a little more attention than we were before. It's amazing how you can be doing something you think requires a lot of thought. You return to find out you were in autopilot almost the whole time you were doing it.

An example would be going to the grocery store in town, where I could be sitting in the parking lot and not even remember how I got there or what traffic was like, or did I stop at the red light at 54th or not, or how many bugs did I see? One of the reasons I play slug-a-bug is because the occurrence of Volkswagen Beetles in the traffic flow is essentially random. For me to notice a random occurrence of the Beetle as I'm doing something you would think would require attention…you're supposed to be paying attention when you're driving right? What I find is sometimes I don't react to the bug when I've already set the intention to point it out. What this means is that I'm on autopilot. I'm not paying attention to what I'm doing. Part of me is paying attention. That's the formatory, mechanical part. I might be paying more attention to the music in the car or the cars on the side of the road than actually driving. I play slug-a-bug as a conscious exercise to monitor random occurrence and take the charge of my machine away from the driving octave. That's why I do that.

J: And here I thought you just loved playing slug-a-bug with me.

Dr. J: Aside from the fact that I want to beat J everyday in slug-a-bug.

6. Practice Generosity.

Dr. J: Pay generously for what you get. We get into mechanical expression that includes reciprocal exchange of energy as if it means something. We want to pay what something's worth and no more. We don't want to overpay because somehow that means we're being taken advantage of or we're not as sharp as we could be. It could mean all kinds of things.

There's a work idea that we are to, with conscious intention, be generous in all things. One of the features of "tramp feature" is that "Tramp" is stingy. Tramp wants to always get the best and lowest price no matter what. Tramp wants to get two for one. Tramp wants you to give them something and then wants to ask you for twice that or something more even if it's completely unreasonable. "Well, I just thought I'd ask." This happened maybe twelve times this last year or more. I had someone ask for a full tuition scholarship for class and tell me their sad story. Then I would say okay. The next thing they did was to ask for free housing, food and in at least six different times, they asked me to reimburse them for their gas or airfare. That's tramp feature.

It was really funny in two different cases. Not only did they ask us to feed them, but then even before they got the answer they went into a long list of all their special food preferences. Not only were we going to have to feed them for the month after teaching them for free, we would have to follow their very specific dietary restrictions and cook separately in order to feed them. I tried to explain to them that the whole purpose of having a school was not to treat everyone who called as if they were my long lost cousin, son or daughter. Part of our program was about encouraging people to be professional and responsible. To try and scam the school out of everything they own is not being professional and responsible. You have to give and be generous.

The school principle says we are honor bound to give more than what is proportional to what we receive. That's called the third line of work. That's how third line of work comes into effect. If people aren't being generous, there's no third line of work. It means you need to give back more than what you received, and not because they deserve it.

See, we all have these external criteria. "Well I will be generous if I feel like you really deserve it." That defeats the whole purpose of the exercise. I'm being generous because it's an exercise. There's a benefit to me.

The other day we were driving down the road. There was a homeless guy looking kind of shabby and had his hands out. Immediately I decided to be generous. I instantly dug in my pocket, rolled the window down and handed him some money. Now, in the past, I would see someone like that and have this whole conversation in my head. "Do they look like they deserve me to give them something? Are they really homeless or just scamming me for drug money? Are they really…" I'd have all these criteria relating to this person, which really had nothing to do with them. Sometimes I would come to the conclusion I wasn't going to give them anything so I wouldn't. The other day when I looked at him, I started to have that thought, "What is this person…" then I just thought, "You know what? What do I care? There's someone on the street asking for money. I'm going to give him some money. I can afford to. I don't really have to know what's going to happen with it or where it's going to go." It's just a practice in generosity.

Sometimes I give people scholarships and not because I think they deserve it. In fact, I know they don't. I get that confirmation, for example, when they show up in class in their Hummer or Cadillac or new BMV with the new car smell wearing their designer shoes and yoga outfits, talking about their big house and swimming pool and husband's fat business. I know they didn't really deserve it. I give it to them as an exercise for me.

Everything about me would say I shouldn't give somebody something for nothing. I should never give something that has value to someone who doesn't deserve it. As a work idea, sometimes I have to do on purpose things that are exactly the opposite of everything that's about me—and for no other reason. That exercise is very difficult because you have to be paying attention.

7. To awaken you must be able to suffer and endure much humiliation.

Dr. J: Whoa. It means voluntary suffering. There is this idea of knowing you're suffering and knowing there is a way out of the suffering but not taking it so that you can get to the other side of where humiliation comes from. Where does this feeling of loss come from when we're in particular situations that cause us to feel like we're suffering? What is the genesis of it? Because it is natural, it is part of our machine to avoid pain. When the burner is on and you accidentally stick your hand on it,

114

you instantly pull your hand away. It's instinctive to move away from pain and suffering. Instinctive is another word referring to machine-like and formatory. We try to avoid pain and suffering in every way.

It is a Herculean task to see suffering ahead of us and not try to avoid it. It is also Herculean task to know if you say something or do something or put your self in a particular situation that you will be embarrassed or humiliated, but to go ahead with it anyway to see what's on the other side of it.

This ties back to another statement about approaching emotionally difficult tasks. For example, there's a conversation I need to have but I don't really want to have it. There are words I need to say but I'm not going to say them. I know if I say them I will probably be humiliated or embarrassed. My viewpoint might not be validated or it might be diminished or start an argument.

I'm not advocating starting arguments or creating situations that feed your poor self-image or lack of communication or issues about expression of being, etc. What I am saying is sometimes when you see that curve coming, you don't take the exit ahead but let it happen. You go into it, say what you have to say, or allow your self to remain in the situation a little longer than you might ordinarily have done so—not because you're a dirty dishrag or co-enabling, not because you're codependent or helpless and hapless. You are doing it on purpose because you want to see what's on the other side of it if you were paying attention.

It's a very sophisticated exercise. It's an advanced exercise. Jesus submitted to being nailed on the cross. Whether or not the story was true or really happened is irrelevant. Sometimes you let your self be led into a dark place at the mercy of people who are less conscious than you. In the example of Jesus, you let them nail you to the cross. Why? The only way to see what's on the other side is to submit to the process of suffering on purpose. It's not pretty.

Of course, if we're going to practice this kind of exercise, we have to start with small things. We don't start with "let's get nailed to the cross and see if we can sustain our focus and observer mind while someone is hammering nails through our hands". Start with something smaller.

Voluntary suffering and how we start creating opportunities for it is on the road to paradise. Let's use our parents for example: "I know if I say something to my mom or dad or have a certain conversation with them, that because I know they're going to demean me or not respect my opinion." This is hypothetical. I could never say those words or have that conversation. I would have a pleasant experience with them, relatively speaking. I could just bite my tongue and, if things are too intense and might drive me to say something I'm going to regret, I'll extricate myself and go hide or go outside to smoke a cigarette. Instead of practicing avoidance, go the Samurai way. The conscious Samurai says, "You know, I'm just going to stand here and be myself. I'm going to say what I actually think and deal with the consequences, no matter what they are. I'm going to be here, full on, eyes open, observing myself and how I react to what happens. I'm going to pay attention to what emotions come up, what words come out and the parts of me that want to fight, defend, run away, and the part that observes all the parts."

8. Embrace that which makes you suffer.

Dr. J: Intentional suffering will become a way for your progress.
 Good news and bad news. It works. The bad news is that voluntary suffering is part of the work ethic. We constantly reassess our comfort zones. On the one hand, we work hard with our communication and way of being to make each other comfortable and have a comfortable place to live and work. On another level, that's not my job. Part of my job and eventually your job (I'm being positive that way) is to make people uncomfortable. It is to challenge them. I know that different philosophies have different viewpoints. Some say you can always challenge people in a positive way.

I don't think challenge is positive or negative. If you stimulate people and have them do one thing not in their natural inclination at that moment to do, or think a thought they haven't already agreed it was a thought they should be thinking, it will create friction. It will create a push and pull. It will create suffering. Sometimes the result looks like a breakthrough. Sometimes the result looks like a breakdown. One way or the other, we have to look for opportunities to, in a way, make each other a little uncomfortable.

Because we are living and working together, we don't want to make ourselves so uncomfortable that we try to hurt each other. Now you forgot the objective. It wasn't to hurt each other. Sometimes it might feel like that.

That's this whole idea of administering corrections and creating situations where there's friction without negative emotion being the motivation for them, or coming from a reactive frame of mind (tit for tat). "I'm doing this today because you did that yesterday" kind of thing. That would be an offense, not allowing someone to be self-determined at all times.

From a work point of view, it's not possible to be self-determined if you're not a fully self-realized, conscious being. If you're not, most of what you think is self-determination is just the playing of tapes, the role recital of mechanical inclinations of likes and dislikes, attractions and repulsions and the voices of organs and the tissue being expressed in some fairly random manner. Occasionally we pipe in and think we are doing it all on purpose. For that moment when we think we're doing something on purpose, we think that means we're always doing everything on purpose. That couldn't be further from the truth. Having that interjection of external pressure actually goes against the grain of self-determination.

In our way of working, only advanced practitioners or students have the privilege of being self-determined. That's not determined by some external resource. That's still determined by them. In every school at the beginning of training, students are given very little right to be self-determining. The reason why is, according to the latitude you give for self-determination, students always deviate and go to another denominator of action not complimentary to working, practice or to the school. They tend to then pull energy away from the school.

For example, let's say I did a CTP [Certified Thai Yoga Practitioner Course]. As people came to the class and it developed, I gave them permission to sit anyway they wanted to, to talk anytime they wanted to, to use their phone any time, to eat any time, to come to class any time they wanted to. Very quickly, I would be the only person sitting in the class. Their self-determination would very rapidly bounce off the walls. One of those random bounces would go out the door or two windows in the classroom. One of those phone calls would take them outside. On one of those meal trips to the grocery store, they would meet someone they would run off with. Very quickly there wouldn't be anyone in class, proportional to the amount of self-determination I gave in class. There might be one or two people who would step up but maybe not.

I did an experiment like this one time where I did that in class. I had a small group of about four people. I told them there were no rules. We are all independent, self-determined adults here. Class was going to go from ten to six. They would determine exactly when they came, early or late. They could leave whenever they wanted to. At the end of class, I would only give them credit for the hours they had been in class. We did this for two and a half days. No one in that group got full credit for the class. Three of the people ended up only getting a certificate for half of the hours. One person left during lunch on the second day and didn't come back. By the end of the last day, everybody had some issue that came up. It was family, job, personal or health for why they had to leave early on the last day of class. They all did. I didn't say anything. My intention for that class was to do an experiment in how much latitude and determination I would give students. After that, I started giving students less latitude for self-determination and I've been on that curve ever since.

It's really hard to be a disciplinarian in a structured environment like a class. It's too easy for you or me to not be constantly paying attention to what everybody is doing. Everyone, in their own way and head, ultimately have the right to determine whether they are coming or going, sitting or standing. There is constant secrecy of trying to get around the discipline all day long.

All I want to do is try and find the balance between discipline and self-determination that allows us to make concrete progress. Giving too much latitude looks like spinning wheels and eventually no school. With too much discipline, you start to lose people because they feel like the environment is abusive. There has to be a happy medium. That's our practice continuum. It varies from group to group.

9. Higher powers give you suffering. You are intended to transform it voluntarily.

Dr. J: This process can only begin with unconditional acceptance. Judging or resenting creates a condition of unnecessary suffering on top of the real suffering. It's enough to take the discipline or correction. Higher powers bring us discipline or correction, whether they are your teacher, elder, or their teacher or elder, whether it is based on agreements in the school or working environment or what not. They all represent higher powers because they are structures from outside of us and are natural laws we need to conform to in order to get something. That something is the opportunity to work on our selves and develop different skills and qualities practical and beneficial toward that end.

How do we accept the practices and the discipline without always wanting to elaborate on the suffering? "I know you're asking me to do something right now and I really don't want to do it. Not only am I just going to have the friction that resistance will give me, I will also elaborate on that with judgment, criticism and other unrelated issues and grow it like a tree." The hardest thing in the world is to simply take the discipline, correction or shift of change and observe the friction, unwillingness, defensiveness or sluggishness. "I'm going to do it but only when I get around to it and as slow as I possibly can. I'm not going to do a good job."

It's like on the last day of class when the administrator gives students the task to do chores to restore the environment before leaving. You notice some people will go to it and have a positive attitude. Some people will not like it but will keep it to themselves. Some people won't like it and they will grumble about it the whole time. Some people will do it, grumble the whole time and complain about how unfair it is. They shouldn't have to do it. Someone else should do it. Then some people will agree to do it and start to. As soon as they feel like someone is not watching, even within a minute or so, they are off somewhere completely different. If you were to ask, "What are you doing way over here?" there would be a long list of reasons. Some still will refuse to do it and take some principled stand on how they don't deserve to do it and shouldn't be asked. There is this long continuum. We would call it the octave of cleaning the bathhouse, for example.

In reality, it's not pulling teeth to clean. Yeah, we don't like to do housework but we also don't like having to take a shower on top of a gooey fur ball left by some anomalous creature. The same people who would avoid the task would probably be the ones to complain the most and the loudest if there was a big, hairy fur ball in the shower.

J: Even if it was their hairball

Dr. J: Everyone does this to some degree. This is what we want to try and avoid if we are paying attention. The self-remembering shows us we add to the source and friction unnecessarily. As part of self-observation we see how we take something a little uncomfortable and turn it into a flaming breakdown or make it way more uncomfortable. What are the mechanics behind that?

10. Non-identification, non-attachment, and non-qualification can transform suffering into something higher.

Dr. J: Suffering can be anything that takes us away from being in tune with our true nature or essence. Even something that in some circumstances might be pleasurable, if that takes you away from your true, non-divided self, you will suffer. It explains why we are not happy when we are doing exactly what we want to be doing. We'll go through a lot of effort to create environments or opportunities. We'll dress right and make time. We do what we want to do and guess what? We are not happy. Even something we might do on purpose, if the end result is that we get lost in it... For example, we might plan to do something that seems like it will be really beneficial for everybody involved. Because there is resistance to it or because it doesn't go the way we imagined, we get unhappy. We then become attached to being unhappy and it turns into a failure. Conversely, of course, if we are acting at the whim of external events, which might include other people and the way they look at us and think of us, if we are identified with them being a certain way, we are going to be unhappy, and that means suffering.

Non-identification. The hardest thing in the world is to come to an understanding that everything we see, think or feel, is us, comes from us and is reflective of us. We attach to and identify with it. I might have a thought go through my head. I then attach myself to that thought. I have a feeling in my body and I add the word I to that feeling. I feel this. I think that. Yet in the very next moment, there is another feeling and another thought that can be completely contradictory. I instantly go, "I think this and feel that too." I don't even have a problem with the contradiction. I don't see the transition or how they are diametrically opposed to each other. I identify with both as if they are somehow me. I don't get it. That's a cause of suffering. Since those emotions and thoughts, for example, are both coming from the past and are reflective of buffers (tapes playing, multiple I's, transient I's or emotions reflective no more of the room temperature than what I actually believe) I identify with them. Of course then myself is messed up. I have no control over who I am. In other words, whoever I am is not deliberate. I am not deliberately conscious at any particular moment because most of the thoughts and feelings I experience are random, being caused by external or internal events. Those thoughts and feelings are not reflective of a self-directed consciousness. I hold onto them as if they are real but they are not because no matter how hard I try to hold onto them, they will leave no matter what.

I am angry or anxious or sad. I will hold onto that feeling like a terrier dog. There's nothing anybody else can do about it. I will do whatever it takes to maintain that because at least I have the sense that, when I'm in a particular emotion, it's as if I feel a little more real in that moment. The problem is, as soon as I look away for a second or as soon as the external environment changes the least little bit, it goes away like smoke. If I'm attached to that, I'm going to notice it's absence and I'm going to suffer.

Non-qualification can transform suffering. Qualification I think, in this regard, is this idea of justification and defending thoughts and feelings which are not real, defending and protecting, if you will, justifying aspects of false personality and ego that are completely unreal and you know while you're defending them they're not real. You know the whole time you are making the excuses, you are arguing the fine points, the pros and cons, etc. etc., you know the whole time you are having that conversation that you're arguing for something you know is not real about your self. Simultaneously, a part of you knows that in about five minutes, it's going to change and be completely different. I'll fight you to do the death on it right now and right this minute. Five minutes later I will have a different point of view. All that qualification, justification and defending supports suffering. Not doing it is a way to reduce suffering.

From this perspective, there is no reducing suffering. There is only transmutation of suffering. Transmute is an old term used in alchemy to denote changing one element to another, as in converting a base metal such as lead into a finer substance such as gold. That's the possibility. It's not that we're going to reduce suffering, because as long as we're in the tissue and subject to whim and event and the law of accident, as long as we're subject to influence and pressure and even conversations of people that we live with and are around us, we're going to have suffering—and also people we don't have control of. I hardly have control of myself. I have no control over you. Any control I have over you is an illusion. We either work in some form of cooperation or not. One way or the other we're going to have suffering. There's no way around it. There's always some source of friction. What do we do with that friction? Do we identify with it? Do we attach to it? Do we justify it? Defend it? Do we try to maintain it when most of the ideas and feelings we have are temporary? Sometimes people ask, "Well wait a minute. If all of these emotions and thoughts are false and reflective of false personality and ego, what about true emotion? Is there such a thing as a real positive emotion? A genuine thought that's reflective of original, fundamental or objective consciousness?"

We think that there is, hypothetically. If there is such a thing, it's on the other side of being completely owned by everything that's not real. Whatever is a true and positive emotion, it's an emotion not completely controlled and on the other side of an emotional sea that's completely negative. If there's a true thought or vision or clarity of mind reflective of original, authentic true self and essence, objective consciousness and magnetic center, well, then it's going to look very different than here one minute and gone the next associative thinking and random thoughts, which are the ordinary consciousness kind of thoughts. It's going to have a very different feel and a very different flavor. We don't really worry about that so much. Initially, in the beginning, all we are trying to do is learn about ourselves and identify what a mess we are.

The fact is we live in what is equivalent to a garbage dump. It's like waking up in the middle of a landfill and realizing that's our home. Worse than that, not only did you wake up in the middle of a landfill and realize that's your home, you realize you actually made that landfill. You are the person who dumped all that stuff in the landfill, which in every direction is junk and disgust. Here and there, even in a landfill there might be some nugget that has value. What you start to do is sort and sift through all the junk, which is everywhere in every direction, looking for something of value. Whenever you find that, you gather it together and right in the middle of the landfill you begin to construct something unlike the landfill. It's completely different.

There are a couple different ways I could go with this metaphor. It might be that you build a space in the landfill that's pristine and is reflective of a whole different organization of life and consciousness than what the landfill represents. It might also be that you build a vehicle you climb in to take you to another place. This escapist thing is kind of limited because a lot of systems are based on escape. In other words, if you follow this principle or do this daily discipline, you will escape your normal life and you will arrive in the blissful blue crystal land of Samadhi and nirvana. The problem is, the system tells me, when we do that, we take the landfill with us. In fact, the blue crystal medicine Buddha land is an illusion for a state of mind where you have successfully and completely repressed and suppressed all the unresolved issues. The system says either we resolve the issues presented to us by false personality, or that's what we always are. Whatever reality we're in is reflective of that false personality. If we try hard enough, we can imagine ourselves into a better place than where we really are, at least for a short amount of time.

The problem with the blissful land of nirvana where everything is rosy is that it's temporary. The thing about it is, even when we read books and people talk about how they achieved enlightenment and how they got to their blissful land and so on let's say a book was written in 1998 and the author's on a popular talk show in 1999. You look at them in 2009 and they've been divorced and remarried twice, bankrupt and are now suffering from some disease, etc. The bliss they were talking about on the popular talk show didn't actually last longer than the show. I could give you example after example of people who are very famous, as far as being able to talk about visualizing and completely perfecting their lives and all this kind of thing. At the time the book comes out, they're on top of their game and they're exemplary. It's just like the guru who has millions of followers and everything is just right. There are many examples of this if you consider many charismatic teachers and "gurus" of the past few years who, after amassing hundreds of thousands, if not millions, of followers, were found to be less than their public persona and marketing suggested, and went through immense downfalls from grace into disrepute. We see this in every area of life, religion, self-help, economics and politics—role models who are not what they appear to be.

Just before these collapses and falls from grace, these icons of some kind of enlightenment were writing books about how they had achieved perfect enlightenment and the blue crystal medicine land in this life and was giving instructions to people on how to do that. The next thing you know, they are running for their life.

Any kind of blissful possibility of achieving a state where there's not going to be anymore suffering as long as you are alive is unrealistic. You are still going to be in your body subject to the "hoopleheads" like the IRS and/or pollution, corporate misadventure and, if nothing else, the vagaries of our tissue, as we don't live forever in the physical body. One way or another we suffer. The suffering is just the difference between the inner harmony and what's actually real. The idea is that it doesn't matter what's happening to us if we could find that equilibrium of non-identification, non-attachment and non-qualification. If we maintain that while we are going through stuff, we start to see the benefits of transforming suffering.

11. The worst scenario you can imagine could be the most beneficial to your evolution.

Imagine what's the worst scenario you could imagine for me? Perhaps being embarrassed in public. That's terrible. Sometimes that scenario could be the best for you. It could be something else that is really hidden. On some level we all have our worst scenario. From a work idea, it's always about this: our worst scenario is having our negative features drawn out into the light, our most vulnerable, weak or negative features being brought into the light and in public. However, this house and the school are not public. There are actually different rules. Even in that case we still want to be able to keep our counsel, cut some slack and not be called out when we're not behaving in highest way we can internally or externally. If that comes out, it's a nightmare scenario because in the short term, there is nowhere to hide. That's where the justification comes in. Immediately we try to cover up and escape. We try to get out from the scrutiny and avoid the light of revealing what's going on. That's a worst case scenario. However, whatever that is, whatever you can imagine, even worse than that, could be the most beneficial to your evolution. We have no control over this because nature will out and win. I might decide I'm going to take my lessons in soft little bits in very comfortable circumstances with lots of rest breaks.

Nature turns around and wham, lays that stuff on me like a blanket. It pulls all my shortcomings out into the open, all out in public, and that might just mean one person. That's too public for some issues. No one is really supposed to know what I'm thinking or feeling, right? If they do, it instantly feels like a violation. We instantly try to cover, run, justify and hide in all the great variety of ways we are absolutely expert at doing. It's quick. It happens faster than thought.

One of the purposes of a school is to make each other uncomfortable. We want to support each other in the most loving and un-judgmental way we can, considering we are completely messed up. A school is an environment where we agree to embarrass each other and challenge each other. We agree to poke each other with a sharp stick. Part of the theory goes like this: let's say there are three of us. We're all working on ourselves to one degree or another. Part of the work on oneself is awaking from sleep. Being completely consumed with mechanical nature is the same as being completely asleep. Being less mechanical is being more awake. At this particular moment, maybe all of us are more awake than normal. Part of it is because if I prick one of you and you squeal a little bit, that tends to get everyone's attention. If nothing else, the attention is to decide if it's good or bad. What then happens is one of us might go completely asleep and literally nod off. In a school, when we notice each other asleep at the wheel, we pick up our sharp, pointy thing and we go, "poke, poke, poke," and we jab until they wake up. It's just like if I was taking a nap. I'm having a really good nap, not a casual nap. Right in the middle of that, you come and wake me up with something I'm not dreaming about. Chances are I might be a little irritated and cranky. Why are you waking me up? What? What is so important? I might have a little disassociation. I will probably not be able to relate to what you're talking about even for a minute or two. Why? I was just asleep. I might even be mad at you. Why? That's the way people are when you interrupt their sleep.

Here we are. We're going through our day. At different points, we pass out and go to sleep. In a school, part of the reason for the other people in the school is to wake you up and poke you a little bit. The agreement is that if they go to sleep at the wheel, you will do the same to them. The idea being that between the three of us, if we can function in a healthy way like that, then what happens is that all of us tend to sleep less. We're all paying slightly more attention than we would if we weren't in this place of agreement. We're less likely to drive off into the weeds. The problem and downside is that we keep getting interrupted in our sleep. We keep getting caught doing things no one is supposed to know or notice.

How do you know someone is sleeping in real life in a normal state? They are curled up in a fetal position. Their eyes are closed. They're breathing deep and rhythmically. They're snoring. We have all these clues that tell us someone is asleep. In normal life, other than on the job, if you see someone sleeping, you leave him or her alone. That's what we do most of the time. We notice someone sleeping and being less than thoughtful or conscious. We observe it and leave them alone. However, in a school that doesn't work. In a school, we have an ongoing agreement that we are going to prick each other and get on each other's nerves and be abrasive, in a sense. There's no way for me to wake you up without being abrasive. At some point, I have to push, poke or talk to you hard enough that I get your attention out of the sleeping mind into the conscious mind. You need to wake up now!

There is a lot of resistance to that because when we are asleep the inclination is to stay asleep. It's not to wake up. There is always resistance. "I was right in the middle of a wonderful dream and you interrupted that and I'm now mad at you." Guess what? That sleepy dream and unreality is your life. You wouldn't be here, if at some point you hadn't asked to wake up and be able to find your real life and who you are in the real world.

12. When falsely accused, do not reciprocate or escalate.

Avoid identification and justification. Accusations from other people are events no different than any others. They are always more about the person making them than they are about you. All people communicate from the level of consciousness they are currently in and according to which I's are currently in control. If they have flipped in the Queen of Hearts (i.e. have become negatively polarized in the emotional part of the intellectual center), then everyone outside them selves is responsible for every imagined slight or injury. When one is in that negative polarity it's not possible to be self responsible at all, and as a result the accusations externalize and fly about. See the play as one of a polarity shift, a mechanical shift, and work to not attach personal significance to it.

Q&A

Dr. J: Can you remember what you were going to ask?

STUDENT: Umm, I notice that I tend to avoid…where I see something and don't point it out in the moment. Sometimes it turns into resentment and sometimes it doesn't. In that case, I can see and I've seen other people point stuff out. For example, what happened earlier with the dryer. This is what I saw. You started talking to her about stuff. Then it almost looked like you could have been avoiding your own issue. Can that happen where you start pointing someone else's stuff out and it originally starts as a good intention but then becomes an avoidance of something that came up for you?

Dr. J: Well, not an avoidance. It's actually quite easy to have the idea you're going to point something out and then get caught up in an issue you have. That's actually quite possible.

STUDENT: In that moment, what do you do? The whole of it originally was to wake someone else up but then you fell asleep in the process. You kind of wake up to it. That's one of the reasons I avoid pointing it out.

Dr. J: Hypothetically, if that's in reality what's occurring, it's actually impossible to "wake up", as you say, another person by pointing out their stuff. Most of the time even the urge to do this is coming from some lower part of a center and or false personality. The answer when you feel the urge to "point out" is that you stop thought and you start self-remembering. In other words, you have to just stop.

Another point of it is, in a school that is ongoing we've been having a conversation for five years before you came. There are certain patterns we are working on, that I'm working on with J, for example, of which you are unaware. You haven't been here long enough to know. It might appear I'm doing one thing when I'm actually doing something completely different. You won't know that because you don't have enough information yet to be able to say one way or the other whether someone like me in this situation is making a sincere correction or not. You have no way to know. You don't have enough information. Sadly, you won't have that ability for quite some time. That's the reality of it.

In most schools for developing consciousness, new students aren't allowed to give photographs or stops to other students for some period of time. The students could be constrained in this way for years. They are not allowed. Not only are you told to resist the temptation, if you're caught doing it, an advanced or senior student will go, "Whoa, whoa, whoa, what are you doing? Remember the part where you don't give corrections until I or we tell you that you can do this? Normally, we don't allow it for one year. There's a reason for that. It's because your judgment as a new person is still 99% based on pre-existing ideas and understandings about what certain behaviors mean. You haven't practiced having other behaviors and other understandings. You can't help it. You interpret it based on your previous experience."

Let's say it's on a sliding scale. People who have been studying and practicing longer have more practice in the way of being able to do corrections and to photograph and to make the call one way or the other, whether something is concurrent with what we're doing or not. New people virtually can't at all.

This kind of schoolwork is not the kind of school where new students walk in and they have an equal voice, vote or say in how anything at all is done. The learning curve is too gradual. It takes a long time. For example, just in talking about basic principles. If the basic principles are in five different books and you've only read the intro to the first book and a hundred pages in the second book and you have 4000 pages more to go to cover the basic principles, then if someone is communicating based on some ideas in book 3, you'll have no clue where they're coming from, why they're saying what they're saying or what the exercise is or what they're doing or why they might be doing it. You will try to interpret that based on what you know, which is completely different. You will be wrong.

One of the things about schools is that we try to keep the conversations and corrections as close to the level of understanding of the people who are present as possible. That's not always possible. For example, J and I have been having this conversation and working on certain issues for seven years ahead of you. We've made some progress on some things. Other things we are still working on.

J: One of my biggest things is that I don't take corrections well. It has an impact on my ability to be in physical class with other students. Sometimes when I receive a correction I melt down. I start crying in the middle of class.

Dr. J: You also need to understand that this was not a pattern invented with or by me. This is different. In real life, in my past I was resistant to taking corrections, too. One of the hardest things I had to learn was how to take correction in school life. I wouldn't let you correct me over virtually anything outside of school. Where it saved me, where I was able to make the adjustment was when I realized it's a special environment, so there are special rules there. It's not out in the world. We're not doing this out in the world or in public. It's not for public consumption.

J: Except for occasionally at Wal-Mart when it's necessary.

Dr. J: Well, it's between us but it's not for public consumption. It's not about that. If I'm getting corrections out in the world, I might be equally as resistant as anybody else, but in the work, if that correction was coming from a teacher or one of my peers or seniors, I would take it to heart. Why? I agreed to do so as part of the process of learning how to do this. It's necessary.

Another reason we do not encourage newer students to correct each other too much is because the corrections need to be balanced and cannot always be emphasizing the negative. There has to be a proportional emphasis on positive qualities as well. Otherwise the whole process of giving corrections or photographs is just another form of negative reinforcement.

Corrections are proportional to the level of being and consciousness of the person giving them. You can always tell where there is mechanical resistance in how quick the defense comes. For example, if I give a correction and there's a delay, and then there's a studied response, well, then we may have something to talk about. If I give a correction, however, and the defense happens instantly, you're not going to win. What's going to happen is a little time will settle and you'll say, "Yeah I know. I could've been more attentive or done this differently." It's a time delay idea that determines whether the response is mechanical.

Although you know, I have to say this. If you're really smart, you can learn how to delay. The challenge is the false personality can learn how to delay. In other words, you give me a correction and I can just learn how not to respond immediately and then respond more thoughtfully. Guess what? That's better because that little time lag in your response at least creates the possibility to observe your self a little bit before you start to respond.

STUDENT: I didn't really understand, so this can be another discussion. You said, you can leave anytime. Anyone can leave at anytime. How does that play into the working on your self where you make commitments and stick to them no matter the external circumstances, which could be people.

Dr. J: Right.

STUDENT: How does that work?

Dr. J: If you do leave, then you do abandon the work in the particular school and perhaps the internal or self-work, as well. It takes a certain amount of work before anyone is able to be self sustaining, and some never get there. However, at all times you have the right to choose.

STUDENT: Then when it's not mutual, it's still an external circumstance, but then it has to be mutual.

Dr. J: No, it doesn't have to be mutual. For example, anyone can decide to not be mutual at any time. That's their right. They can just get up and leave. The thing that's really important is two things. The first is that this may be literally where their work in the school stops. The second is in my response to that. If the school continues, I'm still under the obligation to respond to even that in the best way I can. That response has nothing to do with the person who's leaving.

We have to have an understanding that it's always voluntary. Everyone is always free to go, to quit and to step away. Why? People do and people will. That's an external event. If I'm tied up to the idea that everybody can keep their commitments, then I'm going to be really unhappy because most of the time people don't keep their word. Remember, the only thing we can guarantee is a person's weaknesses. What can I absolutely guarantee about person A, B or C? The list is going to contain something about a weakness. That's what I can absolutely guarantee. Can I guarantee a person will be consistent or mean what they say and do what they say or keep their word? No, forget it. It's not going to happen.

We operate in spite of that. We know it's not negative. It's the nature of the beast. The only way you can ethically keep a promise is if you're working on your self. A lot of people think they make promises or commitments and keep them. They don't really consider that it was still all about external environment. As long as their external environment was positive and supportive and non-challenging they stayed. They think that is the same thing as having kept their commitment. That's not it. The only time it counts is when you hold commitment in the face of adversity, when you hold that commitment in the face of challenge when everything in the world says you should let it go. Then it counts because there is a struggle. If there is no struggle, it doesn't count. Does that help?

STUDENT: A little bit. In the context of you in particular saying you can leave at any time, does it make any difference how much responsibility you have?

Dr. J: No it doesn't.

STUDENT: Thinking about, like if I was going to be a teacher.

Dr. J: For example, you have a congressman who has worked his whole life to develop a career and goes through a competitive process to become elected as a congressman. He has to have sponsors and acquire millions of dollars of revenue and donations. It may take hundreds of thousands of people to put him into office, then he goes into office and throws it away entirely with ten minutes of bad behavior. Well, he had the choice. It was voluntary to remain true to his ethics and keep that commitment and continue to be the congressman. Honoring the effort and contribution of all the people, many of whom might have devoted a large part of their lives for many years to get that person into that place where they could maybe do something good. He had a choice. It's voluntary. The congressman acts badly, gets caught and next day, gone. On to the new career. Golf or boat captain in the Bahamas maybe.

STUDENT: What I'm trying to ask is, does stopping a commitment mean you're stopping working on your self?

122

Dr. J: It could be. Certain work you can only do in certain environments. Regardless of why you leave that environment, that work stops. If you're not in that environment anymore, then that work stops. Now what's the condition? If you've gotten to a point in the work where you are self-sufficient and self-determining, then you are less dependent on the external school. Here's where we get off into fantasy. Everybody thinks they were there the first day they showed up. That's what fantasy life says. I was already there the day I showed up. They are lucky to have me.

"You're not the boss of me. I can leave anytime I want and I can keep doing what I've been doing." Well, the answer is, yes that's true. Yes you can and yes you are. You're going to stay right where you're at chasing your tail like you always have and that's not going to change. Or maybe you stick to something and achieve something a little more permanent. Eventually, if you have that permanent core, which we call magnetic center, you might get to a point where it's actually irrelevant where you are. It's no longer important whether you are in a school or not. Why? You have a magnetic center. You are now a self-sustaining, self-motivating, self-generating entity. That's quite rare. Most of the time we need dedicated environments to do very specific work. What is typical at a certain level of being is for students to cherry pick schools. They go to one school for a little bit to get a little of this. Then they go to another school for a little bit to get a little of that. Then they go to another school to get a little of this and that. They are under the assumption that having a little tit and tat from here and there and in between is the same thing as having something substantial. None of that ever does add up to anything substantial, from the point of view of this work. Certain kinds of results are based on consistent, singular efforts over a period of time. But the false personality says, well I made a little progress so now I can move on. The problem is that the false personality is who's determining whether you made a little progress or not.

False personality always wants to stop shy of learning or acquiring any facility that might lead to its death. We're always jack-of-all-trades and master of none. It's why the strongest inclination of the greatest number of students is to have the lowest level of mastery and competency they can get by with without making any commitment whatsoever to actually conquering or mastering anything at all. Occasionally, rare opportunities exist with special people who are able to be a little more awake, a little more conscious and to have a little more of a magnetic center in development that it can actually work into a situation in a sustainable community where they can make a commitment to do a certain kind of work and last long enough in the work to actually achieve something substantial, which will last hypothetically forever. Most students stop short.

That goes back to the question: why do we leave the work that we do? We leave because at some point we get attached to some negative idea or emotion and we draw a hard line in the sand, and then that becomes the wedge that drives us away from what we're doing.

J: That's what I was asking.

Dr. J: There's always justification later. I left for a good reason. I stopped working on myself because they weren't working on myself the way I wanted to. Even though I am a total beginner and I have no idea what they're up to or what they mean by what they say, I have determined it is not correct for me. Therefore, I am leaving. One time that happens. Two times that happens. A hundred times it happens. Over a lifetime it happens over and over again. Individuals who have this behavior will have very good patter. They can talk freely and deeply about a lot of different things, yet in their actual personal life they're not making that progress. The demons are still running amuck because they didn't get far enough in any particular area to make certain, permanent changes.

All this is hypothetical, especially with students or novices, because it's all contingent on a lot of work, which is hypothetical until the work is actually done.

J: Persuade without destruction. I don't really understand that.

Dr. J: It's about the concept of nonviolent communication. Persuade without being violent and without destruction. Just like I said. Don't use threats as the basis of your persuasion. In other words, it's like coaching versus being a dictator. We have rules and things we want to be strong about. There is a little bit of latitude as to how we want to come to agreements about these things. It's better if we can come to agreements with persuasion versus threats.

STUDENT: That ties into being diplomatic rather than blunt, right?

Dr. J: Right

STUDENT: Because it reduces the reaction on either end.

Dr. J: Right. diplomacy may reduce the negative tendencies on both ends. For example, we have to be hard about some things because that's how we in a sense establish the borders of the school and inner circle versus outer circle. Yet, we want to do it in the most diplomatic way possible. Again, even if someone is doing something that is a violation of principles or rules, we don't want to necessarily resolve that with threats or coercion or anything destructive. We want to come to it in the most diplomatic way we can using persuasion.

That's a practice because it's much easier to say, "Oh, you broke the rule so you're out of here." Man, that would save me a whole world of discussion and headaches and diplomacy. It's quite simple. There are schools that choose to be efficient in that manner. They're just like, if you break the rule, you're out of here. Sorry, if you wanted to be here, why did you break the rule? You agreed to this before you came. There's really nothing to talk about. Hope you have a nice life.

Most of the time I choose not to do that. I will bring up the rule but then I come back and say, let's talk about this. What is going on? Why is the inclination here? Why are the boundaries being pushed or challenged? Where does that come from and what is the end result of this process? We try to bring in rationality and diplomacy. The end result is that we come up with an agreement, which is either a correction of some kind or an understanding or even apologies sometimes. The idea is that it keeps us engaged longer. It keeps us engaged at a higher level. It keeps us engaged in a more positive way. It possibly opens the door to more communication, which I think is always important.

Persuade without destruction.

So make a correction. Just making a hard correction by saying no, actually notice you were being disruptive. That's not disruptive. That's a hard correction. That's very clear. Now, because we made the correction, there is no excuse to beat somebody up. For example, if I point out a student is breaking the rules or is out of line in concordance with what was agreed, it still doesn't give me the right to beat them up. If I get proactive and try to hurt them, then I would be wrong. That would be some mechanical expression on my part. Talking about where this gets funky is when I've had to bodily remove somebody from the property because of bad behavior. How do I do that without anger and without becoming destructive and emotionally involved and reactive? That takes a lot of practice. Where that starts is in the little things. We have little disagreements. We work on how we handle that. If we learn how to do that, then we can learn what to do when someone is being violent. I can physically remove someone from the property without the attachment, retribution and resentment. That's part of life.

That is part of having a school because we are open to people coming from the outside to the outer circle. People come into the outer circle who are going to lose it because something's broken. It's not going to get fixed fast enough for it not to be an issue. Being in a school presupposes we all have a certain level of development that allows us to accept a certain level of discipline and correction, and to apply ourselves with a certain amount of enthusiasm. If that's not there, if we're not willing to do a certain amount of research, do the reading, do the study, do the practice, it's not sustainable. We have to have a way to understand that because eventually people who are in our system and not committed and practicing at a high level have to be moved out, in order to keep the central focus high. That doesn't mean to hurt them. I don't mean to do anything that's negative whatsoever. I mean that we have outer and inner circles.

We have outer circles of people who are positive and occasionally doing a little bit of self-work, and we support that and they support us. They are not in the inner circle and they have no idea what kind of conversations we have in here, nor will they ever because their level of participation is what determines that. I don't care, for me, two students or a hundred and two students. I don't care. The same standards apply. Why? I've been taught that's how these schools have been able to survive for many generations. I cannot personally verify that because I haven't been in those many generations of schools. I have seen consistency in the schools I was in, over twenty, thirty years. I've talked to people who were thirty years ahead of me or even forty. Their stories are absolutely consistent. I look at the writings and teachings from a hundred years ago and it's consistent with what the real life people tell me. I have a lot of evidence to suggest that's true. I don't spend any time trying to sort out new ways of doing things, in this regard. I call that re-inventing the wheel. I don't spend a lot of time trying to re-invent the wheel. For example, I'm not trying to invent a new system of acupuncture. I'm pretty happy with that. I think they probably did a pretty good job inventing acupuncture. Now what I'm doing is exploring alternative and novel ways to use the understandings, like in the EDS, the electro-acupuncture and electro-dermal. These are new and novel adaptations. Why they are possible is because of new technology which did not exist four thousand years ago. They certainly exist now. Trust me, if the old ancient Chinese Reishi had had the technology we have now, they would have been using it up one side and down the other. Certainly, all the who's who of acupuncturists today are into the technology.

124

When I think about Fourth Way consciousness principles, healing, martial arts and all these different disciplines of meditation and mindfulness, that all come together here, I'm not interested in reinventing the wheel but rather finding what is the best way we are going to apply these things. That's what I care about.

STUDENT: Have no expectations from anyone. You were mostly emphasizing expectations of good. But you can have expectations of their weaknesses all the time, just like you said you assume everyone is iodine deficient, you would assume negative as a way to work with it so you're prepared. Because I've noticed that a lot of times, I've assumed the negative but then it turns into imagination and keeps me from talking to them or something...

Dr. J: Well, it is imagination if you assume the negative and then you elaborate.

STUDENT: So what do you do then?

Dr. J: In other words, it's one thing to assume the only thing I can absolutely guarantee about you is your weaknesses. I just know that. Now, it's imagination to go into all of what they might be. To go off into that is imagination. Then, if I make decisions and actions based on that, that's identification.

STUDENT: So, what's the point of having expectations that.

Dr. J: So I'm not disappointed when you disappoint me. I'm not sidetracked when you disappoint me.

STUDENT: So, expect the worst? No?

Dr. J: No. Actually, there is no inverse. It's not really helpful to try and think of what's the opposite or is that just being pessimistic because those terms don't mean anything.

STUDENT: Just basically knowing we are all mechanical most of the time.

Dr. J: Right. It's a work idea. In other words, don't take it outside the four walls. It's a work idea, that by having that perspective it allows us to have access to insight about ourselves, because other people are just like us. We can always see the weaknesses in other people. We can never see them in ourselves, not really. We hide the best ones because they are too special for us to see. We can see them in other people. We want to see them because I have to intellectually keep coming back to the idea that your weaknesses are no different than mine. It might just be where we are in that wheel. You might be on this side with this issue and I'm over here with this issue. I think I'm superior because I'm not experiencing your issue at this particular moment. Man, wait ten minutes and I am. That ten minutes could be another lifetime but it doesn't mean we are superior. From the point of view of practice and work we are not being pessimistic. We are trying to get the clearest picture that we are absolutely and completely machines. If we don't really understand that at an emotional level and get emotional about it, there's no incentive to look for the possibility of what is not mechanical about us. Is there anything at all about you that's not mechanical? Prove it. You can't because it always comes back to everyone having their own perception of what is real.

STUDENT: You can't at this level, right? I mean, when you first start. There's no way.

Dr. J: Correct. There is a way. That's what we're practicing. There is a way, possibly, but if it is possible, it's not at the beginning. It's at the end. It's not something you do at the beginning. If it's possible to have a particular way of knowing or way of being that is not mechanical and is representative of positive emotion, the possibility of higher consciousness is not manifest at the beginning. It's the result of a process. In this system, deconstruction is the source of the process. For example, you go into an old, abandoned neighborhood and you want to build a new housing project. Well, you can't just go in and start building new houses. You have to tear all the old stuff down. You might have to rip up all the sewer pipes and all the power lines. Literally, you might have to rip up all the existing superstructure and infrastructure and start from the ground up running new sewers, new power, etc. After you've done all the deconstruction and demolition work, you might have to blow up buildings with explosives. That's messy, loud, big and dangerous! Everybody run! Be far away when it happens. That's absolutely what's required to make something new and utterly and completely different. That's us. We're still in the demolition stage. We are nowhere near enjoying the benefits of the point of view of the high rise view point of the new construction. It's like in Vegas where they wanted to build the new MGM pyramid. They had to destroy like two city blocks of casinos to build that one hotel. They did it with explosives and dynamite. They shut the whole city down and set off air raid sirens because they expected bricks to fly as far as half a mile from the explosions. They did that and of course sold it and sold tickets to it. It's Las Vegas, so even when they destroy something it's an event worth charging admission for. Then they had to clean up the debris and start building.

For us, it's like we are sitting in the architect's office and the hotel is still there. I go ahead and move into the penthouse suite in the model and think I'm there. The actual deconstruction hasn't taken place and the new building hasn't been created. In my head, I'm already in the penthouse and none of the work has been done. It's all imagination. In Fourth Way, the work says most thoughts about these higher states are imagination. We didn't do the work necessary to demolish the building, reconstruct the neighborhood, build the new building, furnish and then move in. We don't possess it but we think we do. That is delusional.

Not being in delusion is hard. It's rough and not pretty sometimes. I'm not successful building the new building, the higher consciousness. That's okay. If I can just clear out some of the debris, I'm ahead. If I just knock down some of the junk obscuring me from being able to see what's going on in my life, I'm ahead, much less if I build this superstructure, this hypothetical, higher level of being or consciousness. Who cares? I need to simply start getting rid of some of the riff-raff keeping me from being present and being myself. Then I am successful. It's not easy.

J: I know that for me it's helpful to hear that there's going to be chaos, confusion, and you're going to feel out of sorts and out of balance. It's more exciting to me to hear that than it is to hear the pink, fluffy slippers and clouds with the silver lining. The soft squishy stuff doesn't seem to have an effect on me at all, no matter how many times in my past I've done yoga or sat for a couple years doing meditations, it didn't help clear the trees. It's like I had a chainsaw but I didn't know how to use it. So I just sat down and played with it, lalalalalala.

Dr. J: Well who knows if you had a chainsaw? You might have had a Wiffle bat.

CHAPTER SIX: Exercises for Dealing with Others

Dr. J: Man do we need that. It's been my experience that these kinds of things are almost worth memorizing. If not memorizing, at least learning until they are second nature. I'm just going to run through the list here.

1. Avoid violent emotions. You diminish your self if you take small things seriously.

We really have to work on putting the brakes on taking very small issues too seriously. When we do that, we diminish our capacity to even consider the big ones because we are caught up in the minutia. A lot of times we miss opportunities to miss something big because we were distracted with something small we were overemphasizing.

2. When you are censored, do not justify.

Again, this is for school. This is not for life. We have established there are different rules in a school or work house (a community of people working on themselves) than out in the "chaotic world not about that". When you correct, or take a snapshot of, someone that very clearly illustrates a state of sleep, you hold it up and say, "Hey check out this Polaroid I got." A lot of times we don't want to see that photograph or we say, "That's not me. I wasn't doing that." The person who took the photograph says, "But you were the only person in the room. You are the only person in the picture. I kind of think that was you."

The trick is to just take it. Don't justify it. Just acknowledge it. That's why I say things like "the proper response to a correction is…" When you get a correction and immediately go into justification and argument, which feeds the false personality. That is the most normal thing in the world everyone does. It's not about accusing, because there's really no big crime that was committed. For example, when I was talking about the buzzer. In the picture of the world, it's no big deal. It's interesting how the most normal thing about our false personality is that when we are caught, accused, photographed or censored in any way, small or big, the instant reaction is to justify, defend, argue and Immediately prove it's not deserved, appropriate, applicable. It's special circumstances. "I did it on purpose. I don't care." It goes through this whole litany of things. It's instant. There's no delay. It is a mechanical feature. Everybody does it.

It's not about right or wrong. The justification coming from ego and false personality says, "I don't have to agree with you if you're wrong. If you're correcting me, you have to be wrong. You can't be right by definition." I'll start defending before I even really think about what the conversation is. I'll already have a perfect defense to that censor, photograph or correction. The work idea is when we are censored to just accept it and not to justify it in the moment. This is completely contrary to your natural, mechanical inclination.

That's why in class I sometimes say, "Actually, that's a story. The correct response to a correction is, 'Yes, I accept it.'" Later we work out whether or not there was some justification. Most of the time it turns out there wasn't and we can move on. By not justifying a correction with a story of why you were doing what you were doing, there is a possibility of a moment where the justification is not there. If I can have a moment when that justification is not there, there is friction and I might learn something about myself. I might see something I would never get to see by always justify.

3. Be benevolent even to unjust men.

Here's a practice. How do you turn the other cheek? When you can't do it to your self or the people you live and work with, how are you going to do it to people you don't know who are unjust, wrong or dangerous. The truth is, you can't. We need to practice on many levels.

It's really easy to have an "us and them" type of scenario. The practice is that when you notice your self going into that mode of "This is right. This is not right. Us and them. We are righteous. They are not. Our point of view is correct. Theirs is not. The work idea is to think and react to them in a benevolent way. To understand and project that unconsciousness is on a continuum. Irrationality is on a continuum. Maybe at this moment, they are not the most dominant parts, but in other circumstances, I know for a fact I've been irrational. When I look out in the world and see people behaving irrationally, I have to have compassion. Had I been as publicly displayed at my most irrational moments, I don't think I would appear any more sane or stable or loving.

When I was having, at one point in my life, a violent outburst, had that been recorded on the video and flashed on YouTube and front lined on the news and in the paper, it wouldn't have come across any less rational or benevolent than Sadam Hussein going after someone. For me it wasn't as public. I had my meltdowns in private, and I was trying very hard to keep them private. When people are unjust and doing bad things in public it is no different than doing those very same things in private. I don't condone it. The way to relate to it is to be benevolent, less judgmental and more compassionate. The worst behavior others exhibit is still reflective of fundamental parts we always have in our nature because they are common to our machine.

4. Reproach neither others nor your self.

This continues with #3. Don't talk smack. Don't belittle. Don't demean others or your self. Don't be critical in a demeaning way with others or your self. Don't beat your self up. If you have a bad minute or a bad day, observe it, acknowledge, forgive it and move on. Come back to the present moment and do the best work you can at this moment. Don't beat your self up because an hour ago you were having an issue. Don't for one second beat up someone else because you think his or her efforts are not superior.

5. Do not blame others.

That's different from taking a photograph or correcting. Giving a correction is like catching someone asleep and prodding him or her with a stick. Blaming is a tool or technique we use when we're asleep to divert attention from our selves. That's different. When I say don't blame others, you need to know you are going to do it. "I'm unhappy because of you. I'm attached to this feeling because of you. I'm being distracted right now because of you." That's blaming someone else for what you are doing or not doing.

Part of the reason we respond to other people the way we do is because of hormones. We exchange pheromones and have attraction and/or repulsion. We have mental and emotional states that follow. Of course, we are aware of this. After the fact we try to justify that there's some reason for it. If it works out, it's a blessing. If it doesn't work out, it's their fault. This is a way of covering the lack of control biology creates. It's also a really big way we fail to take responsibility for our own internal dialogue. When I blame others, I fail to take responsibility for my own internal monitoring, for my own responsibility to observe myself and to practice self-remembering, to not express negativity, to create aims, to practice building discipline, to be a good householder and whatever I am working on. It is just another reason, a good one, for not working. It's a good one because it's never about you. It's always about them.

6. Choose to serve rather than rule. Never push your self to the front.

In conscious schools, the responsible people end up being in charge. The function of them being in charge is that they are working on themselves as a first priority. Their second priority is to help as many people as possible to get to as high a level as possible in order to have partners who can help them work on themselves. That's the point. It is not for any particular group of people to benefit from everyone else's efforts. That's not the point. It's a service point. Serve your self by working on your self. Serving others may help them be partners to help you work on your self.

Never push your self to the front, but if you are in front, you have to accept that. Being in front is not bad or good. Don't push your self to the front. If you find your self there, how do you accept that and integrate that into your work life? Trust me. Being in front is the hard place to work from. It's not the easy place. It's a lot easier to work on your self when you are kind of in the back of the room and out of the line of fire and direct sight.

The challenge with small groups in a school is that there is no place to hide. In bigger groups, you can go at a much slower pace and have a much easier time because it's possible to hide. It's possible no one notices you weren't even present in a class or in a work effort. In small schools that's not possible, so the pressure is much more intense. It also means the benefits in the short term are potentially much higher because the quality of the work can be much higher.

7. Laugh at the boring expressions of self-esteem, especially your own.

It's a really good practice to take your self with a great deal of humor. We are so serious about ourselves. If you really think about it, how funny it is the way we're made, the way we interact with each other and how we work, I mean come on, it's funny. We're just like one of those Masonic Shrine Clown Circuses running through our day on our little tricycles as big as a hand bag scooting around the house trying to get things done, pulling rubber chickens out of our butts and blowing our little horns, all the time taking ourselves seriously.

8. If anyone wishes to be in false personality, let them. Do not fight or challenge.

If we're working on something and someone is in false personality and you try to correct them or give a photography or bring it to their attention and they are super resistant, just let them be. Don't fight or challenge. If you pointed something out to me, for example, what I do is give you the perfect excuse and justification for why I'm being the way I am, which of course is obviously not true. You can see that as clear as a bell. I'm adamant about my righteousness to be in false personality. Once I prove really hard that I'm going to hold to that argument no matter what, then back off, unless the issue is threatening the welfare or wellbeing of the house or personal safety. Basically, we have to walk away sometimes. It's not a bad thing.

Usually what happens is that I'll get a correction and defend and justify it. You'll try to communicate to me that it's not really working. I disagree and will be judgmental and defensive and maybe even proactively aggressive, or I'll be defensive to the point of withdrawing and shutting down completely, both are the same. When you realize I have stopped responding one way or the other, your work is to try and let it go. Walk away for a minute. After a few minutes, I see the part of me that was paying attention, because I'm committed to observing myself. That observer tape is playing even when I don't see it. After a couple of minutes without the external pressure, it comes back and it goes, "Oh, actually they were right. I don't really have an excuse. I wasn't really paying attention. Okay, alright. I'll come to that realization and make the correction." Then we'll move on.

There's a point to where we can wrestle with each other and it will work. There's also a point to where we dig our heels in and there is no progress being made. At that point, we really need to let it go. The inclination of the machine is to go to the end of a thing. It's always to take it to its final conclusion. We want to work against those inclinations.

9. Balance negative I's about someone with positive I's.

If you find your self thinking negative thoughts about someone, then a work idea is to on purpose think positive thoughts about them. It's very telling that if you are out of sorts with someone and you can't think of a single, positive thing, that's an indication you are in a very mechanical and reactive mind. It's not conscious. You might think it's conscious, but it's not. You should be able to find something positive about the person you are thinking about.

Here is an example of how the principle can be applied. Most people think of Adolph Hitler on their top ten list of most negative and or flawed people. Let me tell you a positive thing about Adolf Hitler. He apparently loved his girlfriend Eva Braun. Apparently, right to the very end, no matter what, through thick and thin, from the beginning to the end, he was consistent with her. He seemed to be very devoted to her. Everybody else was expendable, but not Eva. This guy was messed up, don't get me wrong, up one side and down the other, but if I think about it and apply the principle, I can actually have some positive I's about him.

129

You should be able to be positive about anyone if you're not being knee-jerk mechanical. Even the person you think has hurt you the most in your life has positive values. Even if you think a relationship was an utter and complete failure, because in the past I could describe one as my nuclear holocaust of relationships. Yet, when I'm in a work mind, I can come back and acknowledge that it wasn't all bad. There were periods when things were working and I felt very satisfied. I realized I might have been nappy and asleep at the wheel. That's why it was so comfortable for me, because I really didn't know what was going on. I can come up with some positive I's.

This is no easy exercise. It's right up there with Jesus asking for forgiveness for his jailors while on the cross. Do you think that it was at that moment when he decided to take up the practice? I think not.

10. Never redress slander with slander.

You hear someone talk smack about you, don't talk smack about them. You hear someone say something bad about the school, don't say something bad about them. Don't do it. Be aware of how you react to perceptions of threat. Slander is a perception of threat. Why are they saying these things if they are not being threatened? Don't react in kind.

11. Do not argue with the many I's. Silence is the best answer.

When give you a correction I'm kind of acting like an I outside of you, then you argue and justify and defend with me. If you're doing that with me, you're doing it inside your head, too, with more I's. You are having discord. It's like that illustration of the angel on one shoulder and the devil on the other. One I wants to do this and another I is saying no, don't do that. Another I is saying, no no we have to do this, it's a really good thing. The other I is saying, to hell with them, let's do this other thing.

The best thing to do when you observe this back and forth with these I's is just to find a quiet place. What is that quiet place in your head if the I's are arguing? It's the observer mind. It's the I that can observe. Go to that place if you can. Watch the fistfight happening. Observe there are two parts of you having an argument right now. How interesting is that? If you can observe that, it means there are three present. That's very important.

12. Be diplomatic rather than blunt.

I have to work on this myself a lot because my machine, my natural inclination, is to be blunt. That's a really big one for me—to practice being more diplomatic in my communications since my natural inclination is not to be.

When I was a fighter, other people's natural inclination when they fight is to come at their opponent gradually from the side angles and wear them down and strategize and work into it until they find a position of advantage while getting hit as little as possible. Mine was to walk up to my opponent and knock them down. I spent a lot of fights just chasing people because they would be trying to get away. I would be very upfront and nose to nose and not so from the side. That's my machine's inclination.

Other machines' inclinations are, when confronted from the front, to divert and go to the side, shift the energy, be elusive and come at it from another angle, to be more diplomatic.

13. Do not bluntly say, "None of your business." Be kind.

I think as a practice we do pretty well with that. The trick is don't draw hard lines in the sand when you are in a work environment, because whenever you bluntly draw a line in the sand by saying, "This area is none of your business," as of that moment you shut off the possibility of working on the issue, whatever it is. You pick one issue and then another and another and then all of a sudden "none of your business" will turn into everything.

One of the ideas we work on in a school is not drawing hard lines in the sand for what we will allow introspection of, or what we will work on or not work on, because whatever that issue is, we can work on everything, we can talk about everything but my relationships with other people. That's off limits. That's a line in the sand.

If the chief place where you display false personality and negative emotion is in my relationship issues and I just made a hard line that we can't even talk about that because it's off limits as my private space and private time, well that will become the primary issue that separates you from being able to work on your self. That will become the primary issue that will separate me from being able to work in the school.

What if I say, "We can work on anything and everything and I will work on myself except I will not allow you to challenge my ideas on religion"? If my ideas about religion are where I have the most ingrained aspects of my false personality and negative emotion because of my history with religion and my family's religion and how religion has been a force in my life, which is why of course I'm drawing that line in the sand, then that's going to be an absolute Impediment at some point. It has to be. If I say I'm going to work on everything but my negative emotions, that's the end of the work because most of the things we have to work on in ourselves, one way or the other, deal with negative emotion. If I say, we can work on the mind, the body, the spirit, attitudes towards life but we cannot work on sex. Well, as soon as I say that, sex will be my primary issue. I will realize that's where I hold the most expression of false personality and negative emotion. That will be an absolute impediment. That's where I'll stop.

The machine has this instinct for self-preservation. False personality also has this instinct. It doesn't want to die. When we start bringing energy, attention and consciousness to bear on negative emotion and false personality, false personality will look for any hiding hole, any place it can build a fortress, any place it can declare off limits. Why? To weather the storm. Right now, we are working on ourselves at a very high level. False personality is under attack from all sides. It's fighting for its life. What is it going to do? It's going to find a place to make a fortress or a place to hide. We can always identify those places. Those are always going to be the places we draw our hard lines in the sand. False personality is going to hide where it feels most secure, where it has the most control, where it can preserve a nugget of negativity that cannot be dissuaded, that cannot be challenged, changed or what have you.

Again, just like in the samurai way, which is a different manifestation of this kind of school we are talking about. I'm saying maybe there was a core of conscious school in the Samurai tradition. Maybe not all samurai were practicing it, but there was a core. Some of it is expressed in this writing, the Hagakure or the Bushido Code, in the way of the warrior and the resolute acceptance of death. That's always been taken to mean separation from life. In other words, if the samurai said they would accept they are going to die in real life, what they were actually saying is they would accept any pressure to be real, to be true to themselves up to and including death.

I was saying this to J yesterday, the ways I interpreted the Bushido Code was: I will give up my life before I lose my mind. In other words, my true self and my ability to be transparent to myself are more important than my physical life. I will give up my life before I will give up my self. As a samurai, that means I don't have any lines in the sand. Everything is up for grabs. Everything is up for introspection. There is no part of my life that is taboo. There is no part of my personality which cannot be looked at or worked on. When I find areas where I hold out, I know that is chief negative feature.

When I'm listening to the photographs and the comments coming from my work partners (my family and friends who are in the work with me) I start to notice areas I avoid. When I start to notice those are the areas I avoid, if I'm mapping out this false personality, I now know that's where it lives. Whatever those areas are, they are going to be the strongholds for the false personality. Normally, those areas are invisible to us. We have all kinds of ways of hiding in them. For example, here's one. You agree to work on something but never do. Oh, that's a brilliant tactic.

We just went over number 13 with this idea, "bluntly, none of your business, etc. etc. and be kind." The idea is not to draw hard lines in the sand. We want to be aware when we do this. We want to be really aware. Where do I tell you to back off? The last thing I had mentioned is (I say this in class a lot), helping is another way of hiding. In the work, one of the ways we hide is by agreeing to do work we never intend to do. It could be as simple as house keeping. I agree to keep the kitchen clean, then there are the 25 ways I don't. I agree to help keep the books organized on the shelf, but then there are the 50 reasons why I don't do that. It could be little things. It could also be that I have a lot of issues with relationships. I know that's one of the primary things I need to work on in my life. Guess what? I'm going to work on, focus on, emphasize, everything but. The whole time I'm doing that, I'm going to be talking about how important it is to make progress in my relationships, but I'm not actually going to do anything different. It's anything we want to pick. It can be mental, psychological, past life or trauma issues, repressed issues, injury issues, disease, emotional, physical, sexual, or anything. False personality is creative.

14. If you are unjustly treated, stop the I's and use the energy to remember your self.

In other words, we are coming from a point of view in which we wouldn't be together in the first place if we were here to try and hurt each other, to be unjust. If we thought that was true, we shouldn't be here. It's not why we are here. Sometimes we get the feeling like, you know, you're not really treating me right. You're being unjust to me.

If you are unjustly treated, stop the I's and use the energy to remember your self. The truth is that you are not really being unjustly treated. It might be that somebody else is not being as conscious in the moment as they could be. Alright, so what? Everybody is mechanical. The trick is, the question is, how do you respond to that? If you are out in the world, when someone is unjust to you, you react and you escalate and/or you react and run away and/or you react and then bad mouth him or her for six months. In the school, if you are unjustly treated, the discipline is to stop the I's. What are the I's? All the defensive, all the justification and reactive I's, you can't treat me this way I's, in all their variety. Stop on a dime. Stop it when you notice it. Then use that energy, that Impetus to remember your self. The appropriate response is to remember your self.

15. Have no expectations from anyone.

You can absolutely depend on a person's weaknesses. Every time we depend on each other's strengths and consistencies, we are disappointed. No one ever treats us quite the way we expect them too. No one is ever as consistent as we would like them to be. No one is ever as strong consistently as we would hope they would be. Therefore, we are always reactive, disappointed and in a situation where we are going to start holding accounts.

The only thing you can absolutely depend on is a person's weaknesses. If that's what you can depend on, then you can't be disappointed. That can't be grounds for criticism, that they are not consistent or that they are weak. It can't be a reason to be critical because everybody is inconsistent.

16. When accusing others internally, stop thought, and self-remember.

I say it different ways. Sometimes I say, just let it go. What do I mean by that? I mean to stop the thought. Don't have the next thought. It's not about just coming to stillness like slamming on the breaks and coming to a screeching halt. Stop and self-remember. What you are doing is like a train on track A. All of a sudden you realize there is an on coming train heading straight for you, also on track A. Rather than just slamming on the brakes hoping the train doesn't run into you, you hit the brakes as you change tracks and get on a completely different track. That train misses you and life is good.

When accusing others internally, stop thought and self-remember. Cease this internal mental activity and accusing others or having "bad thoughts" about people or being critical or judgmental about them. "I don't like how so and so is treating me. They aren't being respectful of me. They aren't listening to me. They aren't validating me. They aren't paying me enough attention. They are all accusatory. They're in my business. They don't respect my space. They don't pick up after themselves. They expect too much of me."

When you are observing your self and you see, whoa, I'm in that state of mind, you'll just notice you are in an accusatory state of mind. The discipline is to stop thought and self-remember. In other words, STOP! Change tracks and put the emphasis back on you. Up to that moment, it's all about them. You are allowing a chain of causation in your head to continue, which has nothing to do with you. They are now the external event.

You want to change direction to transfer the energy.

17. Persuade without destruction.

In other words, I want to encourage you to be a certain way or do certain kinds of things. I want to do it as much as possible without threats. I want to do it in the most peaceful way I can. That's why I say, as long as we are in agreement, we can do anything we want. If our agreements change, and you were to decide you wanted to do something completely different, even something not complementary to me, my commitment is I will work that out in the best way possible. That's my commitment. Why do I do that? Destruction and violence, push and pull, antagonism and accusations and all these kinds of things are not conducive to me working on myself consistently in the way I want to work on it. It's my commitment to myself. I've learned, for example, that over time, torture doesn't work. You can't get the truth through torture. You can't get commitment through threat. You can't get people to keep their promises or to follow through and do or be anything at all based on external situations whatsoever. It is completely irrelevant. You can't say, we have to do this or the school will fail. You can't say, we have to do this or the marriage will fail. You can't say, you have to do this or you're going to get kicked out. We really can't do that.

If what we are doing is right and validly with merit and meaning, then whatever persuasion is brought to bear has to be nonviolent. It can't be coercive or manipulative.

Everybody always has a way out. I build that into the equation. When we are talking about apprenticeship or marriage, I say our relationship is by agreement and is voluntary. As long as we are in agreement and maintaining those agreements voluntarily, then we continue. If at any point it's in our best interests to no longer be here, we simply make an agreement not to be here and we move on in the best way we can. We don't fuss or fight, no threats or coercion, manipulations. The truth is, every step of the way the work we are doing on our selves has to be in agreement and voluntary. We have to remember that.

I have to remind myself all the time, me being here and me being a teacher in the school and all that is voluntary on my part. I don't have to do this. I could bail. I could change my mind. You might say, oh no you can't do that. You have commitments. You have contracts. Well, so what? When has that ever stopped anybody from not doing something? People make commitments, contracts, promises, agreements, and treaties. When has any of that ever stopped anyone from changing their minds or doing something different in a different direction? It doesn't because it's all external.

Either the motivation is internal by agreement or it's not going to last. Unfortunately for working on your selves, attention has to be sustained for a long period of time. Part of this idea here with these principles is how do we do that? By following these principles, we may actually be able to sustain attention at a high level over a longer period of time than if we don't. Certainly persuading and working together by agreement is very important.

18. Do not try to fight false personality. It will defend itself.

Bypass it by appealing to something higher in the other person. To do this, you must self-remember. It's not good enough for me to point out you are in a low place or that your behavior is not very thoughtful or appropriate for the level of work you are professing you want to play at. Those comments, that photograph won't mean anything if I'm locked up in my own ego in false personality while I'm pointing it out.

Step number one to working with others in being able to combat the false personality is always to come back and remember your self first. Check in first. If you feel like what you're doing is correct, then go ahead and do what you have to do.

19. Share your troubles as little as possible.

This has to do with useless talk. Troubles refer all the little, inconsequential, negative things to which we are attached, constantly talking about the kinds of things going on in our head which are all negative, about a job, a relationship—we want to share that as little as possible. If you are in a group and you notice the discussion is mostly what we call a "bitch session", where it's mostly about complaining about this or that or this person or that person, try to withdraw from that conversation. Don't feed it or give it energy. That conversation is 100% from false personality.

Okay, I was bitten by an ant this morning…and? In the big picture of life, who cares? Honestly, it's going to go away in a little bit. "It was so terrible I actually had to scratch for a whole minute. It irritated me and then I had a bump and my toe wasn't perfect for half an hour or even a whole couple of days. Everybody could see my spots. I felt really bad. I had an unconscious inclination to scratch and it was very distracting to me. It made me feel like I didn't have control of my life. As a result, I had to express that to every person I ran into that day."

Do you know how many times I've been in class and people walk up to me and point out they got a bug bite? You can't even begin to understand how important it is that people express to me that on their second toe next to the big toe, yesterday an ant attacked them without mercy and left a mark, with a tone of voice of "what are you going to do about it". People ask me, "What are you going to do about the ant problem?" I go, "Ant problem? There's an ant problem?" Then they will point to their foot to prove the problem. That's just the ground attack. There's also an aerial attack of mosquitoes. We are under attack by land and air. What are you going to do about it? They really want to know.

Share your troubles as little as possible. These are not substantial. We have substantial issues. We have things that really need work. Dealing with your bug bite isn't one of them. It's not wrong. Put some tiger balm on it and let it go. Think positive thoughts about the ants. Visualize them being in cooperation with your environment. Be glad they're here. They serve a function in the bio-system. They are part of the recycling apparatus. If you don't want to be mistaken for compost, don't stand on top of the anthill.

Ants force us to be a little more conscious of how we walk and how we stand when we are on the earth. Guess what? That's hugely valuable to be aware of what your feet are doing while you're outside. There's life on the ground. When you are walking around outside, you don't own that land. It's living. It's alive. The Native Americans say, we need to learn how to walk on the living body of Mother Earth. Part of the job of fire ants is to teach us that. Pay attention. We are walking on something that is alive. We have an Impact on it and it has an Impact on us. What a great lesson the ants have to teach us. It's a beautiful lesson.

Share your troubles as little as possible. When we get caught up in constantly talking about the little things, we waste a lot of energy that could be applied to something more important.

20. To externally consider, subdue your chief negative feature.

Chief negative feature is sometimes called "the chronic". We use those two terms interchangeably. To externally consider comes back to the idea of getting outside your head, your particular issues and emotions, thoughts and feelings on any particular thing that could be dealing with a work aim, another person or another person's idea. It means consideration that is outside of you. In order to really do that, we work on subduing chief negative feature. In order to do that, we have to have some idea of what that is. What is our chief negative feature? What is our chronic? The simple definition is the primary front or face of the false personality. It's the forest for the trees. It's where we encapsulate and identify most with those mechanical and formatory parts of us.

It's difficult because we mostly live in false personality in our negative emotions, identification and imagination. It's the last place we really want to pay attention or bring energy to. If someone gave me ten choices on negative or mechanical features of myself to pay attention to, it would be on the bottom of the list. I would make sure to arrange that list in such a way that it would always be the last thing, because what I'm hoping is that it will never come up. All the other smaller features and issues will be more dominant and present and get more consciousness and attention, so to speak. Where I live in my negativity, that's the one place to which I don't want to bring attention and consciousness. Of course, this is reiterated over again in various workbooks that that is one of the functions of a school, to reveal to us what are the parameters, descriptions, examples, what does it really relate to, to be a mirror for us. We can say the word confront, but it's not confrontational, it's revealing. We don't confront chief negative feature. We reveal chief negative feature.

That's significant. How do you subdue chief negative feature? You subdue it by revealing it, because the one thing the chronic doesn't like is attention, light, anyone else knowing it exists, not even you. The last thing my chronic wants is for me to be aware it's there. It will do anything to divert attention and drive attention away from it. Of course, it's expert at that. The only way it will be revealed is in an atmosphere where there are other people who are looking at it and seeing it and then reflecting that back to me. How do I see that reflection? It can be in some form of behavior, conversation, corrections and so on.

When I see how people in the school respond to me, it can give me clues as to my chief negative feature. When I see how I respond to the way people respond to me, that also gives me clues to my chronic.

21. Photographing is your way of remembering for another.

If you are not trying to appeal to the highest in another, refrain. To photograph means to bring attention to the wrong work of a center to someone else. It is a way, a technique, a method and an exercise. We have several centers. The photographs and little snapshots of behavior, attitude and emotion will each be different depending on which center it is originating from. Overtime, we should reveal the work of the centers through this exercise.

Another phrase we use for photograph is bringing something to light, not necessarily pushing it or trying to change or correct it. I notice right now you are angry. Why are you angry? Well, I'm angry because I'm angry. Well, exactly. Maybe there is no particular reason you are angry right now. Something is angry. Part of you is angry. If the circumstances don't warrant it, that means the anger is being generated from one of the centers and is not actually a reflection of anything going on. It is completely mechanical.

22. If a misunderstanding occurs, wait patiently for the right time to reopen communication.

To press too soon or in the wrong way will spoil rather than heal. One of the mechanical behaviors we have is that when we misunderstand each other, we try to instantly correct it completely. If the communication is coming from the wrong work of centers and being driven by negative emotion, trying to make it go away sometimes reinforces that way of being in the moment because you have that resistance to correction. There is always resistance to correction.

Because there is resistance to correction does not mean we should not do them, observe them, or photograph them. It just means that if there is too much resistance and a pushback disproportionate to the correction or the photograph, then the practice is to let it go in the moment. Back off and wait. Since it was mechanical, it will change. It might take a couple of minutes for some things, or a couple of days.

In individuals who are not working on themselves, it may never correct. Certainly, if we are practicing and working on our selves, there is a return to another I or another state of mind more conducive to having certain conversations or corrections or photographs. What is the timing? What's too soon? There's no rule because it is completely relative to the pushback in that moment. What's the level of attention of the person you are with?

Whenever you work on this idea of communication when you receive resistance, don't give up. Check your self and self-remember and then be patient. Practice patience. One of the hardest skills in the world is patience. It is learnable, but with practice.

23. To rise above the mutual weaknesses, which spoil your relations with other people, you must self-remember.

There is no other way we know of. It's not enough to try to be a good person. It's not enough to try to get along and to try to say and do the right thing. Key in on the words here: "rise above the mutual weaknesses…" That means we have to take some responsibility with the relationships in the school that are not growing and functioning due to mutual weaknesses contributing to them. One of the ways we signify our understanding of mutual weaknesses is to take individual responsibility to self-remember and self-observe. It's not about apologizing. Apologizing doesn't work unless it comes from a higher part of centers and the receiver is also in a higher part of centers. If both of those things are not happening, then we have the saying, "the apology falls on deaf ears". We've all experienced this. We felt genuine remorse. We overstepped or misspoke or acted in a non-helpful way. We apologize and the other person is like, "I'm not accepting your apology. It doesn't help. It doesn't change what you said." That's not the way to work to rise above what spoils our relationships with each other. The rule and recommendation is not to first apologize or seek apology, but to self-remember. It is not to seek someone else to apologize to you when you've been slighted or wronged. The first is to go back to the basics.

In a sense, it's not about you. If you don't get anything else from the Fourth Way, the one thing you should get is that it's not about you. In order for it to be about you, there'd have to be one. There'd have to be one you. There is no you. There's a you all.

24. Advise rather than reproach.

The first, mild and friendly, corrects the erring. The second only convicts. The word convict is a legal term. It has to do having been accused of something when a law has been broken. After consideration, it is determined that the rule or law was broken and you are errant in whatever deviation there is. You are convicted.

Our goal in making corrections is not to convict. That reinforces negative and mechanical aspects with voices that sound like low self-esteem or guilt and shame.

The purpose of corrections has to come from a good place. The purpose is not to prove somebody's wrong. Out in the world, that's what we do. We are taught to do this from our earliest childhood, when there is some aberration from some standard, which is usually not communicated in the first place.

This idea of advising gives a good way of bringing correction into use. It's not enough simply to point out someone's breaking a rule or doing something wrong. It has to be in the form of advice in the sense of what can be done to correct it or what is seeking after the context or the root of it? It's not about simply declaring that some mechanical behavior is bad. What's the end of that? The end of reproach and conviction closes the door to further communication. We try not to do that unless it is our intention, which is a justification to close the door.

25. Instruct the willing and dismiss the unwilling.

Open the door and close the door. Open the door means to instruct the willing. Instruction is only for the willing. Being a student in the work is a voluntary position. Being a student in the school, in the inner circle, is voluntary. The fact we're in the school is supposed to indicate we have decided to be here. Being here is intentional and based on the best kinds of decision making processes we are capable of. As a result, we put ourselves in a position where we can receive instruction and share information. Only by being willing can we receive instruction.

The second part of this is equally as important. Dismiss the unwilling. This idea deals both with the inner and outer. On the outer, I take it to mean how I determine students that can be part of the work. A student has to appear to be interested and available. To be willing means to have a will and capacity, at least at that level of intention for participation.

There are people who come to the work and come to the school. From the minute they get here they are the most intractable, difficult, resistant and unwilling people they could possibly be. It's as if they went to court, lost a case, and some judge sentenced them to class for thirty days. They have to do it or join the army and go to Iraq. That's why they're here.

It's ongoing right? Instruction stops when we become unwilling. That's why I talk about this proverbial line in the sand, where we throw issues up in the way of teaching and the work. Right there is a good example of a declaration of being unwilling to participate at a high level. It can come across as lots of conditions. There can't be any conditions. Either what we're doing is authentic and genuine and is coming from higher sources and is leading us to a greater sense of awareness and integrity to unify the I's, deal with the negative emotions, or it's not.

We've decided, at least for us, that it is, and so we're here. That's the outer. I also look at this from the inner. Inside myself, I have all these different I's. Some of them are willing and some are not. I notice, overtime, that who's in charge changes from time to time. Sometimes, without notice, no memos were filed that a new group was taking over. There were no letters to the editor that change was on the way. Literally, I wake up in the morning and I don't want to do it. For no other reason than that's just what was in my mind when I woke up. Those parts of the mind, those I's, are not suitable for instruction and self-work. They are not suitable for self-observation and self-remembering. Those I's will be equally as resistant to working on negative emotions, following practices and exercises, or anything required in school.

A funny thing occurring sometimes, when I have this scenario in my head, is that these I's don't have anything better to be doing. They're just against everything else, but they don't have anything they want to do.

In the past, the unwilling I's had stuff they wanted to do and it was all bad and counterintuitive to my life, my health and the integrity of my relationships to other people, my family, my job and schoolwork. In fact, they would engage in sabotage. It's one thing to be unwilling. It's another thing to engage in sabotage. That's another level of unwillingness.

What I'm instructed to do here, in the inner, is to dismiss the unwilling almost like a military term. You report to your commander and you give your complaint. The commander goes, "Noted. You are dismissed." This assumes there is something greater than the unwilling parts that have the power and the authority and the right to dismiss them. With practice, we practice dismissing the unwilling parts. As they show themselves, we play whack-a-mole and dismiss them.

We can take this as an external thing to judge who has potential as a student and who does not and what do you do with them. All schools have the double-edged sword. One side of the sword is to cut away the Impediments keeping you from being able to move forward to those doors that give upon liberty, to cut the Gordian knot, to strike the lock from those doors. The other side of that sword is to cut away that which is useless. All true schools occasionally have to do this. They make extraordinary efforts to support and bring students together and create work environments. A great amount of energy, thought and spirit are used to bring about a healthy, reliable, conscientious and safe place to be able to practice. Sometimes, they have to excise and cut away students who show up and turn out to be completely unsuitable for the work. Unsuitable is not a character indictment.

Just because you are working doesn't make you a better person than someone who is not working. A lot of times people will fall into that conversation. It becomes a character judgment. Someone thinks they are better than someone else. That's not it. Back to this idea of unwilling, resistant and even sabotaging behaviors threatening the very existence of the school on the external. Internally, up to a point, those behaviors will guarantee no productive helpful work can be done. Even if you have two or more people who want to work together, they have to at least want to work together. If half of them don't want to work, then there's no school because it becomes a self-practice rather than a school.

26. Wish nothing that depends on others.

We have the external and internal ideas. In one sense, with a school we are dependent on having people who want to be in the school. Progress, stability and ability to remain are dependent on some level of actually having students who want to participate.

From an external point of view, no matter how dependent the school might seem to be on one or more individuals in the school, if at some point they stop working or decide to not participate or work at a high level, they have to go away, even if that means the school has to reorganize or even move. The school cannot depend on anyone who is not working towards the benefit of the school. It can't be that way.

On a personal level, wish nothing that depends on others. If I wish (there's nothing wrong with wishing when it's not lost in imagination) in a sense of magic with intentionality, as I wish for my own internal progress, I never wish in such a way that progress is dependent on someone else. Ultimately, my progress is up to me. Don't make your progress contingent upon another person being any particular way because people are absolutely, utterly and completely mechanical. People are so consumed with negative emotion there's hardly anything not mechanical about them. People are associative. Virtually every thought that goes through a person's head is the tumbling result of whatever random thought happened to be there a minute ago. For me to create a situation where my internal progress is dependent on your random I's, attitudes and emotions is not sustainable. It will not work.

When I wish for qualities or attributes or insight, information, understanding or correction, I want to wish for it in such a way I am still responsible for all of the work I do. We are all individually responsible for all the work we do and all the work we don't do. When we don't make the extraordinary efforts it takes to do something exceptional, which is to craft a soul out of garbage, then we have to take responsibility for that. We can't blame someone else for not being the best mirror they could be or the best teacher or the best student (whatever our relationship is).

27. The first reason for your internal slavery is ignorance of your own psychology.

Therefore, welcome sincere photographs from others. Cultivate an attitude of gratitude. When you get a correction or photograph that works, that catches you with your pants down in a wrong work of centers, (this is the proverbial "thank you, sir, may I have another"), try not to justify. Accept the photograph with graciousness. These photographs are a cure for ignorance.

We're ignorant of our own psychology. One of the tools we have to overcome this is the sincere photographs and corrections of those in our community who are doing similar work and are committed to their work and our progress together. As we work together and photograph each other and acknowledge when we do good things and make progress, these are cures for ignorance to our own psychology.

Every sincere photograph, which reveals something hidden to you or which you suspected but for some reason you were avoiding paying attention to, cures ignorance. Ignorance has to do with willfully not knowing. It's not that you just don't know. You choose not to know. The chronic is ignorant because it functions knowledgeably with awareness of what's happening and ignores it on purpose. The root word of ignorance is "to ignore". That means you know what's going on. You're choosing not to pay attention, not to bring energy to it, not to self-remember or work on your self.

When we catch each other in little unconscious moments where we are not being as observant as we could be. It's nothing personal. It doesn't mean you're bad. That's part of the chief negative feature, the formatory idea that we can't take any correction without taking it as a personal criticism. Every correction or photograph is likely to cause a response as if you've been punched in the stomach or poked in the eye with a sharp stick. That's our mechanical side. That's the false personality side, which has already determined that if you are not right, you must be wrong. The idea of voluntarily submitting to photographs and corrections is right in the face of false personality and chief negative feature.

28. To get along better with your friends, make more of their services to you and put less value on your own favors to them.

There's nothing wrong with acknowledging the work and effort everybody does. There's nothing wrong with taking credit for your accomplishments, depending on where it comes from. If it comes from ego and false personality, then the self-aggrandizement is worthless.

Out in the world, we have marketing. Its practice is that things are blown up and fluffy and made to look larger than they are in order to attract customers and clients. As we get to know each other better and we're working in a friendly environment, we want to be fair by acknowledging everyone's service and effort, and not disproportionately so.

Put less value on your own favors to them. Favors are the little things. Try not to make too much of all the little things you do for others. There's part of me, a formatory I, that wants to keep a list of every little thing I do for someone. It has another list of every little thing they do for me. If my list is longer than theirs, then obviously they are not trying hard enough. The problem is that I'm in charge of the list. I put all kinds of stuff on my list. I put even Imaginary stuff on my list to make it really long so that I will always be able to do that. It's an intentional practice to whittle that list down and realize, actually, I'm not being as helpful as I think I am. Left to my own mechanical devices, my list will always be the longest and the greatest and nobody else is ever going to have a list equivalent to mine.

Now of course, that goes back to other conversations we've had in the past, which has to do with this idea of holding accounts. One of the biggest things you can do to be able to continue to work on your self in a good way is to come back to this idea of holding accounts. An account is a list, keeping a running dialogue of slights and offenses and where the ball was dropped, where someone didn't do what you expected them to do the way you expected them to do it at and in the expected time. You wanted them to do it in a happy way but they did it in a depressed or sad way. All this stuff finds itself on the holding accounts list. Then when we try to work with each other, we have this running dialogue of how disappointed we are for that reason.

If we continue to hold accounts, these lists gather weight. They have enough weight to start to push buttons. As the lists get longer, the buttons get pushed harder. Eventually, even if nothing external happens at all, the weight of that list will be so much that at some point it will tip the scale toward the side of escape, justification, defense, unwillingness and even sabotage. It is all justified because of this long list over here. The unwillingness or resistance to do the exercises or work are justified because of the long list.

We have to keep working on letting go of attachment to things which are on this account list of slights, things that don't make us happy, anything really, little offensives, disorganizations, little misconnects or disconnects, maybe some big ones—those really help fill out the list when you have a really big breakdown in communication. You definitely throw that on the list. We have to constantly work to whittle it down. How do you know if you are holding accounts? When you are thinking about something you need to do right now, and the first thing that comes up in your head is something that happened yesterday or the day before in your decision making process, that's an account.

How can we make decisions in real-time about who we want to be and how we want to be with each other if every time we go to have a thought about something, it's weighted with every little, imagined, slight offense or disconnect that's happened previously. The thing about those lists is there are pros and there are cons. Even I was taught to do that by my mother. Take a sheet of paper when you are trying to make a decision and write the pros and cons on either side. List all the good things here and the bad things here. Whichever list was longer is the one you go with right? That was probably one of the most useless pieces of information my mother gave me. It was ignorant of any process on how to make decisions. You will always make the side you like better longer because no one is objective. There is no one to be objective.

Ideally, the only way that kind of decision making could work is if the person making the list was actually conscious and self-objective and wasn't adding in negative emotion, false personality, identification and imagination. Since there is no one like that here, that technique simply doesn't work.

29. If you look after the faults of others and are always inclined to take offense, your evil propensities or mechanicality will grow.

There are reoccurring themes. Some of these exercises tie in and relate to other, similar thoughts. It's one thing to give you a photograph or give you a correction. That's one thing. If I am staying in a state of mind looking for something (looking after your faults), I'm paying attention to your faults and even your hypothetical and possible future faults. In other words, I know you are going to mess up, so I'm going to be alert, so when you do I can add it to my list because I'm keeping accounts.

The only reason I would want to be hyper vigilant about your propensity to make a mistake or to not be completely perfect at some moment in time in the future is if I had this list thing going. That's the only reason. In order to keep that list going, that means I have to be inclined to take offense. If I'm inclined to take offense, it guarantees I don't have to be willing or receptive. I'm inclined to take offense. Who would be? That's false personality, back to that chief negative feature or the chronic. Part of the way we identify the chronic is the part of us that is inclined to take offense.

When you don't behave in a way my expectation and imagination say you should and I get offended, guess what? That's a good time to photograph your self, because what you're seeing in that moment is chief negative feature. Your evil propensities or mechanicality will grow. By the way, evil and mechanical mean the same thing.

You want to know who Satan is? Satan is chief negative feature. Satan is the sum of all the mechanicalities and formatory thinking, feeling and being with low essence, without will or discipline, without observation or consciousness. That's why Satan is in the dark and not in the light. That's why Satan is in a deep place and not in the air. That's why the voice is inclined to take offense. Everything about chief negative feature is about creating a state of offense, which pays more attention to the fault of others.

By others, we could take it internally the part of us that finds fault with all the other parts of us, the part that keeps the list. It's one thing to be objective and self-observing and self-remembering to observe these weaker I's and negative I's and so on. It's another thing that we take offense at it and keep lists in order to support being offended. Being offended is another one of those perfect states of mind that is completely contrary to being able to do self-work. You can't work on your self when you are offended.

30. Dig up the desire to conquer others if you would free your self.

We say this, "Well, you can't really change anybody." Of course, who acts like they believe that? Everybody tries to change everybody. We want to work together. We don't want to change each other. Conquer is the idea of forcing transition or change. It works all kinds of ways. The teacher has to be mindful to not force the student into submission. Students have to be mindful of not trying to conquer and force the teacher into submission because one way or the other, the end result of that process is nothing gets done.

The one thing we have to constantly keep reminding ourselves when we are in a school, a work-school, is that we want and need to make progress. Something has to always be in play. There always has to be movement, friction, give and take, and progress. If one group or another just dominates and conquers the other, then that give and take and progress stops.

Submitting to the work is not about being a victim of conquering. We are not a conquered people. We choose to submit to the principles we agree to work with. We don't do it because we don't have a choice. We don't do it because we are forced to do it. If that's why we are doing it, that's just another form of slave labor and it doesn't matter if it's internal or external. Slavery is one of the things we are trying to work against. We are so used to slavery as a mindset in the world and we've grown up with this idea of how to be a good slave and a good slave master. In a more conscious environment, it's very hard not to fall into those roles of slave, victim, master, conqueror. We have to be vigilant in constantly coming back to establishing good, healthy work equilibrium.

If a misunderstanding occurs, wait patiently for the right time to reopen communication. To press too soon or in the wrong way will spoil rather than heal. What about it?

Q & A

J: You mentioned "too soon". Is there a too late? Like if it takes you a while to sort it out?

Dr. J: Well, certainly there is a too late.

J: Is it a day or an hour?

Dr. J: There is no time. You can't put time on this. That would be formatory and mechanical to think you have to do it within a certain time period or it can't be done or if it's done later it won't be effective.

Things come and go. They have a life and time of their own. There's no arbitrary time.

J: Mostly I'm relating to the collapsing of distinctions.

Dr. J: Of?

J: If say, for instance, you have a miscommunication or misunderstanding and you're fussy about it. You try to work it out and realize you can't in the moment, is there a waiting too long where then the principle of collapsing distinctions comes in?

Dr. J: That can happen immediately. It probably has already happened. That's usually why the disagreement is happening in the first place. There's no time period. There's no time required for anything mechanical to happen. Generally speaking, the mechanical behaviors happen instantly and automatically. Time doesn't make a difference.

The only thing that takes place overtime is when you are in that negative, offended, holding lists and accounts mode, more time gives you more ammunition to add to your list. If you are working on your self, giving your self or the other some time, there is space to make a correction. As far as what is the right amount of time? Who knows? Whatever seems to work in that particular situation for that particular issue with that particular person.

There is a saying, "time heals all wounds". I hope you know by now, just from the research we've done so far, that that is a complete myth. In fact, time doesn't heal anything. What's really funny is that usually that statement is used in relation to emotional issues like grief, loss of a loved one. The truth is it doesn't. The only thing that happens overtime is we tend to repress the issue. We repress our emotions relative to the wound. I deal all the time with people where we go back in time to

140

bring energy, attention, consciousness, breath and pressure to old, unresolved issues going way back in the past to when they were children. We deal with formatory issues that happened at a young age. If time heals all wounds, then certainly by the time someone gets to be 30, 40 or 50, 70, 80 years, these injuries they received when they were five and six years old would be healed.

The work says that nothing gets healed unless it's healed with consciousness. The physical body is the only part about is that has the ability to unconsciously heal itself. If you get a small cut, you'll notice it and pay attention to it for a little while. Then you forget about it. Next thing you know, there is a scab. Next time you look, the scab is gone and it's pink. Then you can't even remember where the wound was. The physical body has that capacity. Our matrix body, the mental and emotional bodies remember everything. They store everything.

STUDENT: When you talk about holding accounts, what do you do with them? How do you let them go?

Dr. J: How do you let them go? The first thing is to be aware that we do it. Everybody does it. The chalkboard in the back of our mind with the magic marker at the ready and script, script, script, oh, ahh…there's something…on the board it goes. The first thing is to observe we do that. Wow, I just wrote something down. I just made a mental note. I'll go, "Note to self! So and so just messed up." I make a mental note. We might even discuss it amongst ourselves. "Did you notice yesterday that so and so was not right? Did you notice this afternoon that somebody lost his or her temper? That means they're not conscious and not in control. They are not as consciously elevated as they might otherwise pretend to be. Did you notice that? Quick, let's all write it down in our notebooks. Let's put it on FaceBook. Actually, I took a video while it was happening. Why would I do that? It's a video in my mind. I then have it for future reference. What's the future reference? It's holding accounts.

Sufficient unto the day are the evil thereof. In other words, yes on some level, behavior patterns mean something. Yes they do. It's the point where we keep the list and use the list as ammunition for justification, for unwillingness, for imagination and identification, for expression of negative emotions in their endless variety, that this note taking becomes unproductive. It interferes with our ability to practice.

Observe that you do it. Observe you just did that. You just put something on the list and it's critical. You already know it's going to be used as part of an excuse to not do something else. You have to become clear. The lists are not about anybody else. The effect of the lists is how they affect our own abilities to function. My lists affect me. My lists are in the way of me being able to do what I've already determined I need to do to keep making progress in my life to keep working on myself.

Work on adding to the positive side. Make it an exercise, part of everyday, where you look with intention for something that someone else is actually doing that benefit's your life and helps your practice and is supportive of who you want to be as a person. Make a mental note of that. Look for the positive aspects, make a mental note and do it with intention.

We think that because we hold accounts accidentally and spontaneously that somehow it is more valid. It's exactly the opposite. Mechanical anything is not better than the conscious equivalent. Anything you can do with more attention and consciousness will have more value than anything you do automatically without thought. I know automatically without thought that I keep these lists. I know I do that. I'll put them aside and pick them back up. I'll crumple them up and throw them out the window and run all the way around the house, pick up the crumpled list and flatten it out and start adding more to it, a list I already threw out that isn't productive, helpful or even real. Everything on it was Imaginary. It was my own perceptions based on imagination of what people meant when they said this and that of what they were doing based on past negative experiences and other conversation and programming. I already determined that. That's why I threw the list away. I have to run out and go get it. It was a good one. None of it's real, but it was nicely written and it has a lot of weight.

One of the antidotes is to notice the friction when trying not to make the list. Another thing is to be proactive and instead of being in this negative frame of mind where you are looking for a slip up so you can add it to the list, look for something really positive or really good, even the least little thing. Make a list of those.

If you want to make a list with intention, as a more conscious person, that's different from an automatic list compiled from negative filters and imagination and so on. Create the intentional positive list to give some counterbalance.

When you get caught up in looking at the list and you notice, wait, wait, I'm looking at the wrong list. This one's all bad. That's not the list I decided to keep. That's the autopilot's list. Where's the one that I decided to keep? You might have to rummage around for it because chief negative feature constantly takes those intentional lists and shoves them off in the corner, puts them under the pile of folders on the desk and keeps the negative one right on the top so it's easy to get to and see.

I find myself doing that. Sometimes I want to think positively about someone. I do. I want to have a positive consideration. I look at them and nothing comes to mind. That conscious list is not handy. If I consciously said, "Can I think of ten negative things about this person right now?" I could probably do that like bam, bam, bam, because it's mechanical, automatic and not actually conscious. If that's what comes up on the radar first, I know what it is. That comes from false personality. I have to come back and say, "No, no, no. Let's do it." Sometimes it's like pulling teeth, because when you're in a negative frame of mind, it's very hard to acknowledge something positive and right in front of your face. We struggle with it. It's in the struggle and friction that we gain energy, which allows us to be more awake.

This idea of work with accounts is quite valuable as far as gaining energy.

J: You were just talking about the holding of negative lists and the making of positive lists. Sometimes I notice myself thinking oh look, how nice that person is being with this other person. Then I go, they never do that with me. Oh, I just can't stand that because I see a really positive thing, but then I have the other list right next to each other.

Dr. J: That's not a list, that's a tape.

J: Okay.

Dr. J: "They don't treat me the same way."

J: I put it on a list.

Dr. J: No, the thought, "they don't treat me like that". That's a tape. Now because the tape plays, that now will qualify what you see as an item to be added to the negative list.

J: Right.

Dr. J: The trick there is to say that's a tape as soon as you hear that voice. That's not me. Whatever me is, that's not it. That's a tape. Then, work hard to not do anything based on the tape. As we create these lists, holding accounts and what not, because they are such powerful Impediments to being close and working closely together, it's something we all have to work with in real-time, to struggle with, to whittle away and try not to get into a state of mind where we acquiesce and give in to the weight of those lists.

As soon as we start to go into that frame of mind, we're no longer working. What's the difference between this and being unwilling? The unwilling is what happens when you get to a point where someone's list shuts them down and out so they are asked to leave. The whole point of trying to keep equilibrium in that process is to prevent that from happening. Again, who's in charge of that? Well, not us. Not me. Not the school. The individual is in charge of that. The school observes.

The school acts like the observer mind. It is like the surrogate observer. The school is everyone, not you, who's observing you. Every individual, of course, is working on him or herself. That's simply a function of the school. To dismiss the unwilling is when the school determines a student has gotten seized up, is no longer practicing or participating, and then that person is moved along. Usually that doesn't happen. Most of the time, when people get seized up and attached to their issues and stop working, they just leave. That's the way most schools experience it. They have what's called turnover.

Think about how funny it is. Put your self in a conscious school in a group of people who are working on themselves, and then absolutely refuse to do anything. How funny is that? It is a resistance thing. They can't help it. The harder you push them, the more they resist, though they will not go away. It is usually internal. We think all the pressure comes from other people and it doesn't. We think, oh so and so is putting so much pressure on me. No they're not, unless they are sitting on top of your head. Unless someone is sitting on top of your body, there is no pressure on you. Most of what we think is pressure from other people is based on our own resistance, tapes, and it's our push back. I might look at you and say, "You are pressuring me." Actually, what I feel is not you pressuring me. What I feel is my resistance to you in the moment. I just don't know the difference. I think that's what pressure is. I'm not aware of my own psychology. Since I don't have a clue about my own psychology, how would I know if you were pressuring me or not? Hell, I feel pressure when there's nobody else in the room and sometimes more. We have to learn ourselves better to know what the difference is.

31. Hold no accounts and be without hesitation in forgiving your self and others for lapses.

Dr. J: It's very hard. Holding accounts relates to patterns in the way we store negative emotion, okay? So, if we were evolved and self-realized we wouldn't be negative all the time. We would be more consistent. We would have the ability to be more consistent, the ability to be more truthful, the ability to have more disclosure, to have more integrity and honesty and be able to work with each other. To whatever degree we're identified and encapsulated in that mechanicalness of our nature and the expression of personality and so on, we mistreat each other and we deviate from high standards of integrity and high standards of honesty and disclosure. We are storage apparatus. We have this infinite ability to store negative energy and trauma and even perception of it, and so that's our record keeping system. We call that holding accounts. For example, every time you disappointed me, I store a little record of that in my "every time you disappointed me" file. Little things, big things, woosh, go into my drawer. The interesting thing is, we do not store or hold accounts the same way for when people do the right thing, when they are right with us.

J: Why is that?

Dr. J: Because it's the way we're made. It's part of the machine. So, we don't have an equal file drawer to balance this out. We can't say this file folder is this big but the good one is this big and they cancel each other out. That's not how it works. In fact, we have the ability, when we're in a negative place, as in we're having an argument or something like that, to bring up every little thing you've ever done I feel somehow caused me to have a negative feeling.

It doesn't matter how far back it goes. All of a sudden, some word you said five years ago in some odd circumstance, at which I got offended, we're having an issue right now, and that somehow is relevant to what's happening.

You know you're doing this, holding accounts, because generally speaking we always refer to them with the word "all" or "always". So, we'll say things like, you always this or that. Well, that's just crazy talk because we don't always do anything. We're so inconsistent we don't do anything always. We couldn't do anything always if we wanted to. Nobody could, so me accusing you of always being critical of what I say refers to holding accounts.

One of the things we try to do as a relatively intentional community is to not hold accounts and be without hesitation for others for their lapses. Now, we hold accounts against ourselves. Right? I see my own inconsistencies. Especially and more when I try and start remembering myself and I'm put in an environment where I have to pay more attention to myself. Guess what happens? Because of my bad training and my bad habits, I track them. I count them. I list them. I label them. I store them. I accumulate them. Basically I'm accumulating and holding accounts against myself. Eventually, I might find I have enough accounts against myself to justify me not taking care of myself. In other words, I might come to the conclusion, if I have enough accounts, enough listings on this account, then I'm a worthless, dirty dishrag and there's no hope for me, and why even try because I never get it right.

See, the problem with that accounting system is that it's completely imbalanced, because we, generally speaking, only keep accounts of the negative things. Now, as much as we're negative, we're not always negative. We often have possibilities of being a completely different way. Those don't go into the same filing system. The negative filing system is in the tissue. If you want to say where's the positive filing system? Well, it's not in the tissue, it's in the consciousness. Those two are at odds with each other. The positive expressions of our being are not stored in the tissue. They are found more in our consciousness. In a way, they are less tangible. It is also situational whether we even have access to them, because if we're identified, justified, defensive, negative and so on, we don't have access to our consciousness and we're not self-remembering.

Getting access to the positive side of the equation is actually conditional on being in a more conscious state of mind. Then when you're in that place, guess what? You are more empathetic. You see more how you have genuine qualities. When we are in the tissue life and we're identified with the machine, all of that information is stored in the tissue so guess what? Easy to find. Easy to find. I can tap into your filing cabinet for this holding accounts and negative expressions. I can just kind of push on you a little bit and get that drawer to pop open. I don't even have to create much pressure. And then all you can think of is everything I've done that wasn't right, or conversely, everything you've done, all of your lapses. So, what we want to do is know we're going to lapse. We know we're going to occasionally say things that just don't make any sense. We know we're going to occasionally have behavior that's not a perfect expression of unconditional love. So what we do is A, we don't want to keep a list going and B, without hesitation forgive your self and others for all their lapses. Literally be in a mind-set of being forgiving. You just have to do it. I know, I'm kind of irritated with you right now. Okay. Well, I have a choice. I can catalog it. Oh, here's another irritating thing. Or okay, obviously they're not really paying attention right now and I forgive them. That act of forgiveness steals something away from the negative energy inside you.

It doesn't necessarily change anything about them. We also assume that if we're working on purpose and we're being in a relationship on purpose that our intentions are good. In other words, the reason why we're trying to cultivate intimacy in a relationship is not because we are trying to hurt each other. When you hold accounts, you can come to a point of thinking that actually the reason a person wants to be with you is because they are trying to hurt you. You have enough evidence. Now, it doesn't mean there are not people out in the world who won't try to hurt you. There are people out in the world who will try to hurt you. You want to be able to identify them and you want to be able to pay attention to them and you want to be able to react appropriately and be safe. That's not what I'm talking about. I'm talking about being in an environment where you are intentionally, on purpose and consciously engaging others in relationship and intimacy and discovery of love and discovery of practicing your self. In that situation, you can't keep the records quite the same way as you can out the door. You have to be more forgiving. You have to allow for lapses and then recover. You have to make those kinds of efforts you would never make out in the world because you would just cut people loose. As soon as you cut them loose, you can't work with them anymore. Certainly, in a work and relationship environment, where we say openly we are trying to work on ourselves and we are trying to practice certain things, then we cannot hold accounts against each other and we have to be very quick and very forgiving and very quick to be forgiving.

J: What if you notice that, and I know you notice this a lot with me where I'm not paying attention and I'm doing certain things over and over again, how, in the moment, when it's happening, do you positively express that that's a pattern, that you're noticing a pattern in that person.

Dr. J: That goes to another subject we talked about, which was photographing and stop exercise and so on. How do you, as you're observing your partner, and they're not in a good space or they're kind of off track, or they're identified with something really negative, how do you interrupt that? How do bring attention to that? The answer is however you can, without being identified your self. As soon as you are identified with their negativity and you're trying to control them or correct them, and you're coming from a place of identification and justification and defensiveness your self, then it's a moot point. Everybody's out. Everybody out of the pool.

We can be identified with virtually everything. This is actually sort of after the fact. You know, in other words…

J: After you realize you're out of the pool.

Dr. J: It's the idea of: you lost it yesterday and I'm going to take note of that. Then a week from now you lose it again and I take a note of that. Then a month from now we are having a discussion where I'm identified and I bring up every time you've lost it in the last six months, as somehow some basis for my argument, as if that's all you've done, in the whole six months, is try to make me mad. It's been the sum total of your existence. All you've done from morning to night for the last month is try to irritate me. Well, that's what we're talking about.

144

CHAPTER SEVEN: Exercises for Curbing Lying and Becoming More Sincere

1. Avoid guessing and speak only of what you are sure.

Dr. J: We want to work on creating an emphasis in speech where we speak in a more sure or knowledgeable fashion. It goes back to exercises on stopping useless talk. Simply guessing for guessing's sake is useless. In daily practice, when we're working on ourselves, we want to avoid that as much as possible.

When you realize you are having a conversation or speaking about something by guessing what it means, how it works, or what one should do, it's better to not do that and keep the speech focused on things you are sure of.

We have references. If we are not sure about something, then before talking about it too much or getting into a lot of imagination and guessing about it, go back and reread a resource, double check a fact and practice validation. Practice guessing less in speech.

2. Do not exaggerate or magnify people and events.

Dr. J: This one is really hard because the inclination is to exaggerate, especially from false personality. The inclination is to make events, people, or descriptions of either to be bigger, more dramatic, or take up more space than they actually are or do take up.

After a point, exaggeration is another form of lying. Anytime we can come back and reduce a story or an example to more specifics as far as to exactly what happened, exactly what the place or position that the person we are describing holds, we curb lying and practice condensing our speech in such a way we tend to speak more truthfully. Why would I care to do that at all? Exaggeration fills a lot of conversation. Part of what I would like to do is know my true self, yet exaggeration feeds false personality and ego. It feeds ideas of self-importance.

Relate this to the opposite, as well. We also don't want to exaggerate on the negative side or diminish things on it either. It's just as unconscious to downplay or to not make significant things which are significant. The trick is to try and find the middle ground where when we are speaking of things, we think of them more correctly with the weight they deserve.

3. Minimize your talk of friendship and love and substitute deeds for words.

Dr. J: To minimize your talk of friendship and love doesn't mean to not talk about friendship and love. It doesn't mean that it's okay to say you are friends or describe your friendship or to say you have love or to communicate you're being loving. It just means, minimize it in proportion to your deeds. It's better to substitute deeds for words.

It's one thing to say you love to something. It's another thing to act as if you really believe it. When you act overtime and act what you really believe, then your actions should be different. It's normal for people who are not focused or working on themselves to exaggerate or talk about friendship and love magnanimously in definite and even infinite kinds of terms. For example, because I love you now I will always love you. In fact, much of the time, those expressions are really just expressing an emotion, which is contingent on everything going a certain way. If things don't go that way, it is no longer true. I loved you this morning, but I hate you this morning. Loved you yesterday but I hate you today. Even just a glance or tone of voice or some other behavior, which is really quite subject to change at any time and maybe even random. It is better, if you want to communicate friendship and love, that you constantly bring your attention to bear in such a way you consider ways to demonstrate the love, connection and friendship. Work on having confidence in the ability to be satisfied with that.

For example, we have a lot of ego attached to this kind of interaction. I say I love you. Now I want you to say you love me back. If you don't, then I'm going to get my feelings hurt because you didn't respond the way I wanted you to. My expression was somehow conditional on your reciprocation of the same expression. The thing about being loving versus constantly talking about loving someone is that it places less emphasis on real-time communication of reciprocity. I love you so I'm going to act a certain way. If my way is concurrent with the words, then I don't need to emphasize the words as much. The problem with the spoken communication of friendship and love is that the conditionality and reciprocity of it is conditional on how everybody is in the moment.

It might be different a moment before or after. Either way, even if we do agree, I look at you and go, "Oh I really love you." If right that minute you are not in a concurrent space and don't reciprocate, then I might go into this whole chain of thought that might trigger tapes. "What does it mean when one doesn't reciprocate love?" I've collapsed the words with the action. If I really understand this correctly, you could tell me you hate me and disagree with everything about me. Yet, if you act in a loving way with me, I'll get it that you actually have love for me or that you're sharing love with me, regardless of what you say. No matter how much I say I love something, if I don't act in a loving way, then that's what I'm communicating no matter what I say.

It's the most common thing in the world for people to talk about how much they love each other. There might be some meeting and good conversation with someone. Next thing we know, everybody is telling everybody how much they love each other. There's going to be no behavior in support of that past that point. Is that love and friendship or not? I think it's a friendly encounter. I think it's a compatible moment. It might be a moment of synchronicity.

This is another thing we always misconstrue. We misinterpret attraction for love.

Attraction and love are two completely different things. Not to say that if you love someone you will not be attracted to him or her, but also, I want to say, just because you love someone doesn't mean you will be attracted to him or her. There are two different things. The attraction part is much more complex. You can be attracted to someone mentally, emotionally, physically and instinctively. Instinctively simply has to do with hormones, just getting a shot of pheromones. The emotional part might be more about synchronicity in concurrence of feelings. The mental part is having a satisfaction of being able to share ideas, vision and creative expression and so on. There are many ways we can be attracted or not.

Love is not dependent on that because you may find overtime you are more or less attracted in a physical way to people you really love and care about. There might be periods of time where you are not attracted at all and other times when you are. Then that goes away and comes back. If our ideas about our expressions of love are dependent on our feelings or our attractions, then that is going to be completely unreliable. That will come and go accidentally. It will not be consistent.

4. Reduce subjectivity by not voicing your arbitrary views.

Dr. J: In Ayurveda, there's this idea that the constant expression of like and dislike is a sign of imbalance. I'm attracted to this; I'm not attracted to that. These are arbitrary views because they are what we call knee-jerk responses. The compulsion to constantly express these arbitrary positive and negative I's is very mechanical. It's completely subjective. It's entirely based on what you were thinking and feeling at the moment you had that opinion. One minute later, you can have a completely different opinion. You can like something one minute and not like it the next. You cannot like something one minute and like it the next.

I don't know how many times I've run into to people who have told me about the significant things in their lives, the revelations, the new things they were up to and completely engrossed in, and it might even be new people and relationships and what not. Then I talk to them a month later and they are like, "Oh, yeah. I'm not doing that anymore." You said you had researched this and that this is the most important thing to you. You had twenty reasons why this is what your life is about. Then a month later, they go, "Eh, I changed my mind." The amount of rational thought and exploration in the "I changed my mind" was not even close to what was being justified before.

Really listen to your self. I will monitor my conversations. If I notice I just did a string of "I like this and I don't like that", I make a note that it's very mechanical. That's a voice false personality uses. When we are in that expression of "I like this" and "I don't like that", it is an expression of false personality. It's good to notice this and reduce it as much as possible.

5. Do not express your likes and dislikes.

Dr. J: False personality dislikes. One of the things I've noticed is that when we're doing this, I like and I don't like, most of the time, the I don't likes far outweigh the likes. Part of discerning false personality is in rejection, rejecting anything new, for example, or that challenges the status quo or anything or anyone that makes it or you uncomfortable. The false personality constantly expresses a list of things that make it unhappy, a list of things that it doesn't like. It is almost a continuous conversation. When you observe that conversation pattern, make a mental note, "That's false personality." False personality dislikes. It doesn't like. It is constantly comparing everything around it with what it doesn't like. "How does this fit my list of things I don't like?"

6. To be more sincere, be your self. Do not imitate others.

Dr. J: This is a really interesting one because it presupposes you know what your self is or how your self should be. Already, there is no possibility of doing number 6 unless you've already done a lot of self-work. You have to have some idea of what your self is and how your true, authentic and genuine self would choose to be.

You've heard this saying, "What would Jesus do?" It's a way of saying, if you don't know what to do in any given situation, ask your self, "What would Jesus do?" Then you imagine this Jesus person or the idea of the Christ and you try to model that behavior in some way. This is like that except the model for the behavior you want to move closer to is your self. It is not some external image, model or a guru. In other words, what would Swami G do? What would the Guru do? What would Jesus do? What would the Buddha do?

This is different. In our work, we come back to the idea we do have an authentic self. It's buried most of the time. Somewhere within us, we have a genuine self, an authentic and true self to communicate with.

Sincerity starts with being your authentic self. We are in a continuous state of exploration learning what that is. This is progressive. My sincerity in this moment is limited to my ability to communicate from my authentic and true self as I understand it and as I am in the context of it.

The flipside here is "do not imitate others". We have role models. Even our role models are still not us. Quite often I talk about my teachers, my elderly teachers and their lives of service and work and how I have good role models. On some level I want to emulate them, but with a grain of salt. My life is nothing like their lives. My life circumstances are nothing like their life circumstances. My family history is nothing like their family histories. In other words, we may have common points of interaction and belief and practice and so on, but there is more different than there is the same. I could never actually be successful ever in truly being like them. That's not my goal. That's like saying your goal is to be another person who's not you.

Take these words literally. My former teacher Dr. U Maung Gyi stated during a class "No Nation Has a Monopoly of the Sunshine"! Of course by "Sunshine he meant TRUTH. Implied in "No Nation" is no teacher, no system, no program, no group, no church and no teacher. As a teacher I make no claim to exclusivity to any particular truth. I control no access and nor do I have secrets which no one else has. I have experience, my own experience to share. I was taught to question everything, to validate and or verify everything and as a teacher I am not exempt from this process. All teachers need to be questioned or considered in this way. So, don't clone me. Don't want to become me. Certainly entertain no illusions about serving me as I am a student still in many ways and make no claim to being evolved. For the record this is why I'm not a big fan of "Guru's". My inclination is to run away from any person or group that claims specific higher evolution and or exclusive and secret knowledge that can only be obtained by paying membership dues or personal favors.

We want our goal to be ourselves, our own role models. This is why I say in Thai yoga that it's like a time machine. When I do a session or program with someone, because I'm taking them through postures with less antagonism, not completely, but with less defensiveness, less self-protection, less control than they normally have over every little thing they do in their body, I can show them ways of moving and being in their body they might not be able to get to for one or two years in the future. The role model for this Imagery of what they can do and how they get there is them selves.

The down side with teaching a yoga class, where you have the teacher in the front of the class and monkey see, monkey do, everybody follows along—the downside is that your Imagery and model of the physicality, the physical expression in motion, is not you. It's someone else. We try to emulate them but our bodies and physiologies are completely different. Our emotional make-ups are completely different. Our body types are completely different. There will always be a gap between being able to do what you see the teacher demonstrate and what you will have as your own, personal experience in going through the postures. This is a big thing for really good yoga teachers to understand. The students are never going to be able to it exactly the way you can do it. In order for that to happen, they would have to have your history, your scar tissues, your injuries, your emotional inhibitions and all of those things the same with the same body type. Since none of these things are concurrent, they will never get there, to do exactly what you are showing.

That's not a bad thing. You want to work on having your own authentic expression and less imitation. Part of the reason I teach the way I teach and push students the way I push them is because I don't want to see people just imitating me. In a way, I feel like it's self-serving. Unfortunately, that imitation tends to feed false personality. What I want is concurrence and sympathy, in the sense of sympathetic action. Overtime, what I want to see are people, in whatever they do, acting with an authentic expression of their understanding and their genuine way of being in relation to what we are doing and teaching, not just mimicry and being really successful in acting like the teacher. Here's what happens, at some point, if this process works the way it's supposed to work. That authentic expression will eventually be completely unique and will in fact no longer even look like the teacher. If the end result of this process is students, after 20 or 30 years, who look like clone teachers, somewhere there was a breakdown. Where is their authentic, genuine and original expression based on what they've learned and the progress they've made? There should be something entirely new. Every generation of practitioners should have an entirely new contribution to the work, because that's what happens when we authentically express our uniqueness and individuality. In the beginning, maybe not so much. Even I do this. Do it this way whether you understand it or not. If we stay in that space after one year, two years or ten years, we've missed the boat.

The "do what we say the way we say it" is training wheels. If we're paying attention, as soon as that student is at a point of stability, then we take those training wheels off and say, "You know what? You need to now explore the model you have and find your way of expressing it that's completely genuine and authentically you." This is expressed in the Sifu Bruce Lee algorithm. "Research your own experience, absorb what's useful, reject what's useless, and add something specifically your own." Those four steps are Bruce Lee's formula for mastery. This is under the umbrella of an organized system or methodology. At some point, the end result of that process is utterly and completely unique. This is very personal. The end results have to be appropriate for you personally.

7. Learn sincerity by not justifying.

Dr. J: The justification is the instant conversation to qualify or defend any particular thought, feeling or deed. Certainly, anytime you are caught either by your self or someone else and there is a photograph or a correction and there's that first string of thoughts, "Well, that's not right. I disagree. This is why what I said or am feeling is justified." That first blush of expression of apologia is justification. The practice is to not do it. When we have a photograph or correction, just for kicks and giggles, try to not do that. In fact, try to accept it, even if you disagree. That's the thing, maybe even especially if you disagree, because that is one of the ways false personality gains power. It believes it has the right, because it disagrees with something for any particular reason at any particular moment, that it does not have to accept a correction, direction or instruction. There's a pop-up thought that "I disagree and here are the reasons, so because of those thoughts and associations, I don't have to pay attention, agree and, in fact, I have perfect justification to not take the correction or even see what's being revealed in this photograph and moment." If we can practice not instantly justifying, it is an exercise toward building sincerity. In the moment, it doesn't matter if you agree or not because we are practicing certain kinds of behavior. If we constantly second guess and challenge every little effort to create a behavior that models higher consciousness, then we never actually get to practice and develop the behavior. Justification undercuts doing what we need to do.

8. Learn sincerity by NOT assuming that you know better.

Dr. J: I have to work on this all the time. I have these I's that automatically put the thought in my head, "I know better than that." Boom! That way of thinking is an expression of false personality because the truth is that I may or may not know better. To automatically assume in any particular thing that I know better is ego. Whatever comes out of that expression is not as genuine as it could be, because if I'm going to have this opinion one way or another, the only way to find out would be to test it or examine experience.

I know better about this because I've done it ten thousand times in ten thousand different ways. That's not justification.

Let's say it is something that doesn't fit that profile. I don't automatically know what's better. If there are ten choices and I had an automatic choice, there might be one or two other ones that might be equally as good that I'm not even considering because I've already decided I know better and this is what I want to do. That's not objective.

We want to practice mental skills that lead us toward more objective states of mind. We need to practice observing when we are in this associative thinking, that the I's are not objective at all. You may or may not know better, but do not assume you do.

9. Be more sincere by being less subjective with likes and dislikes.

Dr. J: I like this and don't like that. Why do you like that? I don't know, I just do. That's totally subjective. I don't like that thought, behavior, exercise, practice or person. Why dislike this or that? I don't know. I just don't. Again, that is subjective. We want to practice being less subjective and more objective about our likes. When we, in our heads, say we like or don't like something right now, it's a good exercise to come back and ask your self, what about this "fill in the blank" creates the thought, "I don't like". Already, by questioning the thought, you start to separate from identifying with the I that is being expressed. One way to be more objective is to place less emphasis on the I having the thought. Stand off in the self-observant, self-remembering space and ask the question, "Why does this one not want to do this? Why does this I not like this? Why does this one or I like this so much? What about this makes one want to run away? What about this makes one want to do it without thinking?" Bring that self-observing attitude toward your likes and dislikes.

10. To be sincere, you must remember you are not one.

Dr. J: It's lying to pretend you are one. As long as I've studied the many I's I notice how easy it is for me to fall into this easy, imaginary way of thinking that I am any particular thing or that I believe any particular thing whole heartedly or that I want to do any particular thing or not, that there's just one I. It's so easy to fall into that. That's the inclination of the machine and false personality. It is a really good exercise to remind your self there is more than one I. There are many I's. We don't know how many. Remember that whatever you are is not necessarily the I being expressed, which might be an opinion, a feeling, an attraction, repulsion, an agreement or a disagreement. Whatever you are is something other than that. It's lying to pretend you are one.

To really have a definite opinion about I, in other words, "I definitely never do this or that". That's a lie. I can't say that about anything. I can't say I don't have an I capable of thinking or doing just about anything. It would be lying for me to say otherwise. I have violent I's. I have I's capable of expressing any harmful thing, thought, word, action and deed. I have I's I like to think are the good guys. I have my white hat I's and my black hat I's. The white hat I's are humanitarian and want to help, be generous and give you the shirt off their backs without thinking twice about it. Then I have other I's who would negotiate your shirt off of you so they could sell it to someone else. These all coexist at the same time. At any particular point or moment, to pretend there is just one of me is a lie. I have to understand that and see it as clearly as possible and constantly remind myself. I have to constantly come back to, "I am not one. I am many. I am legion".

11. Do not have hidden agendas. Make the inner as the outer and the outer as the inner.

Dr. J: This is a super important one. Do not have hidden agendas. When we are working and living together, when we are developing relationships together, we have to acknowledge there are parts of us which always want to have something going on the side, outside or in the background. There is always a part of us forming contingency plans if it all goes wrong and belly up. Those are the "what if" I's. "What if" I's lead to agendas. Agendas are when we start noticing we have groups of I's doing something completely different than what the rest of us are supposed to be doing. Those are the agenda I's.

At least within the context of our practice, we want to practice not having agendas. It's very difficult to do that, I know. It means we cannot manipulate each other. It means in order to not have agendas we have to practice disclosure. Disclosure is anti-agenda, unless the disclosure is part of the agenda. "I'm going to disclose something to you because I anticipate a certain reaction from you, which will give me justification to do something else." That's an agenda. Generally speaking, disclosure is good because it helps to practice our self-observation and self-remembering, at least with each other.

With your work partners in life, you want to practice not having agendas. In the world, it may be very functional to have agendas. For example, there is such a thing as a business plan. That is an agenda. There are marketing strategies. Sales promotions and programs are agendas. In the context of our lives and those we are working with, we need to constantly come back to asking, "What is my agenda with this person? Is there one?" If there is, we want to work on letting it go. Part of it is in disclosure.

One of the reasons I do regular check-ins is to create opportunities for disclosure and to work on our differences and negative emotions, which lead to agendas. There are different kinds. You might have an agenda you will hang on to a certain list of negative items against someone no matter what. You don't disclose it. It's like a gothic Santa Claus where you have this list of naughty and nice and you check it twice and by god you are not going to let go of it. That's an agenda of holding accounts. We have to struggle with this.

Make the outer as the inner and the inner as the outer. I don't want to think about what I've said to anyone. When I talk to you and we talk amongst ourselves, I don't want to worry about that. I don't want my actions to be so inconsistent with my words or that I have some agenda with my words that I have to keep track of so I don't slip up and accidentally say or do something not in accordance with my agenda. As much as possible, I want to live authentically with what I know and believe. We want to be what we know. That's part of being authentic.

12. Translating knowledge into being and making efforts to be what you know will curb lying and generate sincerity.

Dr. J: Practice to verify. Initially, when we try to practice a new way of being, it is very difficult and quite hard because it runs contrary to our habits, whether they are physical, mental or emotional. The practice gives us verification. There is something that is a result of our practice. Don't take practice for granted. "Oh, I practiced the other day." Well, that's good. Everyday, ask yourself, "What's my practice today?" I want to look back and say, "I practiced yesterday." I don't want there to be big gaps. Sometimes I want to have practice in the morning and practice in the evening. Why? I'm trying to create a thread of continuity of consciousness. I'm trying to string intentional moments together like pearls on a necklace. I believe, if I can string enough intentional moments of practicing being what I know and being who I want to be together, that I can craft something quite beautiful. By cultivating practice as part of my way of life, it curbs lying. I no longer have these longs gaps where I can go off into negative imagination and into other directions and get off base too much. Why?
Because I literally only have a few hours before I have to practice again. It tends to keep one moving between the curbs a little better.

School is important not just because it's a place to practice. It is important because it is an environment where you get to practice quite often. Overtime, that has an effect. We will be different if we sustain our practice. We can't even imagine what that difference is today. All we can say is, "Well, I've been practicing this last year and I feel very different. I think different thoughts. I am in a different place than I was a year or two years ago." What has transpired in that time is a result of practice. I've been practicing disclosure and cultivation of integrity and sincerity. I've been working to be a more authentic expression of the possibility of who I am. I am different because of it. I can only assume this will continue. If I keep practicing, I will be more myself in the future.

CHAPTER EIGHT: Exercises for Harmonizing Your Centers

1. Make your acts follow your decisions. Fulfill your agreements.

Dr. J: There are two parts to this. In order to fulfill agreements, we have to make agreements. That is why I say that I strive to do everything by agreement. This is a principle of the work. We practice creating agreements, making agreements, agreeing to agreements and then acting as if those agreements have weight and merit. We then do whatever we can to fulfill the conditions of our agreements. It means that when we find ourselves outside of our agreements, we make a note, observe it and make extra-special efforts to correct and come back to our agreements. It's so easy in the world, when you are not working on yourself, to not keep your word. We agree to all kinds of things and then literally the next minute, turn around and go, "Eh, I changed my mind." We have all kinds of reasons and justifications for not keeping our word. Things like, "Well, meant to keep that agreement, but I thought it was because you were a certain way. Now that you're not a certain way, I don't feel like I should have to keep my agreement anymore." Here's one I hear so many times. When I mention to someone they are not acting in accordance with an agreement we made, they will look at me, or maybe through the phone or email, and they'll go, "I changed my mind." There is no justification whatsoever here. There's the idea that because you were in one mind when you made the agreement, later when you are in another, it doesn't matter. It's as if the left hand can make an agreement but the right hand doesn't have to keep it. This will happen even when we try to work on ourselves. We will write a check from one part of ourselves that another part of ourselves has to cash. When the time comes to put up or shut up, the part of us that's present at that time doesn't want to do it and doesn't acknowledge the agreement another part of us in another time and space actually made.

It's important to observe this because, if nothing else, it is another way of validating or proving there is not one of you, there are many. We are all a little bit schizophrenic because we can wholeheartedly look someone right in the eye and make a commitment. We shake hands and spit, lay hands on sacred texts and by all the powers and gods that be. A moment later, an hour or a day, it's as if that vow never took place and that agreement was never made. It's as ephemeral as smoke. We all do this.

The practice and work idea is to fulfill your agreements. This also means that you pay attention to yourself and work on not making agreements too casually. Sometimes I've made agreements for every little thing, even when I'm not paying attention or when I have divided attention. I'm really thinking about one thing, but I'm talking about something else. I hear off in the distance my mouth making words that "I intend to" or "I aim to" or "I agree to do this, that and the other thing". Because I'm not paying attention, I think that it's not like a signature. Why we do sign contracts? They state, by that action, that they were present when the agreement was made. When we have contracts and write them out and sign them, it is a reminder we were there. We even put a statement in the agreement that "I am of competent age to be able to determine for myself whether or not knowledgeable, informed, lucid, present and whether or not I have the ability to make agreements. I sign this agreement, with full knowledge that I am making a commitment and I will be held according to my word, which I am giving here." Then you sign something to say you are competent to sign something to make an agreement.

I have that on some of my own agreements. In our daily lives, we make agreements all the time with no intention of keeping them. We make agreements for all kinds of reasons. We make agreements because we don't want to disappoint someone, which of course, on some level we have to realize if we don't keep the agreement we will disappoint them more. We don't think it through. We don't take responsibility for the causative nature of our actions. Making agreements gives us responsibility for the causative nature of our actions.

Karma, a natural law, is a fulfilling of an agreement. If every thought, action and deed we do has a karmic consequence, and previously in our lives we were subject to a great deal of what we think of as accidental and incidental karma (in other words, things happen and we have no control and that's just the way it is because we weren't consciously part of the formation of our karma), agreements are a tool to change our karma. When we make agreements with consciousness and intention, knowing there will be a consequence as the result of our agreement, and then we fulfill that agreement, we get a karmic benefit. A benefit is karma we consciously create.

We make small and big agreements. This is one way to bring conscious control into the way karma manifests in our daily lives on an individual and group level. You can use the ability to make and keep agreements as a barometer of your ability to remain conscious. If you are tripping or checking in and out, if your level of consciousness is constantly going into sleep or near waking sleep, then you'll notice it's almost impossible to keep your word. In fact, the word of individuals who are always in sleep or near sleep means nothing. It doesn't matter what they say, how emotional or heartfelt or apparently conscious or intentional it is, it is guaranteed 100% they won't keep that agreement.

The only possibility we have of fulfilling our agreements is that, when the time comes to do so, we are in relatively the same state of awareness or consciousness that we were when we made the agreement. That means we have to work on maintaining that over a period of time.

We might make an agreement to work with each other in clear communication with honesty and clarity to the best of our abilities. Guess when payment for that agreement comes due? Anytime you are challenged with any other kind of communication other than what I just described. All of a sudden, you find you are not communicating clearly, honestly or with disclosure, openness and compassion. You are now in violation of the previous agreement.

It would be really helpful to be able to notice that. If we found ourselves not fulfilling our agreements, the prudent thing to do would not be to abandon the agreement but rather to do whatever is necessary and possible to come back in line and in harmony with that agreement. There are no excuses. Nothing else is acceptable. Unless the agreement said something like, "I'm going to speak with you about our personal lives and relationships as clearly, honestly and openly as I can at all times except if you're being resistant or except if you're not listening to me." I didn't put that as a caveat before. I didn't put into the agreement that it was conditional on you responding a certain way or that you look or sound a certain way. Technically speaking, how you respond to that communication is irrelevant to my agreement. The enforcement or fulfillment of the agreement comes from myself and is not dependent upon you because it wasn't part of the original agreement.

"Make your acts follow your decisions." The acts are all the little accommodations and corrections we do to try and bring ourselves back into harmony with our agreements. All this behavior, both making agreements, correcting of aberrations and the fulfilling of the decisions is crafting and creating karma. We can be a functional source of creating karma for ourselves. These actions are also validation and verification for us internally that we have something substantial that can make a decision. In order to fulfill agreements, you have to have a certain amount of will and being. If you don't have the will to do and a certain amount of being to carry through, you will not be able to follow through with decisions and agreements.

It's a practice. It harmonizes centers and brings me energy every time I keep to my agreement. I develop integrity within myself. The root word of integrity is "one". To harmonize our centers is the same as cultivating a state of "oneness" as opposed to a state of fractured lack of oneness, our ordinary state.

2. Do not sleep too much. Work hard.

Dr. J: This is both literal and figurative. It literally refers to physically sleeping too much. Don't be too attached to how much sleep you get or don't get. It is one of the most common justifications in the world to be out of sorts and not be present and conscious to working on yourself because you didn't get enough sleep. I can use that as a justification of any darn thing. I could be in a cranky, bad mood, negative and resistant, all day long. Every time it is pointed out, I can say, "Well I'm this way because I didn't get enough sleep last night." Everybody would nod their head and think that was perfect justification. What I didn't say was that I'm being out of sorts because I'm not observing myself and working on myself today. I just said I didn't sleep enough. What's enough sleep? When have I ever had enough sleep? My machine loves to sleep. In fact, all things being equal, my machine thinks virtually anything that takes it out of the bed is an Impediment to its well being. The bigger and the more comfortable the pillows are and/or my bed company, the more I like being in that sleepy state. I'm attached to my naps.

I plan classes and have the course day of the class start about one or two hours than I would ever normally want to have to do anything? Why do I do that? I'm in charge right? You know what I did for years? Let me explain this because it is telling. I didn't really appreciate the value of this comment. For years, I wouldn't start teaching a class before 10am for all the tea in China. People would say, "Why can't we get started earlier? We get up at 6am. We get up at 7am. We get up at 8am. Other schools do their morning meditation at 5:30 in the morning. Why do you not even want to start class until 10am?" You know why I didn't? It was because I like to sleep late. I like to stay up late and I like to sleep late. Since I was in charge I would think to myself, "To heck with it. I can keep my own schedule. If you want to learn from me, then guess what? The day will start a little later and go a little longer because that's what serves me. That's what makes me feel good." I realize that when I made myself, on purpose with intention, get up earlier and have a little less sleep than my machine was naturally inclined to get, that for short periods of time my attention and energy for class was a little higher than when I didn't do that. I didn't do it for the students. I learned about this principle of not sleeping too much. When I'm teaching, I wanted to engage in that.

The other is "work hard". Work hard means whatever is hard for you. It is not necessarily according to someone else's definition. What is a little over and above, a little beyond, a little extra effort from you? You are doing a task. Ordinarily let's say you work for an hour or two hours or three or five. That's normally what you are good for and where you want to quit and take a break and do something completely different. A work idea is to not stop then. When you are very clear you've come to a point where you want to quit, make an aim and go a little bit longer. Go a little further and harder. This is the only way you can increase your capacity to work. Let's say we were working by a time clock and get off at 5pm, but everybody actually quits working at 4:30pm. A work idea would be to work at the highest possible level you can until 5pm and maybe five or ten minutes longer, as opposed to 4:30pm in anticipation to stopping work in 30 minutes. That's an example of working hard. If it doesn't cause you personally a little discomfort, you haven't worked hard enough. If you are still within your comfort zone, you haven't worked enough.

3. Do everything the best way you can.

Dr. J: That is so tough. When I think about the different things I do during my day, if every single day I went back and did a little check list of the various things I did, worked on or conversations I had with people, and then asked myself, "Did I bring my full attention to bear with everything I did during the day?" unfortunately, it is quite sad how often I would have to say I didn't. This is an aim, "to strive to do everything the best way I can". It doesn't matter what it is. If I work to make money, I want to do a really good job of that. If I'm writing something, I want to write as well as I can. If I'm editing something I want to be the best editor I can. It's all relative.

4. Exercise, eat properly and eliminate wasteful habits.

Dr. J: We all need to do some kind of exercise. We are a yoga school so technically we choose to emphasize yoga. It can be physical activities like martial arts, stick fighting, kickboxing or kung fu. It could be jogging or running. It could be Hatha yoga. It is anything that really engages your physical machine on a daily basis. You want your physical machine to be engaged in activity because we build up energy in our bodies. It manifests as a kind of anxiety. That anxiety and restlessness is distracting. When we exercise, we feed the machine. We dissipate static electricity (as a metaphor). By doing so, the machine quiets down and gives us a little space. By doing a little exercise frequently and consistently, we gain energy. We do get stronger. It improves circulation, resistance to disease, mental, emotional and physical stability, but only up to a point. If we get all fanatic about it and go crazy exercising all day every day to solve our emotional problems, well now we've become compulsive, and that creates another problem. Some exercise is necessary. By reducing susceptibility to injury and disease and increasing well being, we create a more harmonious working environment that balances our energy centers. When we don't exercise we are not as strong, durable, energetic, and we tend to not sleep as well. We have more irregular energy through the day. It makes it harder to work on yourself when you feel like you are in a coma.

Eat properly goes without saying. Nutrition is our fuel. If we run our machines on low-grade fuel, the pipes get choked up. The exhaust gets nasty. We are slower and not as efficient. We have lower energy and are more inclined to have to rest more because the fuel is not being burned as efficiently. Poor nutrition can cause disease, which further inhibits working on us as efficiently as well.

Eliminate wasteful habits. This refers to any mechanical habit that interferes with any ability to keep your agreements to eat properly, exercise and work on yourself.

5. Develop ability in one of the arts.

This is a really useful exercise. I think it's useful for everyone to have something they do that's creative. That's what we mean by art. It doesn't matter what it is. It could be music, sculpture or performance. It could be writing. It could be your exercise. Cultivate your exercise as an art. Bring an art mind to the way you practice your yoga for example. You can think, "How can I use this practice right now to express who I am as a person right now? How can I use my practice to express what I really believe about this practice?" It could be almost anything.

Music especially is a good choice, as it has the capacity to combine the efforts of multiple centers in harmonious function all at the same time. It can stimulate or calm, sedate and or balance. It can influence one or more centers over others specifically. Consider how drumming may engage the physical center, awaken the instinctive, bring emotional awareness and the play of the intellect all at once.

6. Choose the middle path between extremes.

Dr. J: When you identify an extreme behavior or an extreme point of view, whether you understand it or not, make a decision and an aim to pursue a middle path in regard to that extreme. We justify extremes. We identify extreme points of view. We place all kinds of conditions on moving away from them. That's the antithesis of being and working. When you are working on yourself, you cannot afford to hold onto your extreme positions. You can't afford to have too extreme of a behavior of any kind. It takes you away from yourself. It takes you away from your work. It ties you up in one particular area in one little compulsion, one little negativity, and because of that you can't move forward. It puts you into a loop of a certain kind of repetitive thinking and actions, which are recurring. The work idea is when you identify extreme positions, thoughts and behavior, that on purpose with intention you make an agreement not to do that. I didn't say stop. I didn't say throw it away or abandon it completely. What I said was that it's a mind thing. What is the middle path? What is a compromise path I can do, think or feel in relation to this and move toward it? Just do it for the sake of the exercise. Why? It harmonizes your centers. In extremes, one part of a center over the others is being emphasized in relation to that issue. Whenever we hard focus on one center, we Imbalance the others. Because of that we lose and waste energy.

7. To get rid of imagination, be less identified.

Dr. J: Identification leads to imagination. When we say imagination, we talk about a leakage that occurs in the machine, which reduces your energy and distorts the function of the centers and interferes with their ability to work with each other in harmony.

Be less identified. Whenever you catch yourself in imagination about something you are identified with, bring attention to it. First observe it, because of course you can't possibly make a change if you are not aware of it or can't see it. If you are clear about it and you see you are identified and there is no real basis for that identification, or you see you are spending a lot of energy Imagining different circumstances, results or analyses—if you notice you are in that mental loop, bring your attention to something more concrete.

I find it's really helpful to practice letting go of my compulsion to be right as an initiating factor to doing something that could be very helpful. I find it very helpful to let go of the idea that I have to understand something completely before I make a change. Here's the funny thing. If you were really rational about your life, one of the things you would see as a pattern is you've never used the criteria of complete understanding to make a decision about anything. That's an illusion. That's imagination. We all make decisions all the time with less than a perfect understanding of what it all means, where it's all going to go and what the consequences will be. Where we select to apply this criterion, which in an imaginary way we say we do all the time but we don't; in other words, I say, there is something J has asked me to do or a way she has asked me to be. I say I'm not going to do it because I don't really understand why J wants me to do it, what the benefit is to me to do what she wants me to do. I tell J, "You know, I'm not even sure I want to do what you're asking because I don't understand it completely and the benefits to me." I use that as a way to keep from making an agreement with J. The truth is if I then set that aside and think about the hundred other things I did during the day rapidly and willy-nilly without one thought whatsoever of whether I understood it or not, the application of those criteria of understanding is purely subjective and arbitrary.

We have to understand this in order to say that is a process of identification. I'm identified to the idea I have to understand something completely in order to commit to it. I commit all the time without understanding, so it's never stopped me before.

154

Why is it stopping me now? I have identification and imagination about whatever is in front of me right now. It's bringing up something for me. This is the justification I'm using not to confront or address it.

8. To be less identified, do not think of yourself as "I" all the time, especially from calling unstable or over emotional I's "I".

Dr. J: The I's that demand to be referred to as I the most are the overly emotional I's. "Ahhh. I think. I believe. I feel."

One school I was in had the idea a teacher would sometimes do this. When they saw you expressing opinions heavily laced with the word I, they would tap you on the knee and they would say, "Try using the word 'one'. For the next five minutes, don't use the word 'I'." Then you would have to express whatever opinion without using "I" and watch what happens. We will do that as an exercise. Sometimes as an exercise, you realize that yes, you had emotional I's that really believed and supported your point of view, but when you started thinking about it in this meta-mind, third person point of view as in "one has this opinion", you might realize there are other parts of you at the very same moment which don't agree with what you were saying. In fact, they might have completely different and alternative points of view. We are like that. We can have two, completely opposite points of view functioning in our head at the very same moment.

The emotional I's get to express theirs. Emotion is the most powerful thing we have. It drives us and always dominates. It's just like using too much hot pepper in a recipe. I like spicy food. I don't want Habañeros in every meal even though I like spicy peppers. Habañero is emotion. If I put too many Habañeros in my food, after a point it becomes unpalatable. In fact, if I put too much pepper in it, it no longer is food and could be used as a weapon. My love of spice might lead me to create a weapon of self-destruction in my kitchen. I have over spiced the food before and then could not eat it. Extreme emotion can do that. You might have a valid point of view more in harmony with yourself than not, but because there is so much emotion in it, you invalidate your position and lose power.

9. To avoid identification in unstable and overly emotional parts of you, remember that things change and will be different tomorrow.

Dr. J: Don't panic. No matter what it looks like in the moment. Yesterday we were doing some self-work and most of the time we were at a very high level of attention, and it was good practice. At the end we were getting tired and kind of lost it there. We spent our coin. You only have so much attention, or "money", to spend on a certain level of work at any point of time. Once you spend it, you're empty. You don't have any more. It'll look like that. "What happened?" It's like you ran out of gas and now it's bumper cars instead of a race. We are going every which way. That's typical.

When you find yourself locked into this hyper-emotional, extreme state of mind, remember to remind yourself that it will change. Those emotional I's say this, "Well this is how it is. It's always going to be like this. It's never going to change." Guess what? It always changes, if you just wait an hour or two hours (that's the value of time outs, by the way). Sometimes by just taking that little break, the edge comes off the emotion. You have a little restoration of the balance of your centers. Then when you come back, you don't relate to what you were relating to the same way. That always happens.

The next thing is, don't panic. I call it the roller-coaster of escalation. In other words, we have the building of anxiety up to a point. Then we have the freak-out. That's where the roller coaster tops the hill. Now we are all going to die. We throw the baby out with the bath water. That's the downhill part. Guess what? On a roller coaster it doesn't just go down. There is a point to where it levels out and it starts going up again. There is always a wave-like characteristic to the way emotions play out. When you get locked up into identification and imagination, designate some I in the background to go, "Don't panic. It is going to change."

Imagination is when you have a negative thought and you imagine and play out in your head the complete, worst possible consequence if it came true. In other words, you tell me you don't love me anymore. I immediately imagine what the worst, possible result could be in what that might mean. I don't think automatically, "Well, obviously we need to work on our communication." That's not my first thought. My first thought is, "My life is over with this person. We're done. We have nothing else to share." That's more like my first thought. Then what do I do? I elaborate on it. "Now I know why you've

155

been treating me the way you've been treating me. Now I know what this means." I start going off in six different ways in imagination, somehow trying to string them all together like some twisted string of pearls, where no two pearls are or can actually be connected to each other.

Don't panic. Take a breath and wait. Things will change in a little bit.

10. To diminish negative emotion, diminish the self-justification that feeds it.

Dr. J: I see right now I'm experiencing a really strong emotion. If I'm working on myself and I've been studying and trying to get these ideas into my head and I remember to diminish negative emotion, diminish the self-justification that feeds it, I start to look for how I am justifying how I feel right now. "How am I resistant to letting it go right now?" Whatever that is, it is justification. That is what I have to let go.

To let go might be another way to say, "Stop paying attention to it". Stop holding it in your mind's eye. Stop ruminating over it, what ever "it" is while running around and looking at it from every possible direction. It can also be thinking about something else. Stop emphasizing the self-justification. As an exercise within the exercise, to first notice I'm in a strong, negative emotion regarding you or me, instead of justifying why I'm in the negative emotion, I'm just going to agree with your point of view, even though I don't agree because it's contrary to my self-justification of my position. It doesn't matter if I believe it or not.

STUDENT: I've noticed I've used that negatively just so someone will stop talking.

Dr. J: That's not what I'm talking about. When you use that on purpose to diminish your own expression negativity.

STUDENT: Consider they might be right.

Dr. J: Whether they are or not is a moot point. Agreement is an antidote to self-justification. "I don't have to agree with you because you're wrong and I know you're wrong. I know blah, blah, blah…and you don't agree with that." This is an excuse to continue to be in this negative state of mind. When I find myself in that position and I consider for a second the exercise, I might go, "Actually J is a smart person. J is an emotional genius. If she is expressing this, there might be something valid in it." The whole time, in the back of my head there is something screaming, "To hell with her point of view and the horse she rode in on." With consciousness, willfulness and intention I try to think thoughts that are not self-justifying and more positive toward J, even though she might be completely wrong. That is irrelevant. What does it matter if she is wrong if I use that as an excuse to be wrong myself? What higher position have I actually succeeded in obtaining? I haven't. I'd be allowing her being wrong to be an excuse for me to be wrong. Now together we become a dog chasing its tail. I don't know if I'm the dog or if she's the tail. One way or the other, we are not making progress.

11. To increase control, externally consider.

Dr. J: Practice random acts of kindness. To externally consider means to have compassion. When I'm feeling selfish and thinking a lot about my needs, I notice I've been thinking about what I want and what feels right to me a lot. I'm turning inward and I'm being self-centered. I'm identified with that. Whatever that is will imbalance me.

To increase control, when I notice I am in that self-directed, self-motivated, introspective mode, one of the practice ideas is to get up and do something for someone else you think would benefit them. It's especially valuable when you don't want to. Where that exercise has the most value is when it is the last thing you would ordinarily want to do.

I'm mad at you and I'm holding on to that anger. Of course, the last thing I'm going to do is be nice to you. Of course, the last thing I'm going to do is be close to you. I don't want to be close to you. I hate you right now. If I'm working on myself, I'm going to observe that attitude and I'm going to make an effort to do something good for you. I will be kind to you. I will do something that in ordinary circumstances might even be inappropriate.

156

What I mean is that it's really not inappropriate to be loving with someone when you're really mad at them, really disgusted with them. That's not the appropriate time to show love. We're supposed to be passive-aggressive, repressed, defensive and argumentative. Or, if we're really progressive then we just keep our opinions to ourselves. If you can't say something good, don't say anything at all. Right now I don't like you very much and don't have anything good to say so I'm just not going to say anything to you. If you talk to me, I'm not even going to look at you because by making eye contact you might be able to read me. You might be able to know that I'm withholding from you and trying to avoid you because I don't like you very much right now. If you ask me something, I'm going to grunt and give some monosyllabic answer. If you persist I'm just going to get up and go somewhere else. I'm going to invent some job that suddenly needs doing that is somewhere else other than where you are.

The exercise is that if you observe yourself in that state of mind, then initiate a spontaneous act of kindness and/or generosity completely in opposition with what you feel and what you think. Just do it as an exercise and not because you anticipate getting some particular benefit. It harmonizes your centers. That's why you do it.

We do things to give us energy but we cannot be attached to feeling that we are getting energy. These are two different things; feeling that you are getting energy and actually receiving energy, whether you feel it or not. The feeling is irrelevant. For example, by sitting here in this room we are constantly and continuously exchanging energy. Do you always feel it? Have you been aware that for the past 40 minutes I have been sharing energy with you? Whether you feel it or not is irrelevant to whether or not you are receiving it. I've been getting energy from you. I'm aware of it on some level but I don't always feel it. If you are paying attention to anything at all, you are exchanging energy with that which you are bringing attention to bare. That's how attention works.

Even when you are mad at someone and you are self-consumed with your madness and anger inside your head and you think you want to be separate from them, the more disturbed you are, the more mad you are, the more you are exchanging energy with them. It's not necessarily the kind you want. What resists persists. The more you push back, the more you receive.

We do this unconsciously all the time. We want to try and harmonize and give and exchange energy with more intention instead of incidentally and by accident.

12. To be less identified, give up attitudes that condone negativity.

Dr. J: Right now, even today, almost everyone here in this room has expressed an attitude, which if you hold on to and cling to that attitude, it is guaranteed that you will express negativity in relation to it. As long as you have that attitude, you will express negativity.

Sometimes it feels like giving up a cherished possession. How about this? As an exercise, instead of giving away, like taking to the goodwill the things you absolutely know you have no use for anymore, try once and a while throwing something in that you actually value, as an exercise on giving up something you value. Most of us wouldn't consider this for a second. Why would we give it up if we value it? It doesn't make any sense. That's the way we are with our attitudes. It doesn't matter that certain attitudes we have always create negativity. These attitudes may always be a barrier between us. They are our cherished possessions. We know them so well. We have to practice giving up small to give up big. How are you going to give up your life when you die and give up your body and move into your transition when you can't even give up a simple attitude? How are you going to give up big things requiring sacrifice on every level of your being when you haven't practiced even giving up the smallest things? We have to practice giving up small things.

13. Lessen identification by working on other people less with your own requirements.

Dr. J: What requirements are we going to substitute when working with each other? We call them work ideas. In other words, the further we go along in our daily life of practice, as we work on and with each other, we want to substitute more of the personal affectations of the work we do with ways of working which are principles based on the work.

You have to learn the work ideas. As you work on other people, work from those ideas and less from your own personality and self-serving interests. My reason for helping you and coaching you should not be just to make my life more comfortable. That's not a work idea. As I work on you and coach you on working on yourself, if I have as an outcome to make my life more comfortable, well that's not a work idea and it's not sustainable. Over time, it won't work. Whatever I'm giving you as an initiation into the work and exercises and so on over time have to come less from my personality and more from work ideas and principles. If you don't know what those are then that reveals your level of practice. Study until you know what they are.

We've already covered some of them in great detail—this idea of self-observation and self-remembering, not expressing negativity, etc., etc. When I formulate work ideas for you or for someone else, or if you're doing the same for someone else, before you give them the task, try to think, "How does what I'm asking this person to do relate to the work? Does it relate to the work?" If it clearly does not, then you need to consider that. It might be coming from false personality or ego.

14. Resist identification by not pretending there is anything noble, strong or justified about it.

Dr. J: Most people relish in their identification. We teach our kids how to do this. For example, identify with religion. This is one of the first ways we teach our children that being identified with something is noble or strong or justified. "Your religion, our family's religion, is the best there is and it's the only way that counts. Nobody else's way counts or matters. If you do it this way, the only way, then you are noble and strong and you will always be right because our way is the right way. Any other way is the wrong way." That's a way to teach kids to be utterly and completely identified. Then we have sports. We have this idea that the sport is America's pastime, like baseball for example. Is it really? How many people do you know actually play baseball? We don't even own anything baseball. We do have baseball caps though. That's why it's cool to where a baseball cap. When you wear one, you are identifying as an American, as showing symbolically your support for America's pastime. The rest of the world does not wear baseball caps. They have their own kinds of caps. Thais and Vietnamese and Cambodians don't wear baseball caps. They wear triangle hats that sit this high off the top of their heads. They work because they create airflow around the top of your head. You go to Africa, which I've never been to Africa, but I've seen pictures of Tuareg tribal people. They wear turbans made of cloth on top of their heads. They don't wear baseball caps. Can you imagine a Tuareg in the middle of the Sahara with his baseball cap? You'd have to know he works for a US company and is showing support for America's pastime. I'm using this as an example.

There is nothing strong, noble or justified about being identified. When we are completely identified with anything, no matter how good or bad, we are not objective. We become it rather than separating from it. What do we wish to be? Do I wish to be the icon of baseball? Is that the evolution possibility there for me? Do I wish to be the world's most perfect husband? Am I identified with that? Is that noble, strong or justified? Who gets to define the world's most perfect husband? What is the definition? In different cultures, they have different definitions. There are cultures that say it's perfectly appropriate for a husband to have wives and girlfriends on the side and have no disclosure between any of them. The husband's job is to make as many children as possible with as many women as possible, irrespective of what the women or the children think. If he does so he's considered a real and successful man. Is that the definition I want to use for myself? No, it's not. I don't necessarily know an ultimate one that's better. Until I might have such a thing, I don't want to be identified with a concept for which there is no definition.

If you think about most of the things with which you are identified, if you were in an objective moment and you wrote down on a piece of paper a word or concept, my guess is that you would not be able to define it. Now you are going to prove me wrong because that is a typical thing we would do. You will write a really good definition. You won't believe, however, what you wrote. It's subject to change. Do you want to be completely identified with something you don't actually believe, understand or can define, and which will change over time as subject to circumstances? I want to be something other than that.

15. Transform negative emotion by realizing you are the one who observes rather than what you observe.

The whole point of self-remembering and self-observation is to create the possibility of objectively seeing that you are not that which observes. Whatever you are is what sees what you are being identified with. You are not that which is identified.

The real you is the other. I believe this is what Swami Vivekananda was referring to in his treatise on Jnana Yoga, when he said "That Thou Art."

16. Develop intellectual parts of centers by listening rather than speaking.

Dr. J: This was one of the really good things "L" was having us practice yesterday. We were giving practice to a listening exercise. Notice how hard it is to practice a listening exercise. Here we are as people who pride ourselves in a way as being good listeners. If you ask me, "Are you a good listener?" I'd answer, "Pfftt! Of course I'm a good listener. I'm a great listener." Right up until we have to do a listening exercise and then it's like, "Whatever, I don't have to listen to what you're saying. Well I would listen better if you said something that made more sense or was more interesting or if you would stop lying. I don't have to listen to you because what you're saying is not correct."

Develop intellectual parts. When we practice the listening exercise, it feeds the intellectual part of our centers. That way of feeding the intellectual center is different than thinking about things. Thinking about things does not feed the intellectual center. In fact, a lot of "thinking" steals energy. It does the opposite from what you might think it would do. Part of the way you feed intellectual centers is by listening. This is also why, most of the time, we don't really function in the higher parts of centers. How much time during the day do you spend listening? Most of the conversation in your head is not listening. Talking about listening is not the same thing as doing it.

17. To begin to correct what is wrong with you, cease to justify.

Dr. J: Every time we point out something we know is not right with us we throw in the word "but". "Well, I know I do this and that's not good. BUT, I know I'm not really relating to you in the right way now, but…I know I really should be responding different now, "but" We need to cut out "but". Catch yourself "butting". Can you do it a different way? How about when you are expressing something you know is not right and you know you are not doing to the best of your ability, instead of saying the word "but", just say it and let it be. "I'm having difficulty with this. I know I need to work on being closer to you. I know I need to work on being more open." Don't say or even think "but". Whatever follows is justification. "I know I should wash the dishes right now, "but" Whatever it is, handle it and don't qualify it. That is very important, especially if you know it is negative and doesn't make you look well. Allow yourself to not look so good. If you can correct it, then do so without justifying.

18. To eliminate wrong work of the sex center, give up useless activity.

Dr. J: Bring the same level of attention to your sex center and functions as you do to the other kinds of functions and centers you are working on. The sex center is important. It is one of our three primary centers (Instinctive, Sexual, Emotional and Intellectual). We are working to harmonize all of the centers, so we have to find an appropriate expression for all of the centers. We have to find how to bring energy to all of the centers, including the sex center. This is one of the areas many schools have issues with. Everyone talks about the sex and the sex center, but there is very little in the way of practicing bringing energy to it. The sex center, like any other center, has instinctive, physical, emotional and intellectual parts. All the parts have to have energy and information. You have to care and feed the sex center. We have to negotiate amongst our community and ourselves what the healthy expression of sex within us is. Then we make agreements based on that and work to hold our agreements. We cannot ignore it because now it's the gorilla or the bull in the china shop. The more we ignore it and repress it, the more space it takes, the more influence it has. By bringing energy and consciousness to it, we reduce its potential negative impact to distort all of the activity of the other centers. The Sacred Sexual arts of service and healing practiced in the ancient Sumerian, Egyptian, Greek and Hindu temples, traditional Vedic, Yoga and Tibetan schools and the modern so-called "neo" Tantric schools, are all dealing with practical ways of supporting the integrated and ethical expression of sex energy and the consciousness which it expresses.

The expression of sexual activity and what Wilhelm Reich calls "Genitality" is a proper function of the Instinctive/ Moving Center and not a symptom of imbalance. According to Reich, "*Gradually it became clear that it is a fundamental error to try to give the sexual act a psychological interpretation, to attribute to it a psychic meaning as if it were a neurotic symptom. But*

this is what the psychoanalysts did. On the contrary: any idea occurring in the course of the sexual act only has the effect of hindering one's absorption in the excitation. Furthermore, such psychological interpretations of genitality constitute a denial of genitality as a biological function. By composing it of non-genital excitations, one denies the existence of genitality. The function of the orgasm, however, had revealed the qualitative difference between genitality and pregenitality. Only the genital apparatus can provide orgasm and can discharge sexual energy completely. Pregenitality, on the other hand, can only increase vegetative tensions. One readily sees the deep rift which formed here in psychoanalytic concepts."
— *Wilhelm Reich, The Function of the Orgasm; Sex-economic Problems of Biological Energy*

19. Physical work puts centers right.

Dr. J: It can be virtually anything that gets you out of your comfort zone. That's why, for example, physical expression of sensual and sexual activity, and consensual, mutual and healthy expression is balancing to the centers, because it does multiple things at the same time. It brings energy to our physical, emotional, intellectual selves. We get to express and dissipate some of this anxiety type of energy. What we come away with is an opening, a window, a calmer place and a more integrated place to continue from.

I'll read this again, "18. To give up wrong work of the sex center, give up useless activity." Useless activity concerning the sex center is anything that expresses that energy in a negative way. Coercive, manipulative…anything not healthy and positive about the expression is wrong work. "Bring the same level of attention to the sex center as your other centers." This goes with "19. Physical work puts centers right."

It's not enough to talk about these things. We have to find practical ways to exercise them. It's not enough to talk about putting positive energy into the sex center. We have to find actual, physical, practical ways to express them. This can be anything that gets you out of your comfort zone. If our condition to practice is that we are always comfortable, the work ideas say that will not be as effective at giving you the results you want. It has to push your boundaries a little bit. It has to push your comfort zone. You can't be completely comfortable. If we find ourselves completely comfortable in our expression, we have to shake it up. We have to deliberately find a way to push us a little further out of our comfort zone. Does this mean to the point of annihilation? Am I talking about being pushed so far out of my comfort zone to where I think I'm going to completely fall apart or lose control? No, but it might be heading in that direction. Why? Because anything that pushes me out of my comfort zone is pushing me in that direction, because I'm not completely in control.

If I was completely in control at all times, well I would be comfortable at all times. This is a hard one. This takes a lot of attention and intention.

20. Behave decently by suppressing extremes of joy and grief.

Dr. J: Avoid excessive laughter and tears. Extremes of anything are equally out of character for the machine. In Chinese medicine (TCM) we talk about the depth of depression and the height of over-joy equally creating illness or the inclination toward illness. If you find yourself extremely happy, come back to the middle. If you find yourself extremely unhappy, come up to the middle.
Notice when you are laughing too much or crying too much.

21. Pay attention to the cycles of the moon.

Dr. J: We should all know where the moon is and what is the cycle of the moon. Lunar astrology is the "our astrology" because it correlates to our emotional rhythms. It has a very strong correlation to instinctive and physical rhythms as the tides within us follow the external tides. Until we can see that and see how that affects the way we are from day to day, see how emotional ebb and flow changes in harmony with the lunar tides, then we are still at the whim of those lunar tides acting in waking sleep. I want to see my lunatic tendencies, my lunar tick, trends and issues, because I want to see what doesn't change. What does not change with the lunar ebb and flow is more akin to my true self. The lunar influence is planetary and cyclical just like the seasons. Therefore, it's mechanical in any expression of emotion or particular kinds of imagination or fantasy that happen to coincide with full moons and new moons, are utterly and completely mechanical. If you track them

160

over time, you find they are repetitive. This has to do with our periodicity of menstruation and ovulation cycles. You need to correlate your fertility and menstruation cycle with the moon because there is the double whammy of emotion and physical expression of energy you are caught between, the hammer and anvil. Whatever is in between is you.

Notice what changes to notice what doesn't change.

Q&A: Exercises for Harmonizing Your Centers

STUDENT: In #20, it talks about suppressing extremes. That sounds negative. All I can think of is "repress". Does it mean to not express?

Dr. J: Suppression is different from repression. Repressing is mechanical and is the normal way you handle uncomfortable things. In this context, "behave decently by suppressing extremes of joy and grief. Avoid excessive laughter and tears." This means to intentionally take the edge off and modify the behavior to move the emotions toward more a moderate expression as a way of harmonizing the centers and not wasting a lot of energy.

STUDENT: #14. It's not related to exactly what it said, but rather what you said about religion, how we teach our kids, "this is the only way. This is the only way." Where do you find the balance, for example, in Fourth Way where you've come to a point in your life where you feel like this is the best way. How do keep from thinking it's the only way versus the way that works for you?

Dr. J: For me, I've come about it through a process. I didn't decide it was the best way. No one told me it was the best way. I don't know that it's the best way. All I know is that it's the best way I know right now. I can't speak of all possible other ways. I can only speak of what I know.

We are taught this idea of identification without consideration. When we flat out say, "This is the best way," you ask, "How do you know it's the best way?" I answer, "Well because I said so or because if you don't agree with me I will hurt you or you will go to hell." That's very different than what we are doing, which is to say, "Here is a way and these are the principles and you have to experiment and practice to see what the benefit will be. You will come to your own appreciation one way or the other." It's very different.

Of course, there is some identification in it because there is a person studying it. I'm nothing but full of identification. I wouldn't be who I am if I didn't get identified just about all kinds of things. The purpose of this work is to try and untangle that mess. Other systems seem to thrive on the identification. In fact, they'll go to a point of even saying, "Actually, you don't even need to know how this works. You don't need to understand it. All you need to do is believe. You don't need to understand. You don't even need to practice. In fact, you can do everything wrong and it's all going to turn out right as long as you believe it will turn out right."

This system does not say that. This system says, "Actually, nothing ever turns out right. It's not right on purpose. If it's not right on purpose, it's not right."

J: I have something about #14. "Resist identification by not pretending there is anything noble, strong or justified about it." When you said it, the first thing that came to mind was that in my family we have a saying, "blood is thicker than water". No matter what is going on out in the world, your family is dependable, good for you and who you support, love and care for. I did that only to realize at some point that this identification with my family's saying was harmful.

Dr. J: Is blood thicker than water?

J: I don't think so.

Dr. J: Here is a statement that says, "Your personal welfare and happiness as a person and evolution as a person is irrelevant to the welfare of the family." Usually what is most important is that the family continues. What if the family is completely dysfunctional and in every way is keeping you from evolving. To whatever degree that is, you have to separate from the family. In some cases it might have to be complete separation. In other cases, it might just be externally. In some cases it could be emotional separation, while in others it might be smaller. Every family is different.

"Blood is thicker than water." This is an example of a cultural identification. "No matter what, J, you have to understand this, that no matter how abusive the family is to you, you have to be loyal. Even if we kill you, you have to agree to it because if we kill you that means we believe that by killing, destroying, diminishing or controlling you, that that's better for the family."

This idea, #14, says that's a myth. Personal evolution is personal. There may be a role for the family or there may not be. The actual role of the family may not be the one assumed by the ordinary interpretation of the biological relationship. We can't be identified one way or the other. You can't say your personal evolution is contingent on the participation and support of your family. If your family is not engaging in the same process of personal evolution as you are, then that reality is not there. That doesn't mean it's good or bad, because we can't justify it. I can't look at my mother's evolution as less than mine, even though I might look and say, "Well she does everything different than me, or is it that I do everything different from her? I'm confused. I don't know." Her path is her path and my path is my path.

J: There was something in #17. "To begin to correct what is wrong with you, cease to justify." Are you saying that when you notice when you're out of sorts and you want to make the correction, you said you say something with "but" and then you say something else.

Dr. J: To justify being out of sorts.

J: Right.

Dr. J: In other words, it is to justify not correcting yourself.

J: Is that also the same as using the word "but" taking away everything you said right before it.

Dr. J: No, it's still there. It just means what follows the word "but" is the most important thing. When you justify, you're saying that what you're justifying is correct and shall remain unchanged so it must be very important.

J: Is it more important than when you say things like, "My aim is to" or "I'm having this issue about", but nah, nah, nah." Is the blah, blah, blah, more important?

STUDENT: I think it depends on your intention of why you're justifying. Are you justifying to bring up a blockage?

J: This one has me a little stumped.

Dr. J: When you are confused, let's come back to the simplest example. "It frustrates me when you are slow to try and understand something, but it's always going to be that way because that's just how I am." That's a complete justification. I've just declared and justified the negative state of mind, which is wrong and not correct or justifiable, so that I don't have to address it at all, by saying, "but it's always been that way and will always be that way." My experience has shown me that it won't change.'

STUDENT: Isn't there a point where you can bring up a justification like I've done before to say, "This is the justification I've been using to not do this. What can I do about it?"

Dr. J: That's different. That is working with this idea of ceasing to justify. In other words, you are looking for a way not to justify. Before we are able to not justify, we have this intermediate process, which is to seek to not justify by exploring the possibility of how I could think of this without the justification. What would that look like? How can I practice without the justification?

J: I've caught myself saying in my head, "All my experiences with men have created this place for me not to be able to trust them, like them, have a decent relationship with them, but…" So that's what I do with them.

Dr. J: You have to be more specific. Name a behavior you do because of that experience.

J: Not trusting.

Dr. J: Here's an example. "I can't trust you because you're a man and because my experience has shown me that all men are not trustworthy." That's a perfect justification. It's completely wrong. There's no truth in it at all. Has the man at the grocery

162

store who checks your groceries ever robbed you or caused you harm? Has the man at the grocery store who volunteers to push your cart out to the car ever done you wrong? Has the man who takes your admission ticket at the movie theater ever done you wrong? Has the waiter at the restaurant…if you started to think about it, you could make a list of ten thousand men in your life who have never done you wrong, who have never hurt you. In fact, maybe they've only shown you generosity and compassion and care and support.

When we justify, that's not what we do. Justification has to believe that that doesn't exist. It has to exist in a world of fantasy. "I can't trust you because men have proven to be unreliable." You are not "men" in my life. You are unique. You are just a man, not all men. For me not to trust you now because all men in my life have been untrustworthy is a non sequitur, because I have no experience with you. I don't know that you're untrustworthy. There's no way I could know without knowing you. That is what's required.

What is required to know if someone is really trustworthy or not? You have to get to know them. If you don't really know them, you can't really say that. When we say it like that, "because of my experience, this is why I…" it seems rational. It feels rational. If you really look at it and break it down, it's not.

The justification is how we make a rational leap of connection to avoid being present how we otherwise could be in the moment. We tie this moment to all past moments, both imaginary and otherwise. Yes, maybe some man in the past did lie to you, was not trustworthy, hurt you and even worked against your advantage. Maybe that is true. There is such a thing that did happen, and that won't change. Did all men and have all men done that? Absolutely not. That's the truth. To then make a judgment about all possible men based on the expression or character of one or two, "Oh no I have more than one. I have two examples." Oh, okay so you have a couple of experiences and you are now going to judge three billion humans and their character of life and their ability to express truth in their life based on the couple of bad apples, which might be very true. You can't make progress this way.

Ceasing to justify, like L was saying, is not possible to just stop on a dime because it's our habit to justify. That "but" happens in my head faster than light or sound. When I'm in that space and I don't want to change, consider or address something, that "but" is there faster than light. L had a really good idea, which is to practice this expression, "I am aware of this. In order to not justify this, what can I do?" Then try and explore possible ways of expression that are not entirely limited by our justification. Part of the answer is to be the behavior and the consciousness we aspire to, with intention and on purpose regardless of the justification. The justification will be there.

J: I have this example that involves you and a past partner. Both of you share this thing called Black Belt. One of them was the shark predator that we talked about this morning and the other was not. However, because of my experience with the shark predator or 5th degree black belt, Immediately when we met and you told me you were a 5th degree black belt, I thought, "Oh no. Here we go again." There's another part of me, that as we started talking that went, "You know, maybe this is a different kind of Black Belt. I've heard there are some that are the good guys." I had to really think about it quite a bit, and then I just decided there was no way for me to think it through. I had to go into the experience and determine for myself what kind of Black Belt he was. I had to take that risk and that chance. Lo and behold, you were different.

Dr. J: I want to say you can take this broadly. Part of the practice is risky from the point of view of when we challenge our assumptions of these buffers and justifications, that in order to get to the other side of them, we have to gamble. It's not a blind gamble. It's an intentional gamble. I'm going to intentionally allow myself to be vulnerable in order to challenge the situation, previous behavior and conditioning, and in order to open the door to the possibility of having a different experience than that which I've had in the past. That's the antithesis to "I need wait until I understand it and can control it completely before I make a change". If we wait, of course we will never make the change because it will always be a restatement of what we already know.

You can't possibly be comfortable ahead of time because you haven't actually been there before. How could I have a condition to not challenge myself or have a practice until I am perfectly convinced it won't challenge me and won't be a restatement of what I've experienced before. This is all my justification for not doing it, when the only way I can become something new and create new karma is to think, act and do something completely different than what I've done in my past. That means I have to do things which are not conditional to all my justifications.

STUDENT: An exercise might be, if you're thinking the concept of intentionally being out of your comfort zone keeps you more awake…then an exercise could be to notice when you're giving a reason to justify, to then ask, "Is this keeping me in my comfort zone?" If it is, that indicates a justification.

Dr. J: It could be. Think about anything when we agree to do that (it could be anything, housework, schoolwork, yard work, personal work, anything) and after the fact, any justification comes up not to do it. Whatever that is, it is what we are talking about. Of course, that can be a long list right?

CHAPTER NINE: Exercises for Dealing with the Instinctive Center

1. Reward the machine after it makes an effort.

Dr. J: Time each gratification. There's a saying from the Bible, "muzzle not the oxen while it is threshing the wheat". When the animal is doing the work it's supposed to be doing, in this case when the machine (when you) are doing the work it's supposed to be doing, reward it. When you are successful, you need to acknowledge that and reward the machine, any time you overcome a substantial obstacle. Renew your focus, commitment and intention to engage your self at a high level. After you have done so, you need to absorb the idea you were one way before and as a result of following the principles you were able to come to a different place. That could be a minute ago, last night, yesterday, or something you've been working on for a week, month or year.

When you do the work and overcome or have a little success and are no longer completely subject to whatever was taking you away from being able to be present, it's a good idea to be very intentional and acknowledge that. Sometimes you can help by doing something rewarding to the machine. It could be a mental acknowledgement. It could be accepting some emotional gift. It could be some restorative, physical expression like taking an extra hour of sleep or getting a bodywork session or treatment. It could be doing something fun and in no particular way relates to a specific practice like listening to music, enjoying a nice meal, splurging with a glass of wine or whatever it is for you. What makes you happy as a treat? Whatever you do, reward yourself with intention. Don't take for granted when you have some little success by letting it pass. Practice being grateful. Have "an attitude of gratitude". Say "thank you" to yourself and in partnership with those you are working. It's very important to do this.

Avoid associating the work with the acknowledgement and let go of identification. All work and no play makes for a dull person. Sometimes that reward looks like play.

2. Be kind to your instinctive center with proper food, rest and impressions.

Dr. J: If we think of the instinctive center as the sum of our physicality, in the sense of our machine, it is the organs, tissue, blood, muscles, brain, nerves, the organ systems and all the individual, mechanical constituents of the machine. When we are not eating well or resting and intentionally taking in constructive and higher impressions, this is disturbing to the machine.

In therapy we call this process disease. If you are not kind to your machine with a healthy diet, the machine starts to deteriorate prematurely and break down. It doesn't operate at its optimum level of efficiency. It's like taking a Formula 1 racecar and feeding it some watered down gas so that it can only function at half of its actual capacity. You have a car built to go over 200 mph. Since you are feeding it bad gas, it only goes 40 mph. Of course, the problem we have with our machine is that sometimes we suspect it is high performance, but because we've been feeding it such low quality nutrients for so long and have gotten used to the lower level of functioning, we then think that's as good as it gets. As we learn more and we learn the sophistication of the nutrition, the food, the way we cook, we constantly seek to Improve and maintain a high quality. Just from the point of view of the mechanical life of our body, it allows that body to manifest its way of being at the highest level it was designed to express.

There is not just one kind of food. Rest is important but it's more than just sleeping. Rest is sleeping and making an effort to get minimum hours of actual sleep everyday. There are little techniques we do like having a safe and calm place to sleep, reducing the light, etc. I started wearing eye shades when I worked with a doctor in Atlanta who ran a medical sleep center. They were doing sleep architecture studies. I learned that the light equivalent given off by an alarm clock is enough to change the brain wave activity. Any light in the room is enough to change the chemical reactions in your brain to cause your sleep architecture to be disrupted. That's when I started wearing eye shades. When I would go to sleep I would have complete darkness over my eyes. Just because we are asleep and our eyes are closed, the optic nerve is still funneling information to the brain. In order to have a complete, deep rest, the number one thing to do is cut off light to the eyes.

Rest also has to do with restorative exercise. When we do yoga and then practice Savasana at the end, we practice going into a deep relaxation state. That's not just something we say. It's quite often possible in Savasana, when it's properly done, to achieve a brainwave or brain activity state equal to or greater than what we normally experience in the bed sleeping. There is a way we can intentionally rest. The idea is that you do the mechanical exercise first, which in this case is the yoga practice. Why? Strenuous and mechanical exercise releases tension and reduces antagonistic muscle reflex, which normally, when we go to bed. If we have a lot of that body tension, we have this higher tonus. What happens is, instead of relaxing, we go into various states of contraction. These contractions have an effect on our brain and pull us away from the delta brain wave activity, or deep sleep. In yoga, when we do exercise and then go into an intentional Savasana, we start to release the antagonistic tension and bring awareness to the different centers in our bodies. We reduce a certain amount of interference. We'll pick it up again later for sure. For the moment we reduce it so when we go into corpse pose, we can now reap the benefits from that by intentionally resting.

There is a difference between going to bed when you are sleepy or tired and intentionally creating a situation of deep rest. Sometimes even ten or fifteen minutes of Savasana may generate more recovery for you and your body than being in bed for eight hours.

Sometimes we go to bed early for 8, 9 or sometimes 10 hours. When we wake up, we are not refreshed. We wake up tired. We wake up tense. We might even wake up with some pain. How restful was that? We are fortunate to have technology, that even if we can't get enough rest in bed, we can actually do a yoga practice and do a meditation or Savasana and make up the difference. It's very important one way or the other that we do it. If you're not getting enough rest in bed at night, then it's really important to do more yoga, including the Savasana practice, because that's where you dip into a state of being that is actually restorative.

When we say restorative yoga, the restoration doesn't happen when you practice. It's what happens when you go into the rest phase immediately following the practice. The deeper and more complete you can get into that, the more profound the benefit of the rest will be.

The last thing in being kind to the instinctive center was this idea of impressions. Food and rest are necessities for the machine's wellbeing at a continued operation at a high level. You want to work everyday at a high level on yourself, on your emotions, with each other? You have to have energy to do that. You can't be sick. You can't be depressed. You can't be overly anxious. There are things and supplements we take. Food is a supplement. Rest is a supplement.

One of the most important ones is always listed as one of the three foods essential to moving energy around your body. It is part of the three points of the triangle you see inside the pentagram symbol. When you look at the nine-pointed symbol anagram and there is a triangle in the center, each one of those points is where a certain kind of food must be brought into the process and the machine. One of the most important ones is called food of impressions. P.D. Ouspensky writes about this in the Fourth Way in great detail.

You want to periodically through the day, at some point in the day (there's no particular time like 2pm or 4pm), before the day is over and maybe even early in the day, bring in with intention an impression of something that represents a higher energy. For example, this is one of the reasons why, even though I don't always do this, I start my day at least with a few minutes of reading something very meaningful to me. In a way, it represents a higher form of thinking than I might be currently inclined to have. It could be anything. It could be a workbook. It could be a poetry book. It could be a reading from some sacred book like a Bible, Koran, Mathnawi by Maulana Jalaluddin Rumi or Leaves of Grass by Walt Whitman. It could be taking a few minutes to look at some art intentionally and absorb the art as food. Most of the little pieces of art I have up have some energetic or spiritual significance. It allows me, at some different point in the day, to stop sometimes, just for a minute, in front of a piece of art like Shivago or the Tibetan Tankas or the Mescalaro Apache art or what have you. I can just consider it for a minute or two. I'm taking in that impression as food.

Impressions are also in nature, outdoors. That's why it's good, no matter how busy we are, to always try to take a few minutes to go outside and find some little bit of nature, which could be a plant, flower, dragonfly, anthill, and just meditate on that for minute or two. It's not about how long you do it. What's important is you do it with intention. We take in nature as a form of impressions. We take in art as a form of impressions. We take in sacred or intentional reading as an impression. It's important we do this everyday. It's important because it gives us energy.

3. Do not believe all of the instinctive center's I's, but do not lie to it or cheat it.

Dr. J: This references the fact the instinctive center, as the voice of the physical machine, is in constant conversation with us. This is the part of our brain that monitors every little sensation, action and activity of every organ, the flow and circulation of the blood, the intake and exhalation of Prana and out-gassing, the temperature of our skin, how our hair feels on top of our heads, our comfortability in every sitting position, like where our toes are or where our fingers are, where our bottom is, etc., etc. This constant information is being offered on some level in real time. What's interesting about it is that the instinctive center's information has a random quality time. In other words, what is being emphasized in any particular moment doesn't necessarily follow any particular strategy. If we align ourselves with paying too much attention to the instinctive center, then we are in a continuous change or loop of conversation about various equilibriums coming and going for which there is no resolution. There is no possible way to get to the other side of it. There's no play where all that stops, especially when we get into a loop of association with the instinctive center and we add to it this idea, the mental idea of trying to sort out what it means, then we get lost in all kinds of associations and can literally be lost for days in trying to sort out what we sense we feel. It can be a real distraction.

The one thing you can say about the instinctive center right now is information. If you wait about a minute or two it will give you something else. Ten minutes after that it's going to give you something else. There are times when we do want to pay attention to the instinctive center. We don't necessarily want to take all that information as if it means something. It's sort of like watching a thermometer from morning 'til night and seeing the little variation in temperature. You'd see what every little variation meant and how come it kept changing and where it was going. It goes through its daily cycle and ends up back where it started. We get so attached to the instinctive center that it won't tell us anything. There's flux in the system, in that the instinctive system and operation of the metabolic body and all the tissues is on an equilibrium. There is no stasis or state of equilibrium that's always the same. There is normal variation, normal high and low, normal play between tonic and relaxed states, more and less circulation, more and less tension, higher and lower temperatures, etc. All these variations are normal. If we get caught up into what all that means, we will be completely distracted.

Then again, don't lie to it or cheat it. When we have a consistent, clear communication coming from the instinctive center, we have to pay attention to it. If we foo-foo it or say that's not important or that doesn't mean anything, it knows we are not telling it the truth. What happens is the instinctive center becomes more dominant than it was. In fact, at some level, it has the ability to shut us down completely if we ignore it when it's giving us a signal of something substantial. Part of what the process is with physical exercise, for example, is to learn with a clearer vision what the normal state of our instinctive function is so that when it gives us messages outside of normal, we can pay attention to it. We don't pretend they are not there. That's what happens to a lot of people. They have no conception of this communication. When this communication happens, good or bad, and the instinctive center is trying to tell them something is wrong with the heart or bowels, it gives a clear and immediate signal. What we do is, "Well, I don't get it. I don't think it's important. I'm not going to respond or even look at it." If we try to cheat the instinctive center, we will find ourselves in a place where we are being injured.

Part of the instinctive center's job is to communicate threat to you. If you feel threatened all the time, checking in on that, well that's not productive because you are not under threat all the time. If you feel like that, well that's irrational. Now if you suddenly feel threat, then don't ignore it, sit up, open your eyes, pay attention and look around because often the instinctive center will perceive a threat before every other sense can define it, before you can hear, smell, see or even feel internally or externally that something is happening or about to happen which might have the ability to kill you. It could be that extreme. That's a proper use of the instinctive center. It is meant to keep you alive.

On the other hand, it's too busy at the job. We don't want to listen acutely to every little message it is sending along because otherwise we would have nothing else to do. It turns into gibberish, like Chicken Little crying that the sky is falling. We listen to all these little, uncomfortable messages, like my instinctive center is communicating to me right now that it doesn't like I'm crossing my leg in this fashion. It would prefer I would cross it the other way. I'm really not going to pay too much attention to that because I just decided I wanted to cross my leg this way. If I cross my leg this way and get a sharp pain in my groin followed by a dull aching sensation, and every time I cross my leg it did exactly the same thing, I would pay attention to that. That would be telling me there is something in need of my attention. If I ignored it, I'm either not resolving something available to be resolved, so it will continue to be a buffer or filter of some kind to me, or I'm not bringing the energy my instinctive center is telling me I need to bring in order to correct or heal something.

4. Make your meals fine impressions.

Dr. J: I want to say I'm pretty happy with the work everybody does on doing this. From the beginning this has been something we have been trying to cultivate about our meals. When we prepare food, the food is not just about getting the substance into the mouth or getting it from the store to the refrigerator to the plate to the mouth. Food is an impression. Food is energy. We get to have a say so of what is the quality of that energy we are taking into ourselves. Just like I might practice Pranayama, some focused breathing and I realize that if I have a very specific visualization while I do my Pranayama it creates more energy in me. If I take the same five ingredients you might have on a plate of food and I just throw them on the plate and wolf them down, I get some nutrition from that. If I take those same five ingredients and arrange them artistically and bring a higher consciousness to the presentation of them, then as I eat them, not only do they give me just the core nutrients of the organic material, but they also give me energetic nutrients, which are from the food of impressions. The finer this food of impressions is, the more energy I need to be able to work on myself I get. The organic material of the food, the body of the carrots feeds my body. The beauty of the carrots—the artistry and beauty of the carrots is an impression. It gives me a higher hydrogen, that's a way Ouspensky would say it. It gives me a finer food nutrient energy which does something else. It is useful for something else other than just running my machine. After all, that's part of what I'm trying to do. I'm trying to avoid wasting too much energy and simultaneously take in and create as much energy as possible. The work I do on myself requires a lot of energy. I'm a high performance machine. I need high performance nutrition. All the foods are important.

5. Self-remember before you take the first bite.

Dr. J: This causes an energetic shift when we remember ourselves. This opens up the centers to being more receptive to particular vibrations and kinds of energy. Just like we say in Puja, the first step in Puja is this idea of acknowledgement. That is to give us access to the exchange possibility latent in the practice of Puja.

When I take a moment, just before I eat that first bite, to check-in and remember myself, I can open up the centers to receive all of the qualities, nutrients both organic, physically tangible, and the intangible impressionistic, energetic, which are also part of the food. By the way, they also come from the person who prepared the food.

One of my favorite movies is "*Like Water For Chocolate*". I like the book too. It was all about that. It wasn't even so important what the ingredients were. For example, there is no reference or mention in the book about organic, local, slow, non-GMO, non-pesticide…all those kinds of things we are fond of commonly using as qualifying criteria for our food, there is no reference to any of this whatsoever. In the book, it's more important who you are when you prepare the food than the constituents of the actual food you are preparing. Not only is it important for you, it's important for the person or persons who are going to receive the food, because the food is an expression of you. It is an expression of your energy and your love. It's an expression of your care or not. If you want to talk about things that contaminate food, the most dangerous contaminant in food altogether is negative emotion. It is more damaging than pesticides. Something of you is conveyed in what you prepare and what you make.

When I eat your food, part of my self-observation and self-remembering before I eat the first bite is I try to visualize the person I Imagine prepared the food, whether I know them or not. If I'm in a restaurant, maybe I don't even see the chef. Before I eat that first bite, guess what I do? In my mind, I go into the kitchen and look for every person who laid hands on the food or the plant and sometimes I do it tantrically, which means I actually extrapolate this back as far back as back goes. I visualize the chef and the kitchen staff preparing my food, their state of mind, and then all the caterers and crafters and vendors who brought the food to the kitchen. Then I see the food on the truck, I see the food on the boat, on the plane, and I see it go back to the field and I see the farmers and I visualize very quickly every person in the field from the farmer and laborer who cuts the vegetable off the vine and probably planted the seeds and watered them to even the atmosphere in management, which was pervasive while this process went on, and then to the land and in one moment I am able to see all of that as if in a hologram, all these simultaneous Images about what happened, what had to occur, how much effort and intention had to come together in order for this piece of broccoli to be on my plate. I also visualize a thankfulness, a gratefulness and a blessing for everything in that chain, because of course a broken link anywhere in it and that broccoli is not on my plate. Then I acknowledge the intention, even if I think there wasn't a lot of intention, and then I eat that first bite.

If you are cooking for me, know that every time I eat that first bite, I think of you. I think of you. I think of everything in your life that has to have been occurring and is occurring in the moment for you to actually be present in the moment in the kitchen making food for me. I'm grateful. People say give thanks before you eat. This is what they are talking about. Some think it means to recite some mantra, "God is good. God is great. Thank you for our daily bread. Blah, blah, blah." This is what we mean by the difference between exoteric and esoteric. The exoteric gift of gratitude before you eat is to hold hands, bow your head and recite a mantra. The esoteric understanding is, in the moment before you eat, to have a visualization of the sum of everything that had to come together in order for this to be able to happen right now. To see it and how this represents the life, not just of the plant but of the people who brought the plant to you, and to acknowledge and give thanks for that. Now I'm connected to the web of the life I'm leading, and not just being grateful for the goodies on my plate.

6. Tame the instinctive center by curbing its tendencies to take up space with loud talking, laughing, singing or aggressive, physical postures.

Dr. J: Step number one is to notice when your machine is doing that. Notice when you just invade space and engage in loud talking, when your machine is laughing for no particular reason and/or when you assume aggressive postures without intention.

I want to say, by the way, that the opposite of these things are equally the same. In other words, to tame the instinctive center by curbing its tendencies also means to not withdraw, speak too quietly to be heard, never express laughter or repress the Impetus to laugh when it seems appropriate. Laughter is a sign of a release of tension at certain times. Not singing or to never sing doesn't make any sense. To assume aggressive, physical postures or constantly find yourself in defensive postures, which are out of context with the environment in which you find yourself, like being very timid or shy, be aware of that also and counter it.

If you notice your voice is escalating and you are talking too loud for no particular reason, take the edge off and lower the volume. If you're laughing uncontrollably for no apparent reason, then observe it, take a breath and stop. If you are humming and singing mindlessly, notice it and try not to engage in it. If you have an aggressive, physical posture, take the edge off and drop your shoulders. Put your hands down. In the timid version, pull shoulders back, push your chest up a little bit and make eye contact.

7. Make your food attractive.

Dr. J: That goes back to making your food of fine impressions. When you look at any food you've prepared, eyeball it, look at it and ask yourself the question, "Is this attractive?" If it's not, then don't serve it. Consider the overall esthetics of what your consuming. Oregamy, Fung Soi, the Art of Placement, Zen or English Garden on your plate all come to mind. Do something to enhance it and make it more attractive. This is the example and origin of the garnish. That fixes it. It's something you add, like an accent or some color or something that just bumps up the energy. It really makes a difference when the food is not attractive.

8. Maintain your health. If it's broken, repair it.

Dr. J: This relates back to number two. Maintain your health. Health is on an equilibrium. There is no such thing as perfect health. There is such a thing as being completely broken down. You want to be more on the side of perfect health, so there's almost a little bit of continuous attention to do that. We all come to the party with scar tissue, viruses, bacteria, long term ramifications of Improper or poor or even destructive dietary habits, toxicity and deficiency and unresolved issues. As we become more aware, we have to take responsibility to continuously strive to repair our machines and bring up their functions to the best efficiency. When we see we've been missing it in one area or another, then that's when we bring the energy and attention to it. It's very hard to work on everything all at the same time. Certainly you pick one or more areas to target with some success. If you get to a bottleneck or plateau, where you've been working on a specific issue for a while and you've stopped making visible success with it, let it go and go on to something else that is nearly related to it. Let it go.

It's a psychological issue I have been working on and made some progress. Now I've flattened out and am stuck there. Give it up. Let it go. Walk away from it and go to something completely different and start over. Anything physical, emotional or mental we get too crystallized in and identified with becomes a limitation and an obstacle at some point because we are always in motion. There will never be a point where there is nothing to work on. We have to keep coming back to occasionally drawing lines where we say, "Okay, I've done work in this particular area as much as I can and that's all that is accessible to me right now, and if I keep being compulsive about trying to conquer it and fix it, then that compulsion will become consuming and will stop my work." I want to notice my compulsions and I want to work on walking away from them. I want the work I do to be intentional and not compulsive. There is a difference.

9. As you do for every other part of you, don't waste the energy of the sex center.

Dr. J: Apply alchemy to the Sexual function. Back to the food of impressions. As we consider our sexual energy in the way we express and relate and give and receive sexual energy, we have to bring intention to it. We want to work on the impressions of it. Giving and receiving sexual energy is a kind of food. We want as much intention in that process as we possibly can. We don't want to take it for granted. I mean that for everything. Even if you are thinking about sex, you need to try and have fine thoughts about it. If you are masturbating, then make it really satisfying. You want to avoid creating situations where you will feel like you are hiding something or that it's engendering some guilt or shame, but rather that it's a healthy expression and activity of your machine. Your machine needs it. It's part of the balancing mechanism for sympatheticatonia that Wilhelm Reich talks about and which I refer to in the *"What is Thai Massage?"* book. It's part of the balancing and correcting mechanism. When we share sex with each other, on whatever continuum we do that, whether it's from conversation to expression of sensuality to the action of intercourse, one way or the other we need to be intentional about it. We have to always bring intention to it. It has to be on purpose. I don't accidentally eat. When I do Pranayama I bring intention to my breath and that changes the quality of the Prana. When I'm expressing myself sexually, I bring intention and breath to it, and aesthetics in order to have some Impact or influence on what the result of the expression will be.

Alchemy is the idea of taking what is fundamentally a biological mechanism and transforming it through a process of adjuncts, in other words, exposing it to various pressures, various impressions, various intentions to change the nature of it altogether. That's what alchemy is about. We want to understand this idea of the alchemic process, as it relates to the process of our sexual energy through our sex centers.

CHAPTER TEN: Exercises for Reducing Chief Negative Feature and Unnecessary Suffering

1. Do not expect anything more than the present.

Dr. J: We are constantly in a state of expectation and imagination and identification with how things are supposed to be right now, how we are supposed to be, how other people are supposed to be, how our life is supposed to be, and what it all means. We are also influenced in this idea of expectation with our history, with our past experiences. There's the overflow of what happened yesterday, the day before yesterday, and the day before. There's rumination of previous conversations and a push and pull, positive and negative, substantial and insubstantial, and confusing. We're completely consumed by that to a degree that it's very difficult to accept the reality of what's happening right now. What are we actually feeling right now? What do we actually know right now? What is our realization about our life right now?

It is an exercise to practice not expecting anything more than what the present is offering. There may be other ways to say this. For example, you could say, "Accept the present however it is." It's not good or bad. It just is. The present moment is not about what happened yesterday. It's not about what happened a year ago or ten years ago. It's not even necessarily about where you happen to be sitting, because if there are any qualifications or criticisms based on anything else than what you're actually experiencing right now, that's unreal. This is a concept in Ayurveda, too. The Doshas are defilements of the ego characterized by likes and dislikes, by affinities and repulsions, by knowledge and confusion. Those are the primary determining characteristics of the Doshas in the present moment. If we think about how much of our thought life and daily life is generated by all these polar opposites, want and not want, I understand and I don't understand, there's not a whole lot left over that doesn't fall into one of those categories.

One of the work exercises is to constantly bring you back. It's like a puppy on a leash that wants to wander. The leash is your aim and commitment to work on you. The puppy wandering is all the parts of you that wander and don't want to work on yourself. When you work on your aims overtime, when the leash gets taut and the puppy starts to drag you off the trail into the bushes, you remind yourself you're not the puppy and you have a leash. You pull on the leash to pull the puppy back on the trail. You want to bring all of your parts back into alignment with the present moment.

2. Do not feel obliged to act on your many I's.

Dr. J: One of the Vipassana concepts is that just because there is a thought in your head doesn't mean it's yours. Just because it happens to be in your head, when you're not working on yourself, and you don't have sophistication and understanding of consciousness, the thought is not yours. We are programmed to assume. An uneducated person with no knowledge of what we're speaking might assume every thought that happens to pass through their brain is theirs simply because it's there. This is the reason why we go into so many different kinds of discussions, practices, exercises and challenges. In one sense, it's because we want to challenge the assumption that because a thought or feeling is in you, it is relevant to you and your life. Most of the time, it isn't.

Let's say a thought is a reflection of the consciousness of an I. We have many I's so we have many thoughts. Most of the I's are based on false personality and are disorganized. The I's that are the reflection of the consciousness of the authentic, true self are more subtle. Again, like the classic Vipassana illustration of thoughts vs. the authentic self, being able to differentiate when you look up at the sky the difference between clouds and the blue sky. The blue sky is the undifferentiated atman and the clouds are your thoughts. The clouds are not a reflection of the sky, of the true self. They are just passing by. They are a reflexive, reactive, associative manifestation of the consciousness of the many I's. That means they have a random and chaotic life cycle. When we feel compelled to act according to every little thought or feeling we have following the lead of those I's, what we do is find ourselves acting in ways contrary to the aims and ambitions and the consciousness of the true self. We act completely out of context with that. In fact, we will find ourselves feeling and acting and being in a way completely contrary to the possibility of manifesting the consciousness of the true self.

Our programming says we are obliged to act based on what we think and feel. We are taught as children that this is valid. "Follow your heart. Be yourself. Make up your own mind." At the very same time, we are not taught that thoughts are unreliable, feelings are unreliable, and that if you base your actions or are obliged to act based on peculiar little thoughts or feelings, just because they're there, most of the time your behavior will be contrary to the way of being your authentic self would have you to be. It's contrary. It has to be. It's random, associative and chaotic. What we think and feel at any particular moment is reflective of the consciousness of the many I's. That is more about things that have happened to us in the past than it is about what's happening to us now. It's more about crystallization and negative emotional patterning or tapes that come from the past than what is happening now. We are not seeing the person we are with because we are looking at them through a filter of everything not about them or about the moment or anything at all relative in this moment, and then we act on it. If I'm doing that and you're doing that, then that's Kali's dance, a dance of chaos. There's no way we can connect. Our past associations, inclinations and karma are different. Let's use this as an example, the way you're being with me right now or another person is entirely based on your karma, past associations, thoughts, actions and deeds and manifestations of false personality, associative thinking and random feeling and so on. I'm doing the same. Where is the point of intersection for us to actually communicate? Where is the point of intersection for us to actually exchange energy in the moment? Where is that? The chances we'd be able to connect, to be sympathetic in any particular moment, are slim and none.

And "oblige", what does oblige mean in this? It's the compulsion to act on what you are thinking and feeling right now. That's the obligation and the compulsion. We feel compelled. "Because I'm not feeling connected to you right now, I'm obligated to act as if I'm not connected to you right now. Because I don't understand you right now, I am obligated to act as if I don't value what you're trying to communicate." I'm conditioned to do that.

You add up all this stuff and no wonder. It is a miracle. This is how we know there are higher powers. There must be higher powers involved in this equation because when you really start to understand this, you have to come to a point where you would have the understanding that the likelihood any two human beings on the planet at any one particular time could actually truly understand each other or truly be connected, bond and be sympathetic in thought, action and deed at any particular moment in time, is virtually impossible. I'm talking about a genuine connection, not about whether we can act like we are in harmony, connected, cogent, like we're sharing an understanding. That's not what I'm talking about. I'm talking about the genuine possibility of that occurrence.

We have to work on this feeling of obligation to act on the many I's in us.

3. Suffer less by thinking about yourself less.

Dr. J: I always like to take these statements and mix and match them a little bit. In other words, I think about the statement first exactly the way it's stated and see what comes to mind. Then I ask myself, is there another way I could express or formulate this that would make it clearer? I'm dealing with someone else's words right? Some of these are my words. Some of them are not. Some of these are words I've gotten from my teachers or other teachers. Some of them are my own cogitations I've come up with.

One of the causes of suffering is the compulsion to consider myself all the time. The first question that might come up for you is, "But wait a minute, don't you tell us to observe ourselves all the time? Don't you tell us to practice self-remembering? How is that different from thinking about yourself?"

J mentioned it earlier today when we were talking about the difference between pondering and wondering. Wondering is an associative, identified, chaotic thought.

Pondering is when you choose to consider something with the higher parts of your faculties. When you ponder, it's deliberate. When you ponder, it's a reflection of an aim or a conscious intention to do so. When you wonder about something, like I was sitting outside and looking up at the sky and I caught myself thinking for about 30 seconds why that cloud looked like a bunny. I did. I thought, "Wow. That cloud looks like a bunny. I wonder why?" First of all, the cloud is not a bunny. There's no relationship between that cloud and any bunnies. No bunnies were harmed in the making of that cloud. Yet, when I looked at the cloud, I saw the head of a bunny with its long ears. I was wondering about it. That is not the same thing as pondering. It was spontaneous, associative, reflexive, imaginary, fantasy. When I think about myself normally, that's the way I think about myself. I have no higher level of consciousness going on than when I'm looking at the cloud wondering why right now it looks like a bunny or in another moment it looks like a battleship. I notice when I catch myself in that frame of mind, the bunny will become the battleship or vice versa. They seem to just morph one into the other and I don't have any issue with that. When I think about myself I don't have any more consciousness about it than that.

When I self-remember, that's pondering. It's a thoughtful, deliberate consideration taking in all of my parts. One thing that makes real self-remembering different than other types of remembering or observing is you also have this intention to try and pay attention to all of your parts. In other words, I'm not just concerned with what's going on in my mind or thoughts, I'm open to an awareness of my feelings, of what's going on in my body. How does my body feel right now? Am I hot or cold? Am I comfortable or uncomfortable? Am I stimulated? Am I depressed and withdrawn? I try to see the whole picture, not just my thoughts. I do it on purpose. There's that element of deliberation. There's also an element of resistance to going off on tangents of associative thinking. Self-remembering is not about going off on tangents.

When I think about myself in the normal way, that causes me suffering because I'm not here. I'm lost in the associations. I'm lost in the feelings, whether it's emotional or sensate. That's the difference between the instinctive, physical and the emotional center. The instinctive center is about communication and coming together from the tissue, nerves. It has to do with pressure, position and diet and what's happening in relation to what I ate an hour ago. Those things are all factors in how I feel, and that comes from the instinctive center. Do I feel safe? Do I feel threatened? Emotions and the mental part are different from that. The self-observing part still is separate from all of that. All of that is transient. It will change for no other reason than that time elapses.

Thinking about oneself, being caught up in introspective loops about what it means, what I understand and what I don't understand, am I comfortable, what do I like? This is all thinking about your self right? This is what you do when you are thinking about yourself. Is it I? What do they think about me or not think about me? What will they do if I do this? What will they not do if I do this? All that leads to suffering because none of it has any bearing on what's happening right now. What is your experience of life in yourself in the place you're at right now without anything else interfering with it? Can you see the moment for what it is? To the degree we deviate from being in the moment now, being real, in other words, being in imagination, negative emotion, associative thinking, to the degree we are separated from being in the moment we suffer. That's what suffering is.

My old professor Dr. Palai said it so simply when he was giving me the definition of Ayurveda. He says, "Ayurveda is science of life, of therapy, healing and medicine, which is to correct, to remediate, to resolve everything, all the Impediments, interferences, that keep us from knowing god now; having a direct, Immediate and personal experience of god right now. That's the definition." When he told me that and gave me that little tidbit, it shocked me. Up to that moment, I thought Ayurveda was medicine, a.k.a. techniques, procedures and technology, yoga, herbology and things like that. I'm sitting here in a classroom with Swami Veroma and Dr. Palai, and several other famous gurus and swamis who are considered to be the grandmasters of Ayurveda, and they are telling me Ayurveda is not about fixing things in the sense of mending and patching. The reason why we do the medicine is, for example, when we have a physical illness we are consumed with the life of the illness. That keeps us from being present to he knowledge of god. When we have emotional illness, we are completely consumed with our emotions and all the activities and actions driven by the emotions other than allowing us to have a direct, higher, emotional experience with god. When we have a mental illness, we become completely defined by our mentation and associative, random and chaotic thoughts that happen to wander through our heads. These thoughts are no different than if I heard a radio station playing in the background and there's country music on and it's some "achey-breakey she left me and took the house, the truck and my dog" kind of song, I would think, because those words are wafting into my consciousness, that that's about me. Those are my thoughts. Whatever that is, it is not a higher mental function that would be cogent with a direct, personal experience of the mind of god. Ayurveda was and is meant to cure that.

The only thing that needs curing is a separation from oneness, from integrity, from the real time, immediate experience of manifesting of consciousness cogent with the absolute consciousness of everything else there is, whether we call it god or the absolute. That's true Ayurveda. Everything else is just window dressing. It's what we do in order to be able to craft this. When we do yoga, we quiet the body. When we do therapeutic conversations and tapping and our psychological processes we quiet the emotions. When we study diligently, learn and then practice what we understand so that we be what we know, that quiets the mind. When they say quiet the body, heart and mind, why would you want to do that? Why would you want to do that? What's on the other side of that? It's Samadhi. Samadhi is oneness with absolute, undifferentiated cosmic consciousness or oneness with god within and without. That's the way the Maharishi Mahesh Yogi used to say it. It's immediate, in real time, in the now. This is the bush everyone is beating around to get to the "be here now".

We have therapy for this. What is therapy? It is practical exercise for the way we live and work with each other. It's the way we practice being what we know. When we are not doing that, when the body is not quiet, we have different names for it.

173

Now the body becomes the dominant aspect in consciousness. In other words, the instinctive moving center becomes dominant. What does that look like? That looks like disease in the body. What does it look like when the heart is not quiet? We are consumed with its issues and emotion, the push and pull and tides of emotion. Our life is all about that. That's the filter. It's what defines your life. When your body or your mind or heart is not quiet, that's what defines your life. Guess what? None of them are up to the job. They don't do it very well. The more dominant that influence is, the more separate you are from your true being, true nature and authentic self, your undifferentiated cosmic consciousness. We call it separation suffering.

What is the function of these exercises? The function is to quiet the body, heart and mind so you can see something that's not the body, heart and mind. You are not the body, heart and mind. Yes, this is your vehicle. This is your stress-adaptive human biological transformational machine, but you are not that. It is the vehicle for your consciousness and the expression of your consciousness. It is the crucible for the development of your consciousness. When we let it run the show, we suffer.

4. Expect to give rather than receive.

Dr. J: Just observe yourself, when we are practicing, how often do you think the thought, "How is this good for me? What's the benefit for me? What have you done for me lately?"? That is the opposite of giving. More often, a healthier exercise, from the point of view of the work is for you to look at situations we encounter in our lives and think about how you can make a contribution now. How can you reach out and step up? How can you give rather than be completely consumed with receiving? We can't be submissive in the process of submitting to the work. It's unacceptable. We need to be proactive. If we want to receive the true benefits of what we are doing, we have to constantly come back and reengage ourselves to reach out and make a contribution.

Granted, there might be times in our lives when we are so overcome with our crap that we can't even find a way to give. Guess what? That's the perfect time to give. I'll give you an illustration. I had a counseling client whom, after I got to know her, I realized was a pretty joyless person. That was a quality. When I looked at her, I saw no joy in her life. She came to me because she suffered from horrible depression, mental anxiety and psychological illness. When I talked to her and did my assessment, I realized she was one of the most joyless people I had ever met. She was an executive, a vice president of a large company in the Chicago area. She had more money than I've ever seen in my life, yearly. She drove a car I've actually seen featured on car shows. She was dressed really nice, but was the most sad, joyless and depressed person.

Apparently she had a boyfriend she didn't have many problems with. I couldn't find any particular history of trauma from what she was telling me. I was meditating for a minute. I was pondering the information from her. The main thing that came up was the lack of joy. Ding! I know the equation: love, compassion, joy and equanimity. I go, "Okay, I have a therapy that can help you." She said, "You do? I mean I'm not saying I don't think you do because I came here to see if you could help me, but I've been to lots of docs and no one has been able to help. The medications don't help. Groups and psychotherapy don't help. Nothing works. This is a last resort kind of deal. I'm only coming to you because my girlfriend told me I had to come at least one time or she wasn't going to talk to me anymore, so here I am." I said, "Well, she made the right choice for you. You made the right choice to be here because I do think I can help." She goes, "Okay, what do we have to do? Acupuncture or herbs or you mentioned colonics? Maybe I'm so joyless because I'm all constipated." I go, "Actually no. Have you heard of the Food Bank?" She goes, "Well I've heard of it. It's like a warehouse kitchen kind of thing where they feed homeless people?" I go, "Yeah, that's it. I happen to know they are always looking for volunteers.

The Food Bank is huge so they are trying to help thousands of homeless people get food everyday. They have big warehouses and they have to have people to volunteer to stock and restock and pull orders. They have commercial kitchens, soup kitchens. They have people who wash dishes all day and package food. They have vans to deliver food. They are always looking for volunteers." She looked at me like nothing was coming to mind. "I'm not following you. What are you saying?" I said, "Here's my prescription for your therapy. At least once a week, twice if you can swing it, even if it's just for half a day, four hours, go to the Food Bank. Volunteer and make a commitment at least one to two times a week that you work in the soup kitchen or wherever they think they need you most and you do it completely for free as a gift. If you make that commitment at least for one month on a trial basis, whatever you commit to, you do not quit until you fulfill it." She goes, "I'm not following you. How is me going to some food kitchen going to help my problems?" I go, "I know. Here's the thing. There's a method to the madness. I think that you will learn something very helpful for you. The sooner you get to it, the sooner you'll get it. Could you go today or tomorrow?"

We got into a little discussion because she was resistant. She's like, "I do charity. I make donations. She tried to tell me some big number she donates." I said, "Yeah but it's not the same. That doesn't count. It's good but it doesn't count because it actually costs you nothing personally. In a personal way, physically, emotionally or mentally you don't have to sacrifice anything. You're just taking a tax write-off by making a donation. That's not what I'm talking about. I'm talking about the health of your mind and heart." Well, kudos to her. She did exactly what I asked her to do and she started volunteering. To make a long story short, she was cured of her depression. She became a happy person. Not only that, after two years of regularly volunteering, because she was an executive, she did have an advanced degree in finance and because she was a very corporate lady with very good organizational skills, she ended up taking a position.

As far as I know, she's still working for the organization. At some point after that, we had a conversation where she said there's a point in time where originally she was resistant and she couldn't understand why I was trying to get her to do this. It made no sense to her whatsoever. She couldn't relate to anybody who worked there. They weren't as educated, as well dressed, etc.

Something happened to her one day while she was working, where she was in the kitchen and she realized that if she wasn't standing behind the line serving up the soup to this person in front of her, most likely the kids in front of her would have nothing to eat that day. Their lives were so hard, a family living in their car. The only place they could get food was at the food bank. That's where they ate. They would try to organize their lives so the parents could go and do day jobs. They would take turns keeping track of the kids in the car. At some point, she connected with this family. She got it that she had to stop thinking about herself so much. She had to let go of her self-consuming life. It was all about her, her needs, her feelings and her understandings. She needed to give to somebody else. She made a genuine gift, not even on purpose. There was a moment where she made a connection and she performed a genuine act of compassion than for no other reason than out of consideration of these kids. What happened was that she got a kick of joy that literally knocked her down and changed her life. She started becoming a different person.

Expect to give rather than receive. We will have expectations because we have all these identifications. We expect things to continue how they've happened before, to continue to be that way. Well, if we are going to do it anyway, if we are working on ourselves, then it's possible for us to craft our expectations with intention, to expect to give rather than receive and then practice it.

5. Replace bonds of fascination with bonds of something higher.

Dr. J: Fascination is attraction and attachment identification. Fascination in relationships is what can be called "new relationship energy" (NRE). Allurement is the initial hard attraction, which we think is mostly chemical. It may be aesthetic. "They smell good, they look good, and they feel good." There are the pheromones we are not aware of consciously, etc. Fascination is like that. The reason why we are together or we do what we do is based on fascination. What's going to happen? Well, of course it will go away. It's not going to last.

We have to work on replacing the bonds of why we do the things we do, even why we are together, with something other than just fascination. That's why I say things like, "Actually, I prefer you didn't like me as the reason you want to be with me. I would prefer the reason you want to be with me is not that you are attracted to me." Why? All of that is based on fascination, allurement, identification and chemistry. That means 100% it will all go away. It is based on event-centered, external circumstances that are going to change. Chemistry will change. Behaviors are going to change. Situations are going to change. Attraction will change. It always does. It has to.

I would prefer the inclination to work with me, to work on you, or to be here or for us to work with each other, be not based on fascination and attraction. That's unreliable and will not survive the test of time.

We have to explore replacing those things, which will exist and come and go. Just because they weren't here doesn't mean they're not here now or won't be here at some future date. They come and go. We want to work to replace those bonds and connections and aims with something, a basis of something other than attraction and fascination, if we want to survive long term and have an enduring work.

6. Think of an area in which you are identified and try to let go. Something may be better.

Dr. J: Already I know, just in the little bit we've all been working together in the last couple of months, we've identified areas of identification. The exercise is to on purpose challenge it and let it go. The letting go cannot be conditional on you understanding it. It cannot be conditional on you believing in it. You let it go as an exercise. The reason we do that is because something better may come. Why is that? If we let go of the repetitive, associative, identified, negative things (thought, feeling, emotion, the tapes, etc.), that creates the possibility we might have the experience of something else, something new. How are you going to experience something new when every thought in your head, every feeling in your body, is a reflection of something old? How are you going to have something new? We create the possibility of something new by letting go and coming back. Again, this is not a one-time deal. It's constant. It's repetitive. You have to let go. Then you come back and the next time you see it, you let go and let go until the habit is gone. Right now our habit is to clutch and contain, to hold on.

Here's the way it works. We are in a situation that challenges an area where we are identified. What do we do? We dig in. We hold on more. We dig in and push back. We get defensive. "Not only am I not going to let go with what I'm identified with right now, I'm going to hurt you. I'm going to push back and challenge you. I'm going to start throwing pots and pans." "Throwing pots and pans" is when your identification in one area is being challenged and you start bringing in unrelated issues and throwing them on the table for consideration as if they are related. That's a diversionary tactic. That's Chaff.

Fighter jets have a defensive technology called chaff. Right now the way you shoot down a fighter jet, because it goes so fast, is with a rocket. The only way a rocket can hit a jet that has the potential to change direction in fractions of a second, pulling 4 or 5 G's times the gravity of the earth in different roles and maneuvers, is to have a weapon that can react faster than the pilot can make changes and corrections ahead of you. They use a smart rocket called a heat-seeking missile or sidewinder, or whatever is the equivalent. You have two jets. One's chasing the other. One jet wants to shoot the other one down. They tell the sidewinder to arm and go hit the target. They fire and let the sidewinder go. The only way the sidewinder can track that twisty-turny object in front of it is to follow the signal of its exhaust to the hottest point, which would have to be where the engine is. It follows the exhaust trail. The missile is launched, independently of the pilot who fired the missile. It is smart, in a sense. It makes its own decisions and corrections. It twists and turns and reacts a little faster than the pilot in front of it until it gets to the other plane and destroys it.

There is this question, "How do we handle the reaction?" I'm being challenged in a way where I'm identified. What's the defense with that? I'm in the front jet. The jet behind me has just fired a sidewinder missile at me. If I don't react really quickly, of course it will get me and I'm dead. I know I can't out-maneuver that rocket. I can't do it. What do I do? I hit a button, bang. It releases a thousand little pieces of foil right out the rear of the jet. All that foil is called Chaff. The sidewinder coming up to it sees its infrared reflected back to it from a hundred different points. It cannot tell where the target is anymore. Whatever is on the other side of that chaff all of a sudden becomes invisible to it. As soon as it loses the tracking, I can now pull away one way or the other and lose the rocket. We say the chaff is a diversionary tactic. When we are working together and run into an area where we are strongly identified and start pushing up against it and we dig in, we are not being successful. The tension is still there; the pressure is still there. What do we do? We start throwing pots and pans. We throw Chaff. We start bringing up issues and ideas. We start bringing up information, concerns and so on that have nothing to do with what we are trying not to be identified with. If we are successful, what happens? We get away. That's what happens. We get away with our issue intact. That's the whole point.

We have to try to let go. This is not a good metaphor all the way through because if that were true, I would say I want that missile to hit. In this case, however, the only thing that will be destroyed is my identification. I want the missile to hit. When I see myself throwing pots and pans and letting out the chaff, if I'm observing myself doing it, I need to then do something exactly the opposite; in other words, not defend, protect or justify myself. I have to do it on purpose. I'm not helpless in that moment. Guess what? I'm powerful. I'm as powerful as I'm ever going to be in that moment. I have more control of myself in that moment than any other time. Why? I'm doing it with intention. The defensive posturing, protecting the identification, is responsive, reflective and mechanical. That is not conscious. Therefore it is not powerful or empowering.

We mistake getting away with our issues intact for having handled the issue. That's entirely different. Technically speaking, from the work point of view, handling the issue means you let it go. You don't walk away with it anymore. That's what "handle the issue" means. It doesn't mean that after struggling with it you've been able to successfully protect it in such a way you can walk away with it intact. We have to challenge these things.

176

7. Make your problems smaller by speaking about them less.

Dr. J: There is more than one kind of speaking about our problems. We often do check-ins. That's where we speak about our issues and problems. That is okay. We have designated a safe area, a particular time where we will do this on purpose. That's okay. Talk about your problems when it's appropriate because you are doing it on purpose with intention and a higher level of consciousness. When we speak about our problems just to hear ourselves talk, and when we bring up our issues when they are unrelated to what's actually going on in our lives in a particular moment, that is a complete waste of energy. It's energy we could use for other purposes.

8. Reduce unnecessary suffering by not requiring other people's attention.

Dr. J: There are two ways we require other people's attention. One is by creating drama. That gets everybody's attention because it is instinctive in us. We are hardwired to pay attention. Drama grabs your attention that for the same reason from birth we are hardwired to respond to the cry of a baby. It's not just the women who have this. When you hear a baby cry, it doesn't matter if you have children or not. It doesn't matter if you are a mother or not. It doesn't matter how old you are. You could be 3 or 12 or 70 years old. It is hardwired into our DNA, that when we hear a baby cry we are unable to be comfortable until we resolved it or know what the problem is. Is that baby at risk? We have to be able to answer the question. We might look and think, "Oh, the kid's just crying. He'll be fine." We can't ignore it. It grabs our attention.

Say you are at a restaurant or on a plane. Someone's baby starts crying and people get angry. They get mad. Why? It's because it requires their attention and they can't not pay attention to it. They might have had the impression they were doing something else like sleeping or resting or reading or trying to have a conversation. That baby starts crying and guess what? The longer and louder, you can't have a conversation and you can't sleep. Why? You are hardwired to pay attention to that cry.

Guess what? When you do the same, I have to pay attention. When I do the same, whatever is my adult version of it, because all the baby is doing is saying it is uncomfortable in some way, you have to pay attention. The baby's hungry, wet, needs to be changed, is not being touched enough. Make a list. You could do that as a homework project. List all the reasons a baby might cry. Then take that list, the ten reasons a baby might cry, and compare to any time you have drama to get attention and tell me how it's different. I think what you will find is no different. As babies it's a reflection of their essence and being. It's mechanical, but that's where they are. They are not crying to be mean or for some agenda. They are genuinely uncomfortable and that's why they cry. As adults, we cry because of our identification or imagination. We cry because we just happen to have some random thought that came through our head we associated with as our own, which made us unhappy.

I said there were two ways we require other people's attention. One was drama. The other way is the opposite, by withdrawing, being invisible, separating, not participating and being passive aggressive. It's a way to guarantee to get attention.

Invisibility is a work concept—trying to not rock the boat, not participating, not contributing, not reaching out, not giving, not making a contribution over what you are required to do, being unresponsive, reducing response. "How are you doing today?" "Fine." And you walk away. That's not a response. That's not a consideration. It's not a connection. Technically, even though we might say we know, for example if I ask you, "Hey how are you?" and I'm not really asking how you're doing. That's not really what I care about. The reason I'm doing that is to try and make a connection with you. That's why I do it, not because I've got some mental curiosity of how you're doing. In fact, that might be the furthest thing from my mind. The reason I ask you how you're doing is as a way to attempt to engage and connect with you. When the response is "'fine' and then turn away", here's what the communication is: shutdown, withdrawal, don't want to engage, not available to be engaged. Here's the thing, do you think in that moment you get more or less attention from that person? You get more because now you just put into motion a consideration of, "What was that? Why wasn't there a connection or reciprocation? Why was there no reciprocal effort to make a connection? What's going on? What is really going on?" When someone reacts that way, they are obviously not fine. The last thing in the world you'd say if you were really fine is that you're fine. This is simply an illustration. Invisibility demands attention.

Being quiet in the background, not engaging, those bring up attention. That's not how we avoid attention. When we are like that, we are requiring people pay attention to us equally as if we were having lots of drama, although we tend to prefer the second to the first. The former can look like fighting. Guess what? They're no different as far as value. They are equally off balance, off center, on that seesaw of disequilibrium of ways of being and behavior. We have to struggle to find the middle ground. Somewhere between drama and trying to ignore each other there's a continuum and balance. The balance is somewhere between being really edgy, controversial and challenging with each other and being like we're in different countries, although we are in eyesight of each other. Part of it has to do with requiring attention. If we could just be with each other more, in that middle space, then you don't have to require my attention because you have it. I don't have to require you to pay attention to me if you already are; in other words, if you are engaged. Then there's no push or pull.

In school, we have to constantly come back to being engaged in the middle way as much as possible. We have to renew our commitment and aims to be engaged. It is constant. If you find yourself not being engaged or pulling away, and/or creating drama, which is a form of diversion by getting lots of attention, you have to step away from the drama or the withdrawal and try to find the middle ground. Yes, in practice you won't be perfect at it because it takes a while to get good at it. It takes a lot of practice, years of practice.

I talked the other day about recovery time. When we are out of sorts, it's important we keep in mind this idea we need to recover. We can't stay out of sorts. We can't stay dislocated, fractured and separate. We can't be in our own "Private Idaho" because we need to be doing something together. That's why we are here. If at any point anybody withdraws completely, then there is no reason to be here. At the same time, if we have so much drama we lose the ability to function, then that has to go, too. We have to avoid both of the extremes. We have to avoid them like the plague.

The exercise of not requiring so much attention is part of how we find ourselves in the middle ground, which is the more productive space for working. All 8 of these things are about reducing chief negative feature and unnecessary suffering, because the lack of these exercises looks like suffering.

9. When you suffer, try to see what part of you suffers.

Dr. J: Usually it will be chief negative feature. Chief negative feature is the personality that is a reflection of your primary negative emotions, the thoughts and the physical states and postures that go with them. Take all those things reflective of that and voila, your chief negative feature. As I've stated, it's what E.J. Gold sometimes calls "The Chronic". I like that term because it reminds me of a bad cold or a persistent cough. It just won't go away.

One of the things you want to do when you are suffering and are very uncomfortable is to try to remember to look at what part of you is suffering. What is the epicenter? We look at an earthquake and how the buildings shook here, but maybe the epicenter is way over there. Even though we might have a personal earthquake right now, we want to be able to step back and see what the epicenter is. What's the source of that? Where is that suffering really occurring? You know what? Quite often, the suffering has nothing to do with what we are doing right now.

Reduce both suffering and your weakness by giving up imagination and identification.

That has to do with the stories. When you are suffering, when we are uncomfortable and not connecting, observe the stories playing in your head about what this all means.

Observe the imagination, the things that don't have anything at all to do with what's going on.

10. Work on chief negative feature by trying to change precisely where it is most difficult.

Dr. J: This is really hard. By definition, I think number ten is one of the hardest. Memorize it. Anything you have identified as your primary issue of resistance, defensiveness, that pulls you into negativity and imagination, fascination and identification—the primary issue that causes you to act contrary to your aims and ambitions, for you to fuss, push away, to act out either in drama or withdrawal—whatever it is, you need to change it the most and bring the most consciousness to bear.

You have to be fearless. I don't mean that in the sense of having a lack of fear. I mean the fear does not keep you from being able to do what you need to do. Do it because you have fear.

11. Try not to meet difficulties with impulsive and negative attitudes.

Dr. J: Instead of driving to the brink of disaster, try instead a trip to the art gallery. That's a metaphor. Driving to the brink of disaster is when we act out an issue with exaggeration and emotional drama, which runs the risk of driving us off a cliff or breaking the vehicle, allowing us to do what we need to do in life. When you notice an issue, try not to take that issue to its furthest extreme. When you catch yourself on the slippery slope of taking it to the furthest extreme—I mean either into drama or into withdrawal, both of which end up with you paralyzed and not able to continue—take a side trip to the art gallery.

Sometimes, if I'm not able to correct myself, then what I do is divert myself to something positive. If I can't distract myself to get to my positive workplace, then there's another tactic. I will take that energy and go in a completely different direction with it in a helpful way. Instead of driving off the cliff, take a right turn to the art gallery. This takes a lot of discipline and strength to be able to do that because, of course, we can't resolve all of our issues with each other in the moment. We go as far as we can and then it's okay to take a break and go in a different direction for a little bit. Because we take a break doesn't mean we're done.

Going to the art gallery is intentional. Find the positive place you can get to from where you are. It means at the next opportunity you have to come back and address the issue that drove you off the cliff in the first place. Guess what? Keep doing that until there is no longer a cliff to drive off of. Then you get to the next issue to work on.

We have to make progress with our issues. If we always come up against the same issues and hitting the wall or going off the cliff, that is not progress. We have to change that somehow. These exercises are meant to do that.

12. Reduce unnecessary suffering by not comparing yourself to others.

Dr. J: Don't compare yourself to others. Don't compare your strengths, your weaknesses, your attractions and repulsions to others, because they are not you. They don't have your life experience. I don't care if it's your family. Every person in your family has a unique, personal life experience utterly and completely different from yours. Because of that, their baggage, issues, tapes, crystallizations, understandings, are completely different from yours even though superficially they might appear similar. When you compare yourself to your family, it won't work because you're not them.

This idea of comparisons to others is not functional. Try to catch yourself doing it and stop.

13. Control chief negative feature by replacing it with essence.

Dr. J: By essence, I mean qualities that originate with the true self. All these exercises lead to the cultivation of essence. Reduce chief negative feature by reducing unnecessary suffering. By doing all the things we've talked about that are not the exercises, that's how we create suffering in our lives. Really quickly I can list about a hundred ways I create suffering in my life for myself and for other people.

This refers to the last line in the Metta-Sutra (Buddhist Mantra or prayer to reduce Karma and suffering), which is where I make an aim to commit myself to no longer participate in the origination cycle for the creation of suffering for myself and others. How do I do that? To remove myself from the cycle of the creation of suffering, I have to reduce the control of my chief negative feature, I have to reduce the control of ego and personality, I have to reduce the control of my negative emotions, I have to be less in identification and imagination, I have to be less in attraction and repulsion and attachment to

179

those. I have to be less in all these things. As I find ways to reduce their power and I'm more coming into the power of my authentic and true self, I, by definition, am withdrawing from the cycle of the creation of suffering. I'm removing myself from the Dhamma wheel.

The purpose of Buddhism is to get off the wheel. The symbol for Buddhism is an 8-spoked wheel. Each of those spokes relates to an exercise one can practice in life that cultivates knowledge of life and will allow one to get off the wheel. What is the Dhamma (Dharma) wheel? It is the causation cycle of suffering for others and our selves. The Dhamma wheel is also a metaphor for reincarnation and how we reinvent ourselves over and over again, but like we were before. It's circular. In other words, every time you recreate yourself, it is like a model of what was there before entirely. In your current incarnation you're subject to all the same issues you had in the previous one.

You're stuck in the cycle of birth and death. Regardless of if we are talking about real life or not, even just talking about moment to moment, every time we have a breakdown, a breakthrough, we have an opportunity to recreate ourselves in the moment different than a moment before. Every time we make the choice to move ourselves toward creation of a new possibility, every time we make a choice to bring to bear a new skill, a new understanding, a discipline that feeds the essence vs. false personality, we are recreating ourselves in a slightly different way. Every time we recreate ourselves a slightly differently, we are becoming something entirely different. We are becoming something new, something not utterly and completely bound by this origination cycle of suffering.

In ordinary life, we are tied to the wheel. We are tied the wheel. We are on the Gerbil Wheel of suffering. We just go from one issue that causes suffering to the next issue that causes suffering. If not for us, for some body else. I might be fine right now but I'm causing you problems. Right now I'm pretty good but you're causing me a problem. You're causing me suffering. We are still locked in the wheel. How do we remove ourselves from the cycle? We can't even talk about new life because all we see before and in front of us is the gerbil wheel. The real life of our authentic selves is everything that's not on the wheel. It turns out the wheel must be pretty small. We can recognize all the recurring experiences in it. It can't be that big because we recognize everything that's there. We've been over the same thing over and over and over again, life after life after life after life. That also refers to who you were a year ago vs. who you are now. You think you are the same person today as a year ago? You're not. This is a different life. Somewhere in the process you went through a Bardo transition from being a certain way in a certain place with a certain life a year ago, and you're not there now. You are in a different place. How did you get here from there? Through the Bardo.

The Bardo is the intermediate process, the transition process, and the space where something can become something different. If you can't go back and see how you got there from here, then that means during a lot of that process you were asleep. You weren't paying attention. If you can maintain consciousness in the Bardo, then not only do you see how you get here, but you get to make better choices about who you are now. You didn't just choose to be here now. I didn't just choose to be here now. I chose to be here now the way I'm here now. If I want to be here now differently a year from now, then the possibility for that is found in this conversation I'm having today. In other words, it's happening right now, this minute, if this is going to determine where we are at tomorrow or tonight or the next day. Every time we get to make a choice, talk about recovery time again, every time we get out of sorts, there's a choice we can make to correct it. Every time we make that correction with intention and thoughtfulness and deliberation, we are choosing a door, a path of incarnation, the level of play that is going to determine where we are forever in the future but especially even by the end of the day, tomorrow, a year from now or ten years from now. We have this possibility a year from now, by practicing these kinds of things, of being substantially different in every way than how we are right this minute.

The question is, is that motivation? Is that interesting? We have to have some reason to be motivated. We want to be able to validate the process. Where does the validation come in? When you consider in retrospect how you were a month ago or two months ago, three or six months ago, three or six years ago, can you see anything different? Even the three of us, we've been working very intensely together since before June, occasionally intensely since January but almost fulltime since June. Is there anything different? There is, in my opinion. Is everything different? No. Rome wasn't built in a day. It'd be unrealistic to think everything would be different in a day. This is no time hardly at all. The fact we can have this conversation and see some progress and understanding in practice and being is actually significant. It means something.

15. In direct measure, as the wish to injure declines, suffering is quieted.

Dr. J: There is a one to one ratio between desires, inclinations and behaviors, which support intentionally causing harm or suffering for others and our own suffering. This relates to when we talk about Karma; thought, action and deed are causative and creation factors in the manifestation of the world and reality we live in psychologically, mentally, emotionally and physically.

This relates to why so many teachings say a state of mind that's suitable to go along with the pursuit of consciousness is a compassionate and loving state of mind. When we find ourselves in periods of time when we are not spending a large amount of time having loving, compassionate, thoughtful, considerate types of thoughts about those we are near, we have to understand that if we have other thinking going on and behavior going on that's not those things, then we are generating harmful karma. That karma at some point will present its own impediments to our progress. We are always about creating our own impediments to our progress.

I'm someone who's thoughtful. I want to make progress. I want to support the elevation of my consciousness as much as possible. Even if I was being selfish, even for that reason alone, if I was the most selfish person on the whole planet in regard to my own consciousness, I would need to realize the necessity to act with love and compassion and equanimity, balance, harmony and thoughtfulness with the people in my life, if nothing else except for the karma coming from behaviors that are not those kinds of behaviors.

16. To revive your spirits under trials, work. Permit yourself little repose or relaxation night or day. –Johann Wolfgang von Goethe

Dr. J: Geothe is someone I consider to have been important in traditions of conscious schools and teachers. His writing and contributions are quite significant.

Goethe recommended that when you are feeling pressure, that's the time to work. The more pressure you feel, the more you work. We've often been introduced to the idea that we need to do exactly the opposite. When we're feeling stressed or are under trials and tribulations and our spirits are down, that's when we take a break or a time out. The problem is that creates stasis. When we're in a trial or tribulation and when our spirit is under some pressure, when friction is occurring, that's when the energies are being cultivated that have the capacity to sustain higher levels of consciousness. When we step away and go to rest or to sleep because it seems like it's too much to deal with and overwhelms us, we also step away from the benefits of working through it. Inevitably we will come back to that same issue again and again and again. Every time we have some repetitive trial that causes us stress, you already know it's something you need to work through. When we have repetitive trials and step away by going to rest or relaxation we need to get back to work. Become like a terrier dog, get a hold of the issues and don't let go until you come to some resolution of it, night or day.

I also want to say "permit yourself little repose..." does not mean NO repose. After prolonged periods of intensive efforts it is necessary to reward the machine with rest and some fun!

17. Do what someone else wants to do because either you don't want to do it or it is something you would not be inclined to do naturally.

Dr. J: I'm not talking about shooting yourself in the head or jumping off a cliff. As always, there's a range. It could be a mundane activity that in the normal course of your daily life you would never want to do. Someone else suggests you do it. Occasionally, make the effort just because you don't want to.

The other thing is something you would not be inclined to do naturally. We are not naturally inclined to address any of our issues. If we didn't work with this, we would never address or work on anything. Our natural inclinations, driven by instinct and false personality, are all against bringing consciousness to bear on anything we don't like. As a result, we are constantly trying to find a restful place to avoid what we don't like.

The work says that if we are smart and want to make progress now, we have to do exactly the opposite. We have to learn to go with other I's that are not our "own". This is different from following random I's of myself. I'll cherry-pick which I's I want to listen to and go with. I do that all day long. I pick my favorites according to my rationale at any given moment. The work is about practicing going with other people's I's even though you know you don't want to, without justification or defense.

18. Allow someone else to win an argument with grace even though you know you're right and they are wrong.

Dr. J: This is one that is especially hard for me. It seems to be a personality type; the stronger, either positive or negative, the number 3 or 5 type, do not want to lose an argument, especially if they feel like they're right. This is a practice. It doesn't mean to do this all the time or every single time in every possible situation. It does say occasionally, on purpose with intention, allow someone else to win an argument. Be gracious about it.

We don't know how to be gracious. We need to keep practicing and bringing care and attention to this idea of graciousness. I also use terms like congeniality, conviviality. These are qualities that make life easier when you live with other people. If you are going to live in a cave or with wolves and/or in a crack-house, then you may not need any of these qualities. You can't work on yourself by yourself. You have to live and work with other people. To do that you have to work on these qualities.

If you find yourself having wandered away from it, acting as if you have no manners and are no longer suitable to live with others either because of withdrawal, aggression, negativity or what have you, it is your responsibility to make the correction. If someone else gives the correction, you need to take it graciously and react to it without a lot of head conversation and justification.

19. Break a pattern just because you see it.

Dr. J: A lot of times we see small patterns we know are kind of old and repetitive. Because they seem to be little things we do, we discount them and don't really give them a lot of energy, as far as thinking they are important enough to want to make a change. I think what we do is to constantly qualify our habits and patterns as good and bad. I like these. I don't like these. We don't divide our patterns into mechanical vs. conscious because that would be too critical. What if you asked yourself this question, "What patterns and habits have I cultivated with conscious intention?" Now make a list of habits you've cultivated on purpose to work on yourself that were decided upon consciously. That's critical because there might not be any.

Sometimes if we can work on this idea of paying attention a little bit to notice things that are repetitive, OCD, and unconscious mechanical little things, break it just because you see it. Right now, I won't do it to do something different.

Some of these exercises give us a lot of energy and some give us a little energy. We don't want to discount the ones that give us little bits because this energy is cumulative. Even the little bits will add up over time and support breakthroughs and realizations.

Q&A: Exercises for Reducing Chief Negative Feature and Unnecessary Suffering

J: If I'm only observing myself when I'm being negative and not observing myself when I think I'm being positive I miss an opportunity. That's one of things that I realized, "Oh I don't really do that. I just think I feel good. I don't notice why I feel good." I don't remember that maybe my feeling good is just some drama.

Dr. J: The thing is when we do that, it is considered a form of sleep. All times when you are not engaged in this, if you want to say introspection, this observance of self, whether we call it self-observation or self-remembering, when that's at this level of play, when that's not happening, you are asleep. Quite often, we find ourselves in equilibrium where everything seems to be pretty nice. Everybody is getting along, things are pretty positive. We think now would be a good time to take a nap.

This means we miss the trigger for the negative push. We miss the trigger for where we lose it because we weren't paying attention. We were asleep at the wheel over here. It's like going on a highway trip, when you're in the curvy roads you tend

182

to pay more attention. When you're on the long straight away such as Hwy. 90 in Arizona, where it's several days and there's not a turn, well it's very easy to go into a complete coma while you're driving. In fact, they now have signs on the highways that are meant to wake you up with flashing lights, for no other reason. In the middle of the desert, there's a big sign with flashing lights. It's because they've noticed that right at about three and a half hours on the straight road with no variation in topography, they had about a hundred car crashes there where people would leave the highway and go off into the cactus for no apparent reason. They went to sleep. That's what we do. Everything's good so we don't need to pay attention.

J: That's what I recently noticed. It came to my attention that's what I'm seeing myself do.

Dr. J: Not only do we go off into the weeds because we are not paying attention, that's why we can't sustain that level of goodness, so to speak. We get nappy while we are doing it. What if some genuine issue then comes up? We are on the straightaway and we've gone to sleep and are not paying attention. Now we've hit a curvy section all of a sudden. Our capacity to adapt to it in a good way is not very high because we don't start paying attention until we hit something. Now all of a sudden it's like, "Whoa what's going on? Wait. Wait. Where did that come from? That's a left turn. I wasn't prepared for that. What's going on?" Now we are in shock. The automatic resistance kicks in and the chaff goes out while we are trying to sort out where we missed the turn. Then it takes us a little while to come back to some equilibrium, depending on how far we went off into the bushes.

One of the tricks is, when things seem to be really okay, you have to remind yourself that now is just a good a time to observe yourself and pay attention to everything as when things are really not okay and you are really struggling.

J: It's like sometimes I do the same thing with yoga. If my body doesn't feel pain in it, I don't really get motivated to do yoga until I have a discomfort, and then I go do yoga and say the yoga felt so good, I don't know why didn't do that sooner.

Dr. J: I know, I'm the same way. We feel like we have to have external incentives. Pain in your body is an external incentive. For example, I'm depressed because I feel fat. I feel bloated and fat because I overate. I'm depressed because I overate. Why did I overeat? I needed attention but I don't want attention from you. I need stimulation. The food is stimulating.

Back to this attention of others, you could apply this idea of extremes for attention from others to yourself on an individual basis. How about this? What do you do to get the attention of my true self to myself? What do I do to myself? I was talking before about what we do with each other to get attention. How about this? What do I do to myself when I'm alone to get attention? How weird do I get?

J: Very.

Dr. J: You don't have to emphasize that. J's like, "Yeah, you get really weird when you're by yourself!" It's 100% true. What am I doing when I'm being extreme in my head or my emotions or even in my body when I'm by myself. I'm diverting from paying attention to something that needs paying attention to. I have extra energy and I don't know what to do with it. Instead of using it to do something concretely productive for myself, I waste it in some mindless activity. In all of those extremes, I want my own attention.

People will say this who have different kinds of compulsive disorders, like cutting. I've had a client who was a cutter. She had cut her wrists more than four times and wasn't suicidal. She was misdiagnosed. She wasn't suicidal. What she told me was that when she feels pain, then she feels real. She feels like she's here. When she doesn't have pain, then she must be off in her head somewhere and she doesn't feel real, like not being grounded, like a balloon without a string. She said, "When I don't have pain, I feel like a balloon without a string. When I cut myself, it brings me into my body. I feel like I'm here now." Guess what? That's not crazy. She's not crazy. She just needs another way. That's just what she had worked out.

When we are by ourselves and have these extreme behaviors, mentally, emotionally or physically, it is the many I's, in a sense, looking for the master. There's somebody here who knows how this thing is supposed to work. I need to hear from them now. I need something to come now or I'm out of here. It's all the different ways we check-out. For lack of attention we check-out. The attention has to come from within.

When I'm by myself, I create drama all by myself. You don't have to be in the room for me to have some dramatic mind or for me to have some memory that brings up a feeling that makes me really sad or unnerves me or makes me anxious or angry. I don't need anybody in the room at all to have all of that stuff. I don't. I don't need to have anybody in the room to be sitting around playing with my toes or masturbating or picking my nose or playing with my hair or just whirling the energy around trying to expend the energy. I don't need anybody else's help to do that. We all have the ways we waste our energy. It's the same. Just one is in private so we don't get to address that as much.

J: So then we cause the drama and withdrawal so other people will notice us to help facilitate something.

Dr. J: That's a pattern in abusive relationships. Part of the reason why they are abusive is there is a compulsion to have the attention of the other person. If I can't get it one way, I'll get it another. The end result is because I don't have anything that feels real inside of me, in other words, it's like I'm not fixed in time and space except when you are looking at me. Consider, does what's behind the house actually exist if I can't see behind the house? Does it exist because I know it's there because I go there and look at it? Is that why it exists? There's this intangibility about our consciousness difficult to verify that you are actually you without someone else observing you. By observing each other, we make ourselves more real. It validates that I'm here. The fact you pay attention to me, the fact you interact with me, validates I'm here now. See, that's why we work so much on the internal, because if I don't have the internal validation process and can't observe myself to verify there is a self to observe, then I'm utterly dependent on that from you, from my external life. If I don't have a person to validate me, then what am I going to do to validate I'm here? I'm going to run into things. I'm going to cut myself. I'm going to have self-destructive behavior because it makes me feel something.

This is the most common thing people say. I don't feel anything. The reason why I'm depressed is because I don't feel anything. I'm suicidal because nothing matters and I don't feel anything. They are missing this internal validation of their consciousness and existence. They look for other people to do it. If other people are not doing it, then they have no choice.

If other people are not doing it, then they have no choice. Does that make sense?

J: It makes sense. It's also the other thing that JG Bennett said in the book, "Transformation".

Dr. J: I don't know if it's helpful or not but I was saying why we act out internally when we are by ourselves…why we have these extremes. Why do we need attention?

One of my ideas in interpreting the Fourth Way, it's about creating tension, a state of tension between the real and the unreal, between the false personality and the true self, creating a state of tension between them that allows me to have a more direct experience of being here. It allows me to have a more direct experience of being in this world through this state of tension. In lieu of having an internal perception of it, I seek it however I can. I seek to create tension in my life because that experience of tension validates that I'm still here. It validates that I am here, that I am having a life, experiencing a life, good, bad or indifferent.

Without education, without a system, without a plan, we seek to create this tension any way we can. It's not organized, conscious, directed, focused, and we miss the point. We are creating tension for tension's sake and we don't know why. What is the subtle anxiety every person has which is a symptom of simply being alive? Everyone has it. That's that tension. When the tension is too high, then we call it anxiety or panic or fear or a seed of compulsive behavior. There has to be a natural reason why we all have this tension in the first place. It is significant of our inability to come from a place of pure being.

When we talk about saints and sages and Yoga Reishis, what we are looking at are individuals who may have found a way to be without the necessity of random occurrences that create extra tension. Essentially, what they've done is they've created systems. Since we are stress-adaptive human biological transformational machines, whether we like it or not, then one of the paths to consciousness is to choose with intention what creates the tension within me. That's what I'm going to adapt to. If what is creating the tension and the evidence of that is the friction, if that is with more intention, more conscious, more deliberate, then that means whatever adaptation is the consequence of that will be more deliberate and potentially more conscious. One way or the other I am adapting to stress. This system requires it. I'm choosing consciously to try and have influence on that which I am subject to anyway, maybe control, too. I think control is far away. I don't know that I can control anything. I certainly know that at this point in my life I have the capacity to have an influence on the things, the pressures I'm subject to. I have some influence, maybe not all the time, maybe not on everything, but sometimes in big or small ways I absolutely have the ability to have some say so in how that stress will come to me. Because I do it on purpose, I'm actually being an influence to myself for my future adaptation. That's how I got here and that's how I expect to get from here to whatever is the next level for me.

CHAPTER ELEVEN: To Become More Emotional

1. Sacrifice imagination and negativity.

Dr. J: This predisposes you notice you are in imagination and are being negative. Rather than give yourself the permission and the justification to allow yourself to be in imagination and negativity, sacrifice it. Give it up. Just stop. If you can stop, then do it.

This is a willing and voluntary sacrifice because you've made an agreement to do this. This is a true, religious or metaphysical sacrifice, in that it has value in order to give up and get something in return. From this point of view, a sacrifice is a kind of exchange of energy. Give up something near and dear, critical and valuable, in return for something maybe more valuable but less tangible. I give up my comfort in return to get access to a particular state of mind.

2. Do physical work longer and harder with others than you can do easily.

Dr. J: Here's an exercise that doesn't have to be everyday. At least a few times a week, do some hard, physical exercise of some kind or another. Do it longer and harder than others. Don't let the group or your practice partner determine how long or how hard you work or practice the exercise. The idea is to bring a personal, self-motivating component to your effort. It could be a yoga class. Just because the teacher says a class is over, it doesn't mean you have to quit. Just because it starts at a certain time doesn't mean you can't go and start practicing a half hour earlier. Just because we have class on Tuesdays and Thursdays doesn't mean you can't practice on Mondays and Wednesdays. You could get up earlier. You could stay up later.

We use to have occasional midnight and after midnight practices even at 3am. My teacher would call me up and say, "Be at the school in 20 minutes at 3 in the morning." We would go to the school and have practice until sunrise and then we'd all go out for breakfast. The thing about it was that it was so beautiful. Everyone would show up to practice mad. Think about a class where everybody shows up angry. Often it would be in the winter time. He seemed especially perverse in this way. His name was Lloyd Gerard. I thought he took delight in this idea. We were all mad because it was so early. Sure enough, we'd have to practice really hard.

For a time, when I practiced with a Korean Tang Soo Do Master, named Yu Jin Kim. At that time he was my roommate Sa Han Kim's father. Master Kim was very fond about once a month calling a midnight practice. He would call the advanced students and do the telephone tree. We didn't have email back then. You either called someone or threw a rock at their window. He would expect everyone to be notified and show up at last minute notice, and we'd have to do a midnight practice. He would guide some of the practice and then tell us we couldn't stop until sunrise and then he would leave. Then we could do whatever at sunrise. Those practices were really interesting. Most of the time when we were asked to practice outside of our normal day and comfort zone, there was immediate irritation and resistance. Most of the time, it turned out there was some increase of being, some feeling, even just a connection between those who were practicing. It was not uncommon to have some particular, little, special insight that might only come about around 4am.

This is interesting because when we study Chinese medicine, for example, we learn that each of the meridians takes its turn in dominating the activity of the matrix body on about a two hour time clock. There are times in the night when we'd normally be sleeping or in unconscious mode where we have access to a different part of our minds than we normally have during the day. The possible insights of occasionally doing this type of practice are unique. If part of the background noise of what is your waking mind is in fact the voice of your organs, like we suspect—part of the chatter of the many I's, not just divided according to instinctive, emotional, physical, intellectual—even among those four categories there's chatter from every tissue in the body, every organ, viscera, bone, connective tissue, nerve, every cell communicating in real time. That's below our conscious threshold most of the time because that is an infinite amount of noise. That is the white noise; all these voices simultaneously occurring. Sometimes various groups of I's poke their heads up, some of which are those of the physical machine. It's not all random.

Different systems of medicine have for thousands of years tried to tell us every part of us has a voice, a message, an essence or vibration energy it is trying to communicate. Most of the time we are oblivious to this communication. Doctors, healers and therapists who practice listening and looking to themselves and others are able to hear more of these voices in themselves and in other people. You can learn how to do that. Harder still is to do it for yourself. It's one thing for me to learn how to listen to your liver and spleen. It's a whole different ballgame to learn how to listen to mine.

This ties into the idea of working longer and harder than others. Why? We create, by doing so, special circumstances where we will occasionally find ourselves completely outside of our normal comfort zone. In that place there is the possibility of having an extraordinary insight, an understanding, a revelation we normally wouldn't have because we'd be asleep.

3. Put your self completely in the hands of higher powers and then be silent.

Dr. J: Do this for more than one second. How often do we say things like, "I give myself to the Spirit. I submit to higher powers"? Then faster than the next breath, I'm on to working it out myself. There's no gap. There's no place where having prostrated myself in the way and hands of higher powers where they can communicate with me has done any good. Where do they do that in all the noise?

In a way, this is one of the old meanings of meditation. It wasn't just about getting quiet as an end to itself. If you look at the individuals and groups that promoted meditation, they weren't just practicing being quiet. They were metaphysically, spiritually and religiously minded individuals. Traditionally I don't know of any exceptions to this. The meditation forms were always a counterpart to a seeking of remediation, reconciliation, communication from higher consciousness. The meditation techniques, of which there are many, some moving, some still, like the difference between Samatha and Vipassana, teach us to be quiet for a moment so that the voices we hear ordinarily are drowned out in the morass of the white noise of all the other, many I's.

4. Try to be a channel for higher influence to others.

Dr. J: Here's a question. For whom are you a channel for higher influence? It's interesting. We have multiple lines of work. First line of work is self, second with others and third for the school. Being a channel for higher influence is in the second and third line of work, just being a teacher in the school and a responsible person to help people understand how to be, how to practice, how to get it, and to support helping them to work through their obvious issues they cannot see, which can be complete impediments to being able to function at a very high level.

The knowledge you have right now or that we have, that we have validated is a thimble's worth. We know something we've experimented with and practiced to verify and acquire validation. That represents a substance of what's regarded here as higher influence. When you pass that tried and tested knowledge on to someone else, by definition, you are channeling higher influences in the moment.

If I really know how valuable it is to work on my negative emotion and I've proven it to myself and within myself and I realize it is true based on practice and verification, then I try to teach someone else and give them examples to co-facilitate with them, practicing working on negative emotions. All of those things channel higher influences.

It's not so esoteric or airy-fairy as we might have been led to believe by some sources. Some sources talk about channeling higher influences as such a sacred thing that it's virtually not going to happen unless you're in magic Serbia, on top of the mountain and Mother Mary Magdalene manifests to you floating over the mountain and gives you some word of wisdom. 99.999% of the time, higher powers are not going to manifest in that way to you. It's not necessary.

There are efficiencies we see patterned in the ray of creation, for example. Why would spirit choose to only be able to give me a certain amount of wisdom or insight or revelation or picture or understanding at a particular moment in time on a mountain 14,000 miles away and almost impossible to get to? That would mean out of the whole mass of humanity there will only be 4 people who can get that insight and their cousin? It's more likely the way spirit and conscious influence would communicate is through the person sitting right next to you. That's what's available. If higher consciousness is going to communicate to us, then it's most likely those communications will come from those around us. That's the environment we are in.

This was the foundational premise for this book, Angels Speak. I had several experiences in my life where I was lost and so messed up and confused, contemplating suicide because I was so depressed, confused and feeling abandoned, not having knowledge, not having understanding or power or anything that would be one single reason to stay in the world a day longer. Then someone would just say something to me. A stranger or someone somewhat familiar, but not someone I would ordinarily listen to. Once or twice it was someone very close to me.

Once, my father said a couple of things to me that changed my life in that moment, but they were unusual. They weren't things I had ever heard my father say in my whole life and they weren't said to me in a way my father had ever spoken to me in my whole life. These words came out of his mouth and I realized at the time it wasn't my father speaking, it was higher influence. At the time I thought it was Jesus speaking through my father, like he had somehow been transfigured and was channeling Jesus. I had similar experiences with perfect strangers in different circumstances. Once, after an accident, when I was in a hospital, ordinary people gave me insight and information about myself and my life that allowed me to see myself in a different way, and from that moment forward my life was different. It didn't change completely. Some of these changes manifested very slowly over a long period of time, but I can still trace the genesis of that change to a communication and conversation with another person. In that moment, that person was being a channel of higher influence or truth to me.

In the Buddhist way, we have the Boddhisatva. Boddhisatva are flesh and blood men and women who are the embodiment of truth. Well, there you go. By definition they are a channel for higher influence. In Christianity they talk about saints, in Yoga it's sages and Reishes, individuals who at some point in their life are the embodiment of truth. In Tibetan Buddhism it's Rinposhes and Lamas. Does this mean their poop isn't stinky? Does this mean that occasionally they don't have lapses of negativity within themselves? All of these saints and sages, including Quan Yin, had stuff to work out. That's also part of why they were able to become the embodiment of truth, because they worked some stuff out. They could channel higher influence. What's higher influence? It is relative. It is simply what is higher than what you have now. We want to skip intermediate steps. Back to the ray of creation idea; Say, I want to talk to god directly. There is a lot of information, consciousness and communication between me and god that's available to me right now. There's higher influence in you sitting here with me. Why would I be so concerned to only listen to god? That means I won't listen to you. Yet here you are in my life. If I do a
"Sherlock Holmes" in how god is most likely to be able to speak today, it's through you and through me to you, unless I'm not working on myself and am overcome with negative emotions and thoughts, imagination and identification. In that case I'm not channeling squat. I'm just concerned with myself today. I am not going to be much in the way of Boddhisatva for you today if that's my state of mind or being. It's something we have to keep working on and coming back to.

5. Accept denying force without resentment.

Dr. J: There will always be denying force. Denying force is "I want it now! I'm unhappy because I think I need it now and don't have it." The gap between my immediate gratification and the reality of manifestation is denying force. It manifests in many ways as slowness. Some things take time. I plant seeds. I want to eat the sprouts today. It makes me angry because I really wanted sprouts today. That's why I planted the seeds. Now I have to wait. The friction in the waiting and the separation between the idea and the immediate fulfillment is denying force.

Denying force occurs when god speaks through those around me normally but now they are being resistant. You're all caught up in your negativity and you're part of my channel and conduit for higher influences. That's hard for me because that means I have to wait until you get right to get my communication. The delay is denying force.

I want something now but it requires that I do something, that I practice some discipline or perform something repetitiously. I don't want to repeat and so there's resistance. That's denying force.

There's something I really want to manifest and it seems like hell and high water are against it. Every little complication that could manifest to keep me from getting what I want or believe I want is manifesting. That's denying force.

I want to go upstream but the current is flowing downstream. My canoe is facing upstream which means I have to paddle. I can't coast. I have to work against the strong current. Denying force is the weight of the current keeping me away from where I need to go or need to be or what I need to have or acquire. It's in everything.

The resistance to flight is gravity. Even the earth, as it spins through space, encounters resistance. That resistance manifests as the gravity of the sun. The sun is under resistance. There is now speculation there is a minor sun that is in orbit around our sun and maybe even an extra solar planet. The sun is in a galaxy inhabited by other star systems and black holes and whatnot affecting the path of the sun through space. From the sun's point of view, that's denying force, the weight of the planets affecting its individual path. We could say that astrology is a measurement of denying force. It's not just a matter of influence.

Anything that can influence you can create resistance within you. Think about that. That resistance is denying force. It's with every "good" thing and "bad" thing. We do have some choice of the influences we want to be subject to. The number one tool we have to choose what denying force we want to be subject to is our attitudes. That's why we have to constantly work on our attitudes.

6. Transform negativity by not prolonging it.

Dr. J: Don't put off resolving some negative emotion until tomorrow just because you are lazy. That's lazy. If you find yourself in a funk and negativity is ruling and you see you have an opportunity to see it clearly and perhaps to do something with it and come to a positive place, face it. We can't always fix everything in the moment. Sometimes it's huge just to make the effort to make things a little better. A lot of times we don't do that. We don't make that little effort to even try and make things a little better because we can't fix everything. That's not a good school idea. That's wrong thinking. If you can make it a little better, then do.

How are we living and working with each other? What really is the nature of our daily practice? This allows us to put the kibosh on so much negative emotion, in other words, to put it to bed. It's no justification to prolong being in a negative state because you know it will recur. That's the worst kind of justification. We knew that before we started. You are mechanical and unconscious and asleep and are not a transformed, liberated, enlightened being, so yeah, your negativity will return. There is no excuse not to work on it to transform it. If we can make small gains, that's really great.

7. To become more emotional, you must give up self-will, which does not mean blind obedience.

Dr. J: It is willingness to defer to the judgment of someone with more being than you. This is the function of submitting to a teacher, school or work. It's even the function of submitting to an idea. Sometimes I have difficulty submitting to my teachers. I've noticed that in the past I've had an appearance of submission but internally was very resistant. I found sometimes it was helpful to focus on the idea of what my teacher was or represented to me. I could submit to the idea, if not directly and completely to the person. Of course, I always hold it against teachers who have faults similar to my own.

Because of fairytales and maybe story books and movies, I've been led to believe that somehow teachers don't share the same faults as the student. Even if they are enlightened, like Jesus, he wouldn't have any of the same kinds of inclinations or weaknesses. Jesus would never scratch his balls, would he? Jesus with halitosis, no he wouldn't have bad breath or ever oversleep or ever forget anything. When you read the stories, what you find out is even he was still a person. In fact, that's the most significant attribute of the story. The theme of the thing was that Jesus was a man, a person. The sacrifice was extraordinary because it was made by a common person. Common people have common failings. If great teachers like Jesus could have common failings and be less than 100% thoughtful at all times and have a personal, irritating quirk, then of course all of us are subject to that.

The statement "To become more emotional, you must give up self will" refers to becoming more emotional in a positive way. There's no hope of breaking out of our negative emotional patterns without help. Help is conditional. It's always voluntary and conditional. It's always based on giving up something on purpose in exchange for something else. We have to give up self-will. Self-will is thinking everything about me is self-determined. I want to keep it that way. The problem is that I'm asleep, unconscious, overwhelmed by negative emotions. My I's are constantly changing. My idea that I'm able to be individual and self-determined, consistent and conscientious is a completely false. Being attached to my being in charge all the time means nothing because, even if I was by myself, I'm not in charge all the time. One part is in charge one minute and another part's in charge the next minute. When it's myself I don't think too much about it. I'm not so critical. I may not be critical of even wild variations within myself. Boy, if you are in charge of me for a minute and you deviate, oh I'm going to crucify you because that's justification for not submitting.

It does not mean blind obedience. Blind obedience is unconscious and mechanical. This is not about faith. When we talk about faith in the work, it is open-eyed understanding. We don't revere the concept of blind understanding and faith. If we had a choice to do something with knowledge and insight and awareness and agreement, we would choose that. We wouldn't choose to do anything that is the result of completely unconscious, mechanical inclination. Only with intention and awareness can we willingly defer to the judgment of someone with more being than us.

CHAPTER TWELVE: Exercises For Work On Will

1. To develop will, control your attention and learn to do what the machine does not want to do.

Dr. J: All these concepts I have been talking about so far work together. Will is the evidence of discipline. Control your attention. In order to control your attention you have to have attention. Attention is not the same thing as identification. They are completely different. Attached to and identified with are mechanical ways of being. Consciously bringing attention to something is not mechanical. To control attention means to wield attention and focus with care, deliberation and intention. Learn to do what the machine does not want to do. Paying attention, observing what our machine doesn't want to do. Where's the denying force? Where's the internal denying force? Where's the movement towards sleep or rest. Where's the part where we fade out and check-out, where we abandon, react defensively, where we push back and where we don't want to go. What we don't want to do. We need to grab ourselves by the back of the neck, bring it to bear on what we don't want to do, and learn how to do it anyway. That takes experimentation and practice.

2. To obtain, give up self-will.

Dr. J: Here's another definition of what is self-will: childish obstinacy, irresponsibility, justification, vanity and lying.

We take a lot of pride in being self-willed as individuals. In fact, there are a lot of schools right now that teach people to develop their self-will, kind of like the popular self-help Guru type, "take charge of your life" and "just visualize and go for it". The problem is, for most people what they are going to walk away with in an increase in child-like obstinacy. That's like when there is something the child needs to do. You need to wash your hands because you were just playing in the dirt. The child says, "No! I don't have to wash my hands," and then runs around and puts their hands all over the walls. You know the child is tired and they are going to have a long day tomorrow so it will be good for them to go to bed now. You tell the child to go to bed and they go, "No! I'm not going to go to bed." We were in the store the other day and this little girl who was probably about 7 years old saw a display of suckers. She zeroed in on the suckers and started going like this, "I want a sucker. I want a sucker. I want a sucker. I want a sucker! Give me that sucker! Momma, give me that sucker!" Mother tried to misdirect her attention and tell her no. The child was obstinate in her attachment to getting a sucker. She did this 20-25 times. She whined and cried. We were about to witness a full blown, cathartic hissy fit over the non-acquisition of the sucker when mom knuckled-under and reached over and bought that sucker and gave it to her. She taught her a lesson. That lesson was self-will.

When that girl is thirty years old, she will still have that. It will still be a force in her life unless she handles it and learns to recognize it.

Irresponsibility is the lack of being responsible and or ignoring responsibilities. If we are responsible for something like a certain work, an activity, for paying attention to something and we simply don't because we can, that's irresponsible. We mistake doing what we want as self-will. We mistake being irresponsible for being self-willed. Justification is arguing over identification and why you have a right to do what you know is wrong. Why you have to do what you know is not going to work and doesn't work and it's not good for you, it's a reflection of how you used to be and not how you want to be. We mistake self-will for that.

What is the role of vanity and lying? Things have to be and look a certain way. It means something because they don't. That's not self-will. We lie because we can. We think that because we can lie we don't have to tell the truth. "I have self-will, I don't have to tell you the truth just because you asked me the question and I've previously agreed to do so. I don't have to tell you the truth because I am in charge of myself and I don't want to right now, or at least these I's, don't want to right now." We mistake that for self-will. That is simply tramp feature and lying.

3. Develop will by putting into practice what you know.

Dr. J: Everyday try to have a practical expression of what you have actually learned, something you definitely know. Think in terms of the three lines of work because there is that selfishness thing. Just because I'm putting into practice something I've learned makes me happy or feel good, if that's the extent of it, that's still just first line of work. That's baby practice. That is still infantile. Putting into practice what I know for channeling higher influences for other people, for the helpfulness of other people and the school, that is to what I am referring. If you do that, you will have more will.

4. Work when you do not want to and don't justify.

Dr. J: When's the best time to work? When you don't want to. When's the best time to practice? When we don't want to. If we are going to say that part of the reason we are practicing is to develop consciousness, and if we say that part of the reason why we practice is to learn how to control our energy, to gather energy and to channel energy and project energy irrespective of environment or circumstances, if any of that is true, the best times to work are often when we are least inclined to do so.

Don't justify. If you don't work, don't say it's because it's too late or you're too tired or you didn't have a break or your practice partner wasn't the best one. There's always a reason not to work. There're always hundreds of reasons not to work and practice. "I'm tired. I worked hard earlier today or yesterday. I need a break today." Okay. Don't think for one second that it is not justification. At least acknowledge the justification and the lack of higher consciousness and laziness and the loss of potentially getting a benefit. I don't care. Don't pretend it's self-will.

CHAPTER THIRTEEN: Exercises for the Moving Center

Dr. J: Why do I want to have exercises for the moving center? It is so I can learn to see it in operation so I can learn how to define it and where it is, how it functions and its parameters. What does it feel like when it's taking charge of the machine? I want to be able to observe the moving center separate from the emotional and intellectual centers.

We might think we are being intentional in a particular moment. Because we haven't learned to segregate or separate the function of the moving center from the emotional center, we might not realize the movement we are doing right now is completely coming from the moving center. There is no intention; there is no mental aspect to it whatsoever. We are being mechanical.

The moving center is interesting because it shows up in all kinds of ways. It shows up in ways we often do not anticipate. These exercises are to bring that out in order to amplify or put under a microscope what is happening.

1. Do not toss or throw objects. Rather, place them intentionally.

Dr. J: The rule was always this: when you set something down, if you can hear it that is called "throwing the cup on the table". If you can hear it make contact and thump, bang or bump, screech, grind or growl, then moving center is not under conscious control. You are simply sort of tossing the item mechanically. Various teachers in my schools would have this as an example and an exercise in different kinds of classes, so that when we are in the house washing dishes, the rule was to not clank the dishes or bang them against the sink or the faucet. If you break dishes while washing them, that was evidence you were in a completely mechanical mode. If you had been paying attention you wouldn't want to be breaking the dishes, would you? You're intention is not to break them because wouldn't it be easier and save you a step if you just tossed or smashed it into the trash without washing it? Another rule had to do with housekeeping. It is really easy when you clean to bump and bang things around like ramming the vacuum cleaner up against the chair leg so much that after a year or two it has a groove in it, or knocking the leg off the coffee table while vacuuming. Ironically, the purpose of vacuuming was to clean the house. It wasn't to knock the legs off the furniture. If while we are cleaning we are breaking things, isn't that exactly the opposite of cleaning things? Yet somehow, because we are vigorous, we get some satisfaction out of it. I was really vigorous with my cleaning, and yeah I broke some stuff.

Another idea has to do with throwing objects. To place things intentionally relates to our bodywork. One of my teachers emphasized that when you walk around the client, you should not be able to hear your foot falls. When you walk around the classroom, you should not be able to hear your footfalls. If you can hear the heel going thump and bang, that is called stomping. Stomping is not the same as walking. Walking implies intention. The Thais really emphasize this a lot because they are the source of Vipassana meditation. Their walking meditation is where one step is broken down into 8 separate steps. To take the right foot and place it in front of the left foot and move your body forward one step in space might take eight, individual, thoughtful, considerate motions done slowly and of course silently. This idea of the silent, conscious walking translated to the Knead, in that when we walk around the client we do so with intention, like gliding. Lift your foot just far enough to allow it to transport it to the next place. Then don't fall down on your heel, but set it down on the floor gently. This translates over to full body motion. When I move around on the mat and when I put my knees on the floor, I'm quiet. I try to do so silently and make a sliding sound versus an impact sound. On some level, the impact and jarring motion is psychically disturbing. On some level, the constant breaking of things in our environment as we go about our day is disturbing because we are distorting our environment, causing mechanical distortion patterns.

Be aware, for example, when we are moving through the house, especially when you are in a hurry, can you move to the phone or wherever you are going and not hear the sound of your foot falls? When you walk over to get a cup of coffee does it go bang as you stomp?

When I put a book on the table I could throw it on or I could, as a practice, thoughtfully place to book down. I notice, for example, when students are in the house and they go through the library books, I find it a little bit jarring to see someone take one of the books, which might be kind of rare and out of print, and go like this with it, plunk! As they toss it on the table when they are done with it, that tells me whatever they were doing with the book was not paying attention. They were holding the book while they were somewhere else. How do you know that? It's because of how they were handling the book.

This goes for all kinds of objects, like throwing versus placing a spoon in the sink. If you are going to throw something, do it on purpose. We call those sports.

2. Do not kick doors open or drawers shut.

Dr. J: Don't kick things into position unless they are stuck and that is the only way to get them to move. Avoid slamming and banging around in your environment. That refers to doors, cabinets, drawers. Be aware. If you hear a door slam behind you, notice it was probably you who did it.

Here is a Tibetan concept: the Bardo Thodol, the Tibetan book of the Dead, is rife with metaphors and illustrations of doors, both in all of Buddhist land, Thailand included, doorways and lentils and thresholds of doorways are considered sacred. In classic temple architecture, doorways always have an obstruction at the bottom of the door, which is called the lentil. It can be as high as a foot high. When you come up to go into the temple, a lot of times people wonder about it because it certainly doesn't make it quite so handicap accessible. "Why does the temple have this big thing you have to step over to go inside?" That lentil signifies that what is inside the temple is not the same as what is outside. The doorway itself is a Bardo space, a place of transition where energy shifts. The lentil is there to create intention. Classically, I'm sure people can trip right through them. It's funny, when you go to the temples that get a lot of tourist traffic and stand off the side and watch, during the day, how many people trip as they go to walk into the temple and almost fall flat on their faces. It can sometimes be a continuous stream. Go to Phra Wat Chetuphon, Wat Pho to the part of the temple with the reclining Buddha and watch people going in and out. They will trip coming out of the Temple just like they tripped going in, as if they had completely forgotten their first fall. At no time in the Temple were they conscious of the doorway.

We have doorways too. The Tibetans said it was a good exercise to remind yourself every time you go through a door that something has changed, whether it is inside to outside the house or from room to room. Bring awareness to doors, because in the Bardo Thodol your path and progress will be determined by your skill at negotiating doorways. You want to be an expert at negotiating doorways. Apparently there are many kinds of doors to go through.

As an exercise for the moving center, it's very interesting how little we do pay attention when we go through a doorway.

3. Do not take shortcuts across the garden.

Dr. J: Follow a path with purpose. Yes, it would be quicker to take the shortcut. Yes it would be eight steps less to take the short cut. How about this? Don't take the shortcut and walk on the path just because it is longer, and do it on purpose.

What is the garden? It can be anything you designate. It could be any place. It doesn't have to be outdoors. I've always wondered, when I built the big labyrinth previously the borders were 3.5 feet wide and entirely made out of wild flowers. At different times of the year it was quite beautiful. It always amazed me the number of people who would take a shortcut and walk straight across the labyrinth or skip rings in the labyrinth because it took too much time. They wanted to see the labyrinth. Instead of doing the labyrinth they would trundle right across all the wild flowers to the middle. You could see the path they made where they pushed over the flowers to get the middle. Let's not do that, as an exercise.

4. Avoid haste. Do not hurry.

Dr. J: You know the old saying, "The hurrier I am, the behinder I get". It's because to hurry is not the same mental state as awareness. To be in a hurry is a mechanical state, which is an anxiety between the emotional center and the moving center. That's why quite often, when we get anxious and do things faster, we do them wrong and we make mistakes. I get behind because I did it wrong the first time, so I have to do it over. I might have to do something two or three times I could have done once if I had originally been paying attention.

193

This applies to many things. Make a list of where you hurry. Observe yourself for unnecessary hurrying. It is a sign of stress and moving center.

5. Do not crush, spindle or mutilate things before you throw them away.

Dr. J: I'm finished with a piece of paper so I wad it up into a ball and throw it into the trashcan. Rather than wad and crush and throw, if you don't need to wad it up, just put it in the trash. The paper takes up less space if it's not wadded up. Think of packing paper and peanuts. If you want to take up a lot of space, you wad the paper up into balls. You don't just lay it in the box, because it doesn't take up any space. To avoid wasted space, don't wad it up.

We've got the throwing thing and the crushing, destroying thing. When we want to remove something from our environment, let's try not to destroy them. Another thing people do…let's say they are going to throw something away and it is going to the garbage. They'll take something that might still have some use and then break, crush or destroy it. That absolutely removes the possibility of it being repurposed or recycled. If we think recycling is more conscious than not, then we want our garbage to be in better shape. Even a piece of electronics might be broken, but the cabinet or switches might still be useful. There may be something about it that could be repurposed.

6. Allow other cars to have the right of way without speeding up to prevent them, even if you were there first.

Dr. J: Don't identify or lose your consciousness with things or events that happen to you. When is that not a rule or something we would like to say is an operative principle? Don't identify or lose your consciousness with things or events that happen to you. In other words, don't lose your mind just because something happens to you. Let's say someone gives me an odd look and so I go off into imagination about what that look means and lose my mind and then I react, and then they react to me reacting and we get in a fuss and fight all day long. What I didn't take into consideration was that first of all, maybe when they gave me that look, they had a little gas. It didn't have anything at all to do with me. It seems silly, but that is sometimes how petty we are.

This idea of allowing cars to have the right of way is because when we are driving, it's quite easy to become very mechanical. It is very easy to have gone 5 miles in the car without remembering a single thing that has transpired over that distance. You couldn't tell someone if you stopped at a red light or what the traffic was like. You check-out in autopilot. Some exceptions to that are when I'm on autopilot and someone cuts me off or tries to pass me, in my mind inappropriately, so it wakes me up out of my stupor and so I'm cranky. You go to pass me so I speed up because "how dare you, trying to get ahead of me." I don't think it through that there's a million cars on the road ahead of me as soon as I pull out of the driveway. Whether one car here or there is ahead of me can't possibly mean anything on the road. There is always someone ahead and behind you. It should have nothing at all to do with whether you go into imagination, lose your consciousness, go into negative expression and reactive mind.

When we are moving, there is a tendency to be assertive of our space. You see it when people are dancing. When the dance floor gets a little bit crowded, the elbows get a little wider and people start getting more aggressive in their moves. That's completely mechanical, reactive and unconscious. It's the same thing when I'm driving and another car is a little abrupt and I react by speeding up to take up the space I was anticipating they were going to take up (instead of simply noticing). I'm claiming space and prestige, if you will, projecting into the future. "This is my lane. You can't get in front of me in my lane."

7. Bustling about may be a buffer and the wrong work of centers.

Dr. J: Calm down and be present. If you notice you've been anxiously moving in a way that's not necessarily focused in any particular direction, remember that's probably a center that is not working properly and that your moving center has a valve loose.

194

A bustling scenario has to do with sitting. We should be able to say, "I'm going to sit still now for a minute, for an hour." This is what I see, especially in groups. We say, "We are going to sit and have a focused discussion for a few minutes." Somebody in the group will have to be busy the whole time. By busy, I mean they are physically doing something. For example, I had classes recently where the whole time I was trying to have a discussion, there was someone moving from the chair to the floor to five different yoga postures, back to the chair, to the water, to the purse, to the water, check the phone, back to more yoga postures, back to the chair, back to the phone, back to water, constantly and continuously the whole time I was talking. That is leakage. It can also indicate resistance to the conversation. This mindless physical activity is a way of buffering and not being present to the conversation.

A small example is when we are having a focused discussion, I look over and this is what a see (thump, thump, thump), pen clicking (click, click, click, click). That's evidence of a buffer, wrong work of centers and that you are somewhere else. We all do this. We all have our little leakages in the moving center. Examples can be hair twirling, gum chewing. Gum chewing is interesting. In one school I was in, you weren't ever allowed to chew gum. Anytime you were near the school, no gum chewing was allowed because the gum creates an excuse for repetitive, unconscious motion, which indicates a buffer. It would be better to clearly see the buffer without justification than to be chewing gum. The gum and the clicker pen become justifications for the constant, repetitive, mechanical motions. Technically, you just have to click once for the pen to work.

8. With intention place yourself in physically demanding situations where you are not comfortable.

Dr. J: If your nature is placid, practice karate. If your nature is dynamic, practice Tai Chi. Work hard. Technically speaking, the physical work most appropriate for you is the one you are least attracted to, by definition in the work. Now, for peace of mind, I like to practice the dynamic work, although from a natural point of view it's probably more balancing for me to practice the more internal and meditative martial arts, like Tai Chi, Qi Gong. The more combative arts, stick, knife and sword, especially kickboxing, make me happier. I love that. It's exhilarating and exciting to me. From the point of view of moving center, I struggle more and therefore have more friction to work with when I'm doing the most meditative and introspective work.

People who think they are not very physical need to be physical. If you are someone who thinks you are really strong, then work on things that require finesse and fine movement. If you are someone who is really good with finesse and fine movement and detail, do something that has strength training with explosive vitality, like power lifting or kick boxing. If your nature is timid, then practice being combative where you get hit and where you have to initiate forceful contact with someone else. There are low impact variations of all these kinds of things. There is a yoga practice that meets all these different types. Ashtanga may be good for passive types. If you have a capacity to naturally be dynamically active, then do Kriya or Integral yoga.

This is not for physical or metabolic benefit. It's not for your health. Your body doesn't care about your moving center, as far as your need for aerobic fitness. Everybody needs some aerobic fitness. Regardless of your type or inclination to passivity and activity you need some aerobics. You also need to cultivate a practice that is not aerobic, if that's appropriate for your nature as a counterpoint to bring consciousness into the moving center.

9. Sit with both feet on the floor.

Dr. J: If you notice during the day you never have both feet on the floor, as an exercise to bring awareness to the moving center, put both feet flat on the floor. It is the sitting equivalent of Tadasana or Mountain Pose. Notice how much you don't want to be there. Your right leg just really doesn't think it belongs there. It would be so much happier if it were somewhere else, like tucked up under your left thigh. It communicates that to you, "Come on. Just for a minute…it'll be okay…come on, cross your legs."

J: It just happened to me. I had them on the floor. When you said that I put everything down. Then when I saw them crossing I thought, "Oh what are you doing?" so I put them down again. Immediately my toes climbed on top of the other one.

Dr. J: As your right leg starts trying to climb up the left leg on its own. That's the moving center all on its own. That's why we want to do these exercises. It is to illustrate what just happened. That's a mind you are not in charge of. That's a group of I's you are not in charge of. They have the capacity to express themselves.

Back to yesterday's conversation on the white noise. Again, the moving center is white noise. You want to be able to communicate with the moving center. Sometimes you need it. You want it to be functional when you need it to be. You don't want all the resources of the moving center to be so unconscious that when you need to move you can't. That's a survival trait, by the way. Being able to just move out of the way when you need to without a lot of conversation. Your body really just wants to do something else because it's so used to doing whatever it wants to. If you can't just simply get out of the way when necessary, that could mean the difference between a long or a short life.

Certain physical habits lead to disease. Certain physical, repetitive motions indicate organ imbalance, disease and in some cases imminent death. Here's an example: rubbing the chest often in angina before there is pain. They might start opening and closing the left hand. You might be watching someone in their late 40s, 50s or 60s and they are a little overweight. They may be diabetic or pre-diabetic. They have belly fat and inflammation with a sallow complexion and low energy. They might have bad breath and shortness of breath. While they are hanging out, they are rubbing their chest. That could be a sign of enlargement of the heart, which is coming on with motion before there is pain. You look at that same person, male or female and you notice that while you are talking to them they squeeze and open their hands like they are trying to work something out.

Sometimes people start moving their arms. It's called spiral or swinging the arms. This is a symptom before you have complete liver failure. When you have a jaundice cerotic liver going into failure, one of the last signs before complete shutdown is this erratic, mechanical arm motion.

Those are extreme examples. Little repetitive motions like ticks can be an indication of organ or neurological damage from a prescription drug. An example is a yawn reflex while sticking the tongue out. These physical habits are not necessarily innocuous.

Sometimes mechanical motions like a tremor, a tick, a shake, a quiver or a thump may be more than anxiety and show a disease. If you can't stop moving, it might not just be that you are buffering the moving center. It might be a symptom of disease. We want to be able to distinguish between the two.

10. Stand or sit erect with good posture.

Dr. J: Avoid slouching or leaning on things. Notice that we want to lean, tilt to starboard. We don't want our boat to sit stable in the water. We like it kind of heeled over one way or the other. That's in the moving center. A way to struggle with it is to create a little friction by telling yourself to be upright and you can't. You notice, "Okay, I'm going to sit up straight in this chair." In about two or ten minutes I take a mental snap shot of myself and I've gone into this slouching, collapsed posture where my foot climbed up on top of my leg. Notice the struggle.

Anthropologists say one of the defining characteristics of Homo-Sapiens is the tendency toward erect posture. I don't get that. I think the tendency is not Homo Erectus but Homo slouches or Homo collapses.

11. Practice Yoga.

Dr. J: A daily Yoga practice is balancing for the centers and is in general a good housekeeping work for the body. There are eight branches of Yoga and literally hundreds if not thousands of different styles and emphases. It is possible to find one that suits you and your lifestyle. Especially Hatha Yoga, as a form of self perfecting practice it has much to offer, having been refined over a great period of time. Of course, I can't speak too generically. Not all forms of yoga, yoga schools and teachers, are the same. Practices vary widely according to many factors such as geography and income bracket. However, once the basics are learned it can be practiced by just about everyone, anywhere.

12. Practice a martial art.

Dr. J: I think everyone should practice yoga and some martial arts. They are not the same thing. They go about bringing energy and consciousness to the moving center in different ways. They have different physical benefits as well. Just as I described in talking about the benefits of Yoga, we have to say there are equally as many different forms of martial arts. There are thousands of different schools representing both traditional and novel eclectic systems. However, similar to Yoga some are more spiritual and energetically focused such as Tai Chi and Chi Gung styles, and some are more intense and combative. There are bridge systems which combine elements of philosophy and spiritual focus with combative application such as Thai Kabri Kabrong, Muay Thai, Filipino Kali, Indian Kalari Payat and Indonesian Penjak Silat etc. Of we must also include the Bruce Lee/ Danny Inosanto "Lee Jun Fan" based schools and systems as well.

Considering the increasingly wide variety of offerings and availability of instruction gaining enough instruction to support cultivating a practice should not be too difficult.

13. Learn to dance.

Dr. J: Yes, I'm resistant to going to dance class. Yes, I also know and have been told by many of my most credible teachers that I need to practice dancing occasionally. Yes, I am a complete hypocrite by resisting going to dance classes. I'm totally aware of it. As I'm saying it, whatever I is in charge of my mouth right now wants to say I will try to work with that, while the others in the background are going, "Liar!" Dancing, by definition, has the potential to balance and bring awareness to all of the centers, all at the same time. Traditionally it was common for schools of consciousness studies to incorporate some form of required studies in movements and or dance.

14. Practice and play a musical instrument.

Dr. J: This is another way to bring attention to the moving center. Everybody should have an instrument they should learn to play. I don't care what it is, guitar, drum, kazoo. I was listening to the radio while I was running an errand the day before yesterday. They played a couple of tracks from a record made in the 1930's of a kazoo orchestra. It was amazing. They said no musical instruments were played during the performance. Of course, it was a kazoo, which is a human musical instrument. It was twenty people and orchestrated like Bach or something. It was just beautiful.

You can learn to play something. Beat, bang, scrape, jiggle, whistle, singing bowls, drums, penny whistle, ocarina, pan flute, etc. Then occasionally play it.

15. Learn and play a part or a role with intention.

Dr. J: This one is kind of interesting. There are a lot of different tactics. It literally means a play or a role, as in Shakespeare. In quite a few conscious schools, students and teachers organize performances. For example, there would be an organized dance or musical performance. People are assigned roles and parts. In Grass Valley, people were given a stack of joke books and then had to pick one, but then had to pick three or five jokes and perform them. If you can't pick them out, then somebody will come up and say, you will do this joke, this joke and this joke. Perform a musical performance, whether you know how to play or not. If you can organize a kindergarten into doing a musical performance, you should be able to organize a group of adults with the same skill level. The only thing that keeps them from being able to do that is ego and personality and fear of failure, rejection and suffering.

Conscious schools organized the plays in this manner: if your inclination was always to play a certain part, like a lead role, male or female, you would be assigned a minor part. If typically you would be the side characters in a play that stand on the side and agree or yell "yeah",once and a while, the extras, in this case, you would be assigned the lead role. The director would say, "Everybody move over that way," until he could find you hiding in your corner before you could scurry and hide behind the curtain somewhere. He would go, "Whoa, you! You're the lead, because you don't want to be." "Ahh, no, no, no."

"Right. Perfect. You'll be perfect." Whoever gets mad at you because they didn't get picked, they get the minor role. "You'll be the stand in. We want you just to stand over there and hold the umbrella. Don't move and don't say a word. Have no facial expressions."

Learn to play a part. Play a role with intention.

Yes, it does mean plays and parts, like roles in Shakespeare, but it also means roles in the house. It means play a different role with intention and on purpose. If normally you are the student, play the teacher. If normally you're the teacher, play the student. If normally you wouldn't work on any particular issue, then pick an issue you wouldn't like to work on and play the role of someone who would do that. If normally you are not so clean, then play the role of someone who is very clean. If normally you are fastidious, play the role of someone less fastidious. There are all kinds of ways we can do this. If normally somebody else always answers the phone, then play the role of being the primary person who answers the phone. If you're the person who cooks everyday, pick a day and don't cook. Play the role of a person who submits to somebody else's cooking, even if it makes you uncomfortable. You do this within reason without causing yourself or others harm.

Q&A: Exercises for the Moving Center

STUDENT: Number 4. It talks about making a list of where you hurry. I was thinking about how it can apply to communication, too, being impatient with someone when you are communicating, and wanting the conversation to be over or wanting them to just stop so that you can make a point and move on. That would be like emotional or intellectual crossing over with moving center? It's not necessarily moving center alone, but there is an impatience and hurry aspect with it.

Dr. J: It could be. Also, is there a physical part of that? For example, I have one. When I get into a haste mode, I have a repetitive, physical motion I do when I'm mentally in haste. You want to see it? Yes, the answer would be yes.

STUDENT: That correlates to "the hurrier I am, the behinder I get". When you're not listening and are impatient, then you lose any potential communication. Then you have to go back, and that takes longer.

Dr. J: I wouldn't say you lose any potential, but you could. You certainly may lose something.

STUDENT: You go into mechanical mode when the other person is, too.

Dr. J: The interesting thing is that we don't know which comes first, the physical inclination toward the movement as evidence of a buffer, avoiding the mental focus to be present, or the physical motion as evidence of the buffer. That's why we do the exercises, so overtime we can begin to distinguish the variations of this. Is the buffer first or the unconscious motion first? The motion is habit coming from the tissue, but it's supporting buffers. Motion can come just from the tissue. Certain kinds of movement like itching, scratching, twitching, blinking, flaring of the nostrils, winking, swallowing, can all indicate disruptions in the tissue itself. That's a cross between the instinctive and moving center.

The instinctive center notices something's not right. How does the instinctive center get your attention? Something's not right with my kidneys. I have a pain in my shoulder. I have a sense of tension here. I don't really know or talk to my kidneys. For some reason, I have a compulsion to itch and squeeze and poke my shoulder. What's happening is the instinctive center notices there's something not quite right with my kidneys. It communicates this to the moving center. The moving center generates through this sensory circuit this motion to want to put pressure on the point, because if I put enough pressure on it, it will catch the attention of the waking mind, of the intellectual center, so that I might be able to sort out that I need to drink more water. It's convoluted. There's a point on the shoulder that can have irritation. That is reflective of renal difficulty due to dehydration. Certain kinds of motion can indicate an organic problem. The tissue itself is trying to communicate. The way it gets my attention, "we need water!" is through some kind of irritation, or absence of sensation like numbness.

The trick is, while we focus on the exercises, to learn how to distinguish between what is coming from the instinctive and moving center as organic (from the organs and tissue) conversation and what is reflective activity generated from emotional and mental buffers. There are two different things. That means there are two different solutions. The organic and visceral solution is to drink more water. If this rubbing my shoulder, head and chest is a buffer from emotional issues, then drinking

198

water will not help. I have to come at it from a completely different direction in order to resolve it. The motion might look very similar if I wasn't paying attention.

STUDENT: In relation to "learn to play a part in a role with intention" from Angels Speak the other day. In remembering we had made an aim as a group, which we never did, to once a week get together and do that listening exercise where there's a moderator, and I would like to do it as a practice again since we made the aim and then let it go by the wayside. I'd like to come back to it and do it.

Dr. J: Well, we could do it because it's your idea and so let's practice doing things that are your idea, and also because apparently there is resistance to doing it, so it might be valuable to do it just from that point of view.

STUDENT: Something I've done before in Wilderness Therapy I think might be interesting to try one day is for me to be the boss, to play the role of the teacher. This is to switch up the roles, like you said in 15, "If you are the teacher, be the student. If you are the student, be the teacher."

Dr. J: I was just kidding. I didn't really mean it. Did I say that?

STUDENT: I think it would be a challenge on both ends to do that and that would be the exercise.

Dr. J: Okay.

STUDENT: I think the sitting with both feet on the floor is one of the harder ones for me. I noticed this past week and a half everyday "you don't want to sit with your feet on the floor, do you? You always want to have one foot underneath your bum." In the past few days, when I've been doing dishes, I've been working on doing it quietly and notice when I bang things and how it goes in and out. I set an intention to do it for a little while and then immediately I resist or forget completely.

Dr. J: Another one on the moving center is to notice, if someone gives you a photograph or points out you are doing something that's in the moving center, how quickly you might get mad or angry. It's almost like being caught with your pants down. Do you notice right now your finger is up your nose to the second joint? "Nuh-uh..." Notice then the reaction to having introspection or having attention brought to it. Even as you're talking about the both feet, you obviously don't have both feet on the floor. Then there's that first reaction. That's the reactive mind, that's the denying force. That's the false personality or the chronic.

These exercises have to be intentional. If it involves other people, it has to be cooperative and by agreement. It's not so effective to do secret exercises because there is no way to monitor and there's no way to have compliance. If I'm doing a secret exercise and I break the rules, no one is the wiser. We don't do secret exercises. We can do the exercise where L is in charge all day for a day with intention and on purpose. All these exercises have to be done with intention and agreement if they involve someone else.

CHAPTER FOURTEEN: Exercises for the Vocal Apparatus

Dr. J: I was doing some of these exercises this morning. It's a good thing. Working with the vocal apparatus in how you speak and use your voice, as a way to gain access to parts of yourself you normally can't get access to, is quite valuable.

When you speak, you hear what you say. Already you have the benefit of hearing information. I know sometimes we say things that might be derisory like, "All I can hear is the sound of my own voice, myself speaking." In a Fourth Way context and/or a conscious evolution context, one of the most powerful things we can do is practice speaking our truth. It's irrelevant whether anyone else is around or whether anyone else hears us. Something you want to cultivate as a skill is learning how to talk to yourself. This makes sense only from the point of view if you really understand that you have different parts of yourself. We have the different centers: the instinctive, sexual, emotional and intellectual parts. We are four-brained beings, right? Those then are divided into the many, infinite I's.

As you are developing parts of you able to be more responsible toward the work of manufacturing yourself, that part has to speak to the other parts. You can't rely on external voices to do that for you. If you are working with other people, you can't always rely on them to tell you what you need to hear about what is going on inside of you. You can also not rely on them, if they do talk to you about what they see, to say it in a way you need or want or think you should hear it. The only way that will happen is if you have that conversation with yourself. One part talks to another part. What you are trying to do is give the voice to the more objectively conscious parts of you. You want to remove the voice of those parts that are not.

When you speak you have power. Whatever part you are giving voice to in the moment is the one I that has the power. Part of how we tell ourselves who is in charge and who is in control is who has control of the vocal apparatus. That's why, when we say things like, "I didn't know what I was saying" and "I didn't mean what I said", that indicates a severe breakdown in internal processing. If you didn't actually know what you were saying and didn't mean what you were saying and didn't understand what you were saying, and what you said a minute ago is not what you really believe, then all you are doing is confirming that you are giving over control and power for yourself to the lesser parts, which shouldn't be in charge or running the show.

Now it's not just the monkeys loose in the cockpit, but the monkeys are loose in the cockpit and they have access to the PA system. They are telling the passengers to abandon ship when there is absolutely nothing wrong with the plane. "We're going to crash! We're going to crash!" The plane is not going to crash, but that's what is coming over the PA system. What do the passengers do? They react accordingly to the word from the cockpit. Whoever is in the cockpit is supposed to be knowledgeable about what's happening with the ship. The voice from the cockpit says disaster is looming and chaos is raining and we are all going to die and crash and need to abandon ship because it's not going to work out. The passengers tend to believe that.

I've been on planes that have literally dropped close to 1000 ft. in a couple seconds on a 747, where people bounced off the cargo area, people who didn't have their seatbelts fastened. Thank god no one was seriously hurt. This happened on an international flight out of Taiwan once. Immediately afterward this voice comes over the PA, "Hello passengers. This is your captain speaking. I want to apologize for that momentary bad weather we just encountered. I would recommend you fasten your seatbelt if you haven't done so, and we're going to climb to a different elevation in order to miss more of the same bad weather. Please remain calm. Flight attendants please check the cabin and make sure everyone is okay. We are here for you." You know what people did in the cabin? Right before he came online people were like, "Ahhhh!" They were frightened, like, "Oh my god! Does that mean the next one will be worse than that and we drop right out of the sky?" The pilot comes on and speaks in a very calm and professional voice, a voice of reason. He apologizes and explains the rationale of how they are going to handle that awkward situation. It was as if they passed sedatives out in the cabin. His voice was like a vocal sedative. Everybody calmed down and even cajoled each other because it was a voice from the cockpit. That voice from the cockpit is supposed to know what is really going on. What is the actual status of the vehicle?

Now what do we do when the monkeys are loose in the cockpit and they've gotten a hold of the PA? They are chattering and talking nonsense and making up stuff. They are doing everything except representing what is really going on with the machine. Other parts of us hear that and believe it and react accordingly.

Using our voice with ourselves is huge. Of course you can extrapolate that to everyone around you. We want to be careful how we speak to each other when we say things we don't know why we said. We need to come back and make little corrections. There is an effect of our words.

In ancient Ayurveda and Chinese Medicine and other Native American systems and so on, they use the sound of the voice to do all kinds of things, from medicine to meditation. For example, we have the science and recitation of mantra and sacred sounds like ohm. These are supposed to accomplish some shift or change in the energy even if you are by your self. We know from personal experience that when we do ohms in groups it's very powerful and may cause us to have a shift in our energy, which is almost immediate.

Simply speaking truth in a clear voice will have similar and specific effects.

We want to train and practice using our voice. It's important to someone who sings for a living to practice. I've heard musical artists talk about training or tuning their instrument. They are referring to their voice. When we speak with intention, we bring online physical and instinctive faculties. In order to speak you have to breathe. When you speak with intention, you create intentional breath syncopation and an intentional breath rhythm. That's why poetry can be so profound and effective. As you read it out loud, it puts you in an entrainment of rhythmic breathing. From yoga science and Pranayama, we know rhythmic breathing can change everything about our energy. It changes the energy in the chakras and meridians. It changes energy in the organs. It can have an effect on the functioning of your immune system. It can have an effect on mental states like anxiety and depression. When we speak in a deliberate manner we change the rhythm of our breathing. That has an effect on the instinctive, physical part of our machine.

Tones have effects on the centers also. Certain tones are sexier than other tones. Some tones are sometimes outright abrasive and irritating. When we speak in those tones, that's what we get. We get resistance because we are being abrasive and irritating. We know just from dealing with children that certain tones will soothe the troubled child or a troubled mind at any age.

As we hear the words, we conceptually consider what the words mean. That has an effect on our mind. That can have an effect on our attitudes. It's amazing how much of our attitudes are reflective of recurring and repetitive thinking. One way to change your recurring and repetitive thinking patterns is to speak different words than those. You have a thought that plays in your mind that is self-depreciating or limiting, reflective of an attitude or belief, and you want to change that because you've determined it is not productive for you. One of the ways to do that is to acquire something you can read out loud at least until you memorize it. You speak it out loud repetitively and you will begin the thoughts of your speaking. This is one technique you can use to control your thoughts.

1. Try not to think or say I, but rather, which I.

Dr. J: This is an act of discipline. We use I too readily and too easily without qualifying it and without thinking. We need to ask ourselves the question, "When I say I, which I am I talking about? This one or that one?" There is this one and there is that one. Which one has the microphone right now? Is it the captain or the monkey? Who's got the mike when I say I?

2. Do not argue with others, especially internally.

Dr. J: This is something we are all guilty of at one time or another. I might have enough self-control not to argue with you outwardly, but I will excuse myself for an infinite argument on the internal. I'll break down everything you said word for word and I'll disagree with it. I don't have a problem with that because you are not aware of it. I think because I'm not saying it out loud I have permission to do it.

One of my I's is fond of saying, "My thoughts are my own." Sometimes when I say that, it becomes my justification for thinking bad and low thoughts, which I know it would be irrational and unforgivable to express. I give myself permission to have that conversation internally. There's a practice. Try not to argue, especially internally.

3. If you show another his or her mistakes in your mind, this is where you're wrong.

Dr. J: This is a hard one. Criticism and just thinking critical thoughts about others just for the sake of thinking critical thoughts without having any kind of attitude of using that information to bring up the energy or improve communication, which you know about with yourself or the person you are thinking about, is worthless. Just being in a critical mental frame of mind where you're thinking about something someone said or did is perfectly useless. It's a waste of time and energy. It tends to create repetitive, negative thinking, which will generate attitudes, which generate emotions. Emotions couple with the attitude and repetitive thinking, which will generate negative actions and then negative karma. That will have an impingement on your life.

4. Do not think or say, "I do this" or "I do that". Minimize talk about your exploits, achievements and suffering.

Dr. J: I'm as guilty of this as anyone. There is in life a constant challenge, especially living in the west in the heart of the market driven economy, where basically if you don't market you don't get sales. You need to generate income and sales. You have to generate interest and you have to create marketing. It's really hard to avoid that carrying over into other areas of life. We get into conversations about exploits, achievements and suffering both positive and negative. It doesn't matter, either one. Those conversations, just like marketing, tend to feed towards exaggeration. That's why most billboards and magazine, television and radio ads are really over the top. They are in exaggeration and overstatement. By definition exaggeration seems to be a premise of marketing, because on some level it captures the attention of mechanical parts of the mind. The repetition of the exaggeration apparently seems to act as a force of motivation.

When we do this in our personal and work lives we are being less than genuine. Work on letting your deeds be what they are. Work on reducing exaggeration in conversation. It's not so important to stress achievements, certainly once it's understood. Yes you have achievements. Yes you may have suffered. Yes you may have had some exploits. In and of themselves, there may be nothing harmful in relating these things, but when they are exaggerated and taking up space of more meaningful conversation, they are not helpful.

5. Minimize deleterious, negative, emotional I's by avoiding course or extreme language.

Dr. J: If you are a sailor there's nothing wrong with sounding like a sailor. If you're not a sailor, then there's no particular reason why, in normal conversation, you should sound like you are. In one sense, it's a conscious exercise to try and speak more cleanly and more clearly using less generic words. Expletives, by definition, are generic. They don't have a clear, definite meaning in conversation. If we are speaking to each about anything that has value at all, we should try to have more clear and concise language. We may even need to simplify.

6. Eliminate the words should, hate, kill, never, always, very and "uh" from your vocabulary.

Dr. J: This is an exercise. I would say start with reducing. If you write this list down and try to go through a whole day without using the words should, hate, kill, never, always, very and uh, you will notice a certain amount of friction and struggle. That's beneficial in the sense we don't really appreciate how much we do use these words, until we try not to.

A good exercise occasionally practiced is to ban the use of the word "I" for a day or even for a week. I wouldn't recommend doing it for longer than that because in ordinary conversation with individuals who are not in the work, it might come across as being very strange. Most people's conversation is nothing but about "I". When you don't use that term, people won't know what you are talking about. They won't know who you're talking about. The reason why we use this as an exercise is because we think we do know who we're talking about when we use the word I. That's not true because we don't qualify which I is feeling this way or talking. I can believe one thing whole-heartedly with every fiber of my being, and at the very same moment another part of me can be going, "I don't believe that at all." I can say I will do something and another part of me will say, "You're not the boss of me." One I will write a check that another I will have to cash and that I won't do it. We don't qualify our I's by saying which I.

202

Minimize the expression of associate I's. Associate I's have to do with "I like and I don't like" kinds of concepts, "I'm attracted to", "I'm repulsed by", "I like" and "I don't like". Those associate thoughts happen instantly.

7. Eliminate formatory expressions.

Dr. J: What does formatory mean? Formatory means mechanical, without thought, such as cliches. Find an original, authentic and clear way to say what you're thinking.

I've noticed since I've been doing this work that when I'm around someone who tends to speak in clichés, it is not satisfying to me. I get the impression I don't really know what they are talking about. I don't really know what they mean. Clichés and formatory expressions are not that specific or clear.

8. Eliminate repeating slogans, jingles, mottos, statistics and opinions other than your own.

Dr. J: This is a substitute for original thinking. In science and medicine, sometimes statistics and numbers can be helpful. If that's all we talk about and that's entirely where our medicine is coming from, then there's a point where that conversation is meaningless because it becomes all about probability instead of reality. The idea is to find ways of speaking that authentically represent your original thoughts and what you are thinking right now, and not what you might be thinking 30% of the time or not what other people think about the topic you are speaking of 30% of the time. This is the issue with politicians. The politician can speak for days and you still have no idea what they actually believe because they are trying to get elected, so their entire speech is based on what they think a certain number of people will want to hear. It may not resemble at all anything they actually believe or think. Let's not be politicians in our personal lives.

9. Do not speak ill of anyone. Remain silent.

Dr. J: This is that whole thing, "if you don't have something good to say, try not to say anything." This feeds into gossip. Out of a group, when you notice there is gossip going on, somebody should be able to remember to hold up a hand or put a little flag and ask the question, "Is this necessary?" It might be fun and gratifying to have these little conversations. A lot of times you think it's harmless. It's just prurient and gossipy, and a little bit negative. The words have weight. They will support attitudes. They support repetitive thinking, which will support certain, emotional orientations, which will manifest as action. What is that action going to look like? Is that action going to be positive and productive for you or anyone else? That's a good question to ask.

10. Submit in silence to the evil deeds of men.

Dr. J: This refers back to the phrase in the bible, "turn the other cheek". This does not mean to be a dishrag when you are being abused. Only respond if and when you can do so appropriately. If some evil person is doing some evil deed to you, it will not help you to react inappropriately. It will not help you to escalate. It would be better to do nothing than to do the wrong thing. This is missed in popular culture. In popular culture we are often given the example of, "it's better to do something than to do nothing." Practical experience has taught me you can make it worse. However bad you think it is, you can make it worse by reacting the wrong way. You can make it worse. It might be better to do nothing than act without knowledge and consciousness. That's what this is referring to. It also refers to this: evil deeds are events. Even an evil event, an unpleasant event, should not be able to take you away from yourself. There's no excuse. Just because someone did something bad to you, there's no excuse for you to lose your mind.

It's the most common rationale in the world and we hear it in conversation all the time. "So and so did me wrong and that's why I went crazy. I had to go crazy. I had to destroy everything because they didn't love me anymore and did something wrong. Somebody had an affair. I had to burn the business down because they fired me." The "evil deeds of others" is one of the most common excuses in the world for bad behavior. In fact, almost anything we don't like, we react to as if it's an evil deed. Most of the time, what we think are the evil deeds others do to us is simply them being mechanical and unconscious. It's really not about us at all. Most of the connection we think other people's deeds have to do with us is imaginary. We want to practice not being reactive to what we perceive to be the harmful things others do around us. Turn the other check is what happens when I realize most of what I would imagine would be the evil you would do to me, and the lack of respect or what have you is in fact in my imagination. It has nothing to do with you.

I turn the other cheek as an exercise, rather than react negatively against you out of my imagination and my attachment to my identification with your motivation. Submit in silence.

11. Bear pain without grumbling.

Dr. J: It might be gratifying to talk about how much it hurts. "Ow that hurts. Oh it hurts so much. I feel so much distress or pain from this event or relationship." This feeds unconscious parts of us and doesn't change anything. There might be some validation for admitting to having pain. In therapy, I encourage my clients to tell me when they are in pain. I want them to be honest and tell me when they think they are in pain. However, it's not the only conversation I want to have with them. If all they did was talk about their pain, I would have to work with that. Even if you have chronic pain, it doesn't mean there is nothing else in your life. We can't just talk about the pain as being the center focus of our life because that narrowly focuses our lives. Our lives are expansive and grand. Bear pain without grumbling because, most of the time, pain is an event and will change and go away eventually by itself. It's what some doctors refer to as a self-limiting disease. Most pain is a self-limiting disease. If you did nothing at all it would change or go away. We act as if all pain is terminal, when it's not.

12. Do not make trivial things important by using the word "negative".

Dr. J: To declare everything positive or negative is not helpful. When we are doing a specific work and maintain a certain attitude and we are practicing with that, we can qualify our speech as positive or negative. That might be helpful. In the normal, daily course of life, for us to declare everything as positive or negative is not helpful.

13. Do not make it a habit to speak to others about your friction.

Dr. J: Everybody has friction. Your friction is not as special as you think it is. Your issues are not as unique as you think they are. They are not as special as you think they are. In fact, it's quite well understood that suffering is common to everyone. In Buddhism, the world is called Samsara, "the world of pain and suffering". That seems to indicate that everything suffers. Even the animals suffer. Maybe even on some level bacteria suffer. Suffering is a conditioning of life. It's the friction between you and whatever is not you. To habitually speak about your friction and how difficult your life and work is, how hard it is to be focused and how hard it is to be disciplined, after a point serves no purpose. It's not helpful or productive.

14. Digest your experiences before you speak to others about them. –Walt Whitman

Dr. J: There's this idea of having experiences. Practice digesting, meditating on and accepting experiences without having to break them down to their finest detail. Sometimes it's good to just let the experience be what the experience is. Sometimes it's best to leave the best untold. You don't have to say everything. There's a fine line between not saying everything and saying too much. We want to say enough to achieve the communication and expression of being that we want and need to. Yet at the same time, it can be a compulsion to say too much or to say everything.

204

15. Observe your I's as clues to formatory thinking and buffers, which requires not expressing them at least for a time.

Dr. J: Remember what the definition was for formatory. Formatory is mechanical, repetitive thinking, like clichés. Observe your first I's for the clues. Notice, when something happens, the first thing that pops in your head, the first I you identify with, where you go, "I don't like. I like…" Quite often, because that first I is so quick, there is no time for cognitive faculty to manifest. There is no time for appreciation of the big picture and what things really mean. There is no time to consider the context of what's happening and what's being exchanged. That first I is often mechanical and formatory and is expressing false personality.

Sometimes we build in a little delay. It's like in broadcasting where they have live shows where they have a seven second delay in case somebody messes up or says something they are not supposed to, or they have a fashion incident. That little delay gives them room to cover up little errors. It's good to practice to have that little buffer where we don't automatically assume that just because something is in our head, it means something and it means we have to stop or go or change or "yea" or "nay". The feeling may just be something passing through. The thought might just be something passing through.

16. Remember, light utterance of shameful words soon leads to shameful actions.

Dr. J: You must give account for every word you speak. The Tibetans say that karmically we are responsible for every thought, action and deed. What a weight of karma. I'm in continuous thought. When I'm not thinking, I'm speaking. Oh wait, I'm supposed to be thinking before I speak.

If the words we are speaking are not pleasant, positive and supportive, they are generating karma. If we are misrepresenting and misquoting those around us, that is shameful. Shameful speech is depreciating. It leads to shameful karma. Shameful actions create shameful karma.

You must give account for every word that you speak.

Not necessarily to the people you speak them to. You can't often do that. It's very hard to take words back when we say something harmful. Words have power. They have wings. They are out there and gone. It's like when I shine a flash light up into the sky in the back yard. That light is traveling at 186,000 miles per second. It's kind of hard to get it back in the flashlight once I've turned it on and off. I can't get that light back in the flashlight because it's already past the moon. Words are like that. The energy and power of our words travel very far and very fast, even though we might think sometimes no one hears us or pays attention to us or understands our words. They are effectively causing the discontinuity, the confusion and lack of response those words and the way those words are spoken is meant to create. If we want to be more powerful in our words, we need to be more intentional about every word we speak, all the time, not just in a serious conversation.

I'm having a serious conversation with you, so right now I'm paying attention. Ten minutes from now I'm not. In the weight of the words, when I'm paying attention and when I'm not, both have weight and power. Sometimes they cancel each other out. I could speak very truthfully and powerfully one minute and ten minutes later I could say something that might discount and cancel the positive effect of the words I was using before.

17. Read literature out loud.

Dr. J: It's a good exercise for a few minutes everyday to have the book you are going through and read it out loud. Visualize you are the speaker and you are hearing the words as if the original author speaks them. I do this. When I'm reading books by my teachers, I have in my visualization that I'm hearing their voice as if it's them speaking. I hear the words in the voice of my teachers. Or if I've never actually heard them speak, I hear the words as I imagine they would sound and consider the profoundness and effect of the beauty of the words. I imagine the beauty of the sounds those words must have had for people. I read them out loud because you are hearing them. The words become a long mantra. There's no reason why a whole book can't be a mantra. Out of the classic Indian mantra, "Om Mane Padme Om", comes a body of literature called the Vajrayana Tantras. The fact that someone just picked that one little phrase from those thousand pages of Tibetan literature, as they are somehow representative of all of the positive energies Tibetan culture is trying to express, means it was a choice. There are many other phrases and words of power in Tibetan literature.

Q&A: Exercises for the Vocal Apparatus

STUDENT: #3, it says "minimize talk about your exploits, achievements and sufferings." In day-to-day exchanges, how do you engage with someone when that's what they are doing?

Dr. J: Make an effort to simply be with them regardless of what they are doing. Someone else expressing them selves one way or the other is not about you anyway. Minimize or bring awareness to your emphasis when speaking.

STUDENT: Then they might ask why you are not engaged in what they are saying.

Dr. J: It depends on what it is. You cannot generalize. For example, in our situation, part of the conversation about achievements and exploits is important because it's part of our marketing; it's part of our expression that we have to communicate in order to be able to express it to other people. That's one thing. If there's too much talking about it in ordinary conversation, then we have to work with that.

For example, personally I know it's something I have to work with. I get into such a frame of mind about the defense and promotion of the work and of the school. That's required because our genuine achievements are what make us different from most other schools. To someone who doesn't know the difference between a teacher who's only had two hours of class and a teacher who's had 100,000 hours of class, then we have to be able to communicate what that difference might be to someone who can't even guess the difference. In ordinary conversation, it's good to try and reduce that.

STUDENT: #15, "Digest experiences before you speak to others about them." When you've had an experience and you're asked about it right away, and normally, for example, I like to digest things before talking about it…then when someone asks me right away without having digested the experience, then how do I stay engaged without going into a mechanical answer of like, "Oh, I should engage so I'm going to talk about it", when I haven't digested any of it yet?

Dr. J: Again, if you're engaged in class, in an experience of work, this does not apply. That's not what this is talking about. It's talking about in the normal course of life, mostly.

If we are engaged in talking about something that has to be done in a timely manner, there is no time to digest.

STUDENT: My question was about day-to-day things, like if I go out and do something and come back. I haven't digested it and then I'm asked to recount. Last night is an example. I hadn't digested the day at all and I had to come back and recount the entire day.

Dr. J: It was a school and work related task. In those situations, the digesting has to happen in the moment. There is no time.

SECTION FIFTEEN: Work on Energy Losses

1. Stop useless talk.

Dr. J: To have it in context, there are two things we're concerned with. One is building energy and serving energy. The other is wasting energy or losing energy. This section deals with all the different ways of trying to curtail or limit losing energy. One of the biggest ways to lose energy is useless talk. There are all kinds of useless talk. Anything that has to do with something negative for the gratification of hearing something negative or reinforcing something negative is useless talk. Gossiping for gossip's sake is a good example. Saying something negative about someone in no particular context or in any sort of useful way is an example of useless talk. Even just simply speaking or talking and stringing lots of words together to hear the sound of your voice is useless talk.

Anything you say where you are better off not saying it is an example of useless talk. To not speak uselessly really takes a continuous amount of self-observation because there's actually, in the machine, no apparatus or filter for our speaking. A lot of stuff that passes through the screen of our mind is not our own. Associative thinking is a replay of tapes and conversations originating from someone and somewhere else. There's no particular reason to actually be talking about it, but we do anyway. That actually does use a certain amount of energy.

In some traditional schools, they would have voluntary rules, that at certain times of the day or year there would be specific kinds of exercises where talking would not be allowed, trying to give you through friction the ability to observe how compulsive our movement is to verbally express every little thing that comes through our head. Having done those kinds of meditations, I've found that's exactly what happens. I will find myself in a situation where I have an irresistible Impulse to talk about something, but whatever that item is, it is not important or necessary or relevant or constructive. There's just this compulsion to talk.

2. Give up worrying and resentment over the course of your play in life.

Dr. J: Worry and resentment are two negative emotions. If you're concerned about something that may be genuine, and the concern is based on rational thinking or comparing of options and an actual consideration of what you know, then that's one thing. Simply having anxiety and worry over almost anything is useless. There's no benefit to that, and quite often it takes away from circumstances because we don't realize how much energy it takes to worry. I might think I need to be sharp or need to be at my most aware state, or I might need to have all my faculties operating in high gear in order to bring myself to bear on a given situation to make a good decision or really understand something. Previous to that, if I spend much time, effort or energy worrying, then what I've done is already spent the energy I might have been using to have deep or long thinking, which could be useful for actually sorting out something. I've already wasted it. It's not available, so I end up approaching difficult situations, people or issues with dead batteries. I'm not as effective as I would be.

Worrying is also a form of compulsion. You know it's based on negative emotion and a form of compulsion because most of the time, when you are worrying, you didn't decide to be that way. Even if you critique yourself or observe yourself doing it, it's very hard to stop. Worrying can use up a lot of energy.

Paranoia, on the other hand, is quite different. If you're paranoid about a possible misadventure or adverse outcome in something, there's a real basis there might actually be a negative outcome or a harmful situation where someone might be trying to hurt you or have some hidden agenda not complimentary to your welfare. That is different. You need to have an alert mind about those kinds of situations.

Having a lot of predicated anxiety or worrying about events in the future which may or may not come to pass, which may not even concern you, eats up a lot of energy.

3. Give up unnecessary haste.

Dr. J: The machine has a joy of moving. Simply moving, brushing your hair, is quite satisfying. "Wooping" your hands around, doing something fast gives us a sense of visceral gratification that's very physical and enjoyable. However, that is completely mechanical. When we slow down a little bit and with intention do things a little more methodically, there's a little friction between the natural inclination of the machine, which is to toss things about and do things fast with an almost unconscious, gleeful abandon, and the slow pace where you can pay attention to everything you are doing. There's friction there. That friction generates good material for self-observation.

For example, in the classroom when you ask everyone to put the mats down and set up the classroom and then step back and watch, you'll see. Watch how many people just grab a mat, and rather than take the one or two steps to put it down on the floor where it goes, they'll just heave or hurl it to some approximate vicinity of where they think it goes, and then walk over and kick at it for a couple of minutes. Watch people put down the carpet mats. There are people that do what I call the "Mississippi gambler style".

STUDENT: Yeah, it's just like dealing cards.

Dr. J: "Mat distribution", where they fling them out like playing cards and just toss them around and then kick at them until they are in position. At the end of that, that is what it looked like happened.

Dr. J: It's the natural inclination of an untrained, undisciplined machine to virtually everything like that. You can name any task. The task could be to clean up the garden area. If you're not paying attention, there's going to be, at points, a momentum that occurs, where something gets completely out of control, and it is interesting to watch it in yourself. It is definitely easier to see in other people.

We've always practiced this idea of trying to slow down a little bit and do things a little more methodically. Why? There is this friction created from paying attention to what you're doing. Avoiding allows the machine get out of control, unless that's your intention. If your intention is to see how far you can run and jump, you want to coach the machine to be able to let the governors off and let it fly. That's perfectly appropriate. When your intention is simply to get from one step to the next, it might not be so appropriate. There's a lot of potential to waste energy and opportunity, just like setting up a classroom. In this case, there is an opportunity to be almost ritualistically methodical to bringing energy to the placement of things.

In Feng Shui, or the Chinese art of placement, you can bring that to setting a dinner table. Rather than hurling the plates on the table, you place the plates on the table. Instead of plopping food on a plate or throwing things together for a salad into a bowl, you place the food on the plate or in the bowl consciously and bring intention to it. By definition, everything you do with those parameters is artistic because there is intention in it. When you set up the classroom with intention, it has a different aesthetic and feel because now the placement of the mats and sheets is artistic. It demonstrates the intention. You look at the salad and say, "Oh, man, we have to take a picture of the salad." Why is that? It is art. You can see and feel the effect of all the intention.

That carries over to whatever you are going to do next. Intentional action also keeps you from wasting things and breaking things. It solves the equation of running around in circles, which we do when we get in such a hurry to get in the car that we forget the keys to operate the car. Because I'm not being thoughtful, I run back and forth inside the house two or three times, looking for the keys, which are hanging off my belt. It lends itself to all those funny types of situations. Those situations waste a lot of energy, a lot of time and a lot of effort. Accidents can happen. Most of the time, that's how we lose things. I lose my keys, my shoes, my glasses, because at some point I got into some rushing, mechanical activity where there was a gap in consciousness. There was an empty spot because I went completely into whatever the machine was doing. When I try to replay the tape to review in my mind what was placed where and so on, well it's simply not there because of the gap. That works with just about everything.

STUDENT: It's great, because you can think of so many examples of that. I mean, it's so obvious when it happens. I think that, for me, one of the biggest exercises in being mindful, especially when we did our juice fast in early December, beginning that the first morning I woke up, every step, I don't know what it really was, maybe putting my intention into something. Every step I took and everything I did was somehow completely different. I can actually bring more consciousness to what I'm doing when I'm doing something like that, something to my body so that I'm in a different place.

Dr. J: Oftentimes, it's not even a matter of bringing more consciousness to things; it's about having any there at all. I like to think…and there again, that's an ego thing. I like to think of myself as more or less conscious and bringing more consciousness to certain things. Actually, it's more like, there are sometimes things I do where I'm not home at all. I am asleep. I am not present. All the lights are on. The TV is blaring. The radio's in full volume. The washing machine is going, yet the house is completely empty. I come back in the house and see all the activity and mistakenly assume I've been there, busy watching the TV, listening to the radio, washing the clothes, vacuuming the floor. In reality, the house is on, but I'm not. I haven't been on.

There is this idea of not being able to rush around, especially when you first start trying to do this with intention. In other words, let's give up unnecessary haste on purpose. There is so much friction there that can actually cause a lot of suffering. You can see, for example, by giving up haste, you can have a range of emotions. You can see anger. "What do you mean slow down? What do you mean be more thoughtful? I'm the most thoughtful person in the world. I can't believe you would accuse me of being less than thoughtful. You must think I'm a horrible person. Nah, nah, nah, nah, nah…" All you were saying was, could you just slow down and think about what you're doing while you're doing it? It had nothing to do with anything that comes up. It's really quite bizarre to notice the chains of associations when you give up unnecessary haste.

It is a form of voluntary suffering. We all have it somewhere, and when we start to look for it, where we are unnecessarily hasty, it is pretty interesting to see what comes up. It's a good exercise.

4. Give up negative imagination and fantasy.

Dr. J: That's a recurring thing about negative emotion and about fantasy. Fantasy, in that context, you want to relate to the concept of negative emotion. So it would be negative fantasy. In other words, taking a feeling of a negative emotion and then crafting various kinds of scenarios and various kinds of possibilities based on that in a chain of association. It's like you're weaving with negative yarn. "What can I do with this negative yarn and negative knitting needle? I know! I'll knit a negative sweater or a negative afghan."

STUDENT: How about a negative hat?

Dr. J: I will make a negative hat out of all of this negative yarn I have. The next thing you know, you could have spent years, not just a few minutes, weaving this negative fantasy. What happens sometimes is we get a little bit of information, help or insight and realize, not only have we been engaging in negative emotion and imagination, but actually that is what defines our life. We have made ourselves a little, negative house and we're driving a little, negative car and we've got some little, negative friends in our fantasy. We then project it into the future.

One of the ideas is, when you have negative emotion, and you start to go off into scenarios of expression of that negative emotion, that you apply some tool to work on to simply stop it. Sometimes it's as simple as asking a question or having information. One of the reasons why we encourage and practice disclosure is this: when I have a question I ask it, when I have a concern I try to communicate it, when I need information, I make an effort to get it. This is because by doing that, I don't spend a lot of time, effort or energy on imagination of what that question or thought means or might mean. Then you don't go off into a negative interpretation of what it might be or might mean or what might be going on. If I can just simply check-in, ask some questions, have a little bit of clarity, whatever that whole process is, I'm not going to waste any time or energy there by applying a tool.

Having an experience of a negative emotion in a moment and applying a tool, like tapping, robs some of the momentum the negative emotion has to carry us away. We want to apply tools in that place rather than go with it. Even if you can't stop it, it's best to identify and observe it. "Hey, I know what that is. I can't really stop it right now because unfortunately Team Crazy is in charge of my mouth right now. I'm going to have to wait until they give up their seats so I can exert some control over the negative stuff I'm saying. Team Crazy's advertising and marketing crew is in charge of fantasy right now, so I'm going to have to wait until the clowns are out of my head so I can bring some energy to it." If I could stop it by asking questions or bringing attention or tapping, well, then I should do that.

J: I catch myself doing this a lot. You make subtle corrections. Like, you say, "We're not going to imagine that. We're just going to find out the answer." I'm like, "Oh, okay, that sounds like a good idea."

J: And fantasy for me, I had mentioned something to you earlier about it, but sometimes the negative tapes will start for me and then I go through the whole fantasy life of the story I've had with that tape, and I'm trying to apply it to him, meaning Dr. J, and it just doesn't fit. It's very frustrating. I try it all kinds of ways and it's very frustrating. It's like when you put your pants on backwards and then take them off and try again. It's like that, your shirt is inside out.

Recently it has started to occur to me, when I'm catching it, "Well, wait a minute, why are you withdrawing, why are you doing this or that?" Somehow I find, oh, I'm following a tape. Then I make the correction and I feel better, therefore everybody else seems to change. I had mentioned to him earlier, that you know, I feel like I withdraw and then I see the landscape of what's happening and even with school, everybody else withdraws. Then this emotional withdrawal occurs. Once I make the correction, I notice that changes. I think that's pretty interesting. But I don't know what it means. Apparently, it means this because we're talking about this right now.

5. Give up useless, automatic actions.

Dr. J: Useless, automatic actions can be lots of things. It can be any mechanical movement, like flexing your foot or curling your hair or chewing on your lip or tapping your foot. It can also be laughing for no apparent reason. In other words, you're saying something that's not funny, but you laugh. Why are you laughing? The laughter is some tape playing over what you're saying that somehow is qualifying it in case it's not taken in the right way, so you can always come back and say it was a joke.

We justify useless, automatic actions by saying, "Uh, that's uh…it's just my habit. I always nah nah nah" Fill in the blank. This is mechanical. There are very strong, hidden, mechanical parts of us that are almost always invisible. Some of these habits we might be aware of. A is aware he bites his fingernails. He might not be aware while he's doing it. He might just notice he doesn't have any. It's not magic. Somebody else might observe that and say, I notice you're biting your fingernails. In one school I was in, in different lectures, there would be a physical posture Imposed. For example, both feet have to be on the floor the whole time we are talking. It would be really interesting how much effort that would take. It would get to a point where you couldn't pay any attention at all to anything anybody was saying because you could not pick your foot up. It's your unconscious habit to crisscross and uncross and play with your toes. That's part of the machine. Another one they would do is, when you're discussing (it wouldn't always be the same. It depended on the teacher), your hands have to be on your legs or folded across your stomach. It cannot be one hand on a leg and one hand on the stomach. You can't have your hands anywhere else. You don't realize how much mechanical action you have until there's an intentional prohibition against spontaneous, mechanical movement. The machine is going trying to find what's a comfortable place until we nail ourselves down.

One teacher, a lady named Catherine, had an exercise that was to have no emotion in your voice when speaking about emotion. In other words, if we were talking about or reading about or having a lecture or discussion about emotion or negative emotion, you couldn't have any rising tones or any verifiable emotion in your voice. What she would do is, if you got animated or started to be emotional while you were talking, she would just reach over and touch you. You had a pre-agreed signal that if you reach over and touch me, that means there is emotion in my voice. I'm supposed to do something about it. How hard was that to do? It was very hard to do because there are even emotional expressive habits that are unconscious and mechanical. There are physical and moving habits.

Instinctive center has habits, moving center has habits, emotional center has habits, the intellectual center has habits, which are competing for space all the time. "No, no, I want to show my habit." The instinctive center says to the intellectual center, "I know you're trying to make a good point right now, but my bottom is not comfortable so we're just going to adjust, okay? Deal. You deal with that." All these habits can work against each other or compete for space. Eventually they can be so disruptive that, while engaging in the habits, you forget what your intention was you were trying to express.

Other people's habits are also distracting to us. I think that is part of a survival mechanism in the instinctive center, that we pay attention to movement. We can be having a discussion about a particular topic, and if one person is sitting over there and doing this, flippity, flippity, flippity, during the entire talk, at some point, everybody's attention is going to be drawn to observing this person going flippity, flippity, flippity. This is true for everything, for any little or big, repetitive movement. Sometimes I'll point it out and when I do, they go, "Huh?"

210

6. Give up defending personal history or your imaginary picture of yourself.

Dr. J: Become invisible. Give up defending personal history or your imaginary picture of yourself. Become invisible. If you're playing a role, then be Shakespearean and get into the role and express the role as best you can. If you're not playing a role, then stop giving up, reciting and defending your personal history. This is something we do when there is no attack. There is no reason to be defending where you come from or who you are most of the time. It is proactive defense and can take up a lot of energy. There is an inclination to elaborate and an inclination to embellish. There's an inclination to engage in fantasy. It can be a great opportunity for negative emotion, because heaven help you if you say something about your history in defense of yourself that is contrary to someone else's idea of what you're supposed to be like or should've been doing. Some judgment is expressed, and then what happens is you get into a push-and-pull and lose the moment.

Giving up defending an Imaginary picture makes sense because we really don't know who we are in the first place. Being defensive about who we are as a person right now doesn't make any sense. As a result of the process of self-revealing, you find yourself to be completely other than what you originally thought you were. How much time will you have spent defending a person who you now realize you are not? How many times have you found yourself defending a position you don't actually hold or have or believe? Just because there is something contrary going on or someone is judging you? How much energy can get locked up? Relationships can be devastated with this kind of defending of pictures. "You know, you don't see me the way I am…or you don't understand me…or you don't know me…" A lot of effort goes into trying to correct that. The problem is, if you are working on yourself and in a more objective state of mind, you might actually think they are correct. Whatever was the criticism about the picture of yourself you were defending, in another state of mind, you would admit, "Well I actually, I am a little bit lazy. I am a little bit selfish. Selfish! You call me selfish! I'll teach you selfish!" In fact, violence trumps selfish. "You can't accuse me of being selfish or I'll beat you up." But then later, you admit, "Well, yeah, I am selfish."

I did actually eat all of the chocolate. "What? You can't accuse me of eating all the chocolate! Only a selfish person would eat all the chocolate. I did eat all the chocolate. I am a selfish person."

7. Give up self-importance.

Dr. J: Perhaps in developing business and trying to work in the world, we have to have a sense of self-promotion. In the context of the work, we have to work from a different perspective. We have to give up a sense of self-promotion of our importance. That's quite different than acknowledging that you're a significant or are part of something or have a role to play in the bigger picture. That is very different than the thoughts and emotional constructs that build you up as being important. That's different.

We often mistake one for the other. Self-Importance is a sense of inflated ego. The problem with inflated ego is that it can just as easily be deflated. If you are important, and if you are significant and genuinely an integral part of something, then no amount of pinpricking can change that. You can't be deflated. No amount of external influence can make that not be so.

8. Give up negative emotions.

Dr. J: Giving up negative emotions works on energy losses. Why is giving up self-Importance an energy loss? Spending time inflating your ego and puffery, puffing yourself up, is different from building yourself to be a more substantial part of what you are doing, as far as working on yourself.

Energy gets lost from the expression of negative emotions. Most of the workbooks and most teachers say that is the number one way we lose the vital energy, the chi, the Kundalini necessary to sustain higher states of consciousness. Giving them up, often times, we can say, "Oh yeah I can give up my negative emotions." Actually, I can't. Saying you can give them up and giving them up are very different things. They reflect the false personality, and the false personality exists as a result of the negative emotions. Simply giving them up without expressing them is very threatening to the false personality. We can't imagine ourselves without expressing negative emotions, but we have to. We have to give them up.

Negative emotions distract us. They are not real or who we are. If we are engaged in this process of seeing who we really are, it is important we constantly be vigilant in order to bring energy and attention to the things we know are not who we really are.

9. See yourself as neither hero nor victim.

Dr. J: You are neither hero nor victim. You are a player in your life. You are in whatever position you're in. There is an ebb and flow to it. One minute you are the hero and the next minute you're the victim. You can get stuck in either role, neither of which is real. Trying to avoid these extremes of perceptions saves a lot of energy.

10. Spend time in the presence of fine art.

Dr. J: Intentionally spend time in front of beautiful things. If you're an artist and are able to make beautiful things, then do it. Not only do these help us gain energy, because we gain energy from the food of impressions, but spending time in front of beautiful things and focusing on aesthetics inhibits energy loss. Both of these happen at the same time. Art is a really cool thing as far as studies of consciousness. It can be garden art, performance art, media art, music art, whatever it is, as long as it's crafted with intention.

Of course, we see art according to our alchemy. That's another conversation.

11. Explore intimately the beauty of nature.

Dr. J: This is a valuable skill to acquire. When we're in nature and when we're intentionally exposing ourselves to nature, in that moment, we are not losing energy. We are gaining energy. To do, like I saw you guys doing this today, to go outside and have joy in the sky! Noticing how beautiful the sky was and how wonderful the sun felt. Like the Thais say, "Sphāph xākāṣ thī̀ thảnı khuṇ pěn xȳāng diī", "weather that makes you well." That's the beauty of nature. If we're crafty, we can actually get some of that just about everywhere we are.

12. Visit and pay respect at the shrine or temple of a religion you do not practice.

Dr. J: We have many mechanical attitudes and tapes connecting us to how we were raised and educated religiously from childhood. Usually upon introspection we find there is actually little or no basis for why and how we believe what we believe in regard to religion, other than those ideas we received as indoctrination as children. These tapes and beliefs are sometimes very hard to examine. By putting ourselves "out of context" religiously, we give them an opportunity to surface, giving us something useful to work with. Whether our religion of choice is valid or not is not important in this context. What's important is to examine why you believe what you do.

It's part of the reason why, in some of my stories, I talk about these different temples and these different kinds of religious places I visited. I learned this a long time ago. I started out doing surveys of churches and finding what kind of things were around. I've always sort of had an interest to at least visit and notice what kind of shrines people make and what kind of altars people worship at. What kind of religious icons do they see or worship?

13. Be quick to forgive. Do not hold grudges or accounts against anyone.

Dr. J: "Holding accounts" is when you make a list of negative things that someone else has done to you. If I use the term, "holding accounts", what I'm saying is a literal, mental list of everything wrong, every little snit, every little moment you weren't given due respect or weren't treated the way you think you should be treated, or you didn't get what you deserved (like we really need to get what we deserve).

The untrained, undisciplined person has many account lists. In fact, it's a given they have an account list with every person they know. I have a list of every unkind word, every little snide remark, every little snub, every time they left me holding the bag, left me behind, showed up late, abandoned me, you name it, gave me an odd look or that look they do. We have a list for everyone we know. We also have other lists that are just like that. We have "holding accounts" lists against our boss, our industry, our competitors, related industries, the governments, other governments, racists, the Mexicans, the Nazis, etc. We have these lists going on. It takes a lot of energy to manage these lists. If you think about it another way, think of each of these lists as a computer file. No matter how small or big the list, it takes a certain amount of energy just to keep it in the machine, in your head. The bigger the list, the more energy you need to keep it.

It is interesting to note that holding accounts can eventually lead to a point where the account list begins to be a rationale and basis for development of a personality construct, and it's negative because the list is all negative. When you hold accounts, it's all negative.

The funny thing is, when things are good, when you are interpreting things as good, you don't keep those lists. That's the funny thing. We don't have a running list in our heads of every kind word, every kind phrase, every loving glance, every positive thing everybody has ever done to us. We have a general sense of whether they are good to us or not good to us. If they are not good to us or if we are not sure, then we keep very meticulous records, better than any private investigator would hope to do. We'll even put on our account list, tone of voice in conversation or whether they were looking at me the right way. "They gave me a hard look. Oh, well that goes on the list. When they look at me, I don't see respect. Oh, that goes on the list." Eventually we start to create whole personalities around these lists and we become completely consumed with it.

That is why, in one sense, just so that you can understand how I do things in class, as it related to this, I want to bring people's awareness to issues which might directly relate to their health. Yet, at the same time, it is not my intention anyone should be completely overwhelmed to the point they can no longer consider anything else in their lives but that one thing. At a point, that thing becomes just as dysfunctional for them as some other health concern. It is all negative.

Be quick to forgive. The way to handle the list idea is to notice we make these lists. Let's say, in the morning, you notice there were some list items that were added. What you want to do, as quickly as you can, is forgive them with intention. You don't want to invest energy to store them, right? What's the point? What do I care to store, as some life long list against you, that this morning you got up and went about your business without giving me a hug and grumbling a hello at me? What is up with that? "She didn't give me a hug this morning. Well, I've noticed, that over X amount of time, that there are lots of days where I don't get hugs." In fact, I might even get to a point where say, "You know what? I don't even think you ever do hug me. Even when you're hugging me, you're not really hugging me. Don't touch me."

How do I get there? Well, I'm accumulating these lists. Rather than that, when there is some imagined or even genuine act less than thoughtful, the work idea is, "You know what? It's not worth it to me to hold that on my tally sheet because I am working on myself, trying to conserve my energy so I have energy to do the work I need to do on myself."

Just keeping those lists uses a lot of energy. It's a loss of energy. Overtime it's formative for our character. If you pay attention, you can look at individuals who may never have even heard of this concept and can see how long their lists are. Sometimes all you have to do is say one word, and all of a sudden, you get this litany of all the list items. "Well, so and so, he's like this and he does that. I don't like the way he does this and that and nah, nah, nah, nah, nah, nah." What you are doing when you hear that, what you're observing, is someone reading their account list, as if that list is having communication with you in real time, which is not true.

The only way, the fastest way, I know to not do Hold Accounts, is to be quick to forgive. Then there's nothing on your list when you pull up the file. It won't have much on it. As you forgive, you erase those items. They no longer take up energy or space. Go ahead, J.

J: I was just going to say, because when you say that, quick to forgive, I think the propaganda in our culture says forgive and forget. You can forgive but you don't have to forget. It's kind of like, well you say you're not going to put it on the list, but you still eventually do, in the form of some sort of memory I'm trying to keep.

J: The whole time you are talking about this, I can think of like a million lists I have.

Dr. J: Right. If you forgive but still make the list, you are still holding accounts. That's a game we play. The game is, I will pretend to forgive. Then I have an excuse to externally act in some way. As long as I'm adding line items to the list, as long as those notes are being made, you know they are all negative. That's how you know this is what's happening, because whatever is on that list is negative. It's not as if we are being objective, and as we are holding accounts, we are also putting down the wrathful deities, like Vajra-Haruka, by throwing down the white stones as we throw down the black stones. It's not like that. All we have to throw down on that account are black stones. It's always going to be unbalanced, biased and unfair. That has nothing to do with the energy losses all these lists support, because every list, in and of itself, requires maintenance in order for it to be maintained. It takes energy. That is the coin of the realm. That is the coinage of consciousness.

We are really trying to be green about raising our consciousness, in that we are trying to find where we waste energy and stop that. That automatically gives up more energy. Then we do the things we know can increase our energy, so we have some reserve. Unfortunately, we don't know, from one minute to the next, when we're going to want to spend that coinage. We have to have a reserve. Be quick to forgive.

The more the dramatic the situation, the more dramatic the forgiveness has to be. The more immediate it has to be.

J: What if you are aware of your accounts list and they are all based on past accounts and not current accounts.

Dr. J: Well, they are all based on past accounts.

J: How do you handle the list, like say, for instance, you're past relationships?

Dr. J: Well, you can't be generic. As they come up, specific issues, you have to forgive them. You have to consciously go back and look at that. What is the point of maintaining the list? What is the point of maintaining this old file on old relationships and all the dirty deeds and mistreatments? What is the point?

Dr. J: "Oh yes, they've used me." Oh, okay, great. What is the point of keeping that safe and sacred and keeping a list of all the things they did to abuse you. How does that help you be the person you need to be right now? The fact is, it doesn't.

There's really no loss to let it go, but we are attached to our negative stuff. It's another form of attachment. We are way attached to our lists. Everybody is attached and everybody makes lists. This is a Fourth Way concept. Holding accounts is what everybody does. We need to start bringing attention to that, just like every other part of our mind. We need to start bringing forgiveness. That's the eraser. That's the preferred tool, pardon and forgiveness. Those are the two things you do. Just like the governor will say, "Yes, the man committed the armed robbery and yes he killed the clerk 50 years ago. He went in there, robbed the store and killed the clerk. He shot him dead." He's now been 50 years in jail and been completely transformed into a completely different person. He's worked on himself. He's become educated. He's become someone whose life now has value and merit. Yes, at some point, he made a horrendous mistake. The governor steps in and says, "You know what? Let's not execute that person. Let's pardon that person." Even at the last minute that can happen.

What is the effect of that pardon? The effect of the pardon is tangible forgiveness. Rather than forgiveness as a concept, the pardon is an embodiment of forgiveness. It is an actual example, a practical expression of forgiveness.

I'm holding accounts against my ex. What I have to do is forgive my ex. If I keep having specific lists come up, I might have to detail those lists, even action by action. "You know, my ex ran off with my dog!" What kind of person would steal your dog? Not a good person, but she did, "she ran off with my dog!" You hear that? There's an account on a list. I'm giving you a real example, okay? If I want to take away that list's ability to steal my energy, I have to forgive her for taking my dog. More than that, I have to pardon her. It's not enough just to forgive her. What I have to say in my head, in a sense, is, "I give her my dog. I give her my dog. Not only do I pardon her for taking my dog, I give her permission to have taken my dog. I forgive her because I understand I have done things, in certain states of mind, where I was not being very conscious. I was operating under a lower alchemy, which was not very pretty or nice." I've done things like this. Just like I would like to resolve the negative karma of those harmful and less than conscious actions, thoughts and deeds, I wish there is some support that comes to me from the universe. I realize that by forgiving my ex for taking my dog and pardoning her and giving her my dog, on some energetic level, I'm supporting that same process in my ex, even though we are not connected anymore.

When you pardon you develop a habit of forgiveness. Somebody cuts in front of me. So what? I forgive them. I make it my habit, my first response, to forgive them. I don't pull up the finger or call them a name or react. This opens up the door, so that if I do need to react, that reaction will be based more in objective reality and what's actually happening, as opposed to my emotional interpretation of what's happening, which is coming from the accounts.

14. The most noble revenge is pardon. (Plutarch)

Dr. J: The most noble revenge is pardon. It's pretty interesting. A lot of sacred teachings talk about the Importance of forgiveness. Pardon is a form of forgiveness but more proactive. It's more than saying, "I forgive you. I'm not going to hold accounts against you." Let's say you were a death row inmate. You are supposed to be executed at midnight and are waiting for the phone call from the governor. The only thing you want to hear from the governor is that you're pardoned. Not only does it mean you won't be executed, it also means all of the accounts held against you will now be set aside. In fact, if you are pardoned, not only are you not executed, you are reestablished to your original position of being a citizen. From that point forward, you can carry on your life as if the offense never happened. Pardon is more than accepting apologies. Forgiveness, we might think it means the following. You realize you've done something wrong. You express remorse. You make an apology. I accept your apology. Then we go on. Pardon is one step further. You don't just accept an apology. You set aside the original offense as if it never occurred and then reinstate that person to where they were before the whole issue came to the table. It is dramatically different than what most people think of in forgiveness. A lot of people will forgive but still keep the account. I reserve the right, if there are future offenses, to bring it back up and into play. This does relate back to the holding accounts concept.

The value of the pardon is that it completely frees you from the source of negative emotion and mechanical, unconscious behavior that might result from that. It frees you from the sort of karmic connection to what was perceived of as an offense.

Noble revenge is pardon. It's interesting because I can pardon someone who has offended me without his or her consent or cooperation. Even without their apology, I've done something from the world point of view that is kind of crazy. Why? It's unconditional pardon. It is not subject to someone else's remorse. This is something the great saints and sages refer to, which people might hear and think sounds really good. Pardon the offense and whatnot. In reality, they might not consider how strong a statement that is. I absolve you and your offense as if it's external from having an authority or control over who I am in this moment. I am able to, independent of your coming to consciousness or awareness of what you've done wrong or inappropriately, aside from all that, step out of that paradigm of waiting for that to occur as a condition to forgiving you. I'm going to proactively forgive you. I'm going to pardon you for the offense for which you haven't even sought apology yet.

What happens in the moment I do that, whatever that conditional filter would be that would affect my way of being and interpreting what's going on in my life changes. It goes back to this idea of how much we are at the whim of events. People are events. Things people do to us or around us are events. Pressures we are subject to from the people in our lives are events. The events push us and pull us very strongly. We are constantly in a push and pull situation between perceived, little encroachments or perceived offenses, which come to us from the environment of the people we live with and encounter in our lives. It's really hard to quantify how much of our state of mind and level of consciousness, at any given point in time, is affected by this pressure.

Being proactive by identifying an offense, an encroachment, an injury, a slight, a disrespect, something not appropriate in some way, as far as how we perceived it in how we are supposed to be treated, and then setting those aside and kicking them off the table as they are identified creates the possibility of being different. That "different'" is the way we are when we are not filtering our perceptions and thoughts and cautioning our emotions based on this conditional, ongoing need for apologies, resolutions, closure, or a lot of things people think are very important in common psychology.

I seek closure for certain kinds of things. I think closure is important. At a point where you then rely on this process of closure, where you get it and you make some correction on your side, you show remorse, or you apologize. In this case, where's the opportunity for the closure? When is it going to happen? That lack of closure, if you don't do any of those things, becomes another one of my buffers or filters that keeps me from being unconditionally myself in the moment. I've placed a condition that I am not going to be free of whatever impediment until you do something or change something. Who knows when and if that will ever happen? Who knows if it will happen in the right way or in such a way that will allow me to give myself permission to give you closure or to have closure with you?

This is a really strange idea because it's stating the process of seeking closure when it depends on others is not effective. In fact, in pursuit of consciousness, it may even be counterproductive. It is dependent on an external circumstance over which I have no control. I will never have control over whether other people get it or have remorse or understand what they did or want to apologize or want to have closure with me. I will never have control over any of that. To have any part of my mind dependent on the external circumstance creates an Impediment.

The idea of issuing pardon is how we handle that pressure of such an event.

15. Do not give or share authority over yourself to others with less being.

Dr. J: How about that? Do not give or share authority over yourself to others with less being. There is such a thing as the difference between knowledge and being. Just because someone has degrees or just because someone has fame or just because someone is important doesn't mean they are supposed to be in authority over us. We have to also use our discernment to judge whether or not they have sufficient being to be an authority over us. If they don't, then that is not an equitable relationship, and we have to not give in to that. Don't give in to authority.

This doesn't mean if a cop pulls me over and tells me to get out of the car with a gun that I'm not going to do it. I'm going to do it even if I think he's a complete yahoo, because of the situation. This is talking about real authority, authority to make decisions, authority to determine depth of your work or kind of work you are doing. Authorities do exist. There are people with knowledge and being. They are not always the ones who claim to be. We cannot automatically give ourselves over to authorities. It is just like, where you could say, for example, that we talk in class how everybody is looking for a shaman. What they are looking for is someone who has authority to tell them what to do. What we want is not authorities to tell us what we need to do. What we want are individuals with superior being to show us the way by example.

You don't want someone who says, "I'm just going to tell you how you need to be or what you need to do or what the solution is for x, y, z program." I'm just being an authority when I do that. If I can express it in a different way, which is more from my character, from life experience as a being, then that's "true" authority. Overtime, we need to learn what the difference is. There are big differences. There are people who are very expert in what they do who have very low being. They are very expert. Why? It's about the intellectual function. They might have a really high intellectual function, so they have a good memory and they've been able to learn patterns of speech and they are good at role-playing. They may in fact have a low level of being. I'll give you a typical example of a politician who is an authority and a powerful person in responsibility over big projects and lots of people. Then we have the expose, which shows that, on a personal level, as a person, they are just totally messed up.

See, there is a schism between authority and being. What we want is to submit ourselves, not to those people, which millions of people do, but to find people in our lives who actually have being of substance and then submit ourselves to them.

16. Avoid overindulging in anticipation and speculation regarding future events and or speculation regarding events in the past.

Dr. J: Speculation is associative imagination. It is not necessarily with any kind of intention. It has to do with imagining variations of events from the past and/or the future. There is not necessarily any context of the aims and ambitions you are trying to create and craft in your life right now. For example, it wouldn't really serve me to spend a lot of time being in imagination about what my life would be like if I was a mafia hit man. In that imaginary world, if I invest in that, there is nothing in that life or circumstance that serves me in who I want to be now. If I caught myself developing this complex fantasy of my life as a mafia hit man, I am crafting a way of thinking that has no substance based on who I am. The type of being I want to craft myself into right now is a person whose values are based on love, compassion, joy and equanimity. It is not based on finance and murder for hire. That kind of fantasy is an example. I could use other things. It can be little or big things.

There is a place for directed imagination, like creative visualization. What we want to do is try to cultivate the ability to project our imagination in line with the reality of who we are striving to become. We can then use that creativity to find openings and opportunities. There is a teaching that says as your level of consciousness raises, you begin to develop extraordinary faculties like a better facility to predict the future. We develop a better facility to actually understand our past and what really did happen, what it really meant versus what we always thought it meant. We can project ourselves backwards and forwards in time.

To project myself forward in time, from one point of view, is complete imagination if you think we don't really have the ability to move through time. As my consciousness develops, I find I can project myself forward in time. What appears in that moment, to the imagination, begins to manifest in the real world, to a lesser or greater degree. When I look back at this period where I was projecting or imagining into the future, it turns out it wasn't Imaginary and was a prognostication. I was seeing something that was an actual possibility of occurrence in the future. This is a different kind of imagination than simply random, associative, fantastical thinking.

In the *Tibetan Book of the Dead*, it says one of the impediments to making progress through the Bardo is being in denial about where one is and imagining one is in a different place. If I'm in a Bardo space now, in order to move from this place to the next, it's very important to be able to see as clearly as possible where I'm at right now. What is the nature of my current life? If, in this now, my head is full of all kinds of fantastic, imaginary variations and possibilities that are random, associative, negative or positive, and that's what I'm paying attention to, by default, I have not seen where I am really am.

There is a right use and a wrong use of imagination.

Let's take the first part. First is overindulgence, but overindulgence in what? Overindulgence in imagination about possible events in the future. How it's all going to go, what it's all going to mean, who's all going to be there, what are they going to be, how are they going to respond to me, they're going to like me, they're not going to like me, I'm going to do well there, I'm not going to do well there, I'm going to nah, nah, nah, nah, nah. It's overindulging in negative fantasy about, but it could be positive, too, like imagining how flappy the flags will be on top of the castle walls we are going to build.

Regard the past with an open mind. In other words, going back and realizing there are things you know and things you don't know. You may have had a difficult situation in the past. You spend a lot of time going back and imagining what all the motivation was behind everything that happened. That's not really helpful. You spend a lot of time and energy. If you want to go back and look for clarity and practice forgiveness, that's one thing, but going back into endless speculation into what it all meant and why it all went down, coming up with rationalizations for why somebody else did something and why you did what you did is not valuable and wastes a lot of energy and time.

I like to talk about and plan for the future. I like to talk about possible things we can do in the future. I don't want to overindulge in speculation of those possibilities. Why? Because if I put too much energy out there, I take it away from the present moment and I might miss something critical I need to be paying attention to right this second. Getting there is dependent on us being here right now, isn't it?

17. Accept who and where you are and begin to work.

Dr. J: Do not wait for a better time. This follows on the heels of the last comment I made about being able to see who and where you are. When you are in imagination all you see is how you want things to be or how they could be. You do not see what is real. We want to be able to have this awareness of who and where we are and to accept that. That's really important because that determines the next thing we need to do. What is the next step? What is the next exercise, bit of information, issue to work on, thought? If we are in imagination, we are working on things unimportant because they are not real. We end up spending a lot of time, effort and energy handling the issues that aren't really issues because they have come out of our imagination. We might try to work on unrealistic skills because we don't know our current level of practice.

As a teacher, it is really important for me to have discernment about the competency, intellectual and being level of a student. If I'm in imagination about where students are, I'm not going to give them the next thing to practice to get to the next place. I might start them too far ahead or too far behind, in which case, the work won't connect with them in the right way. This is a constant struggle about being with students and being able to see them accurately. For example, what is their actual intelligence? What is their actual, emotional stability and their actual availability and openness to new ideas? What is their ability to be disciplined or to learn how to be disciplined? With certain kinds of work, you have to be disciplined to practice.

There are hallmarks of practice. You have to do a certain exercise 30 times or 300 times to get to that level of competency. I can't describe to you what that feels like until you've done it. If I were to then act as if you just learned and had done it twice and then I Immediately start to relate to you as if you've done it 30 times and have that level of awareness, which you don't, that is unrealistic, imaginary and there is going to be a disconnect somewhere. The disconnect will happen everywhere, in many ways.

Accepting who and where we are is not good or bad. It may have elements that may seem positive and other elements that may seem negative. If I really accept who I am right this minute, there will be a mix of things that are not done as well as successes and progress. That is really important to understand, too. It is not about constantly comparing ourselves to some future standard of evolution we might obtain someday in the future. It is really important, in our present acceptance of who we are, acknowledgeing that we have made substantial progress. Where we are right now is very different than where we were a month ago or six years ago.

I said it in class today and I think a couple of people might actually have heard what I was saying. All the stuff I'm talking about, I'm not talking about it as if it is some hypothetical thing to do someday in the future. I don't see any reason why we can't take everything we are doing at the very best of our ability and practice those things right now this minute. I don't see any reason why we can't do that. In fact, everything I know says that's what we're supposed to do. We are supposed to make our commitments to work on ourselves, to raise our consciousness, to be loving and forgiving, and to practice our healing right now this minute. There is no reason not to do it. There's no reason to wait. Even if we are in class, that's not a good enough excuse to do it. How about that?

There is actually a time when even I would have said, "Class is not about healing. No healing in class. There is no therapy in class. There will be no therapy in class." I realized, at some magical point, this was just crazy, if in fact what I'm actually teaching is real healing technology. How can it not get the ball rolling? How can the doors to the necessity of healing everybody has not start creaking their way open in the presence of genuine healing? How can that not occur? It has to happen.

As far as working on ourselves, well, there's never going to be a better time than now, in an environment like this, with all these wacky people, who don't know how to do anything and are not paying attention and have all their own agendas and are going in such different directions. Well, what better time to practice working on your self than in an environment like that, like this.

As far as working on myself, how could I possibly craft a better environment to work on myself than to do it in a public forum in front of the introspective and critical eyes of a bunch of strangers. How humiliating is that? How humbling is that? And to actually try and give it a good shot, when is a better time to do it? Am I going to save working on myself for after class, as if some artificial environment, where no self-work is allowed, has the circle with the bar through it?

J: I'm putting on my "no self-work" T-shirt. Don't ask me to do it.

Dr. J: "This is a no work zone. No self-work. There is only idiocy in here." What's the alternative? The equanimity and "Promiiwihan-sii" is what we're working on right now, the mental part, the psychological part, the emotional part of what it means to be a balanced person. That's the equanimity part of the equation. Where's a better time and a better place to work on it than where we happen to be sitting or working?

That's the hard part for me. I've come from a place where I used to compartmentalize all that and think there was a better place, as if there was a better place. I then realized everyone went home. "Oh, rut row. Class is over. Now, how am I going to work with them on their self-observation, their expression of negative emotion, on learning how to grow and practice alchemy and magic in their lives, to develop themselves and liberate themselves from the bonds of their preconditioning, if they're not here? I have to try and do that while they're here." That's when I realized I had to start changing things, both for myself and for the students.

Accept who and where you are and begin to work.

We can't have any preconditions about where is a good place to start working on ourselves. All that is just gibberish. Do not wait for a better time, because there is no better time. It doesn't exist. This is it. As I say sometimes, "This is what I'm doing while I'm waiting for a better place for my life to happen. This is it. This is actually my life happening." Right now, believe it or not, J, this is the peak of my life experience with you guys right here, right now. This is it. This is really the peak. I know I'm going to have other experiences and I've had other experiences, but right now, this is the finest hour of my life and you're it, you're here, tag. I'm committed to make the best of it and really pay attention and get the most of this beautiful experience I'm having with you.

18. Overindulgence in life aims steals energy from our work. (Mr. Joel Friedlander)

Dr. J: Overindulgence in life aims steals energy from our work. Householder, which is the broad umbrella concept of tending to the necessities of life that allow us to live, like acquiring food, clothing, shelter, companionship, community, producing income, reliable transportation, computers, technology. If these aims become more important than the work, which is the idea of bringing intention to uplifting and liberating oneself from limitations of consciousness and spirit, then the work is no longer productive.

If I just took one aim like, "I have to make money in order to support the school", the point where I become all about the money as the primary activity, to produce income—marketing, getting people to sign contracts, to commit to paying and to buying things and networking—when that becomes exclusive to where I no longer function as a teacher or as an individual working on myself, as of that point, that aim interferes with the work. If I became all consumed with a hobby like automobiles…I have to have the best car, I want to collect cars, they have to be the finest cars, I'm going to have to build a garage to put those cars in…I start spending the bulk of my time, effort and energy on cars. In and of itself, there is nothing wrong with that. There is nothing wrong with having a hobby of appreciating cars. If it becomes a substitution for working on my aims toward consciousness and evolution of my person in every way, liberating myself from the bonds of programming and the lower parts of myself, at that point, that hobby would become completely counterproductive. If I'm practicing being a conscious person, this is something I have to monitor.

There is a concept we haven't talked about a lot called allurement and glamour. Glamour is the idea of being distracted by something shiny. For example, maybe I'm working on a yoga practice or a healing technology or my psychology, and I see something shiny or meet someone shiny. I am now strongly attracted to that thing or person. It becomes a force of allurement, which pulls me away from what my aim and purpose for being one minute before that. It has the capacity to pull me onto a completely different track as if I was never on the previous track. Allurement and glamour are interesting. When we are in that state of allurement, we think quite strangely. We could have been on one track for an entire year and literally, at the snap of a finger, we see someone shiny and we are on a different track. It was as if nothing that happened before that was valid or real or substantial.

The thing about allurement and glamour is that what attracts us now will soon be substituted by the next shiny thing, which can be anything in life. It can be an event. A trauma could happen and I am glamoured by the trauma, what happens to me as a result of the trauma, or the attention I get after the trauma. From the moment of the trauma, which could have been an external event, like an assault with a person, a financial loss, a divorce, a car wreck, a sudden onset of illness, as soon as that happens, I'm all about that. Whatever I was up to one minute before that, it's like it never happened.

This is one of the reasons we practice self-remembering and self-observation. These practices tend to be helpful in the avoidance of succumbing to glamour and allurement. We can observe the process and as we are pulled this way or that way, part of us will say, "Whoa, I know what that is." Initially, we are so whimsical and subject to glamour. That's why it's talked about. We are whimsical because we are attracted to the new shininess, especially if it's Imaginary. Sometimes what is Imaginary is more attractive than something or someone real. If we are self-observing, we will see the shift. That part of us will realize it is not continuous with what came before. The contrast will be evident to us, so that we say, "Well wait a minute, where am I going? What am I doing? What is happening?" We can identify the process even though we may not be able to stop it.

It may on some level be impossible, because some of the attraction has an instinctive basis. It happens faster than thought. For me to then persist in it and go after it and develop it, it's as if we weren't even having this discussion. We didn't make the decision to sit here and have this conversation. I never made the aim to be focused on the discussion. Now I'm all about something shiny. Next thing you know, it might be a month from now when I start thinking, "Wait, isn't there something I was supposed to be doing or working on?" I am not as distracted by the glamour perhaps a month later, so then I start to think again about the work. I think, "Oh no. I lost the train. I got off task." I was completely separate from the work I was doing for a period of time because of the allurement, glamour, imagination and all the activity that followed. In the short term, it's virtually Impossible not to be subject to it.

The idea of self-observation means we can observe the process. If we see this deviation the glamour brings on is not going to feed back into the work we're doing, at some point there comes a slow or weak place where we can bring energy back into the equation. We can bring ourselves back to task. We can come back to the aim. That's the way the work progresses overtime. It doesn't go in a straight line. We work, work, work. We make progress and then we have distraction. We then remember to work again, grab ourselves up by the coat tails and reapply principles to come back. We make incremental and rickety progress as we bounce from one distraction to the next attractive distraction, whether positive or negative. It doesn't matter, relative to the conversation on aims.

What are life aims? Life aims are jobs. Life aims are income. Life aims are…
J: Looking for the perfect partner.

Dr. J: …looking for the perfect partner. Life aims are driving the right car. Life aims are living in the right neighborhood or the right country or the right part of the country with the right people. Life things are life aims. Overindulgence in life aims steals energy from our work. Why? Because, if we're concerned with that too much, then we are not paying attention and acknowledging the value of where we are right this second.

Being overindulgent and even being successful in your pursuit of life aims does not guarantee happiness. Happiness is something that is going to occur in the moment at every stage of your life. It has nothing to do with your work, your job, your income, your whatever you have. I'm not saying all these things are not important, because we do have genuine life aims. We do have to put some attention to those things. We want to be good at it. We don't want to be stupid about it. We want to be good at it. Why? We want to be able to accomplish them without too much obsession where they take us away from our lives. We want to be able to get the money we need without losing ourselves. We want to be able to get the vehicles operating and the kind of vehicles we want without losing ourselves in the process.

19. Dost thou love life? Then do not waste time, for that is the stuff that life is made of. (Benjamin Franklin)

Dr. J: Dost thou love life? Then do not waste time, for that is the stuff that life is made of. I always like that quote from Benjamin Franklin. He's on my list of suspected conscious beings. That's why I include him in my work, Notes On Evolution. He said some very interesting things concurrent with work ideas. This is one of those things.

"Do you love life? Then don't waste time, for that's the stuff life is made of." (Benjamin Franklin)

There's this mistaken idea we have an unlimited amount of time to not work on ourselves. We can take it for granted we can always come back to it at some future time, pick up where we left off, make progress. I want to be elevated in the sense of being able to explore higher levels of consciousness and more sophisticated ways of being as an individual, of having more control over my machine, of not being ruled by negative emotions, about exploring my true faculties of what I might actually be able to experience in life, yet I might simultaneously think I don't necessarily have to achieve all these things today. I don't have to work on myself right now. I could do it later. The thing about it is the sands of the hourglass are running while we are here. We don't have any claim to one more minute of accessibility to work on ourselves than the one we are engaged in right now. That's it. The only minute we have to work on ourselves that we know we have is the one we're in right now.

The idea of working on myself has been, at times, pretty difficult. Sometimes working on myself doesn't seem like the most fun thing in the world to be doing. In fact, sometimes I've had this experience, where even to think about working on myself I got this bounce back in my head which said, "Oh no. That's not fun. Let's do something fun." Glamour, allurement, I'm on this other track where I want to focus on somebody else instead of me. There have been several times in my life where I've experienced that. I had a much stronger attraction to work on somebody else than I had on working on me. Then I found some lapse of time had occurred where not only did I do that but it was almost as if there was this whole empty spot. It's not like I picked up and continued. There was a big gap where I got lost in some activity or some person or something that happened to me. From the point of view of developing myself as someone of sophistication to be able to experience life with greater facility, I was right back where I was before I started.

I love life. I want to be here. I'm here on purpose. I want to explore everything this life has to offer me in the moment and everything extraordinary in every future moment later today, tomorrow and the rest of my life. In order to enjoy and participate in life at the highest possible level, I believe I need to be more balanced, self-aware and evolved as a person. To not work on myself for any reason is the same as acquiescing to the idea that good enough is good enough or, with all of the impediments that I have to being who I am in the moment, that I should be able to have this great life with all of those.

From this point of view, the statement is asking, "How much do you love life? Do you love life enough to be present while it's happening?" Do we love life enough to bring our highest attention, our best side, our clearest thinking and our most loving nature to it? If we aren't up for that, then is that the same thing as saying we don't care about life? Then I have to ask myself, "Well, what else do I have to be doing right now?"

220

Dost thou love life. I love that.

There's no place where students could learn more or be more productive or learn to be more themselves or be more powerful or have more powerful skills than here. That place doesn't exist in the world while they're here. To keep projecting out, over and over, in so many directions leaves very little attention to being present in class. It's whatever is left over.

If I give a group of students the option to take an open practice, what is the percentage of students who actually want to practice? How much do they value the experience? Have they been paying attention to the fact I'm watching. It's like a test. Oh yeah, if you want to practice, practice. If you don't want to practice, do something else. Here's the interpretation: "Oh, he said we don't have to practice and we can do anything we want." That's not what I said. If you were paying attention, you'd get it. That's not what I said. What am I going to do? I'm going to be working on myself, working on my program, working on being in a good place for the class to bring good energy to class. Even a day off is not a day off in that sense. It doesn't mean there is anything wrong with taking off and having a frivolous day here and there. Again, I live here. I'm here all the time. Some of them have traveled a thousand miles to be here. They have the most to gain and the most to lose from every minute they have here.

J: Right.

Dr. J: How did I get so much from the time I spent in Asia? I'll tell you one of my secrets. When I was there, I wasn't here. Ta-da! That's it. When I was there, I wasn't here. Literally, when I was training in Thailand, I didn't have a life. I didn't live anywhere else. I didn't have a family. I didn't have friends. I didn't have anything. When I was there, I was there 100%, so I got everything available. I got exposure and interaction. People reacted to me, after a time, not right at first but after a time, as someone who they could share valuable things with because they knew I wasn't having a hit and run tactic going on. I wasn't playing grab and run.

Sometimes we have students who are wasting time. They are doing a slow motion version of a smash and grab. "Can I just slow down here for a second, grab some goodies, and then run out the door?" Sadly, they're not going to get very much. Those who are here will.

CHAPTER SIXTEEN: An Act of Power Is a Careful Act.

Dr. J: I put this in. It's a poem and song. It's called a warrior's song.

"I'm already given to the power that rules my fate. I cling to nothing so I will have nothing to defend. I will fear nothing so I will remember myself. Detached and at ease, I will dart past the eagle to be free." (Anonymous)

I'm already given to the power that rules my fate. I've already accepted the fact I'm here with intention. My life is not a mistake, a fluke or a random chaotic event, a glitch in the universe. I'm here with intention and consciousness. I'm here in harmony with nature and am part of nature. I'm rightfully here. I give to that and accept that because that is my fate. Whatever is the power which led to this occurrence, which is me happening now, I acquiesce to that because I'm here. I cling to nothing because I realize all of the external circumstances are temporary. Everything that happens is temporary, even my thoughts. My body, the world around me and everything in nature are temporary. There is nothing in the tangible, organic world that is permanent. Yet there is something inextricably tied up with nature. There is something which does abide, and that I acquiesce to.

I cling to nothing because I have nothing to cling to...yet. I don't cling to anything temporary. I don't cling to anything I've already identified as temporary. For example, I don't cling to my life. That's why this is the warrior's song. The person who wrote this was one of my former students who gave it to me as a gift. It was after we had done a reading on the Hakaguri Bushido Code: The way of the warrior is found in the resolute acceptance of death.

I cling to nothing because the way of the warrior is to acknowledge and know everything is Impermanent yet something abides. We don't cling to what is Impermanent. We cling to that which abides. The work is the discovery process in trying to determine what is that which abides in the world of Impermanence. In my opinion, that is one of the definitions of the work.

I will have nothing to defend. There is nothing for me to defend, protect or rationalize. There's no reason for me to be violent or proactively negative because it is all going to change anyway. Even if I manage to find a way to secure, preserve, nail down and guarantee every little thing in my life, in the next minute it could all be different. I'm not in charge of that. We have a law of fate. In simple terms, it is our soul's mission in the world. We also have law of accident. Law of accident is acknowledgement of where we are in the ray of creation. There is a chaotic and entropic element to nature, where at some point nature destroys and consumes itself. This is like the female principle of Khali, the destroyer. In nature, we have a natural phenomenon that exemplifies this.

We have a black hole. What is one of the speculations of what a black hole does? A black hole undoes everything. So there's part of the universal phenomenon that creates everything. There are galaxies where stars are created or born, how stars are born and how worlds around stars are born. That's the male part, the creative expression of the possibility of being. But then we also have the female part, the destroyer, which is the black hole at the center of every solar system. Everything that was created over there is uncreated over here. It's a cycle between creation and un-creation. The crisp edge of that chaotic, entropic line, that is what's so fascinating in mathematics; the study of fractals and fractal theory. At the finest edge of anything, there is a border where that which is becomes that which is not. There's an infinite border of chaos on the edge of everything. For example, this table here appears to be solid. There is a point where this table, at a subatomic level, is in continuous destruction mode of becoming not a table and becoming a table all at the same time.

I have nothing to defend. I fear nothing. Well, which "I" fears nothing? Only an "I" who knows everything is temporary and cannot have any real Impact on my spirit, soul or whatever is the atman and fundamental objective. Only that part of me and only an intuition and understanding or consciousness that comes from that could not have fear. When I act fearlessly, when I act out of a sense of non-fear, I am acting more in harmony with that part of myself. I will remember myself to act more in harmony with that part of myself. When I talk about remembering myself, I am determined to remember who I am. I am, just like Swami Vivikananda states in his book on Jnana Yoga, "I am that thou art". I must remember that I am that which I am and I am that I am. The "I am" I'm trying to remember is the I that is eternal and immortal. It is the I that has real time, conscious communication with multiple dimensions that are not so intangible and impermanent that they change with every whim and whimsy of external pressure, including my whole life as an event.

"Detached and at ease, I will dart past the eagle to be free."

Even though the eagle is high and represents in Native American lore (as well as other cultures, even going back to the ancient Sumerians) an almost godlike vision of higher consciousness, because of the ability to see past current circumstances forward and backward, and present to see the future and past because of the lofty advantage of the eagle, the eyesight. This was one of the metaphors for Ajna Chakra, the 6th chakra (Third Eye). That's the part of us that has a slightly different view point that can see a little bit ahead into the future and can see more accurately into the past, which means now we are actually seeing the present in some context. This is more helpful than only seeing the now. Here we have this idea that "I will dart past the eagle to be free" because even the eagle's lofty viewpoint is relative consciousness. What is the point of view of that which intentionally crafted this world compared to that of the eagle? Well, the eagle would be slow, blind and dumb compared to a creative intelligence that would be part of the organizational principle to manifest this life. I want to tune with the eagle part of myself, but not as the absolute goal.

In yoga, you hear people talking about the pursuit of nirvana and Samadhi. If you read all the descriptions about those, the experience of nirvana and Samadhi is short. There might the odd individual here or there who claims to be in a continuous state of bliss. My experience has been, with these conscious beings, that to be in a continuous state of bliss was contingent on everyone around them doing certain things to support that state.

...or else they're on drugs of some kind. Just seeking bliss and nirvana is not enough. It is another temporary state of being that comes and goes. It is also very dependent on circumstances and specific practices, like doing the right meditation or being in the right Savasana or posture for the right length of time and thinking the right thoughts and having the right environment where there's not too much distraction. It is hard to maintain your Samadhi when someone is trying to rob you, for example. It is hard to maintain when right in the middle of your meditation the phone rings and you remember you forgot to turn it off. Obviously that's sabotage, right? If you were a unified person and you knew that external environment is critical to going into a state of deep bliss, you wouldn't be interrupted by the Macarena theme on your phone ringer. You would remember to turn the phone off. But you didn't so that can be a form of sabotage. Even if you did everything perfect, it turns out that right when you're in your state of needing to be almost there or you're in the Samadhi state, that's when your ex decides they have to have closure with some past issue. You know what? They don't care you're being all yogic. They will bring you to their level of consciousness in order to address their need and necessity. It could be anything else.

This happened to me. I was doing a very long and deep meditation on achieving a specific, higher level of consciousness. I practiced this for a couple of years and had gotten to where I could really get in the state of complete bliss and separation from my emotions. I was in a space of not having any particular conscious thought, of leaving my body and finding myself in a place surrounded by light. I could actually do this on purpose and had gotten quite good at doing this on purpose. I could lower my heart rate until virtually my heart would stop. Realistically, I think I dropped it down to about 18 or 20 bpm within about 20 minutes. It felt like the top of my head would open and I would leave my body in a ball of light. I would be in this extraordinary place that was completely peaceful, blissful and absent from all the communication in my body, as if I didn't even have a body. Here's a story: I am in this meditation state one day when, all of a sudden, there is this "Bang! Bang! Bang!" on the door. I am in the back of my office. My doors are locked. I have no appointments coming up, so there is a "Do Not Disturb" sign on the door. I bring myself out of my meditation and came back into my body with an irritated, shocked state of mind. I was a little disoriented in my body but I got up and went to the door. There were firemen banging at my door. They were all suited up with their tools and stuff. They told me that two doors down, my neighbor was having a fire in their business. They needed for me to evacuate the building for a little while, but reassured me it was going to be just fine. There were fire trucks and all these people on the street running around, with lots of commotion, people yelling. I had just come out of my meditation, standing on the sidewalk. I'm kind of in a self-observant state and just more than a little bit irritated. It even occurs to me that my neighbor did it on purpose. That actually goes through my mind, because, "They're just like that. They're not very conscious. They don't seem to take care of their space very much. There usually seems to be trash piled up." I'm having these kinds of thoughts. Then I have an epiphany. No matter how good I am at gaining a state of enlightenment and blissful consciousness, I am still in the tissue. I am still in the world. I am still subject to accident, environmental pressure and the behavior of people in the world. They can still impinge upon my reality and "take it away from me" without my permission, from that day to this. I still practice that meditation and am happy to teach you how to do it. However, I realize it's not a solution. It's a tool.

What I'm looking for is more substantial than that. What I'm looking for is the part of me that was the same when I was in the blissful state than when I was slightly agitated, standing on the sidewalk, watching the firemen run in and out of the building.

1. Care and deliberation in your work efforts preserve your life force.

Dr. J: So that's the bottom line of wasting energy. Consider everything we do, in the sense of being deliberate about our energy, in order to not exhaust our life force in vain. Why? Because it's possible that if we can store, build up and create reserves for our life force, we may be able to have some extraordinary experiences that are not otherwise possible. Those are imagination.

See, that's imagination, to think about sit-ups, yogic powers, special abilities, cognitive facilities, precognition and supernormal intuition. When you realize it, those things take a lot of energy. Why can't everyone do those things? Why can't all the advanced yogis do those things? Because even the advanced yogis still spend most of their time wasting energy. They're not conscious of it. Maybe they are conscious and they just don't care. I don't know.

There's something about being careful and deliberate of not wasting energy that gives you energy to do the things you want to be deliberate about, like being compassionate, loving, joyful and able to practically express your consciousness. It takes energy. We have to work on not throwing it away without care, in order to have those reserves.

J: That whole topic just pointed out so much more work I have to do. A lot of the examples you gave were, "I even think I said that", you know? The part that was in the previous section, that I didn't quite understand…maybe it was something you said in one of them. It's in the realm of do not give or share authority over your self to others with less being.

J: How do you determine whether or not they have less being?

Dr. J: I'll give you an example. Let's say we have someone in a community who is "in charge" of something as a spiritual authority, but yet they obviously don't work on themselves. They don't have an elevated being. Well, you may do what they ask you to do, from a point of view of external consideration and cooperating within the community. Do not give that person any authority over yourself to be your spiritual guide.

You know, the last person in the world you want is someone to be your spiritual guide who doesn't practice anything they preach. Overtime, with discernment, you should be able to tell. We should be able to look at someone, especially…maybe…I'm not being judgmental, like I'm passing by and see someone on the stage and make some determination, "Uh, they're a fraud." I'm talking about when you get to know someone overtime and they are in a "position of authority". You will see there is a schism. Their level of being is not in line with their level of authority. If you find that to be true, that's significant. It means do not submit to them in areas that are really important to you. Don't submit to them in areas that are important to you. Submit to them in external considerations that might be necessary, like organizational things.

If this person then begins to advise or counsel you about your progress as a conscious being or your expression of your spirituality, don't give them that power, because you have higher being than they do. It should be the other way around. You should be counseling them.

Authority hierarchies flip artificially, in that you have people who have lower being in charge of people who have higher being, externally. An example being, there could be a policeman who might not have any conscious development whatsoever, but he could be in charge of me in certain situations.

Well, in those situations, externally, I'm going to acquiesce. I will do whatever is necessary to not get arrested or shot. Will I then, while I'm in the back of the police car, take that person's advice on my spiritual development? No I don't think so.

I'd have to make a determination. Are we equal? Where is the parity in our level of being?

STUDENT: It doesn't mean, though, that you can't learn something.

Dr. J: That's not what I'm saying. It says authority. The idea is about having people in authority over you.

Good people get in trouble all the time because they give power over their conscious development to persons who have lower being than them. Those persons take advantage of them and lead them into damaging situations. It happens all the time. You wonder how does a Jim Jones cult thing happen?

224

How does that happen? Well, that's how it happens. People are not judging based on actual being. They are judging on external criteria of authority. The persons authority. They have power. "Okay, we're just going to go with the flow because they appear to be in charge." If their being is not commensurate with the authority, then do not submit to it, because the end is not going to be pretty. At the very least, I'm not predicting some doom and gloom. Probably the most likely consequence is that you will find you've just spent a great deal of time, effort and energy, and you have accomplished nothing following that advice, which wasn't coming from a very fine place.

2. Stimulate knowledge by being impeccable without desire, which requires that one discard everything unnecessary.

Dr. J: Be willing to clean house as necessary and as you have energy and opportunity to do so. In the Bruce Lee system of Jeet Kune Do as related to me by former teacher and mentor Danny Inosanto, Sifu Lee made reference to four steps towards mastery:

1. **Research your own experience.**
2. **Absorb what's useful.**
3. **Reject what's useless.**
4. **Add something specifically your own.**

This topic is about acquiring the where-with-all to actually be able to do these steps in real life. Impeccability is learned and cultivated over time with dedication and practice. No one is automatically or mechanically "impeccable"! It is a relentless process of comparing what works with what doesn't, and then discarding the useless and unclear until what is left is the most authentic version of the possibility of who we could be. In Sifu Lee's terms, by this process we then become masterful.

CHAPTER SEVENTEEN: Work on Self-Importance

1. To diminish self-importance, make conscious, emotional understanding grow.

Dr. J: P. D. Ouspensky defines conscience in the Fourth Way as "*an emotional realization of truth.*" To diminish self-importance or ego, work on the emotional understanding of your truth. Work to bring emotion to your understandings of the ideas. Work to bring emotion to the practices or struggles you have every day.

It's not just random or negative emotion being talked about here. It's the idea of an intentional, emotional attitude. I think the only way to create that is to constantly allow yourself permission to be in situations that are not comfortable for you or are not necessarily what you would have chosen.

2. Think about yourself by judging yourself less.

Dr. J: One of the primary ways we feed false personality and ego is with this constant rumination about our lives. It is a constant thinking, "My this, my that, I this, I that." You are the center of your daily thought life. As long as you are entirely the center of your daily thought life, there is no possibility of considering anything or anyone else for more than a second or two, and then you are cultivating false personality and will continue to do that.

This is an exercise, that when you notice that for a period of time, an hour, four hours, four days, whatever the time period is, you observe you haven't had a selfless thought about a single person in the whole world, grab yourself up and just think about someone else. Think about something or someone else. Prefer someone else to yourself or the thoughts of yourself and see what happens.

3. Avoid preoccupation with yourself by continuing to learn.

Dr. J: This is in the context of submitting to education. All self-motivated education is at some point completely limited. It is limited by the quality and extent of your self. If your self is very highly developed and conscious, then maybe your learning curve or objectives might have more merit. Typically speaking, we follow our educational interests with the same kind of interests we follow everything else, which is completely according to circumstances and events. Any little thing happens and we are on to the next. This is where we see, for example, individuals who claim to be working on themselves, in the sense of having higher consciousness, flitting about from one interesting thing to the next. They acquire lots of little tidbits of information without acquiring any genuine mastery of anything at all. Much time can go by like this. In fact, your whole life can go by like this and you can end up at the end of your life with a lot of little tidbits of information and no mastery of anything substantial.

There is this concept of choosing an educational path and means with criteria not purely personal and ego based. That it is going to take time and will be up and down. It will not always be as interesting or make you happy, because the education should have a longer duration of substantiality than your attention span. If it doesn't have a longer duration than our attention span, then that education does not achieve the goal, which is helping to drive away preoccupation with your random whims and interests.

4. See your weaknesses by dwelling less on other people.

Dr. J: Back to the idea of trying to spend less time thinking about us individually. When we have a whole day consumed with just thinking about ourselves, what are we thinking? What are some of the thoughts we are thinking? We have thoughts about other people as we compare ourselves to them. We have thoughts like, "What have you done for me lately? What has this person done for me lately?" and we compare that against some imaginary, subjective standard of whether what they are actually doing is beneficial to me or not this minute.

We look at other people's faults and weaknesses and slights and lapses of consciousness and so on as a preoccupation. That's different than working together to try and do a practice where we work to in a positive way to photograph each other when we are in a completely mechanical state with the intention of bringing up the energy. That is quite different from constantly observing others and looking for faults. That's completely mechanical. When we do that we miss our own weaknesses, those areas where we need to work on ourselves.

5. Try to deal with others with an absence of self-importance.

Dr. J: It's really interesting that individuals who would say they are the most self-effacing in their thought lives consider themselves to be the most important. There is such a thing as false humility, which feeds false personality. You see it quite commonly in individuals who are really helpful. That's why we say sometimes, "Helping is another way of hiding." If I'm using helping as a way of hiding, I'm going to always help you do something a little bit different than you wanted to do. I'm going to help you go somewhere a little different than where you wanted to go. I'm going to help you in such a way the bottom line is, "Helping you benefits me more than you."

When I'm self-important in that regard, it is difficult or impossible to be generous, because all the generosity or gifts are conditional on some specific kind of reciprocity.

That is how the world goes. Quid pro quo means there must be an exchange of energy for something to occur. That means it is two ways. When we start talking about it from a point of view of consciousness, it is slightly different. It needs to be part of voluntary suffering to practice generosity that is not contingent on reciprocity. That's different from the idea when we are teaching or coaching or practicing reciprocity and right valuation and validation, that we encourage, even demand, that students and others we work with step up and reciprocate and give back with greater largess than they received. Until you see that, you don't have proof they are getting the lessons. This is called the third line of work.

A lot of these exercises are inappropriate for public practice because you will be eaten alive and will fail. It doesn't work like that there. The goal of the outside life is not to raise consciousness and elevate the spirit. The goal of the environment is survival of the fittest.

6. Promote someone else to a position you value.

Dr. J: If you don't value the position or the elevation, then it's not going to be valuable to anyone else. It shouldn't be. If I promote someone to teacher, that means something. Why? I value the role and position of being a teacher, so I'm promoting an individual to positions that are incredibly valuable to me. That is an exercise. From a selfish point of view, I could go into a mindset of comparing teacher candidates with my teachers or my own experience. Nobody would qualify. That doesn't work in the third line of work, in perpetuating the school or system. No matter how elevated or confident the teacher or teacher's teachers, the next generation has to be promoted into positions of excellence and responsibility appropriate for their level. The elevation has to be genuine.

As a teacher, that is one of your first objectives: to look for and create situations where you can promote someone else to a position you value.

7. Submit to someone else editing your writing or critiquing your art, music, dance or practice.

Dr. J: The higher up you are, the more elevated or prestigious or important you are in a given position, the harder it is to submit to other people critiquing and editing. In fact, a lot of experts and professionals don't allow criticism or editing of what they do on the grounds of claiming mastery.

Especially if you are a master at something, it is even more important you find something where you can allow criticism, whether it's your writing, art, music, dance or practice. It is very important to find something you can submit to allowing criticism.

8. Let someone else pick the channel, i.e. handle the remote.

Dr. J: It is interesting in groups how people will take on roles and tasks as small as who changes the channel. It could be anything. Who makes the juice? Who fills the water container? Granted, in a school, we may have designated tasks. That's appropriate and sometimes it's according to nature and capability. Overtime, those tasks should change. Even within the context of that, it is good sometimes to allow someone who would never do a certain task to be in charge of it.

9. Wash the dishes with intention.

Dr. J: There is such a thing as good house holder. In virtually every school I've ever been in, dishwashing has been an issue. It's because, apparently, people tend to want to eat. In the schools, there is always an octave, filed under householder, which has to do with daily organizing and restoring the living situation, especially the kitchen, to some bottom standard. By bottom standard I mean a base organization of cleanliness or preparedness so that there are very definite demarcations between yesterday's meals and today's meals. For example, yesterday is not over until everything is completely put away so it looks like before the meal was prepared. Today's meals and meal plan and preparations in the kitchen start fresh. Today is not over until everything is restored. In most schools, the day is not over until whoever is the responsible person goes into the kitchen and can say it is completely done. Generally, for example, in one school I was in, no one was allowed to leave until the kitchen was done. In itself, that brought up all kinds of interesting situations. For example, what about people who like to snack late at night? The general rule was if you do that, then you have to clean it up as your personal responsibility.

The I's that think it is a hassle to clean the kitchen and food areas and restore are some of the most mechanical I's there are. That's what we've always been taught. That's one of the areas which brings up really mechanical I's. Another area is the bathroom. Things we do in the bathroom. Especially for western students. This was something that was observed, specifically for American students. It wasn't necessarily observed with the Asian students. The reason why was that only in America do we go to the bathroom by ourselves. We invented that idea. In all of the rest of the world, defecation, urination and using the bathroom for bathing was a community process. It was never done in private. In the United States and in our egocentric, American tradition, we have private issues, which we've exported to the rest of the world.

The primary reason we need privacy is so we can do stuff we don't want other people to see. It starts with that and then we continue to have lack of disclosure with many things. For example, we have a lack of disclosure in government, in the military, in finances and many other things. These are extrapolations of fundamental beliefs that we are supposed to be able to have private time. If we are the first culture in the history of the world to teach that as some kind of righteous responsibility, individuals are supposed to have private time. It's an experiment. We don't know if it will work overtime.

Back to the statement about mechanical areas: wash the dishes with intention. You could add number 10 as a step here.

10. Go to the bathroom with intention.

Dr. J: Go to the bathroom with intention. At some point practice the idea that the processes we do in the bathroom are not exclusive or private. As an exercise, this might seem controversial, but think of the most private things you do in the bathroom and occasionally do them not in private on purpose with intention, just to see what happens. There will be friction. Look what happens when you don't have your accustomed privacy.

Many of us who spent a lot of time overseas may experience the disassociation that happens when you have little or no privacy in the restroom. It's interesting if you are not used to that. If you're thrown into that without preparation, it can throw you off your game, so to speak. Even bathing. In most cultures in the world bathing is not a private experience, though that's changing because the western culture is dominant and is taking over world cultures and has been for the last 50 or 80 years. In most cultures, to take a bath was meant to be something you do with other people. You have areas of your body you can't wash by yourself. Even if you think about it mechanically from the point of view of hygiene, it's more productive to have someone else scrub your back. In Japanese and Asian cultures, when people would bathe, other people would assist. It was a community thing. Whole families bathe together. Gender and age were irrelevant. Hygiene is key to living a long life. Staying and being clean is one of the things we learn to prolong our lives.

It's interesting to challenge these cultural patterns and ideas. It ties over into medicine. For example, there are a lot of people who have fungal problems with their feet but they are overweight. Since they always bathe by themselves and no one bathes with them, there is no one to scrub their feet. If they simply had someone to scrub their feet, they wouldn't have the propensity for infections and fungus.

There are a lot of people that suffer from autointoxication syndromes from chronic constipation that could save their lives by restoring their quality of life and reduce disease patterns they have if they would just do a series of colonics. They will never do that, however, because the process of defecation and excretion, elimination of waste matter is so private, and they have so many emotional issues about their bum, that they could never allow it, even to the point of having colon cancer. For many people, that is the first time they ever have anyone examine their rectum, when they are in the doctor's office with suspicion of having colorectal cancer. That can be extreme, even though it might be socially acceptable.

We need to examine a lot of our common physical habits like bathing, washing, eating, going to the bathroom and so on. We want to challenge them occasionally with intention as examples of working on self-importance because our privacy is one of the areas where we preserve the ego and the right to be egocentric and mechanical. No one challenges that.

We often use the kitchen or the bathroom as excuses to hide from mechanical expression. For example, we might be having a difficult discussion about some issue. You want to hide from that. An acceptable way to hide from the discomfort is to say you have to go to the bathroom. When you say that and take off, you're done. No one will say anything to challenge that. We are so mechanically expected to support this idea of privacy that we won't challenge each other's privacy issues, because we don't want to be challenged ourselves. Culturally and socially we have designated areas where we give ourselves permission to be completely mechanical. We know this is true because when we are banging around in the kitchen or when we are in the bathroom, we are not doing anything that might be considered productive from a work point of view. We may in fact use that space to be quite negative.

CHAPTER EIGHTEEN: Examples of Super-Efforts

1. Go to the art gallery.

Dr. J: Once in a while, plan a trip to the art gallery or science museum or an art exhibition or opening just on the principle of the thing. Art is powerful. Art is communication. Art addresses parts of centers that normally the conscious mind doesn't have access to. It is important to occasionally put yourself in front of new art with intention. Literally the act of looking at art is considering different I's, different points of view or perspective. This is stimulating.

2. Smile at someone you don't like.

Dr. J: Make your face make the motion. It's surprising how difficult it is to genuinely smile at someone with whom you are unhappy. It's difficult to think you might have to smile at someone whom right now you don't like and right now you're not happy with. Mechanically, every part of your expression wants to be negative and/or flat. There is a connection between your posture and your emotions. Use this to your advantage and practice assuming positive, external postures when you don't feel like it with purpose and intention.

3. Go with someone else's I even when they are wrong.

Dr. J: Sometimes as an exercise, do what somebody else wants you to do, even when you know they are wrong, without justification, defense or negative expression. The only exception to this is if doing so would cause you harm or violence.

4. Do not answer back even when you are quite justified and in the right.

Dr. J: This is interesting. If you are doing this as an exercise, it can be with your teachers or any person of authority. It can be in any situation where other people are expressing opinions and you feel justified to justify or defend. Part of it has to do with the idea that compulsive defense and instant justification are almost always mechanical. A studied answer seems to be less mechanical.

5. Deliberately choose and hold one feeling out of many contradictory ones.

Dr. J: For example, if in a given situation you find you are having lots of different feelings, and they are conflicted (in other words, the feelings are going in different directions), the exercise is to pick one and let that be your main feeling. Make a decision, because this will teach you something about emotions. You believe your emotions are out of your control even though sometimes you say you have control over your emotions. You'll have an emotional expression. If attention is brought to it, you'll defend it with justification. The bottom line of the justification is that you are out of control. That's like wanting to be in two different places at the same time. "I don't know where I want to be but I don't want to be here now." "I want to work but I don't want to work on myself now." Just pick one emotional state or one feeling out of the contradictory ones to be motivated by, no matter what else is going on. There might be other feelings equally as strong, but so what. This is also an exercise with the mind to hold one thought out of many contradictory thoughts.

You might be at a situation at any given moment where you are having various thoughts. Some are complimentary to what you are doing and some are not. Some are judgmental and some are not. Pick one chain of thinking. Pick one thought and vote it into being the primary thought. For example, if the thought is to be here now to this discussion but I have other thoughts, like what I'm going to do later in the day or food or likes and dislikes about the discussion, the practice is to hold onto the one thought like a terrier dog.

6. Voluntarily absorb the features of others.

Dr. J: This implies attention and discernment. In order to voluntarily absorb some of your features, I have to be observing you. I have to really pay attention to you. Of course, I'm not saying to absorb the negative features of others, but rather their positive features. When we work with each other, we all have strengths and weaknesses. They are individually different, even though we might share strengths and weaknesses.

I look at the people I live and work with and see the strengths and positive features. I can observe something like that and notice it is different from myself. For example, I don't think a certain way you do or I don't have that capacity you have. Whatever it is, whether big or small, it is an exercise to mimic and absorb that positive feature you have.

If we are all simultaneously doing that, it is interesting because we will all be stronger in more diverse ways. I want to absorb the features for myself. It won't come out the same as it was in you because I'm also a filter. There will be distortion of the idea as it is absorbed. My capacity to live and be a person will be larger as a result of that process.

7. For a specified time, submit voluntarily to a teacher.

Dr. J: It is an idea of voluntarily submitting to teachers. There are different levels of this. The submission can be complete and total or it can be qualified. The time period can be short or long or excessive. It is a work idea to submit. Of course I am not extending a Carte Blanche to any or all teachers in general. It is always required to engage in a thoughtful process of discernment in deciding whether or not the teacher is reliable and developed enough to be suitable to submit to. I think this process takes a bit of time and is important to see the teacher in life. However, once you find a suitable teacher, then practice submitting to allow them to give you what they can.

8. Submit to corrections without reacting defensively.

Dr. J: If you don't understand what this means, then play some tapes back and see where you were given a correction and your first reaction was to justify the behavior or the words. In other words, you had a 12-point plausible explanation as to why you should not have to submit to the correction. The school practice is to submit to corrections without reacting defensively, because there are other ways to submit. We have this saying, "thank you sir/ma'am, may I have another". That is different from "I didn't do that. That's my thing. It's private. I have all these reasons to be withdrawn, negative, mechanical, angry, personality focused." There are other ways of doing it. The practice is to accept and do the correction. What's interesting is most of the time, even if you disagree with the correction completely, the proper reaction is to do it anyway. Especially if you think it's not justified or that the teacher is wrong. That's the most important time to do it.

In ordinary life and classes, you can't do this. You don't really know people. You don't know what genuine agendas are. You don't know what the real purpose of corrections is. It's not clear. There's no agreement. There's no function of agreements. There's no philosophy that would allow you to have that kind of power in the relationship. It's exactly the opposite. In the world, I might challenge every correction. "Who are you to even to give me a correction? I'm sorry; I don't have to do that because you're not the boss of me. I'll fight everything." I've even fought speeding tickets where it was two police officers with radar. I went to court and told the judge I thought the radar was wrong and here's why. I gave the list of my justifications of why the radar was wrong. One time the judge told me, "The court understands and pay the bailiff on the way out." Another time, I did the same thing, and gave my rationale, and the judge goes, "Actually, I find that to be reasonable and so I will dismiss the ticket."

That does not work in a school or a work environment, because we are constantly challenged with fighting ego and personality. Ego always wants to justify, defend and fight back. Every time we are reactive and defensive, it is some manifestation of the ego. We work to try and reduce that. It is very hard to submit without reactions.

9. Change from an emotional point of view to an intellectual one on purpose.

Dr. J: One way to handle runaway emotions: I've just been run over by the "Mack truck" of a particular negative emotion. I am out of control. One technique or practice, as far as how to handle that, is to change the point of view you have. For example, if I'm doing a particular kind of therapy and a strong, negative emotion comes up at a particular point in the therapy, and that emotion is so strong I want to quit the therapy or abandon it because of that negative emotion, then one practice idea is to change my point of view and think of it intellectually. "I knew this was going to happen before it happened. I knew there was something there before it came up. I placed myself in this position voluntarily. I organized this pressure and asked for it. What's coming up is exactly what I asked for to work on."

Rather than emphasizing the feelings, emphasize the intellectual point of view of the whole situation of whatever it is. If someone says something to me that hurts my feelings and I get all reactive, and boom, this big feeling comes up that wants to operate my legs and arms and mouth and face and run me around the house like a wind up doll, I can make a decision right then to change the point of view to an intellectual one and break it down. What was actually said and done. What was I doing and thinking when the feeling came up? What is really the issue? 9 times out of 10 when we are offended, the first emotional justification for offense is not it. It is something else. We are holding over an account from some unresolved issue. Maybe earlier this morning I felt slighted so that when you said something to me entirely different later, I lost my mind. I blame it on what you said later but I was in the emotional preparation to get mad at you. When it happens, because it will, reduce and curb the effects by doing the exercise. See the process. Rationalize what is really happening and how you are reacting. This goes back to self-observation. That is an intellectual practice.

10. Make a pledge or promise and keep it until it is complete.

Dr. J: Make an agreement with yourself or with someone else. Don't vary from it or change it on your end until it is complete, no matter what. This is something that is impossible to do when we are asleep because one I makes a promise but an hour later another I has to keep it.

You want to understand as clear as possible the hypocrisy in that. How I can make an agreement with you and then an hour later, I vary or deviate from the agreement simply because I feel like it. The justification is that I don't have to fulfill my agreement or hold to the terms of my agreement because "you made me feel...". That's a phrase we use a lot. An agreement we made a year ago or today is no longer valid because right now you made me feel something and that's the justification, even if it's completely unrelated. We do that with both small and big agreements.

We want to keep working on agreements. Making and keeping and working through the terms of agreements is a conscious exercise. It is, by the way, the origin of contracts in the first place. Conscious schools probably created the idea of contracts to be used as an exercise of the work. The first contracts were probably between school members. For example, the requirements for you to be in the school are...or for elevation in rank and privilege.

These are agreements. We have agreements. I say, which is not always true, that I do everything by agreement. It is something I strive for, to have more agreements in my life and to operate more in harmony with those agreements and to complete those agreements. For example, just doing a class for me, a program is an agreement with a group of people to give them exposure to a certain teaching for a certain period of time from the beginning of one day to the end of another. I make an agreement I will be mindful, attentive and will facilitate the flow of information and experience for these people who are present for a designated state of time. I make this agreement sometimes years in advance. Then the time comes to start he program. I don't go, "I don't really feel like doing this today. I know we made an agreement a year ago. Today you were going to be engaged in a process of experience and information from me, but I don't really feel like it, so I'm not going to do it."

232

I don't do that because that would be a complete lack of integrity. Integrity is this idea you can make an agreement and are integral enough to complete the agreement. It is the opposite of lack of agreement that one I can make a promise that another I can negate. If you have that and your level of development is such that your life is determined by one set of I's making promises and agreements and other sets of I's not keeping them, then you have no integrity. That is a statement of your level of consciousness. To be able to say you will do anything a particular way and actually do it in some semblance is a sign of greater integrity. It is a sign of higher consciousness. It not the definite sign, because some body types are more organized and inclined to work from lists and things like this. They are more inclined to make commitments and promises than others because some types are more intellectual and some types are more emotional.

This is a rule. Make a pledge or promise and keep it until it's complete.

11. Take a role contrary to what you would normally choose.

Dr. J: If normally you would choose to be in the passive receptive, in this exercise choose to be more active. If normally your inclination is to be more active or dominant in a role, choose to be more passive and receptive without judgment and justification. If you choose that role with intention, then if it doesn't work out like you planned, don't go into negativity and justification about it. The whole point of choosing a role contrary to what you would normally choose is to get yourself out of patterns. Any time you're out of patterns you are uncomfortable; you have friction because you don't know how to act. When you don't know how to act, occasionally you do something authentic because you are not acting since it's you being yourself. So much of the time, when we know what to do and how to act, well that's what we are doing is acting. We are not genuinely expressing our true nature.

I'd like to read this poem.

"Our revels now are ended. These are actors as I foretold you were all spirits and are melted into air, into thin air. And like the baseless fabric of this vision, the cloud kept towers, the gorgeous palaces, the solemn temples, the great globe itself, yea, all, which it inherits, shall dissolve. Like this insubstantial pageant, faded leave not a rack behind. We are such stuff as dreams are made of and our little life is rounded with sleep." (William Shakespeare)

There are schools that consider William Shakespeare to have been a conscious author and to have been a member of esoteric tradition of one kind or another. There's a huge amount of information to support that. Even at the same time, there are those who say William Shakespeare wasn't a real person, not even the person who wrote these plays. In fact, Sir Francis Bacon may have been William Shakespeare, etc., things like that. It doesn't matter. It's irrelevant. The words themselves are amazing. This poem is important to me because it illustrates the idea that in normal consciousness, the things we think are most real about ourselves are the least real and most intangible and the most likely to change or fade. This illusion of life about ourselves is by definition the nature of our sleep. One of the functions of the angels speaking to us is to dispel these illusions and to generate energy and information and consciousness to dispel these illusions and to bring us out of a sleeping state into a waking state. We can't imagine what the waking state is like no more than when we are in a deep sleep, in a dream state. We can imagine what our waking life is like. It's much easier for us to imagine what a sleeping state is like while we are awake than it is for us when we are sleeping to imagine what our waking life could be like. To be more precise, that's the whole point of all the exercises and aphorisms of the angels. It is to help us to be able to imagine what we would be like and what the world would be like for us if in fact we were more awake than asleep.

So angels speak and angels say over and over again, *"The sleeper must awaken."* That's the cogent message of the angels.

J: Could you explain further number five in examples of Super-Efforts.

Dr. J: Deliberately hold and choose one feeling out of many contradictory ones. It presupposes you are having a moment where you have multiple feelings. Pick one.

J: Good or bad?

Dr. J: Doesn't matter. The exercise is to pick one. The exercise is not to pick a good one. The exercise is to pick one on purpose and hold that feeling more definitely than the other feelings. That's the exercise. It does a couple of things. One of the things really interesting about that exercise is, sitting here you might think you can't do that. In actual practice, you would be surprised at how often you can do that. If you find yourself where you have mixed emotions and you develop as a practice where you pick one, eventually you'll come to the understanding that you have a lot more control over your emotions than you thought you had. Just because you have an emotion doesn't mean you have to feel any particular thing or not because you could actually choose another emotion.

Now, in the beginning this is not going to be easy and it may in fact be impossible the first few times you try it. It's not going to work but it might and sometimes does. If you can practice this repetitively overtime, you might find you have a very strong possibility of being able to pick a particular emotion out of several and have that be the one you feel. Now we are talking about a conscious emotion.

J: Same with number six in the "Super-Efforts" section.

Dr. J: Voluntarily absorb the features of others.

J: I understand that. Is it similar to picking an emotion, like if you see stuff you like about somebody or would like to cultivate in yourself? Do you just… I don't really know because we grew up mimicking, so I don't really quite understand how to do that.

Dr. J: Do it on purpose. You grew up mimicking but that's completely mechanical. You have positive role model and you have the stick. If you don't mimic you get beat or yelled at or peer reviewed. We do it unconsciously and mechanically. Bio-mimicry is built into our systems. This is mimicry which is intentional. I'll give you an example. You notice someone dresses nice. They consistently dress nice and you don't. Okay. Absorb that feature and put some effort into dressing nicer. You notice someone naturally seems to do better with housework. As you observe them, they have some organization about it. Householder is important. You notice they pick up after themselves and you don't. What do you do? Absorb that feature and start picking up after yourself. It could be little things or big things. You notice in an emergency that someone, instead of reacting or withdrawing or becoming hysterical, alertly responds in an appropriate fashion. You go, "Hmmm…wow that's more productive and I might survive longer if I reacted that way as opposed to withdrawing or becoming hysterical." You practice being more alert and engaged in situations that in the past would have caused you to hole up like a turtle and completely shut down and withdraw. By watching them, you realize there is another possibility for difficult situations. You absorb that feature.

How do you absorb features? First you do so by observing and understanding them. What are you looking at and seeing? The next thing is to mimic it and to repeat that behavior and cultivate that habit until it becomes second nature. Second nature means it's now part of your way of being.

I'll give you an example. Violent people can learn how to be nonviolent people by being around nonviolent people. You can teach violent people, even people who are like criminals, murderers, and felons in prison, how to be nonviolent. You can teach nonviolence to felons. It's been proven you can do this. They have to have motivation to become nonviolent. If they have motivation to become nonviolent, and you have a nonviolent way, you can exchange being, and when we absorb each other's features, that's what we are doing. We are exchanging being with each other. By the way, in a school that's something we want to do. We want to exchange being because by doing so we bring up the being of the school. We bring up the total level of being of the school by exchanging being. When we don't do that, if you're ego encapsulated and I'm ego encapsulated, and my stuff is my stuff and your stuff is your stuff, then the level of being stays constant and low. Obviously you have some being, accomplishment and skills or you wouldn't be here. That being the case, there is something about you I absorb that will make me stronger or clearer or more stable or whatever it might be. Reasonable, alert, productive, relaxed, who knows? That's true for all of us.

Take a role contrary to that you would normally choose.

J: Is that the same as the role we talked about in our last discussion, where we exchange roles or is it just…

Dr. J: It's not the same. It's different. Now you are choosing a role contrary to what you would normally choose.

J: Rather than role-playing, as if we were acting, we are choosing to be a different way?

Dr. J: Choosing a way you would not choose. For example, for me to choose a role of being a student. That's no big deal because I've been a student all my life. Even though I'm a teacher and that's a completely different role for me right now, it's

234

not effort or friction because I've chosen this most of my life. It has to be something I would not choose that I select. The less I like it, probably the more valuable it would be. They are different. The other was talking about choosing roles. I can, for example, choose the role of being a real estate person. I can choose a role of being a web designer and play that role. I'm not really a web designer.

J: The thought that came to me was math. A good example of that because I don't do math or like math or have interest in math…if I choose to be somebody that is more math oriented and worked to do that even though it makes me uncomfortable and I don't like it and sometimes I fail the test.

Dr. J: Which I's? Who's I?

J: The I that doesn't like math.

Dr. J: There's more than one.

J: There's a whole group of them. Is that what you are talking about?

Dr. J: There is no exactly what I'm talking about because I'm speaking in principles. You have to think about it and try and come up with what would be the most practical way to do that. Sometimes we do that in school. I can be the landscaper guy. That's a role. When I put my farmer Johns on with my straw hat and get on the lawn mower driving around in circles I am not being the master of Thai yoga. I'm being Vern, the lawn guy. That's a role.

Remember it's in the context of a discussion about voluntary submission. Quite often, this is a role that's given to you by someone else. That's very different. There are roles you choose that are opposite for you. There are also roles I could choose for you that you would never choose for you in a million years, as in ever. There are roles where I would say, "You will do this and this is what we are going to practice. This is what we are going to do." Instantly you say there is "no way". That's contrary. "No, I'm not or I don't want to do that." That's contrary. You picking a role opposite from what you would normally pick is not the same because you are in control. When the teacher picks the role or the elder picks the role because they know it's going to cause you friction, that's what I mean by contrary.

Qualitatively, they are not the same. On the surface of the words, until you are in the position, you don't get how different they are. When you choose a different role, as long as you are choosing it, you are okay with it. It's like Halloween. I can dress up like any silly thing as long as I'm the one who picks the costume. If we then had a hundred costumes and somebody else picked our costumes for us…well, in one school I was in, that's what they did for Halloween. They had twenty costumes, male and female, and two of the teachers randomly picked the costumes for Halloween. Whatever they picked was what you had to go as to the masquerade ball. If you were a guy and they picked a female streetwalker, then you were the female streetwalker. If you were a female and they picked Albert Einstein, then you were Albert Einstein or Mr. Pumpkin Head. In other words, they just picked the costumes, and you could not imagine how much resistance there was. Some people took it in stride and were like, "Yeah I'm okay with it. That's cool." Other people were like, "There's no way. No, I am not going to…" Mr. Banker says he is not going to the Halloween party as a sexy nurse in the high heels. He's like, "It's not going to happen." Even in a school, doing things like that can be productive to bring this up.

I run into it the most when I assign roles to patients and students relative to their specific issues. If I give someone a task, exercise or practice that does not allow him or her to hide or to not address his or her specific issue, then there is resistance. The thing about it is in the public vein, no one would submit to that because they want to keep that personal integrity of hanging on to their stuff and have the absolute authority and right to say when and how much of their issues are going to be worked on at any particular time. In school, we don't have that permission or luxury because we have to be able to address our issues. Some of the ways we do it is by putting ourselves in situations that are challenging and uncomfortable for us.

One of the ways I do it for me personally is by having students live in my house. By having students live in my house (my teachers did this too but I don't think it was any easier for them than it is for me), it means I have no privacy and all my stuff is out in the plain sight. There's nowhere to hide. I have the same impetus to have to work through issues as everybody else, which I wouldn't have if I didn't let students come to my house for class and to live. That's something I do contrary to my inclination. By nature my inclination is to be much more private. I create a situation of life that is 180 degrees opposite from my nature. It gives me the maximum opportunity to work on myself and definitely more than I would have if I were holed up by myself.

If you are a teacher, guess what, you have to come up with these things for yourself. If there is no one else around you to do it and you are working on yourself, then you have to assign part of yourself to come up with these examples and exercises for yourself. This is the origin of Angels Speak. The origin was that I kept finding myself with long periods of time where I was in foreign countries and also by myself in different situations, and I wanted to have more consistent work. That was part of the process of coming up with this material in the first place. For years this was just my personal workbook. Going through this now, this is the first time I've ever really shared my personal workbook and materials with anybody else. I've shared the notes but not necessarily with any of the explanations.

CHAPTER NINETEEN: Miscellaneous Discussion and Material

Forgiveness. Holding accounts. Dealing with others.

STUDENT: I've told her that one of the things I've found, the two strongest tools for dealing with that and dealing with people in general are compassion and forgiveness. Forgiveness is kind of like compassion in action. You can say you're compassionate. You can really feel for people and see their situations and put yourself in their shoes, but when it's dealing directly with your issues, a lot of times you lose the compassion because your issues cloud your ability to see clearly. You are affected. Since we had that conversation during class about holding accounts and forgiveness, I've been practicing forgiveness. In the actual moment when I feel anything happening that I would have to forgive somebody for, I do it right in that moment, without any hesitation.

You talk about your happiness not being dependent on other people. People really genuinely can't, unless you allow it to happen, affect you in a negative way. Your emotions are all your own. All your stuff and those outside influences are just that. They're outside influences. Yeah, they can get in, but only if you allow them to get in. So if you start with that...I find it to be a really powerful tool of "well nobody's in charge of my happiness except for me. In order for me to be happy, I need to forgive."

The greatest thing about it in what you were saying is that the person doesn't actually have to be there. If you want to talk about something from your past, where someone has done you wrong, and you have this whole list of stuff they've done to you...I've seen this happen to myself in the last few months with things I've been working through. You can, the next time you have an interaction with someone, whether the last time was a year ago or five years ago, have a completely different response and reaction to them because you've been working on forgiving them. It doesn't have to do with anything. They don't have to ask for your forgiveness. They don't have to say they're sorry. They don't have to do anything. But you relate to them in an entirely different way because you're coming from a place not bound up by all the negativity of your past interactions.

Dr. J: And the converse is to see, based on reviewing your past, how much of your thoughts and interactions with people have been predetermined by these kinds of things always being a filter. You only notice it when it's not there. You also see as if you have this interaction, which is unusual, in that if it wasn't there, we know from history that conversation never would've been like that because we would've been...

STUDENT: ...well you would've gone back into the same pattern plus more because all the things they're saying right now would have something to do with everything that's happened in the past, and there would be some sort of association with all of the things that have happened between you and that person. If you are coming at it from a completely different standpoint, this whole field opens up entirely new interactions. It's an awesome way to keep renewing and regenerating yourself in relationships with other people. Let's say you know a person. Really, I mean you can know people for the essence of them. You can really recognize people. You can resonate with people. When you say you know someone, you really don't. Even someone you've known for ten years, when you're interactions are all bound up by all the things that have determined what your interactions have been in the past decade, and you release that and let it go, it's almost like having an interaction with a new person. It opens up the possibility to be able to learn from that person in a better way and learn from yourself in the process.

I've been finding that to be of value. Sometimes during an interaction with someone (say I'm talking to my dad on the phone), I realize I've never actually done that with him and that I now have to do that with him...it's amazing how many times it comes up and how many more interactions...like talking to my mom...you know, I mean that's...those really close relationships you have...those people you've never considered forgiving.

Dr. J: If there's a concept of holding accounts, then we also need to have the process of clearing accounts. In other words, we've been holding accounts because we didn't know or have the technique or knowledge to not do that. We have all these accounts, which are still acting as things that change our minds and interfere with our ability to be present with the person right now. What you're describing is one of the values of forgiveness and pardon. It clears the table as a way of going back. It ties into the time travel concept. Why would I want to travel back into my history? Part of the reason is to be my own counselor. I want to go back to clear those accounts because it gives me an Immediate result in the moment. Once I've gone back and located them, which is actually not so hard to do, and start resolving them, using the tool of forgiveness, things became different. I did this with my dad. I had layers and layers and layers of accounts and negative emotions and interpretations, all kinds of garbage that related to life with my dad. Going back, not only to see what his life was like that made him the way he was, to pick instances that would come up where I could say, "I forgive you for this," over and over again. I realized that as I sat there doing it, I was changing and in real-time. It's about hoping when I do this, that some time in the future, things will be better. In the moment, I'm different. The next moment might then be different too.

STUDENT: The first time I did that was after a yoga practice in the classroom. We had the door open and the sun was setting, so it got dark while we were in there. I had the intention of going back through my life to find a certain spot where something had gotten really stuck. I went there right away. I didn't have to think about it. It wasn't where I thought it would be or anything I had previously remembered. It was a simple instance of me sitting in one place with this one feeling. I think I was 12 years ago. I went back and said all these things to myself. I remember describing it to you guys. Even the words that were coming out of my mouth I had never heard before. It was clearly a really critical point in my life. It changed right away. It was instantaneous.

Dr. J: See, that is one meditation. I call it time travel. It's about trying to find a space where you can go back to find where a pattern or a list was started. Then you can intentionally unravel it at the source. You can anticipate it will have some effect and change on who you are from that moment forward. It's not an exercise like visualization. It's coming from the point of view and understanding that psychologically so much of who we are is based on these issues. It is based on holding accounts and negativity. Technically, we say they are stored in the body's tissue. We work with the tissue to bring them up and resolve them in real-time. We take these tools into the past and apply them. That's a really good meditation.

STUDENT: With time travel, like you're talking about, what I found is that going back to that one, initial spot, I didn't actually have to deal or even think about a bunch of other stuff afterwards that had to do with that exact thing. So, all these other bad things that all related to my dad and stepmom, when I went home for Christmas I noticed I had this whole new way of interacting. I didn't leave, drive away in my car and cry my eyes out. I didn't go there and get all bound up, super anxious and really upset. I wasn't beat up trying to maintain control, while inside I was completely falling apart. That had been the defining factor in every previous interaction I'd had with them for ten years. And it didn't happen. I mean, I experienced sadness, but there was a different quality to it than I had ever experienced.

I guess the hard thing is most people don't practice this, so when you're dealing with someone you've completely cleared your accounts with, but then they have lots of accounts with you, you can't do anything about that. You can't be attached to it. Let it go, but it's still difficult to experience.

Dr. J: The most challenging circumstance we run into is other people who are not working on themselves in the same way we are! This is true even if you're being successful in all the exercises on a personal level.

A lot of people are working on themselves and believe what they're doing is really changing who they are in a positive way and so on, but it doesn't take away from the fact that even these people, who are spiritual and/or consciously doing self-work, won't have friction with us. Just the fact that even if I'm successful and am operating from a different level of consciousness, if I'm not in sync with the person I'm talking to, there will be friction. That friction might actually affect me.

An important thing to understand about levels of consciousness is that just because you are operating at a higher level doesn't make you bullet proof to events, circumstances and people. It doesn't mean these won't cause you to have friction or strain. As long as we're in the tissue, we're subject to that process on some level. The guiding principle is that we may be subject to it but we do not necessarily succumb to it in the same way that we would if we weren't working on ourselves. There are big differences as far as what would be the results of that friction. At one level of consciousness, the friction drives you hard away from working on yourself, maybe even into suicide, which is the opposite of self-work. It is self-depreciation, denigration, depression and even self-destruction. I might take everyone with me at the same time. That's a level of consciousness issue. The idea is that at higher levels of consciousness we're still subject to the same pressure from the external environment, circumstances and events, whether internally or externally derived. It's what we then do with that friction that's different. It's not the same, hopefully and hypothetically.

J: I could see where just normal, every day-to-day moments, where one is working on themselves, whether they are doing self-observation or meditating or doing yoga, where coming back into the world, waking up in the morning and tapping on negative emotions and then feeling as if they've got a handle on their day, and all of a sudden something externally happens that takes them away from working on themselves. We could also say that taking you away from self-work is a form of losing your bliss. You don't really have to be meditating or doing yoga or anything. All you have to do is just be remotely conscious about self-remembering or self-observation and then have someone interrupt that with something else.

Dr. J: The reason I put this picture in here. This is St. Sebastian who was a Christian martyr. The way he was martyred was tied to a stake and then archers shot him full of arrows until they killed him. That's why he is always shown like this, with a blissful look, but he has arrows poking out of his body. He was a saint because even at this time, where obviously the external environment has gone, shall we say, "to hell in a hand basket". If you think this is bad, you know that whatever preceded it wasn't very nice either. This is the end of his suffering and turmoil. At this point, he is forgiving and blessing the archers shooting at him. Even in these dire circumstances, where he is being shot full of holes, with his last breath he is not disturbed about the arrow situation or why he's there. He's not railing or crying. He's there and present. He's conscious and being proactively engaged in serving the principles.

He'd have every right to be offended, angry, horrified, full of fear or succumb to every base human emotion, in this situation. Yet, he didn't do any of that. He volunteered himself to them so they couldn't take him away from himself. "You can't hurt me because whatever those arrows are piercing is not me." Even to a point where he could say that to himself… It would be one thing to say it to someone else, right? "You're not in charge of this. I'm separate from you. You're not in charge of my feelings." It's a whole different situation when you are tied to a post, dying from arrows shot into you in a cruel and unusual way. It is incrementally painful, yet you are able to maintain presence and consciousness to the last breath. This wasn't even substantial enough to take him away from the work he was doing. The only thing that's going to happen here is to be separated from the flesh. "I'm not the flesh. I'm not what happens to the flesh." It doesn't mean there's not going to be a loss or that it's not going to hurt. That's the other thing. I'm sure it hurt. An elevated or conscious being in this same position might hurt just as much as anyone else. It may be more so because they'd have this consciousness of the magnitude of the crime and the suffering that even the people participating in it were bringing on themselves (as karma). In fact, he may have had overwhelming sympathy, thinking, "Not only do I forgive you, but I bless you." He went above and beyond. He did not simply say, "You can't take me away from myself." He added, "I'm also going to help you. As long as I'm here, I will use my faculties, even while you're killing me, to help you." That's amazing. On a continuum from where we're sitting to this guy, we have some work to do.

That goes back to this whole idea of why we keep coming back and asking where are we really and who are we really? It's also good to have role models, even if they are figurative. The reason why we have role models is because they give us a way to model the distance between where we find ourselves and where we would like to head. They help us realize it is not all fantasy or flights of the mind. People do make these kinds of accomplishments and find themselves able to hold onto what is real about themselves even in the craziest circumstances, exemplified by a violent death, which was undeserved.

Then we talk about forgiveness. What an exercise. What possible reason would someone in this circumstance have to be using their last bit of mental presence to be forgiving other people?

STUDENT: It's like the Tibetan monks, you know. I think it's the Buddhist monk Thich Nhat Hanh who tells the story about when they were being tortured. None of them, after this five year period of being tortured daily, had any post-traumatic stress or anything like that because the entire time they were being tortured they were practicing compassion and forgiveness for their torturers. Yeah, it hurt, but they didn't have any residual distortions.

Dr. J: That's the same thing. The Tibetan monk I met, Lama Pauldin Gyatsu, who had been 34 years in prison, in solitary confinement and/or hard labor, also being tortured. When I listened to him in Chicago talk about his experience, there was no animosity, criticism, anger or harshness of any kind toward the people who were his jailors and torturers. There was remorse because he would have liked to have seen more help. Even in that sense he understood. He said this about America, that the monks were waiting for America to come in and rescue them. That was in the 50s, right after the Chinese invaded. It never happened. Even to the last day, they thought the Americans were going to come and save them but they never did. They were curious about why we didn't. After he came to the USA and had been here for a little while, he came to this conclusion, "our level of consciousness did not allow us to actually see the situation for what it really was. Because we couldn't relate to it or see the situation the way it really was, it just simply wasn't something we were going to be involved in. We weren't at a high enough consciousness to even understand."

Once he realized the issue was a conscious or spiritual issue, he immediately forgave us. In the same way he forgave his torturers, he forgave the people who should've been able to rescue them but for whatever reason chose not to. I have to say, when he said that during his presentation, I thought I was going to collapse on the floor. It hit me so hard. I told this to J. It didn't hit me while he was saying it. It was after the meeting was over Robert Thurman and the monk Gyatsu and myself and a couple other people were going to go somewhere to eat. We were in an office building where he did the presentation. Amnesty International sponsored it.

We stepped into the elevator after everyone left. For no reason at all, he reached over and gave me this really big hug. He was in his 70's, a very little man, and had been in prison for 34 years. He had only been out of prison for a few months at that point. I didn't say anything to him. What could I possibly say to this man other than, "Great story I'm really sympathetic. Go Tibet! Down with the Chinese." I'm standing in the elevator and he gave me this big hug. I swear to god, as soon as he hugged me, I lost all the strength in my legs. I collapsed in the elevator and started sobbing uncontrollably. There we were. There was Robert Thurman, the Tibetan monk Paulden Gyatsu and everyone, and the elevator door opens and I'm in a heap on the floor. I was so overcome because I realized I shared the level of consciousness he was talking about. I realized that because I shared that, then I am somewhat of a contributor to that level of consciousness being in the world.

STUDENT: It's like that Amnesty International poster on the wall in the dorm that states, "No One is free until Everyone is free!"

Dr. J: Actually, I found that poster in a dumpster. I went to Lama Pauldin Gyatso's talk on a Friday evening. On Sunday morning, I was out with my dog Tarzan patrolling the alley. I found that poster in a dumpster that Sunday. There was just a corner of something rolled up out of a garbage bag in the dumpster. If you're in Chicago you learn that in alleys you scan the dumpsters. I learned that from my art friends. I saw this thing sticking out and I thought, "Hey, what's that?" I pulled it up and there was this poster. It just hit me like a ton of bricks. I've had it ever since.

J: It's about the allurement and the glamour. Now, I understand a whole different level of what it meant when we first met and you looked at me and you said, "I have to go back to work now." For a moment of several weeks, we were just all in each other's stuff. That new relationship energy was so shiny and smelled pretty and you wanted to be in its vibration and its moment and all its bliss and stuff. Then there was this point where it was like, "Yeah that's fun but now I have to go back to work." I really didn't know what that meant. I realize now that you were going back to school. I just thought it meant he had to start typing again. When I think about how many people I know, myself included, where just in relationships the allurement and glamour are so powerful to pull yourself away from yourself. All of a sudden, many moments down the pathway you realize, scratching your head, "How did I end up doing this? This is not what I was doing before I met them."

Then the negative reaction to that is to first look for all the reasons why I should not be here. How can I go back to where I was before? I'm seeing myself now, instead of trying to be destructive, waking up in that glamorous, shiny state where I'm off doing something else, then instead of destroying that person in order to get away from the glamour, to just attempt to come back to this place of bliss where working on myself happens. When the NRE with new people shows up, I attempt to not get all caught up in it emotionally, even in thoughts. For example, you meet someone and then suddenly you're thinking about what you might do when you invite him or her to coffee. You imagine the glamour and attraction. In relationships, this allurement and glamour can really have a huge Impact on the moments where we're not working on ourselves that seem really subtle. We tell ourselves, "Oh, this is supposed to happen." Once you're in it, you're like, "How did I get here?" It's like whenever you sing that song,

STUDENT: "This is not my beautiful house. This is not my beautiful life."

J: Exactly. This also happens to me during programs. Even during programs I catch myself being glamorized by the fact that I have to have all this time caring for the students. I catch myself noticing that their excuse to run off into this glamour world of programs is a temporary distraction.

STUDENT: As in, "I don't have any time to work on myself now. I have all these things to do."

J: Exactly.

Dr. J: Because I have to take care of all these other people.

J: Right, so I was really grateful during class when we sat and had that one Angels Speak discussion, because it brought me back to this place of what happens before and after CTPs. I realized, "Oh, we're still doing that. Good. I'm glad someone helped me put the brakes on that. I was getting all caught up in the CTP."

Dr. J: You reminded me of something I've thought about quite a bit. Even as far as NRE (New Relationship Energy), but also just this allurement and glamour of anything. It can be anything. It's not just NRE. It's like NRE for cars or desserts or TV shows. There's an idea I picked up at some point, that when I have that NRE, that's a peak experience. That's as good as it gets. Then there's a point to where I started to question, "Well wait a minute. What if it's not?" If the unconscious allurement, this mechanical attraction, can take me away from myself because it's so powerful and it feels so good and so right (every part of me says this is so right, it feels so right), at any other time in my life I would have said this is a peak experience, like if someone were to ask me what were the happiest times in my life. Those days and relationships would come up pretty high on that list.

I realized that what I was saying were some of the most peak experiences of my life were times I was the most asleep to myself, the most mechanical, and was separate and apart from what was happening to me. In fact, those experiences were the most distracting experiences I had ever had. Then I thought, so the idea is that what if it's possible to have peak experience, which is also conscious? What are the requirements and mechanisms for that? What if, instead of experiences that are accidental, serendipitous and entirely mechanical, there was a mechanism to have breakthrough experiences far above that because you are fully present to whatever degree is possible. You were still in touch with yourself and not distracted. You were still in harmony with your inner self completely. That has been on my mind for a long time. Why do I practice some things the way I do? I do so because what they do is open the door to the possibility of me having that ecstatic, blissful, superlative connection or experience. Do you follow what I'm saying?

J: Yeah, because that's what you did with me. I wasn't aware of it. I understand now a little more why when I asked you sometimes how come I didn't turn into a client once you realized how banged up I was. What I got was, and now I'm paraphrasing…there was this potential for me to understand that this was just an experience and we needed to keep going. There were going to be more of these peak experiences. Within those experiences, we're going to practice self-observation so we don't lose ourselves in them. I never experienced that before, which I think is one of the primary reasons why I've been able to, for myself, when the peak experiences come and then we go back down again, why I don't feel like I want to go look for a sharp knife. I'm not having this experience any more. Over time I've been able to see myself do that, and it's becoming less and less. When you and I do things together that have peak experience, I don't get upset when it's over. I'm beginning to come to an awareness that, "Oh, that's just an experiment."

Dr. J: Well, it's not an experiment. When you're working on your consciousness, it's not a straight line. It's peaks and valleys. There are moments and days when you are relatively more conscious than other moments and days. What you want is a trend of these highs and lows so that overtime the highs are higher and the lows are not quite so low. There is a trend toward integrity. There is a trend toward presence in relation to your consciousness. We need to do it on purpose.

There is this idea of intentionality. The thing about glamour and allurement and even NRE is that they are not conscious. It's not a conscious decision. It's not the result of a conscious intention. Let's say I was using cars as a hobby, because cars are attractive to me. I've had really nice cars in the past. I bought a wrecked '56 Chevrolet and I completely rebuilt it from the ground up and restored it and put in a brand new Corvette engine and running gear. I used to cruise around shopping centers and drive slow in front of the glass so I'd look and see the car driving by in the glass.

I actually did that. I was very satisfied in the moment it was happening. I would rev the engine and get some visceral satisfaction out of the rumble and growl and the way the car felt. The point is, when I found the car by accident, I hadn't been collecting old cars or looking for them. Five minutes before I found that car, I had just stopped at a gas station to go in a buy a Coke and some peanuts, a classic southern treat. You take your Coke and you dump the Tom's Salted Peanuts in the top of the Coke. Then you drink it. That was a treat even from my childhood days. That's what I had stopped for. While I was putting the peanuts in my Coke, standing there, I noticed this wrecked '56 Chevy set up next to the gas station and I just asked the guy if it was for sale. He said it was a junker for $500. I just happened to have $500 on me.

As of that moment, I was an instant classic car restorer and collector, where one minute before I was not. For the next five years I worked on cars and restored cars. I was into cars and went to car shows. I even got a bomber jacket from the 50s so I could wear the right jacket when I was driving my car to the car show. It happened just like that. It was very satisfying. Then I think back, well what if it was possible to have this kind of satisfactory experience of life, but instead of having it be accidental or serendipitous, have it happen on purpose. Some people might say, "Well, I attracted that car and the world of cars into my life. On some level, I must have been spiritually projecting that. The universe manifested that." Okay, that's one point of view. In the view of the work, it is unconscious and mechanical. It makes sense because we are blown like leaves in the world of events.

241

If I could cultivate a way of being where I could have a peak experience of life that was a result of an intentional process to be part of life, as opposed to qualifying that the highest points of my life were completely accidental, that's what it's all about.

J: This is where I want to say I find it interesting when I hear about certain conversations where persons on a path of spiritual consciousness will say things like, "I'm not going to have sex anymore until I find the person I resonate with, in order to have that experience." I can understand what the words are, but at the same time I think, "Okay, no matter who I'm in a relationship with, it's very obvious I created and cultivated their arrival into my life in order to have a particular experience so that I could do a particular sort of work." That makes sense. To just say, "In order for me not to have any of those experiences where I find I've lost myself, I'm going to avoid having all experiences with people."

There's a way to go about doing it and then there's a way not to go about doing it. Both are trying to achieve the same sort of goal, which is that somehow you are working on yourself.

Dr. J: Or that I'm going to avoid trying to work on myself until that accident happens where I have that glamour and instant attraction and it takes you away from yourself. That's a more genuine experience than anything else might be. It's the one experience you have no control over, so again it's that peak experience. It's like adrenaline junkies. In other words, I'll know this is my soul mate because when I meet them, I will cease being myself. That's how I know they are my soul mate, because once I hook up with them, I won't think about anything else and I won't have any other association, and it's going to be all about them, with them and all that. The problem with allurement and glamour is they are temporary. They all go away at some predictable point. Just like when I was into the racecars and antique cars, I lent the Chevy to my brother one day and he completely totaled it drag racing illegally after work and left it on the side of the road worse than when I'd found it. I had to sell it for parts to the tow truck driver. From that ride home, I never invested in another racecar or classic car or anything like that. It was over. Where was the consciousness and intention from A to Z in that? I got involved in the moment. It was completely accidental and serendipitous. I got caught up in it and was enamored with it for however long I was. Then circumstances change. There was a wreck. As a result of that, I was not into it anymore. It wasn't even a struggle. I just wasn't into it. That happened in about 20 minutes. Whatever I was into left me.

J: I myself experienced that. The reason I keep bringing it up is because every time you say something, I say to myself, "I've done exactly that in dating." I date people, not realizing I'm doing something unconscious in the moment, like in the past when guys would ask for my phone number. They call. I go out. I have this experience and then crash and burn. "Oh, I don't think I want to do that again." Five minutes later, "Can I have your number?" We go have coffee and disaster strikes again. Now I realize and I'm seeing something…

Dr. J: The situations hardest to see are not the ones ending in disaster. It's much easier to think, after the fact, when things go well externally, that you were more conscious the whole time. It went well so you were more conscious. That's not what it means. It doesn't mean that. The whole interaction might have been equally as unconscious. It's just that when we are acting unconsciously, things might go well or they might not. The idea of bringing awareness to whatever we are doing to raise our consciousness is that we are trying to eliminate the randomness of the interaction, both positive and negative. We are not trying to not have any amazing experience. This is the part where this gets left out. I'm thinking my potential to have an amazing experience is now higher because I'm paying attention. If I'm not in allurement, taken over by glamour and completely swept away with NRE or whatever, I have a higher capacity to pay attention to bring all my faculties to bear with what's happening to me. The end result is not that I don't have an amazing experience. The end result is a deeper experience because I'm more aware of all of the intricacies happening during the experience.

J: I think you can see the person you're with much clearer. I can see where that would have created these interesting and potentially fun relationships, but I really didn't have much interest. I was like, "This really isn't very interesting. I mean, he's very hot and funny and we go places, but…"

Dr. J: I want to say I'm not talking just about relationships. Relationships in this area are particularly attractive. Biologically, it's an area we are subject to in NRE. It is not really what I'm talking about. It could actually be anything. It could be something like I decide to go to the beach today, and by the time I leave I've decided to become a surfer.

J: …and you bought a surfboard on your way home.

Dr. J: I bought a surfboard and shorts before I left the beach and now I'm a surfer. It can be anything.

STUDENT: It could be yoga.

Dr. J: It could be any good or bad thing.

STUDENT: It would be interesting to incorporate that into the yoga conversation.

Dr. J: I thought we were. It is part of our yoga conversation. It's why, for example, I'm not the most militant, physical yoga practitioner. I went through a period where I was. I realized my compulsion toward performance of the yoga was just as mechanical as an aversion would have been.

Dr. J: I remember you talking about that. That would be a good example of what I'm talking about.

STUDENT: I've had that conversation with a lot of people in the last couple of months. I want to write it down and document it.

You know we're still recording?

Dr. J: Yes.

Angels Speak and Demons Shout,
With One Voice
They say *"The Sleeper Must Awaken"*.

INDEX

www.ingramcontent.com/pod-product-compliance
Lightning Source LLC
Chambersburg PA
CBHW081147270326
41930CB00014B/3067